T0322707

SAND, PLANES AND SUBMARINES

SAND, PLANES AND SUBMARINES

HOW LEIGHTON BUZZARD SHORTENED THE FIRST WORLD WAR

PAUL BROWN AND DELIA GLEAVE

First published 2017

The History Press
The Mill, Brimscombe Port
Stroud, Gloucestershire, GL5 2QG
www.thehistorypress.co.uk

British Library Cataloguing in Publication Data.
A catalogue record for this book is available from the British Library.

ISBN 978 0 7509 8370 9

Typesetting and origination by The History Press
Printed in Great Britain by TJ International Ltd, Padstow, Cornwall

CONTENTS

ABOUT THE AUTHORS

PAUL BROWN has been a journalist for fifty years. He started working at the *Guardian* in 1981 and is still writing for the paper. Paul is currently co-editor at Climate News Network, an Internet news service for journalists. He is a Fellow of Wolfson College, Cambridge, the Royal Geographical Society and the Royal Society of Arts, Manufactures and Commerce. He has won awards for investigative and environmental journalism, and is Chairman of the Leighton Buzzard and District Archaeological and Historical Society. He has written ten books on the environment and history and edited *The Secrets of Q Central* (2014).

DELIA GLEAVE has always had a passion for research. She studied French, German and Latin at school in Leighton Buzzard and Italian at the University of Hull. She worked on the *Leighton Buzzard Observer*, tutored a child with emotional and learning difficulties and sang in a folk group at many local venues before moving to Yorkshire. There she continued to perform, studying the history and traditions behind the music. Delia taught, assessed and supported students with dyslexia, and their families. As part of a continuing interest in history and genealogy she undertakes research for clients around the world and was a major contributor to the history of Leighton Buzzard in the Second World War, *The Secrets of Q Central* (2014).

FOREWORD

When research began into the roles played by Leighton Buzzard and Linslade in the First World War, we knew that there had been an aeroplane factory and that sand had somehow been important. We knew nothing of the wire works that made thousands of anti-submarine nets to counter the threat of U-boats, nor just how vital sand was to the war effort.

This book is the first comprehensive and accurate account of what an extraordinary part these two small towns played in the First World War. Nothing could be reported at the time because of the Official Secrets Act but we were amazed that even a hundred years later so much still remained hidden in archives waiting to be discovered.

Many members of the team who uncovered the information at the core of this book are those whose work produced such excellent results in researching *The Secrets of Q Central*, our best-selling account of the role played by the two towns in shortening the Second World War. We hope that readers will be just as surprised and intrigued as we were by this account of how the towns also contributed in a completely different way to shortening the First World War.

There is so much more in this book, not least the stories of life in the towns before, during and after the wars that changed both of them forever. There is also the terrible sacrifice made by the population, a much higher proportion of which volunteered to fight than in many cities.

Delia Gleave and I, as editors, have been part of the team from the Leighton Buzzard and District Archaeological and Historical Society who have researched and written various parts of the book. What has really mattered to make this book new and interesting is the diligent research. Elise Ward, who unearthed a staggering amount of information, deserves a special mention in despatches. Other key members of the team include Sue Baxter, Joseph Cresswell, Kate Crooks, Stuart French, Yvonne Reynolds and Tony Tompkins. Bill Marshall gave us an account of his mother, Lillie, a nurse in the war, and Tony Pantling brought us the heartening story and pictures of his grandfather Arthur Sambrook and his horse Bluebell.

Pictures form a vital part of the book and Keith Burchell, Richard Hart and Colin Holmes organised, improved and added to the Society's existing collection. Thanks are also due to Colin Crooks, Richard Gleave, Chris Goddard, Edwin Herbert, Simon Nicol and Laura Williams for fact-checking and proof-reading. We are also grateful to Stuart Hadaway of the RAF Air Historical Branch, Bedfordshire Archive Service, Doncaster Record Office, the National Archives at Kew, the Imperial War Museum, the Western Front Association and the London & North Western Railway Society for their help in research and in providing images.

To save space throughout the book, any address given without naming a town or village is in Leighton Buzzard or Linslade, since the towns have no road names in common.

Paul Brown,
Chairman Leighton Buzzard and
District Archaeological and Historical Society

CHAPTER 1

PROSPEROUS PLAYGROUND TO WAR MACHINE

Leighton Buzzard and Linslade, two small towns in the middle of England divided only by the River Ouzel, were completely transformed by the First World War.

Until August 1914, they, and particularly Linslade, were at the centre of the most fashionable hunting scene in Britain. As it was only an hour from London by train, the aristocracy, bankers and upwardly mobile Edwardians flocked to Linslade to hunt, mix with the Rothschilds and, in some cases, to enjoy illicit liaisons. Many parties stayed at the Hunt Hotel in Linslade and the Swan in Leighton Buzzard or at their own hunting lodges and country houses.

The prosperous market town in 1908. The cattle market was held on a Tuesday and the coach outside the Swan Hotel on the left used to ferry customers to the station.

Otherwise Leighton Buzzard was a prosperous market town. Its proximity to London meant that it was able to supply fresh milk, vegetables and fruit to the capital from farms and market gardens.

There were two industries in the towns that no one could have guessed would play a leading role in defending Britain and France against Germany and shortening the war. These were the sand quarrying industry and Morgan & Co. Ltd, makers of fashionable carriages and cars for the hunting fraternity.

A third business was already contracted to the Admiralty. Bullivant & Co. with their factory in Lake Street were making anti-submarine netting to defend the British fleet from the new and ominous threat that torpedoes posed.

A century later it is hard to believe the speed with which the town changed to become part of Britain's war machine. Like every other village, town and city, many young men immediately volunteered to fight in the army, navy and in the air. The remarkable stories of these men, the lives lost and medals won, are told in these pages.

Women played a vital role. These were the nurses who volunteered to go to the Front, and the hundreds of munitions and other factory workers who replaced the men who had joined up. The mothers and wives who were left behind must have grown to fear the knock of the telegram boy bearing bad news.

The town also acted as a vast transit camp for soldiers in training ready to go to the Front. The cramped conditions became so bad that some of the troops sent home cartoon postcards showing this, made by enterprising townsfolk.

It is astonishing how much still remained hidden when research for this book began in 2015. The Official Secrets Act was rigorously imposed. The vital industries that were based in the town could never be talked about outside the factory gate or written about in the local newspapers. This history has therefore been pieced together by looking at original documents in record offices and gathering information from local people with letters, photographs and other pieces of background about these momentous events.

The story of the sand industry, which became of national importance for making the moulds for the big guns used by our army in the trenches, has never been fully understood before. There was a desperate shortage of these guns in 1915 and it became a national emergency. To extract enough of this special sand quickly enough, there was a change from horsepower to steam lorries and traction engines to transport hundreds of tons a week to the canal and railways. This destroyed many of the town's roads.

Then there was the conversion of Morgan's from a high-class carriage maker to a production line for aircraft. The factory became one of the country's largest aircraft manufacturers, turning out an astonishing three aeroplanes a week.

The third remarkable contribution to the war effort and a previously untold story is that of Bullivant's, a wire rope company, which specialised in making

Linslade's recreation ground has always been used for church fêtes and other local celebrations. Shown here: children dancing to a local band. Some of the elegantly dressed spectators are using umbrellas to ward off the rain.

products for the navy. Anti-submarine netting made in Grovebury Road was so important to the war effort that a special siding was constructed on the railway line to dispatch the nets to ports all over the country. The nets were used in an extraordinary feat of engineering, an anti U-boat barrier that was planned to run across the Channel from Folkestone to Boulogne, but there were many types and sizes of Bullivant nets deployed across the world to protect Allied shipping.

As in many towns other businesses also contributed to the war effort, but these three industries alone justified the claim that the efforts of Leighton and Linslade shortened the First World War. But there was much more of interest. The town's horses were requisitioned to be part of the war effort, some of them the pampered and expensive hunters belonging to the aristocracy, others the working horses from the local farms. Hundreds were gathered up, transported by train and sent to France to face incredibly harsh conditions alongside the men at the Front, hauling guns, ambulances and supplies of all sorts. One – Bluebell, from the Linslade Post Office – joined the Bucks Hussars with his master on the first day of the war and went to fight in the Middle East.

One of the many surprises in the research was the great variety of roles people of the two towns played in the war. Many men went to sea, somewhat unexpectedly

Lake Street, Leighton Buzzard, 1900. The street has undergone dramatic changes since then; most of the buildings have been demolished. The Corn Exchange on the right was used in the war first as a hospital then as a submarine net factory. The Unicorn on the left was one of the prosperous hunting inns.

for a town in the middle of England. A number were also among the first pilots and ground crew of what were to become the Fleet Air Arm and the Royal Flying Corps (RFC), later the Royal Air Force (RAF). There are stories of families made up of many brothers who all signed up to fight in various theatres of war.

Important, too, are the accounts of what was happening in the town, how people aided the soldiers at the Front with parcels and made thousands of bandages and garments for hospitals there. Refugees came to the towns and, in thanks for their sanctuary, gave concerts at events designed to keep the spirits up, while the indomitable Kitty Towers continued to run the Swan Hotel in great style. There was also a less reputable side to the towns in wartime: a local brothel, and profiteering from food shortages.

The Armistice is not the end of the story; it would not be complete without the aftermath of the war. What was the fate of the workers at Bullivant's and Morgan's who were suddenly surplus to requirements once the guns fell silent? The sand industry survived, but found an intriguing alternative after it was banned from using its destructive vehicles on the roads, buying a light railway system from the Western Front and installing it in Leighton Buzzard.

Although the area celebrated the survival of those that came home, there was discontent from many returning from the Front about the lack of employment, and resentment that women had taken some of their jobs. Many of these women were widows who now had families to support. Committees were formed to erect fitting memorials to the hundreds who did not return.

Despite the victory, life was tough for the majority when the war ended; this was no Land Fit For Heroes, as the coalition government under David Lloyd-George had promised. The two towns did recover but would never be the same again.

CHAPTER 2

HUNTING, FARMING AND FROLICKING

The rolling undeveloped countryside surrounding Leighton and Linslade proved extremely alluring for well-to-do visitors because it was ideal for hunting. An equally great draw was that the towns were only an hour from London by train and close to six stately homes belonging to the fabulously rich and influential Rothschild family; Ascott House at Wing, Aston Clinton House, Halton House, Mentmore Towers, Tring Park and Waddesdon Manor were all within easy riding distance. Perfect hosts, the Rothschild family had their own staghounds and started each hunt by releasing a stag from a horsebox to be sure that their guests would have something to chase.

Lord Rothschild's staghounds, with Ascott House in the background. Several packs of hounds were kept for different hunts in the district; the local papers reported their success in running to ground stags, foxes or otters.

Such was the attraction that two heirs to the throne, Albert Edward, (later King Edward VII) and Edward (briefly King Edward VIII, then Duke of Windsor), hunted locally. In a biography of Robert Grimston, fourth son of the Earl of Verulam, there is an account of his galloping after a stag, accompanied by various Rothschilds, the Prince of Wales, the Duke of Norfolk, lords and marquises, through Linslade, along the High Street and down Lake Street towards Billington. It is a snapshot of the way the aristocracy and rich social climbers used the area as a weekend playground. Not that the town minded, for there was a lot of money to be made from seeing to the needs of the rich.

Among more than thirty inns, public houses and guest houses in the two towns, catering for the constant traffic of wealthy and aristocratic guests, were two large upmarket hotels: the Hunt Hotel in Linslade, which had stabling for 150 horses, and the Swan Hotel in the High Street. The Hunt was described by Grimston as a place 'where peers, Members of Parliament, cabinet ministers, judges, barristers, authors, actors, soldiers, ex-chancellors elbow one another in passages, at the stables and in the coffee-room.'

Kitty Towers with three of her children, taken by local celebrity photographer Theophilus Piggott who had a studio in the High Street. Kitty was to take over the running of the Swan. The hotel was celebrated for the quality of its food and hospitality.

One of the many theatrical acts from London which appeared at the Corn Exchange in Lake Street in the pre-war period for the entertainment of the fashionable hunting crowd. These performers and most others stayed at the Swan Hotel.

The Swan Hotel, the venue for the start of the annual Boxing Day hunt, was run by a remarkable woman, Kitty Towers. Her husband, the licensee, had died in 1893, leaving her with several young children, but she took over and ran it with great flair. As well as her undoubted business acumen, she must have had both a very strong character and an ability to exercise much discretion. The visitors' book of the period is full of praise for the luxury and quality of service. As well as the landed gentry her guests included the showgirls and performers at the Corn Exchange Theatre. Berkelly Perkins, a member of the Carl Rosa Opera Company staying from 27 April 1902 wrote: 'Everything satisfactory. While here broke the 7th and 10th Commandments.' ('Thou shalt not commit adultery' and 'Thou shalt not covet thy neighbour's wife'.) Kitty continued to run the hotel through the war years until 1924 and became a local legend.

The dominance of hunting was such that so many grooms were recorded in the 1911 census as living in Linslade that they outnumbered any other profession. Much of the life of the two towns was geared to providing stabling and care for the horses during the week, accommodation for their riders at weekends, and the entertainment that was required before and after the hunting.

A visiting card advertising the services of
Thomas Handy Bishop who had a shop near
the Corn Exchange in Lake Street, making
and stocking every piece of equipment a
horseman or huntsman might need, all of the
highest quality.

Partly because of all the money brought in by rich visitors and partly because the
town had the Grand Junction Canal and the London and North Western Railway
(L&NWR), independent businesses flourished. As one would expect all the trades
associated with hunting: blacksmiths, farriers, saddlers and even a horse slaughterer,
were also available.

Leighton was moving with the times – there was already a 'motor car garage'
– but it also remained an old and well-established market town which had been
important before the Norman invasion of 1066. The town was very compact. The
common open fields had been close to the town until they were finally enclosed
in the mid-nineteenth century so there was little urban sprawl. Its cattle, horse and
sheep markets on Tuesdays had been the bedrock of the town's fortunes for many
generations and its annual wool fair was a major event.

The arrival of the Grand Junction Canal in 1800 and the London and
Birmingham Railway in 1838 had meant that a fairly isolated town became an
important trading post between London, the Midlands and the North. Fresh
produce for London came from market gardens, and wagonloads of churns
trundled to Leighton station from surrounding farms early in the morning in
time for the daily milk train which helped to supply the city. Coal transported
by canal to Linslade was one tenth of the price it had been when brought in by
horse and cart, and sand, an equally heavy cargo, was being sent north and south

cheaply by narrowboat to help build and enlarge the growing Midlands cities and an expanding capital city.

Although the population of the two towns was small – 6,782 for Leighton Buzzard and 2,262 for Linslade according to the 1911 census – there was a remarkable range of trades and businesses. More than 100 are listed in Kelly's Directory for 1914. The High Street was thriving and there were many more businesses in North Street and Lake Street. Along with the butchers, bakers, dairies, drapers, dress shops, tailors, ironmongers, boot and shoe makers, leather sellers, clock and watchmakers, tobacconists, chemists, hairdressers and gas fitters, there was a pork pie maker, an organ builder, an umbrella maker and a manufacturer of artificial teeth. Alongside these were solicitors, an auctioneer, silversmiths, a wine and spirit merchant and music teachers.

Few of these businesses survive under the same name and with the same family, although John Reid, picture frame maker, still trades at 19 High Street, his father's initials above the shop front.

In both Leighton and Linslade a number of people were described as letting apartments, and it is likely that these were for visitors to the town who had come for the hunting. In addition to the 'ordinary' places of education, a number of small boarding schools for the children of the gentry opened in Linslade, so high was the

Leighton High Street in 1910 with the Fountain Hotel on the right and George Faulkner Green's ironmongers. The posts on either side of the road were for tying up the cattle and horses sold at the Tuesday market. The town was lit by gas, and all important businesses had telephones.

reputation of the town for clean air compared with the smoke stacks of London. The nearby villages of Aspley Guise and Woburn Sands were declared health resorts because of their dry soils.

James Robinson's Basket Works at 43 Lake Street provided their own raw material by cultivating the willows in osier beds, in the water meadows of the Ouzel. The green willow shoots were perfect for weaving into baskets and many of these trees, now very old, still remain. Also in Lake Street, George Brown & Sons agricultural machinery business, then at Victoria Iron Works, was a substantial company still flourishing today. It was celebrated for its Bedfordshire Drill, formerly the Hensman Seed Drill, for which William Brown had acquired the patterns and manufacturing rights in 1874. This had made farming far more efficient, and it sold in large numbers, making the company wealthy. These and other businesses in the town would later be pressed into war service.

Considering the relatively small population of Linslade there was a remarkable number of businesses there too, among them two doctors' surgeries, mostly crammed into the relatively new developments along Old Road, New Road and Wing Road between the railway station and the canal bridge.

Close to the station were two livery stables as well as five public houses where hunters could be hired and stabled. There were two carriage-makers, blacksmiths, farriers, harness-makers, a feed merchant and a veterinary surgeon to care for the horses. The Rothschild family had their own stud at Southcott, which is still in business.

To provide services for both residents and visitors there were three butchers, two fishmongers, a dairy, baker, two tobacconists, a fruiterer, two milliners, two tailors, a draper, three dressmakers, two boot-makers and a separate boot repairer, a hardware dealer, a house furnishers, a watch-repairer, a beer retailer, a hairdresser and a fancy repository in Wing Road. A plumber, a hot water engineer, two cycle makers and an architect were also to be found, and one business, Ernest Lee at 16 Old Road, offered to be a house furnisher, upholsterer, cabinetmaker, decorator and funeral director all at the same time. Two coal-dealers, a miller and corn merchant and a builder had businesses close to the canal.

Perhaps the company that owed most to the hunting fraternity was Morgan's, carriage makers to the gentry. Their works was in Linslade between the canal and the river, with a large showroom where gentlemen and their ladies could choose a new carriage or later a motorcar. These could then be shipped to London on a train which had special flatbed wagons for the purpose.

Morgan's had a highly skilled workforce in Linslade on two and a half acres of land off Leighton Road, with a long workshop alongside the canal. The carriages were hand-built by craftsmen, and among their customers was the actress Lillie Langtry, mistress to the Prince of Wales.

Mentmore Towers, a Rothschild mansion less than 3 miles from Linslade, the home of Lord Rosebery, Prime Minister in 1895; in the pre-war years he was host to the Prince of Wales and many members of his circle who came to hunt nearby.

From Linslade the company supplied its two large showrooms in London – in Long Acre and Old Bond Street – as well as maintaining one in Linslade in front of their works where Tesco now stands. They had seen an opportunity to cash in on the hunting fraternity by providing a service where customers could order their new carriage at either their London home or while they were visiting their hunting residence.

However, shortly after 9.30 p.m. on Tuesday 10 June 1902, Morgan's experienced a disastrous fire, destroying most of the works. In the *Bedfordshire Advertiser* it was reported that PC Lowe, on duty outside the Morgan Carriage Works, spotted flames rising from one workshop.

Local volunteers quickly began moving carriages out of the shop, but only six were saved. The fire brigade was on the spot within ten minutes with three manual engines and a hose truck, but they could not save the main building 'which was an acre of fire'. The firemen played their hoses on to the neighbouring buildings, thus saving Thomas Yirrell's stone works in Bridge Street, Thomas Brantom's flour mill in Leighton Road, the wheel and smith shops within the works and an immense quantity of valuable timber.

By 1.00 a.m. on the Wednesday the fire was under control. However, a gas main in the building ignited, causing an increase in the flames. 'The road was pecked up and the main hammered flat, the supply of gas was cut off.' A large number of customers' carriages in for repair were destroyed and over 100 men were immediately laid off by Morgan's. By the following week the majority of the men were taken back on to assist with the demolition of the damaged walls and the rebuilding of the factory. It was reported in January 1903 that production was back to normal. Confirming this, an advertisement in the *LBO* of 17 February 1903 guaranteed that 'each new carriage sold by them is of their own manufacture'.

Morgan's was unquestionably a resilient company and there is clear evidence of the company's willingness to grasp the new technologies of motor cars and aeroplanes using the existing skills of their workforce and the materials in their works.

In at least one respect the company was far ahead of its time. On 22 October 1901 the *LBO* reported that Morgan's had delivered 'an exceedingly handsome electrical landaulette, to a gentleman residing in Birmingham'. The landaulette was built to carry four passengers and two on the driver's seat over 50 miles on one electrical charge, at speeds ranging from 4 to 20mph – and this was his second order.

Even more surprisingly, in the *Bedfordshire Advertiser and Luton Times* of 3 July 1908 it was reported that 'Messrs Morgan and Co, the well-known carriage builders and motor manufacturers, are to be congratulated on the great success of the two Adler cars competing in the International trials of 2,000 miles and several tests on the Scottish hills, finishing up with a 200 miles race on the Brooklands track, both cars winning first in its class, each taking the silver cup, the 30hp Adler making the fastest speed of the day and finishing with a lead of over eleven laps (or about 30 miles) ahead of its competitors.' Thus these cars proved not only the fastest at Brooklands on Saturday, but were able to stand the terrible strains they were subjected to on the rough roads and severe hills of Scotland and the north of England, the 30hp Adler being the fastest car of its class in climbing Shap Fell. Orders for these cars were quickly given after the results of the final became known, and good results were anticipated. The Adler motor car chassis were manufactured in Germany and imported by Morgan's who added the coachwork.

Morgan's were not only building and repairing carriages and their first cars; in the *Bedfordshire Advertiser and Luton Times*, 17 September 1909, it was briefly reported that 'an aeroplane is being constructed at the carriage and motor body works of Messrs Morgan & Co, which now employ about 220 men. It is being built to the design of a customer, who intends to compete for the *Daily Mail* prize'. Sadly there is no record of the aeroplane's success or otherwise.

The 1910 *Daily Mail* London to Manchester air race was a challenge to fly an aeroplane from a point within 5 miles of the *Mail*'s London office to a point within 5 miles of its Manchester office. Only two flyers competed for the £10,000 prize and both flew Farman III biplanes. The first prize was won by

Building on their success in the motor races and mountain trials, Morgan & Co. took out large advertisements in the newspapers to promote the latest models of Adler Cars. They built the coachwork required to suit the customer.

This high-class outfitters for both men and women catered for the wealthy visitors to the town. Ridgeway & Pledger was one of a number of shops built on a grander scale than you would expect for a town of this size. Note the telephone number: Leighton Buzzard 16.

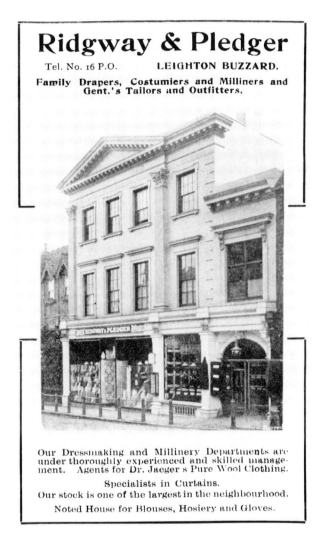

Ridgway & Pledger

Tel. No. 16 P.O. **LEIGHTON BUZZARD.**

Family Drapers, Costumiers and Milliners and Gent.'s Tailors and Outfitters.

Our Dressmaking and Millinery Departments are under thoroughly experienced and skilled management. Agents for Dr. Jaeger's Pure Wool Clothing.

Specialists in Curtains.
Our stock is one of the largest in the neighbourhood.

Noted House for Blouses, Hosiery and Gloves.

the Frenchman Louis Paulhan, with Claude Grahame-White coming a close second. The Royal Aero Club recorded the timing of the flights and reported that Grahame-White had flown over Leighton Buzzard at 6.13 a.m. on 23 April 1910 following the route of the L&NWR. The railway company had painted a large number of railway sleepers white to aid the navigation of both pilots.

Morgan's were demonstrating to their wealthy clients that they could utilise their skilled workforce and adapt their works to build more modern means of transport, while still maintaining the older craft skills of carriage building. This proved to be vital for the company's survival when the war came.

The sand industry was also thriving before the outbreak of war. In fact, sands of the area had been worked for some 150 years before 1914. The outcrops of ironstone in the sand had been used for centuries before that as a building stone. The oldest building in the two towns, St Mary's Church at Old Linslade, is built of it and it is used in many older houses and garden walls. Before the common fields were enclosed the peasants had the right to gather stone from the heath for building.

The sands quarried were Lower Greensand, a type suitable for a wide range of purposes. These included making mortar and cement for building, as well as moulds for metal working, with the highest quality in demand as a material for glassmaking and as filtration for public water supplies.

Much of the sand stratum outcropped near to or at ground level, which enabled people to dig it easily and transport it by wheelbarrow or horse and cart. As time went on, the efforts of the few became the interests of the many, especially after the canal and the railway arrived, and this led to the development of a thriving business in the area.

In 1842 and 1848 respectively, soon after the arrival of the railway, two fields in Heath and Reach, Calves Close and Great Pear Pond Close, had been leased to a Smethwick firm of glassmakers, Chance Bros, and the special grades and purity

A fashionable crowd at the Market Cross on 13 July 1905 to greet Sir George Joseph Woodman, Sheriff of the City of London, an old boy of Beaudesert Boys' School in Leighton Buzzard. This was the traditional place for celebrations and political meetings.

The silver sands of Leighton Buzzard and Linslade were highly prized for glass-making because of their purity. Quarrying was hard and dangerous work because the sand cliffs were prone to collapse. To avoid ordinary wagons sinking in the sand, horses pulled the loads out of the pits on rails.

of silica sand available here led to it being much sought after as that company developed its glassmaking skills in the Midlands.

Ready availability of suitable sands, transported by horse-drawn narrowboat on the canal from Linslade to Smethwick, enabled James and Robert Chance to refine their production to incorporate what was known as the blown cylinder process. This enabled large sheets of clear glass to be rolled out, when previously only small panes could be made. Two early examples of this new technology in use were the 'Great Stove' at Chatsworth House for the Duke of Devonshire, and later, all of the glass needed for the 1851 Great Exhibition building in Hyde Park, London, which became better known as the Crystal Palace. The common thread between both projects was the gardener from Milton Bryan who designed both and who was later knighted as Sir Joseph Paxton.

One early sandpit entrepreneur was Joseph Firbank who supplied considerable tonnages to the L&NWR from his pit at Tiddenfoot. Another was Joseph Arnold, who had already established a flourishing business in Camden, north London, but saw the potential of the pits in Leighton. Although Arnold died in 1911, Kelly's Directory for 1914 for the town describes him as silver and building sand pits proprietor, peat cutter and peat and loam merchant. Not long after, George Garside acquired land and started his company in developing sales of specialised sands. In the few years before the war sales for sand companies increased, good dividends were paid and employment was at a steadily increasing level. Arnold's was to become key to providing the means to supply artillery for the British Army.

The third business important to this narrative, Bullivant & Co., had no particular reason to be in Leighton – indeed, for a business whose main activity was making torpedo nets it might seem a very odd choice. The most likely explanation is that it was suggested by Thomas Selby, a senior employee of Bullivant's appointed to manage the factory. He would have realised the potential of its central position with transport links to ports on his frequent visits to Linslade with his wife, Minnie, whose sister lived in Southcourt Avenue.

The first record of the company in Leighton is a clipping from the *Luton Times and Advertiser* of 8 November 1912 saying that a new firm Messrs Bullivant and Co. Ltd, wire rope and torpedo net makers 'have taken a lease of the warehouse at the bottom of Lake-street, formerly occupied by Messrs Carew as a hay and straw storage.'. Two years later the company's patent nets and new inventions became central to Britain's network of torpedo defences and were key to the defeat of the menace of German U-boats. The Leighton Buzzard operation had to be greatly enlarged and a new factory built. So important had the urgent delivery of torpedo nets become that in 1916 the company had its own new siding from the Leighton Buzzard to Dunstable railway line so that nets could be loaded directly from the factory in Grovebury Road on to wagons to be taken to any port in the country. These small but prosperous towns could have had no inkling of the turmoil and heartache that was to come in the next four years, or what a vital role their industries were to play in defending Britain and shortening the war.

CHAPTER 3

'FOR GOD'S SAKE SEND US SAND'

When war was declared the local sand industry suddenly became a vital national resource for the war effort. The reason was simply that the supply of Belgian sands stopped overnight. These were sands that had been used as ballast in ships returning to Britain from the continent, which were dumped at the dockside before being sold on cheaply to the foundry industry. The sudden loss of supplies was a crisis

Before the war all the sand was shifted by men with shovels, moved out of the pits on horse-drawn skips pulled on rails over uneven ground, then tipped into wagons and delivered to the canal and railway by traditional horse and cart. It took several journeys to fill a narrowboat.

for the government and the armaments industry and alternative sources were needed urgently. Leighton and Linslade provided the answer. Almost immediately, the activities of the quarry owners were taken over by the Ministry of Munitions, who recognised that the specialist sands of the area were of great importance in steel production. These demands meant a sudden and dramatic rise in the need to quarry sand and dispatch it by canal and railway all over the country to munitions factories. Initially production was boosted from 700 to 2,200 tons a week, but this was later further increased. Particularly important were the moulds for big guns, of which there was a desperate shortage. These guns were needed to match Germany's superior firepower.

Sand was moved from the quarries in pre-war England by horse and cart. The existence of around forty stables in and around the town demonstrates that transport of most goods was carried out in this way. The type of cart seen in Edwardian photographs would carry some one and a quarter tons of sand (1,270kgs). A carter

A plan to build a light railway across country to transport sand before the First World War failed through lack of finance. Rails had to be used in quarries themselves to avoid wagons sinking in the soft ground. When the Western Front became a quagmire, all available rails and locomotives were sent to France.

moving this to either the canal or the railway would be expected to carry four loads in a day, taking a full working day to move 5 tons. While this might have been acceptable in times of peace, it certainly was not during the war. Surviving output figures show that later in the war just one quarry owner in Leighton was producing 1,300 tons of sand a month for the war effort, and there were at least four companies working several quarries each.

The options other than horses were lorries, usually steam-driven, and traction engines hauling trailers. They were capable of handling loads of between 5 and 7 tons in every trip, and could make many more trips per day. With them the delivery of much greater volumes of sand could be achieved. This caused huge problems for local people, as the weight of these new vehicles was so damaging to the surface that some roads were impassable to normal traffic. When reporting restrictions were finally lifted, this description appeared in the LBO:

> The tractors worked Sunday and weekday alike, and people who had five to ten ton loads of sand waltzing past their houses every few minutes of the day had long reached a speechless state of indignation. Cottagers said that whilst they lay in bed on Sunday mornings the foundations rocked, and that pictures and ornaments have frequently been jarred off walls and mantelshelves and broken.

Sand in the Leighton area comes in many types and is suitable for a wide variety of processes. The principal need in 1914 and the rest of the war was for foundry work for munitions, where it was used in the production of cast iron or cast steel. Wooden moulds were pressed into the sand to create increasingly complex shapes into which molten metal at high temperatures could be poured. Any large ordnance and artillery forgings and castings needed sand, but this was not sand as we think of it – granular, yellowy-white and featuring in children's play pits. This was sand that needed the alchemist's artistry to achieve blends with other materials, in order to achieve a mould that would give a satisfactory outcome once the molten metal had been poured into it.

Whole books were written about sand, how best to use it and how to prepare it. Professor Percy George Hannall Boswell's book *Modern Foundry Practice,* produced after the Armistice, is a distillation of all the knowledge acquired by him during the war, when Leighton Buzzard sand became essential for providing the means of shortening the conflict. It seems that while adequate supplies of native sand for iron founding were available, the blends for the much higher temperatures needed for steel casting (1,550–1,700 degrees C), were another matter.

War drove many technical developments. Boswell's work for the government included the development of synthetic moulding sands. He brought science to what was previously almost literally a 'black art' of casting metals, and a new market

A steam lorry of the type used for sand during the First World War. This one belonged to William Simmons, the Leighton flour miller who was forced to give up his horses. The metal wheels of this already heavy lorry, combined with the weight of a load of sand, must have caused serious damage to an unmade road.

for Leighton Buzzard sands was born. Of these sands (according to the professor's grading system), the coarse and medium types were deemed suitable for casting steel, while medium and fine grades could be used for malleable iron. Medium grade was also used for another class of metal known as grey iron, the cheapest and most common form of cast iron. The local sands – suitably blended – could also be used for light alloys and non-ferrous general castings.

Professor Boswell received the Order of the British Empire (OBE) in 1918 for his work; he was ultimately the recognised authority by the Ministry of Munitions as the premier sedimentary petrologist.

The importance of the sand deposits in the Leighton area is detailed by the Institute of British Foundrymen, who describe the sands in this area as the Lower Greensand deposits. They are broken down into eighteen types of silica sand suitable for iron and steel moulding. Of these types thirteen were found in Leighton and Heath and Reach during the war.

Moving valuable sand from the quarries to the canal and the railway for distribution to foundries became a serious logistical problem. Deposited in the Bedfordshire Record Office is a bulky file of lengthy and sometimes acrimonious letters between the Ministry of Munitions, Bedfordshire County Council and the quarry owners, showing the turmoil created by the trade and providing an insight into the sand transport situation as it affected the roads around Leighton.

The letters start with demands from the Ministry that no obstruction should be put in the way of the vital delivery of sand, but it becomes clear that the increase in traffic caused so much misery locally that special measures were needed to keep the roads in the area passable. Roads that could bear a horse and cart could not survive traction engines weighing ten times as much.

By 1917 there was no doubt about the priority the government gave to the problem. On 26 February 1917 John Hunter, the Director of Steel Production, Ministry of Munitions, wrote thus to William Woodfine Marks, Clerk to the Bedfordshire County Council:

The sand grading plant in Arnold's pit in Grovebury Road, Leighton at the start of the war. The graded sand could be tipped directly into the horse-drawn wagons off the platform. The well-dressed gentleman in the foreground could be a member of the Arnold family.

Mr Joseph Arnold, Sand Quarrymaster of Leighton Buzzard, has been directed by the Ministry of Munitions to double his output of sand, which means an increase of 1,500 tons per week. This sand is utilised in the production of steel and is of the utmost national importance, owing to the supplies from abroad being unobtainable.

Hunter's assistant visited Leighton Buzzard and reported that the roads used by Arnold's steam tractors were indeed badly damaged with the bottoming of the road showing in some places. Hunter's advice was that:

You should take the matter up with the Roads Committee and have the roads put into good condition. I intend placing on the roads eight additional tractors at an early date to convey the sand from Mr Arnold's quarry to his railway siding, and shall be obliged if you will give this matter your personal attention in the interests of the nation.

Unfortunately these steam tractors, like their predecessors the horse and cart, were for the most part trundling along unmade roadways. Since the motorised carter, like his horse-drawn ancestor, was paid by the quantity of sand transported, these

James Gilbert's foundry helped to make giant traction engines in Leighton Buzzard before the war. Also a steam roller of a type in constant use in Leighton during the war, to fill ruts with crushed granite and keep the roads usable.

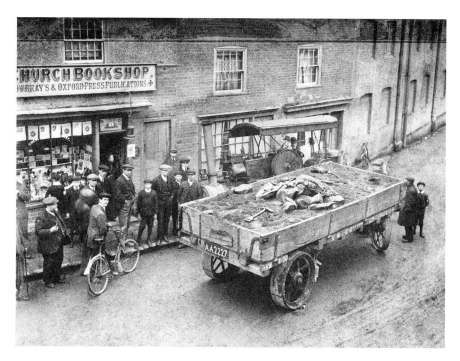

The traction engine, towing a trailer full of sand, which jack-knifed on the steep hill in Bridge Street. The slope caused so many accidents that eventually the street was raised to provide a gentle slope down to the River Ouzel.

heavier loads were also delivered at faster speeds and had a devastating effect on the surface, despite a maximum speed of 5mph being imposed.

Deep ruts and in bad weather the ensuing mud considerably slowed journey times, and therefore the tonnage reaching either canal or railway. Things were extremely unpleasant for Leighton people trying to go about their business. Traction engines rumbled through the centre of town and also had to navigate the then steeply sloping Bridge Street on their way to the canal. On one spectacular occasion the road surface was wet, control was lost and a trailer jack-knifed.

The Bedfordshire County Roads Board, together with the Ministry of Munitions, directed that something needed to be done and some of the main roads in the centre of town were 'metalled'. Metalling involved smoothing a roadway surface, then spreading a layer of larger stones and overlaying with crushed, hard rock – preferably granite from the quarries at Groby in Leicestershire. A slight slope was introduced from the middle of the road, thereby aiding rainfall drainage into ditches on either side. For a while it worked reasonably well, but the constant wear and tear, exacerbated by narrow iron-tyred wheels, drove deep ruts into the

Joseph Arnold's elaborate notepaper advertising his silver sands and the fact that he was Contractor to His Majesty's Government. He had his own private wharves on the canal, and a wonderful address for telegrams: Sandbags, London.

compacted surfaces, which rapidly deteriorated as carts, wagons and lorries swerved to avoid getting caught in the worst of them.

Leighton's two biggest quarry companies, Arnold's and Garside's, were major suppliers to the Ministry of Munitions and did not hesitate to use their influence. In a discussion about the roads, Marks reported that Arnold had brandished letters from munitions companies which asked for more foundry sand, and stated that they could not make guns for the Front unless he supplied the sand.

The Ministry of Munitions was obviously concerned and ordered railway companies to deliver supplies to fix the roads, providing extra men to dig the sand and mend the roads. Despite their importance, although Arnold's company had asked for fifty extra men in March 1917 they were allowed only half that number, six of whom were allocated to repairing the roads. Marks commented: 'Of course the getting of the sand is no use unless it can be conveyed to the station, so that the road work must have first call on the labour.'

This shortage of labour for delivering sand to where it was needed was referred to in one of the numerous Military Service Tribunal hearings held by borough, urban district and rural district councils to hear applications for exemption from conscription into the British Army. These had existed since 1915, formed of local gentry and senior managers of factories who understood the need to produce vital equipment for the army. In Leighton, the sand industry was one of several which had men in reserved occupations who were felt to be too valuable to production to be allowed to go and fight. The military served the call-up papers and the Tribunals decided on the spot whether a man should be taken away for service. If the Tribunal decided against the man, he would immediately be handed over to the military and enrolled in the forces.

These were reported extensively in local papers, the inference often being that those applying for exemption from military service were somehow ducking their patriotic duty.

During a tribunal in May 1916 an employer had appealed against the call-up of an 18-year-old canal boatman. His basic argument was that he was engaged in hauling sand and coal for war work. The lad, who worked two boats with his 'rather feeble' father, was the 'prop for the whole thing'. Between forty and fifty boats were engaged on the traffic for munitions, employing about thirty men, half of whom were beyond military age, and several women. A letter was submitted showing that 'the construction of additional munitions works is delayed for lack of glass for roofs and windows, for the manufacture of which the sand is essential. It is also of great importance for other purposes in connection with munitions.'

Coal boats moored by the canal bridge in Leighton Road next to Morgan's works. In the background, a wharf where narrowboats are being loaded with sand for delivery to munitions works. A traction engine is parked nearby.

One of the tribunal members supported this argument and said he had seen a letter from a 'person of importance in a munitions works saying, "For God's sake send us sand." 'The tribunal was adjourned while an investigation was carried out into the need for labour to get the sand delivered.

There is scant evidence in the records for this period as to the identity of the sand companies' customers, but on 31 March 1917 Christopher Claridge, who owned a pit in Mile Tree Road, wrote a revealing letter to Marks. He was supplying averages of between 400 and 500 tons of sand per week to munitions works and the letter records some of his clients as: Chance Bros & Co., Birmingham (for glass production); Consett Iron Co.; Ebbw Vale Steel, Iron and Coal Co.; Morley Iron Co., Cardiff; A. Percy & Co., West Bromwich; Guest, Keen and Nettlefold, Dowlais Iron and Steel Works; Cardiff Iron and Steel Works (for munitions).

Claridge complained:

I am unable to keep them supplied with their full quantity owing to the rotten state of the roads. In 1913, I was prevented using engines by Mr Leete, but it seems that other people can use them with impunity and nothing done in the matter. The roads are killing my horses, I lost two horses yesterday and have another one laid up with an abscess on the shoulder. My work will be at a standstill if something isn't done soon. I should be pleased to give you any further information you may require.

Ernest James Saunders, Surveyor, Leighton Buzzard Urban District Council (UDC) wrote to Marks on the same day, enclosing another letter from Claridge:

By his reference to the state of the roads, Mr Claridge means, he tells me, the damaged condition in which they have become recently owing to the tractor traffic. And that in consequence his horse traffic has been affected somewhat.

An Arnold's traction engine loaded with sand and the crew during the war; the speed limit of 5mph is newly painted on the side.

With reference to the tractor traffic here, I have noticed a tendency on the part of some of the drivers to considerably exceed the 5 miles per hour speed limit at times. I have spoken to Messrs Arnold's about the same.

Marks' response was emphatic. He was determined to stop the speeding and was concerned to ensure that the proper procedures would be carried out for a successful prosecution. On 2 April he wrote:

If the drivers of the tractors exceed the five miles an hour please report the facts to me at once and I will prosecute them. You must of course be prepared to prove that they did exceed the limit. The speed can only be satisfactorily ascertained by two persons with synchronised stop watches, so as to time the vehicles over a measured distance.

The state of the roads was of concern elsewhere, too, and Marks had decided to consult with other authorities. One of them was Henry Titus Wakelam of the Middlesex County Engineer's Office. In a three-page letter to Marks dated 8 March, Wakelam said:

To put the matter shortly the road, as it stands, is totally unfitted to carry continuous traffic, of heavily laden vehicles, of any kind. I advise therefore, that before any such traffic is allowed the carriageway should be reconstructed, on sound construction lines.

Meanwhile, the District Surveyor at Dunstable, Walter Mann, wrote to Marks on 13 March requesting:

For the maintenance and repair of Mile Tree Road from Arnold's new pit, I shall be requiring a considerable quantity of broken granite, and find it is impossible to obtain this from any of the granite firms unless they receive special instructions to supply the materials, and also the necessary railway wagons, from the Ministry of Munitions. Will you kindly apply for the permit with instructions to supply from one to three trucks per day as may be required to carry the said Sand Traffic for the government.

Marks inspected the roads again, this time with the County Surveyor of a neighbouring county and with Henry Percy Boulnois (Member of the Institute of Civil Engineers, Member of the Advisory Committee of the Roads Board), late Engineering Inspector of the Local Government Board. His first inspection had found that the only road length with serious damage was between the entrance to Page's Park and the entrance to Arnold's siding at Billington Crossing:

Another of Arnold's pits towards the end of the war; three machines for sorting and grading sand that occurs in different layers and colours. Even in black and white it is possible to see the difference between the lighter silver sand on the left and the two grades on the right.

At my visit on Saturday last I found that very serious damage had been caused to the long length of road from the sand pits and therefore serious damage will undoubtedly ensue when your eight additional tractors are put on the roads. I am advised that it will be necessary that the Acting County Surveyor should be supplied with a considerable quantity of broken granite and this cannot be obtained from any of the firms unless they receive special instructions from you and also the necessary railway wagons to supply one to three trucks per day as may be required from time to time.

He anticipated that additional labour would be needed but that this could only be provided by the Ministry of Munitions. This was substantiated by a four-page report dated 26 March from Boulnois:

Roads inspected included: 1) Billington Road from Stone Hill to Billington Crossing, 2) Stone Hill to Union Street, 3) Union Street to Heath Road, 4) from commencement of Heath Road to Mr Arnold's Sand Pits, 5) Mile Tree

Road from Kingsway Pit to Nine Acre Pit, 6) Garside's Pit to the Urban District boundary of Leighton Buzzard [Shenley Hill Road].

These roads had previously been 'well fitted to carry the normal sand traffic of the District'.

Boulnois concluded that:

> All the roads require their surfaces to be lightly scarified and shaped to a proper contour upon which should be laid broken metal [the granite stones], rolled and consolidated to a thickness of at least 3½ inches. If it is possible to obtain tar-slag or a good quality of tar macadam it would be better to use this rather than water-bound macadam, as it is too soft a character to withstand for any length of time the crushing action of heavy and continuous self-propelled traffic.

The services of Ernest Saunders in directing the road repairs were said to be indispensable to the supply of sand, the roads having become 'practically impassable for ordinary traffic' and he was one of the subjects of a lengthy letter from the indefatigable Marks, dated 14 June, to Captain Dowler of the Ministry of Munitions about Leighton's roads. Extracts include:

> The County Surveyor was then and still is in France engaged on road work under Brigadier General Maybury. Two of the District road surveyors were and are serving in the same force. After many consultations with the Director of Steel Production and with the Roads Board it was arranged that the work of re-construction should be undertaken by the Roads Board on the understanding that they should receive the assistance of the Deputy County Surveyor.
>
> Should Mr Saunders be called up for Military Service the work of road construction will come to a standstill and the conveyance of sand over these roads must of necessity cease. I may say at the present time the roads are in such a state that even last week five of the motor tractors broke down and the average weekly output of sand was diminished by 400 tons. The roads are practically impassable for ordinary traffic. I shall therefore be glad to hear that Mr E.J. Saunders will be exempted from military duty so long as he is engaged on the reconstruction of these roads.

Two months later, a letter from Albert Victor Pryer (Deputy County Surveyor) spelled out in detail his inspection of the Leighton Roads Board's roads, made in the company of 'Private E.J. Saunders (late Surveyor to the UDC)'. It would appear that Marks' request for military service exemption for his surveyor went unheeded but that he emerged victorious when Saunders was seconded from the army to the road repair programme.

Pryer reported:

> Union Street to Page's Park entrance – a gang of men and one Steam Roller were engaged in resurfacing this length. Page's Park to Billington Crossing: the work done during Mr Saunders' time has not yet been surfaced. Except for slight depression and unevenness owing to the large material used it is withstanding the traffic very well.

He advised Mr Handford, the Roads Board representative, to bring to the notice of John Spencer Killick (Chief Engineer to the Roads Board) the condition of Vandyke and Mile Tree roads, 'for I am confident that unless urgent steps are taken to improve the present condition the tractor haulage will stop'.

The constant flow of letters between the Ministry, the suppliers of sand, the foundries that needed more and more sand for 'war purposes', and the county council's laments over the state of the roads continued for the rest of the war, and the situation was only truly resolved afterwards.

Many other insights into the complexity of the sand trade can be gained from the letters. In a dispute about responsibility for 30 yards of badly damaged road to Garside's new Checkley Wood Farm pit, the output from the pit was used as an argument for urgent action to resolve the problem. Because some of Garside's other pits had become exhausted it was proposed to extract the required sand from this new pit, but it was to be an enormous quantity. In the month of November 1917, a return of the traffic from all Garside's pits shows that 1,370 tons of sand were produced, of which 452 tons were for steel, 712 tons were for munitions, 26 tons were for glass and 180 tons were for ordinary work.

Gradually the tone of the letters changes. They start by detailing the desperate problems threatening sand production and battling over the possible solutions to repair the damaged roads, and evolve into letters of co-operation and problem solving. It was all about the availability of both repair materials and the labour needed to do the work of re-constructing the badly rutted roads. There was clearly a huge increase in demand for various types of sand – to keep the various types of foundry going and to meet the near insatiable demands of the military for more ordnance – and the quarry owners rose to the challenge. The Roads Board did their very best to keep up the repair work and to obtain granite and other requirements so that the Ministry of Munitions could keep their supply chain going.

When the Armistice was signed on 11 November 1918, the Ministry of Munitions shifted rapidly into reverse. Orders for guns and military hardware of all sorts were being cancelled and production was halted if at all possible, but as far as the sand companies were concerned it appeared to be business as usual. Orders were still coming in and the supply demands had to be met. Men were in the pits digging to fulfil these orders, but in what must have come as a severe shock, the government announced they would no longer be responsible for paying the road repair bills. At the same time they issued an instruction ordering the sand companies to dispose of their steam tractors and lorries before the end of January 1919, not three months after the end of the war.

The *LBO* reported that on 5 February 1919, as the twelve steamers lined up for sale in heavy snow, they made an imposing show, each drawing up under full steam. Ten of them were 5 ton compound steam tractors, the others were traction engines. This was:

> The End of the Tractors: Leighton Buzzard has seen the last of the steam tractors, and there are few people living in or near the roads between the sandpits and the railway sidings who are not devoutly thankful. When the war broke out, there were one or two tractors employed in the transport of sand, but the cutting off of supplies of Belgian sand, which had hitherto come to British steel makers at ballast rates, altered the whole character of the trade. Leighton sandpits were drawn upon for deficiency, and became at once of national importance. By railway and canal enormous quantities were sent to the various munition centres and a dozen steam tractors were pressed into the work of transporting sand from the pits to the railway. No roads could stand such traffic for long. The Road Board were compelled to take charge of the roads affected, and it is no secret that the cost of maintenance has been greater than the cost of constructing a tramway from the pits to the railway sidings. The traffic ceased at the end of January, when the Roads Board handed back the roads to the county and left the tractor owners to face the problems and liabilities of what is legally known as 'extraordinary traffic'.

Their solution was to install a light railway. With the opening of the railway the 'sand carters' were declared redundant and from the description in the *LBO*, this was a group of men whose disappearance was not going to be lamented.

> He came into existence many, many years ago when the sand trade began to develop from a purely local into a national trade. As a type he was unmistakable. He was generally young and hefty, a knotted muffler his neckwear; he wore his cap at a 'don't care' angle and a fag end gave him his final touch of freedom and independence. He might be met at any time of the day between 7 a.m. and 4 p.m., singly or in strings, making one of his four journeys a day between Shenley Hill or Double Arches and Grovebury Crossing, and he had a reputation of beating all records in the twin arts of wearing out horses and the roads. Nothing disturbed him, nothing perturbed him. Old ladies might glare as he rode by, basking in the sun like some eastern potentate on a throne of golden sand. Little he cared.

The war brought him to the height of his prosperity. Whilst lesser fry such as shop assistants and owners of one-man businesses were called up he was protected even after (Class) A men from other businesses had been ruthlessly combed out. But the greater the eminence the greater the fall. Saturday (29 November) saw the dismissal of a big batch of carters and this week will see the sale by auction of 36 of the horses and 40 of the carts. The cheapening of the transport costs from the pits to the railway sidings will provide other and perhaps less congenial work in the pits, but the sand carter as a local institution is gone. Mr Marks of Bedfordshire County Council Highways section will not weep; the aforesaid old ladies will not weep, and those 36 horses 'all out of hard work' as the auctioneer naively put it, will not shed crocodile tears.

CHAPTER 4

GUN CARRIAGES AND AEROPLANES

The start of the war must have been a severe shock to the business of Morgan & Co. Almost immediately after the opening of hostilities the London gentry and the Buckinghamshire hunting fraternity abandoned their field sports and focused their attention on the conduct of the war and what they could do to help. Instructions were received from the Ministry of Munitions that their horses, for both riding and pulling carriages, were to be very quickly absorbed into the army. In addition, their large country houses were quietly closed up 'until the hostilities ceased', or were requisitioned for military use.

For Morgan's this caused a huge decrease in their business. New carriages were not ordered and older carriages were neither repaired nor refurbished.

Morgan's directors, who must have had good connections, looked to the Ministry of Munitions for orders to overcome this adverse impact upon their business. They were soon instructed to construct much-needed equipment for the artillery – limber wagons and gun carriages. The horse-drawn limber was indispensable for towing heavy guns and carrying the ammunition. It was a two-wheeled cart composed of an axle and wheels, with an ammunition chest mounted on the axle containing the rounds for the artillery piece being towed. The lid was designed to seat the driver. At the back of the limber's axle was the tow hitch to which the artillery piece was attached. A team of horses was hitched to the front, and towed the limber and artillery piece when on the move. In times of battle, the limber and horses were left behind the lines of fire and it was then that the gun carriage was required. The artillery piece was mounted on the gun carriage to enable it to be transported to its final position where it could be adjusted, aimed and then fired.

In the *Bucks Herald* of 31 October 1914, less than three months after the start of the war and under the heading 'The War – the Outlook', it was reported: 'The position locally is fairly satisfactory, there being no distress of any kind. Messrs Morgan & Co. Ltd. are now at work on a Ministry of Munitions contract which

Three of the Morgan's girls employed to stitch the canvas on to the wings of the
aeroplanes being built in the former carriage works: Doris Lilian Troughton, May Odell
Dimmock and Nell Underwood.

is likely to keep them fully occupied for some months to come and this dissipates the only cloud which has existed locally…'.

Morgan's were happy to construct these limber wagons and gun carriages but this cannot fully have utilised the skills of the craftsmen employed in the construction of fine carriages before the war. Nor did it need the ability and willingness to innovate the company had shown in the marketing of motorcars and the construction of aeroplanes. This confidence in its skills led Morgan's to approach the Ministry of Munitions for orders related to the newly created aspect of warfare, the aeronautical arena.

The British Expeditionary Force (BEF) had entered the war on the continent with 113 aeroplanes, and it was soon clear that this was grossly inadequate. Realising that aircraft were an indispensable part of modern warfare, the Ministry of Munitions quickly organised a number of individual suppliers into producing batches, each making one type. Morgan's was one of the largest. By the end of the war the Royal Air Force (RAF) was deploying thousands of aircraft of many different types. In total Morgan's received wartime orders for the construction of 700 aeroplanes, of which 640 were constructed and delivered before the Armistice.

With these orders in addition to the limber wagons and gun carriages the company grew in size. Some of its workers went off to fight in the war, and advertisements appeared in local papers inviting women to train in unnamed aircraft factories. By the end of hostilities they were employing 798 staff, 525 men and 373 women.

Censorship had a tight grip on newspapers, so the existence of an aircraft factory in Linslade was a closely guarded secret. However, a curious item appeared in the *LBO* in May 1917 about the delivery of the first 'bus' from Morgan's Works. It was revealed that the 'bus' was delivered to Farnborough, which, although the paper did not say so, was the Royal Flying Corps' main testing station for new and rebuilt aircraft. Morgan's works manager, Charles Richardson, threw a party in Linslade for all 400 employees, including the 100 women. He said that the women (who stitched the canvas on the wings and applied the chemical compound, known as dope, which shrunk this), had worked until 3.00 a.m. to complete the 'bus.' The customers at Farnborough said they had never seen a finer bus and they were going to order another hundred.

Aircraft must have been wheeled or hauled through the streets at least five times a week for the remaining twenty months of the war, but because of reporting restrictions this was never mentioned in local newspapers. The only hint was in a newspaper report in 1917 when an RFC tow truck was reported to have damaged a shop awning in Bridge Street. Although the report did not say so, it was almost certainly the result of an aeroplane being towed through the town and snagging the awning in the narrow street.

The authorities must have feared that if the importance of the work at Morgan's became known to the Germans the factory would have been made a target for a sabotage attempt or a Zeppelin airship raid.

The press is not always to be denied, however, and a way was found of getting round the restrictions. A long article of 25 September 1917 in the *LBO* described the workings of a 'modern aeroplane factory' somewhere in Buckinghamshire. The paper said this description was 'sufficiently vague to tantalise the Hun.' The reporter then described how the planes were made from 'Canadian silver spruce and ash coppiced in Bucks. Steel tubes of paper-like thickness, steel wire of fabulous strength and aluminium alloy, which is very light, very strong and very, very costly. The pilot sat in a bullet-proof seat.' There was also an account of women attaching the fabric to the wings so that the stitches were on the inside, to prevent the plane being torn apart by the 'skin friction' that the plane would suffer while travelling at the speed of 'two miles a minute'. The workers were said to be earning higher wages than at any time in their lives, and the speed with which the planes were produced brought bonuses to the workforce. Every machine made helped to shorten the war.

What little can be gleaned from the newspaper reports at the time includes the fact that Morgan's had a grass aerodrome along the Billington Road. The aircraft were moved from the works and up Bridge Street, along the High Street to Market Square and down Lake Street, and delivered to Scott's Field, a large flat area beyond

One of the 200 Airco de Havilland DH6 machines made in Linslade and used as a trainer by the RFC. They were easy and inexpensive to build and easy to repair after their frequent prangs by trainee pilots. (RAF Air Historical Branch.)

The Avro 504K: a lightweight but robust biplane for warfare which could be flown with a variety of engines to help cope with the national shortage. Later, more advanced aircraft came along and it was used as a trainer until the end of the war. (RAF Air Historical Branch.)

Page's Park. Special silver studs, similar to cat's eyes, were said to be hammered into the road at the junction of Market Square and Lake Street to guide the planes through the narrow gap between the town hall and the shops. On Billington Road there was a special dormitory building where the pilots were housed while waiting for their planes to be delivered from the other side of town.

One of the most fascinating newspaper advertisements appeared in March 1918 for people buying National War Bonds and War Saving Certificates. 'Linslade and District are asked to provide sufficient money to purchase two aeroplanes costing £2,500 each' (at least £110,000 in 2017). Underneath was the line: 'The government is purchasing aeroplanes made in this district. Will you help pay for them?' Morgan's built two hundred each of three types of aircraft for the Ministry of Munitions.

The training aircraft Airco de Havilland DH6 had low maximum and stalling speeds and was deliberately made unstable to prepare pilots for the foibles of the operational aeroplanes in which they would fly. It is perhaps for this reason that the frequent nickname of the DH6 was 'the clutching hand'. The instructor and pupil sat in tandem on basketwork seats in a single cockpit, spartan even by the standards of the time. The instructor had a device which enabled him to disconnect the trainee pilot's flight controls in the event of the need to wrest the controls of the aeroplane from a panicking learner before the machine crashed.

More than 2,280 DH6 aeroplanes were constructed and the RAF ended the war with over 1,000 of this type, many of which were transferred abroad to see further military service in the fledgling air forces of other countries.

The Avro 504K was among the 113 machines which crossed the English Channel to support the British Expeditionary Force in 1914. To avoid drawing attention to the French airship base at Belfort, their destination, these were crated, shipped and delivered by rail. They were briefly used as bombers to attack the Zeppelin sheds in Friedrichshafen. Three Avro 504Ks took off, each aeroplane carrying four 20lb bombs. En route one plane was destroyed by the Germans. However, the attack was very successful, and resulted in the destruction of a Zeppelin in its shed and of the adjacent hydrogen generating plant used for filling the gasbags inside each Zeppelin.

The Sopwith 1½ Strutter was designed in June 1916. Tommy Sopwith travelled to France and, following a meeting in the RFC's headquarters in St Omer, went on to tour a number of aerodromes where he questioned the RFC pilots about the qualities of their existing machines. Later, back in his Brooklands Works, Sopwith revealed his findings to his team of chief test pilot, works manager and the rest of his inner circle. As a result of this meeting a series of designs came off the Sopwith drawing boards.

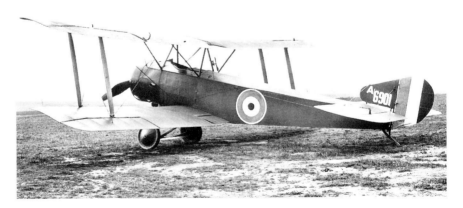

The curiously named Sopwith 1½ Strutter, so called because the central W-shaped struts that hold the wings are attached to the fuselage and are half the normal size. (RAF Air Historical Branch.)

The first operational delivery was in spring 1916 to the Royal Naval Air Service (RNAS) and the aeroplanes were used as bomber-escorts, a type of fighter aircraft. Subsequently the 1½ Strutter had bomb rails fitted beneath the bottom wing and was used also as a bomber. The RFC's first frontline squadron to operate the 1½ Strutter received the aeroplane on 24 May 1916. The first task for these machines was a reconnaissance mission over Cambrai, at the beginning of the Battle of the Somme. One of the RFC pilots, Cecil Lewis, wrote: 'It was the greatest bombardment of the war, the greatest in the history of the world. It was now a continuous vibration, as if Wotan, in some paroxysm of rage, were using the hollow world as a drum and under his beat the crust of it was shaking. Nothing could live under that rain of splintering steel.'

When first introduced, the 1½ Strutter was highly regarded for conducting long-distance patrols and reconnaissance operations with the ability to take care of itself if attacked by German aeroplanes. However, the Germans soon developed faster machines, such as the new Albatros and Halberstadt scouts. The RFC pilots developed a method of fighting the faster Germans by flying beneath the enemy's formation and attempting to lure them down to their lower altitude. As the Germans dropped down to attack, the observers in the 1½ Strutters attempted to shoot them down with machine-guns.

The RNAS planned to use the 1½ Strutter as a naval spotter for their largest ships. A Ship 1½ Strutter was constructed; the machine guns with their synchronisation gear were removed and an Aldis signalling lamp and a simple and light wireless set fitted, to enable the aeroplane to communicate with the Royal Navy vessels below. The machine was launched from a 30ft long wooden platform built over a gun turret. The ship speeded up and angled itself to the wind with the turret facing directly into the wind. Sailors held on to the wings and fuselage of the aircraft, the tail was placed on a special trolley and the pilot revved up the engine. The pilot waved his hand when the engine reached maximum revs, the sailors released their grip and, hopefully, the aeroplane took off. Following the mission the 1½ Strutter was flown back to the ship and landed on the sea, where the pilot waited for a launch to take him off. Sometimes the machine was recovered by the ship. Subsequently, the RNAS used the 1½ Strutter on board the early aircraft carriers.

Sopwith only constructed 146 1½ Strutters during the war, and a number of sub-contractors also worked for the Ministry of Munitions to build the model. Morgan & Co. built 200 of the total of 1,200 constructed during that period.

Finally, there was one other aircraft, destined to be the best known of all the Morgan's aeroplanes even though only forty were built in the town. It was by far the largest, and gave its name to Vimy Road in Linslade, one of the few remaining reminders of Morgan's.

Following German bomber air raids over England, which began on 23 May 1917, and the realisation that the Allies needed to engage Germany on many war

An aerial view of Morgan's works. The enormous building in which the Vickers Vimy bomber was built was erected in 1917. In the foreground, the River Ouzel (now straightened), and behind the works, the Grand Union Canal, Wing Road and Linslade.

The men working on the fuselages of Vickers Vimy bombers in the last days of the war. The planes were equipped with Rolls-Royce engines that had just been delivered and were ready to be fitted.

fronts, a Ministry of Munitions requirement was produced for a British bomber capable of flying to Germany with a substantial bomb load at a height above the range of the anti-aircraft weapons of the day. Three manufacturers responded to the requirement with their designs, the de Havilland DH10 Amiens, the Handley Page V/1500 and the Vickers FB27, later to be known as the Vickers Vimy.

The Vickers aeroplane design team was led by Reginald Kirshaw 'Rex' Pierson, who at the age of 26 had been appointed Vickers' chief designer. The Vickers FB27 was the first aeroplane which was designed in its entirety by Pierson, who moved from his offices in Knightsbridge to Linslade to supervise the construction of the prototype ordered from Morgan's. The existing factory was not large enough to house what was then an enormous aircraft, so it was decided to build the prototype in a vast new shed built on the sports field behind the existing works.

Three prototypes were built by Morgan's. They were so large that the planes could not be squeezed through the gap between the town hall and the shops on the other side of the road in order to reach Scott's Field. Instead the wings were carried separately and attached to the fuselage on the airfield before the aircraft took off for delivery to Farnborough.

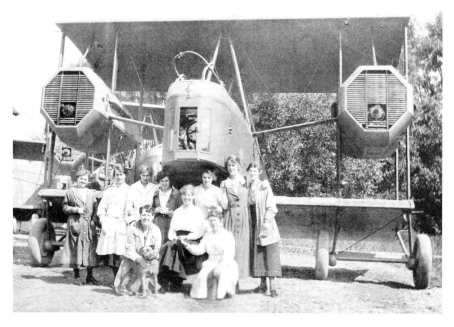

Completed fuselage sections of the Vickers Vimy bomber ready to be wheeled through the town to Scott's Field where the wings would be attached and the planes flown to Farnborough for a final check. Alice Dunleavy and her dog pose with some staff and workers. (Bryan Dunleavy)

A Vimy bomber was used by the RAF as its main bomber until 1925; its stability and strength made it a candidate for other uses, including attempts at distance records.

The prototype FB27 flew on 30 November 1917, a little more than four months from the start date of the design by Pierson, a remarkable achievement. It had a maximum speed of 100mph, and was designed to be armed with a Lewis gun and able to carry 2,476 lb of bombs.

The prototype FB27 was test-flown with a number of different designs of engine until the Rolls-Royce Eagle was selected for the production aeroplanes. In early 1918 the RAF introduced the use of official aeroplane names and the Vickers FB27 became the Vickers Vimy, after the successful taking of Vimy Ridge by the Canadian forces. Although production of the operational aeroplane by Morgan's went ahead, only one example of the Vickers Vimy was operational with the RAF by the Armistice on 11 November 1918.

Most of the Vickers Vimys that went into service after the war were built elsewhere. The *Bucks Herald* reported on 10 October 1919 that 'a new Vimy bomber aeroplane, equipped with two Rolls Royce engines and valued at over £8,000, was destroyed by fire at Messrs Morgan & Co's aerodrome at Leighton Buzzard', thus ending Morgan's links to the aircraft.

When the war ended, restrictions on reporting were lifted. The *LBO* said in its first edition after the Armistice was declared,

One of the romances of the war, which ought to be written when censorship permits, is the work done by Morgan and Co Ltd. Since 4 April 1917 no fewer than 500 'machines' have been produced by those works, including one machine

This Vickers Vimy, piloted by Alcock and Brown in June 1919, was the first aircraft to cross the Atlantic. As they landed in Ireland, the nose sank into a bog, the pair having mistaken the bright green for a grass field. The plane was rescued and now hangs from the ceiling in the Science Museum, London.

which was likely to be a remarkable peace accelerator. For the present at any rate it is believed that work will continue on normal lines, except that excessive overtime will be stopped. When the news of the Armistice arrived yesterday morning a meeting of the workers was addressed by the works manager. National anthems [sic] were sung and the workers were given a half-day's holiday on full pay.

Sadly the 'romance of Morgan's' never appears to have been written.

CHAPTER 5

A VERY SHORT LIFE EXPECTANCY

The flimsy aeroplanes built during the First World War were easily shot down. They were slow and difficult to fly and half the volunteers lost their lives in crashes before they qualified. The pilots who did get to the Front were incredibly brave young men. Once they had started combat missions they had an average life expectancy of just eleven days.

In the early days of the war there were very few flying machines. The Royal Flying Corps had come into being on 13 April 1912 as the air arm of the army and was formally launched on 1 July 1914, although the navy had been using aircraft well before that. After massive growth in the number and types of planes the two organisations were finally merged on 1 April 1918 to become the RAF.

Initially these primitive machines were mainly used for reconnaissance to spy out the enemy positions and troop movements. They also checked that the Allied artillery was hitting its intended targets. They were not armed but German and Allied pilots took pot shots at each other with revolvers, rifles and shotguns. Although the early aircraft were tiny, they were soon used for bombing and the damage they could inflict was more symbolic than devastating. To start with small bombs were simply thrown over the side of the aircraft in the direction of the target.

The Germans had developed Zeppelins and other airships that could fly higher than aircraft and were intended to bomb industrial targets and strike fear into civilians.

Britain's own airships were invaluable for reconnaissance and as a deterrent. Percy William Avery, an RAF air mechanic 1st class from Leighton, was fortunate enough to be a crew member on an airship. His enthusiastic letter about his flight was published on 19 March 1918 in the *North Bucks Times*:

I have had my first flight in our airship, No. 9, 1,000 horsepower. It was simply lovely. We were up in the air nine hours, and covered a distance of 350 miles. Our journey was to London, dropping leaflets. We came as far as Willesden, circled all round Wormwood Scrubs, went all over the Strand and Westminster. I can't explain to you on paper what it was like. I am going up again tomorrow (Sunday), out to sea, by the Wash. I have been very excited since the officer told me I was to go up with them. In a good many places we dropped to 250 feet from the ground, and could see everybody running out of their houses and people stopping their horses and motors to have a look up, because our engines make such a noise.

Airships had considerable propaganda value at the start of the war but proved cumbersome. All sides quickly realised that for military purposes the future lay in fixed-wing aircraft.

By 1916 both sides in the war were building as many aircraft as possible and arming them with machine guns. The Royal Aircraft Factory at Farnborough, which had previously produced most British machines, handed over large-scale production to companies like Morgan's. When the machines were completed in Linslade they were flown to Farnborough, where the aircraft were tested before being sent off to the Front.

The increasing military importance of the RFC led to a recruiting drive in October 1917 particularly for people with the skills needed to build them.

Although the number of people serving in the air services was small compared with those signing up for the traditional services, the army and the navy, at least nine young men from the district are known to have volunteered to fly as the way to fight for their country. Of those, most died in service.

Lieutenant Hamilton Elliott 'Tim' Hervey, served with distinction in the RFC. He was not born locally but is included here because he lived for many years in Great Billington until his death on 30 May 1990, aged 94. He became well known and liked due to his later career in flying, including service in the Second World War.

At the outbreak of war in August 1914, Hervey had recently begun a three-year course in engineering, but on his 19th birthday in the November he joined the RFC, serving first on the ground as a rigger then in the air as a gunner, a gunner-observer and later as a flying officer observer and flying officer pilot. In July 1915 he was sent to France and received his commission in the early part of 1916. In November 1916, while an observer, he was awarded the Military Cross and Bar for shooting down and capturing a German Albatros and its pilot before the plane could be destroyed. The Bar was awarded at the same time for his continued skill as an air gunner. His skill and luck as a pilot kept him alive when many of his contemporaries were killed, sometimes in their first week in action. His total number of flights logged was 175, of which eighty-four hours were as a pilot. Danger increased, however, as the Germans developed superior aeroplanes.

His original flying logs have survived the years, and his last entry for the war records that on 7 April 1917 he was detailed for a dawn patrol as one of a formation of five. His flight commander was Billy Bishop VC, Canada's top flying ace of

G R

5,000 Women

ARE WANTED EVERY WEEK FOR THE

W.A.A.C.

WOMEN'S ARMY AUXILIARY CORPS
for work with the Forces at Home and Abroad.

THE ROYAL FLYING CORPS

REQUIRES IMMEDIATELY

500 SAIL MAKERS to make and repair
Aeroplane Wings—Good Needlewomen who can also use the sewing machine.

150 STORE KEEPERS (Class I), and
women for engineering and other work.

Women are also urgently required as Cooks, Clerks, Waitresses,
Driver Mechanics, all kinds of Domestic Workers and in many other
capacities to take the place of men.

GOOD WAGES. UNIFORM. QUARTERS. RATIONS.

For all information and advice apply at
NEAREST EMPLOYMENT EXCHANGE.
The address can be obtained at any POST OFFICE.

GREAT BRICKHILL.

SEQUEL TO SOLDIER'S SUICIDE

MARRIED WOMAN CHARGED WITH AIDING AND ABETTING.

Emily Mapley, living at Priory Street Lodge, Newport Pagnell, whose husband is a corporal in a Railway Works Battalion, serving in Salonika, was charged at Newport Pagnell Police Court on Wednesday that she did feloniously and maliciously aid and abet, incite, move, counsel and procure one John Charles Jackson to feloniously, wilfully, and of malice aforethought kill himself on the 27th day of August, 1917, at Great Brickhill.

Mr. Darnell (Northampton) defended.

Dr. Cecil Powell, of Stony Stratford, deputy coroner for North Bucks, spoke to conducting the inquest on Corpl. Jackson at Fenny Stratford Police Station on August 29th, when the jury returned a verdict that the deceased soldier committed suicide by shooting himself in the chest with a pistol, and that at the time he was of sound mind.

Capt. John Brown, R.A.M.C., attached to the Royal Engineers' Depot, Fenny Stratford, said on the 27th August he was called to a field in the neighbourhood of Great Brickhill and there he found the dead body of Corpl. Jackson. A revolver was lying about six inches from his right hand, and there was a bullet wound about three inches below the left breast.

Supt. Dibben, (to whose evidence Mr. Darnell objected on the ground that he had not warned the woman before he obtained a statement from her) said that when the interview took place on the day of Jackson's death he had no intention of taking any proceedings against her and knew nothing of the facts of the case. When he told her Jackson was dead she enquired, "Did he shoot himself with a pistol?" and then broke down completely. She said: "Jackson came to live with me on Wednesday, 30th May, 1917. He was billeted here. He told me he was a married man with four children and expected another. He came round enquiring for a billet and said he wished to come here. I told him my husband was away. He said he was on special diet. He came to sleep. On the first or second day he loved me. He stopped with me two weeks and four days. The children and I usually went to bed together. No lights or curtains. One night he called, 'Bring me a candle.' Then something happened which caused me to faint. I told him ...

EVERSHOLT.

STARLINGS. — The starlings have now assembled in large flocks. Thousands go over the village nightly and are very destructive, especially to the damson trees, which they soon clear of fruit.

AIR RAIDS.—On Saturday, Sunday and Monday week the rockets which were sent up during the raid on London were very plainly seen here and looked like gigantic fireworks. The raids have brought a large number of people into the village from London, and they give accounts of nerve racking experiences. Nearly thirty have found lodgings in the village, and all seem glad to be able to get out of London for a short spell.

STANBRIDGE.

HARVEST FESTIVAL.—The service in the church on Sunday week was one of thanksgiving for the ingathering of the harvest and was conducted by the Vicar, Rev. T. Green. The building had been very tastefully decorated by several members. Similar services were also held in the Wesleyan Chapel. The special preacher was Mr. Elliott, of Stewkley, and at the evening service Miss Elliott sang. In the afternoon the choir gave a service of song, "Reaping Time," Miss Rush being the reader. On Monday evening the service of song was repeated, the reader being the Rev. J. Ogden. There was also the

---

Advertisement in the *LBO* for women to help make the fragile aircraft airworthy and
to repair them when they were damaged. Presumably some would be sent to work in
Morgan's factory and some to RFC airfields.

the war, credited with seventy-two victories. The formation was attacked by Germany's infamous 'Flying Circus', No. 1 Fighter Squadron, formed by Manfred von Richthofen, more familiarly known as the Red Baron. Von Richthofen said he liked hunting enemy pilots and claimed eighty 'kills' before he too was shot down and died on 21 April 1918. In this encounter with the Circus, Hervey's machine was badly damaged and dropped 9,000ft in an uncontrolled spin. His log recalls that he managed to pull out of this and fly back to the aerodrome, but the plane was a write-off.

The log entries ended the very next day when Hervey took off on another mission and failed to return. He was stationed with No. 60 Squadron based at Le Hameau, a few miles from Arras. The big Spring Offensive was due to start so there was much aerial activity.

He wrote this:

No. 60 was having a run of bad luck; in fact, during my last week with the squadron we lost no fewer than ten pilots out of a total strength of eighteen.

Four RFC observers training to be pilots at Upavon in February 1917. In the background is a Sopwith 1½ strutter of the sort made by Morgan's. All were shot down; two pilots survived because they were taken prisoner.
Left to right: Lieutenant Thomas Sharpe (POW); Lieutenant William Wetheral Chapman (killed in action); Lieutenant Tim Hervey; Lieutenant Arthur Gardner Brewis (killed in action). (Rosamond Clayton, née Hervey.)

Equipped with single-seater Nieuport Scouts (machines that had done excellent work in 1916), we were hopelessly outclassed in speed and climb by the new German Albatros. Added to that, our daily patrols led us over Douai, the home of Richthofen's famous 'Circus' and we rarely cross the lines without coming up against this squadron.

On April 8, Easter Sunday, I was detailed for early morning patrol. We started at dawn. Climbing through the clouds, we crossed the lines and, on nearing Douai, saw a flight of Albatroses coming up to meet us. In the scrap that followed Bishop [his flight commander] shot down two Huns, Milo (a French Canadian) was killed, and the flight became separated in heavy cloudbanks.

I was making my solitary way back to Arras, hoping to pick up the rest of the flight there, when an anti-aircraft gun opened up on me, and a large fragment of shrapnel passed through my bottom 'plane and lodged in my engine. At first I had a faint hope that I should be able to glide back over our lines, but I had not sufficient height, and eventually finished up on top of a well-camouflaged German artillery dugout. My machine was immediately surrounded and I was unceremoniously hauled out, head first, and was just beginning to think I was in for a 'rough house' when two officers appeared. These two called off their men, arranged for the removal of my machine, and then took me to their billet. Here I had lunch with the battery commander and his officers, afterwards being taken to headquarters for examination. While awaiting this, locked in a small room, I took the opportunity of eating the cover of my pass book, which showed the number of my squadron, having no other way of satisfactorily disposing of it. This was my last square meal for some weeks.

He remained a prisoner of war for twenty-two months, until peace was declared, and was moved between several different locations deep within Germany.

During his internment, along with other internees he made several determined and mostly ingenious attempts to escape, but none of these escapades was fully successful although he was Mentioned in Despatches for trying to get home from Germany. He was also lucky to survive the experience.

On his final attempt to escape, with 21-year-old Brian Horrocks, later to become Lieutenant-General Sir Brian Horrocks, KCB, KBE, DSO, MC, he came perilously close to sudden death. Both were making a dash from the prison camp. Horrocks, despite being shot at twice by a sentry – both shots missed their target – managed to break free and get to within 500 yards of the Dutch border before being recaptured. Hervey unfortunately tripped over a bucket and sprawled to the ground. The sentry ran up to him and pressed the trigger of his rifle, but nothing happened. He was taken off to jug and found himself in a small miserable room, with the sentry in the adjoining cell under arrest for a fortnight for having a defective weapon.

Hervey probably owed his life to being shot down and taken prisoner. Few of his contemporaries survived unless they were captured or too badly injured to resume flying. After Armistice Day, Hervey was released and made it back to England for Christmas.

In 1935 he became chief instructor at the London Gliding Club, based at Dunstable Downs, a position he held successfully until he rejoined the RAF in January 1940 at Haddenham where he taught the army to fly gliders. It was he who prompted MI9, a branch of the secret service based in Leighton Buzzard, to set up an escaping school that aided prisoners of war in the Second World War. He never lost his passion for flying, and not until reaching the age of 90 did he part, reluctantly, with his licence.

Not all local volunteers for the RFC had Hervey's good fortune:

Second Lieutenant Frederick Thomas Brasington, of 9 Squadron the RFC and General List, died aged 23 on 9 October 1917 when acting as observer in RE8 A3663, possibly shot down by Oberleutnant Bruno Loerzer of Jasta 26, between Langemarck and Bixschoote. Since June 1917, 9 Squadron had flown RE8 bomber aircraft with pilot and observer/gunner. The *Luton News* of 18 October 1917 said when they reported him missing 'he took a commission only a short time ago. He had been in France about a fortnight'.

Second Lieutenant Pilot Ernest Thubron Dunford, of 13 Sqdn the RFC, emigrated to Canada in 1911 and enlisted as 17112 of 7th Battalion the Canadian Expeditionary Force (CEF) a month after the outbreak of the war, giving his mother's address as Leighton Buzzard. He reached France in February 1915 and later transferred to the RFC, graduating as a flying officer in September 1916. On 11 April 1917 Dunford was piloting his BE 2d on an artillery observation mission. Also on board the biplane was Corporal George Stewart. Although fitted with a synchronised Vickers machine gun, the slow, heavy 2d was not suited to aerial combat and the aircraft was shot down. According to reports in the *LBO* of 17 and 24 April 1917 they were seen to land behind enemy lines, it was thought safely and that he was a prisoner of war and in hospital. However, in October 1917 his mother was told that her son had died of his wounds, aged 24, on 23 April. He was buried by his German captors, Corporal Stewart having already died.

Second Lieutenant John Alfred Lee, of 55 Squadron the RAF, died aged 18 on 25 August 1918 whilst acting as observer in DH4 A2131 during a bombing raid to Luxembourg. The aircraft was hit by anti-aircraft fire over enemy lines. During July and August 1918 Lee wrote a series of letters to his parents and the following, from an early letter, is a typical extract:

I was pretty lucky in getting put on a raid the morning after we arrived. Observers were a bit scarce; otherwise we might have had to wait a bit before doing anything. … I am not sorry at all to be over here, and it is not at all the

Tim Hervey in his RFC uniform before he became an officer and a pilot in 1917: a rare photographic record of an RFC uniform, few of which survive. (Rosamond Clayton, née Hervey.)

terrifying place described by some persons. It is, if anything, rather disappointing. I came out expecting 'blood, hair and teeth' all over the place, and instead there is little to see at all. We are living in a quiet peaceful place, only worried by Hun air raids which occur pretty frequently, but don't do much damage.

Second Lieutenant Pilot Arthur John Pearson, of 29 Squadron the RFC, was killed in action aged 29 on 9 March 1917 while flying DH2 A2571. He was shot down in flames between Roclincourt and Bailleul-sur-Berthoult, north-east of Arras by the notorious Red Baron, who claimed it as his twenty-fifth victory. Pearson first enlisted in the Royal Fusiliers during September 1914 and six months later was commissioned 2nd Lieutenant in 8th (Reserve) Battalion the Northamptonshires. He was transferred to the Machine Gun Corps (MGC) in 1916, following which his bravery won him a Military Cross. After his transfer to the RFC he trained as a pilot at Central Flying School, Upavon, and joined 29 Squadron (France) in December 1916. On 4 March 1917, he took part in bringing down an Albatros DII, the most modern and dangerous of the German planes within British lines. It was flown by one of the better-known German pilots, Lieutenant Max Bohme of Jasta 5, who was subsequently taken prisoner of war. Pearson grew up in Heath and Reach, where his parents continued to live until their deaths in the 1930s.

Lieutenant John 'Jack' Auguste Pouchot DCM, of 56 Squadron RAF, died aged 20 on 5 October 1918 while on a bomber escort mission when SE5a E5708 was shot down just behind German lines after attacking ground targets near Le Cateau. He was last seen at 13.30hrs east of Cambrai at 9,000 ft. He had moved to Leighton in 1904 with his mother and attended Beaudesert School while she was licensee of the Bell Hotel, High Street.

The stories of four who survived the war follow.

Edward Algernon Ray Hills, second lieutenant of the RFC, had a remarkable escape. The *Luton News* reported on 18 October 1917:

The only son of the Rev. G.F. Hills, Vicar of Leighton, 2nd Lieutenant E.A.R. Hills RFC, is now in King's College Hospital, Denmark Hill after a gratifying but marvellous escape from death. Not yet nineteen years of age, this young officer was leading a patrol over the German lines, when he was struck in the leg and his machine damaged. Starting to return, a second shot hit his propeller and carried part of it away, the fragment striking him on the forehead. The lieutenant had just sufficient consciousness to shut off his engine and land in a wood. He lapsed into unconsciousness, and on recovery found that soldiers were extricating him from the wreckage of his machine, Lieutenant Hills had the undercarriage of his aeroplane shot away earlier in the same week, and when he was wounded he was using a new machine.

His name is on a list of passengers bound for Australia in 1947.

Captain Cyril Norman Seedhouse of the RFC was born at Tavistock House, Grove Place, Leighton Buzzard when his father was a chemist and druggist in the town. He represented Great Britain at the 1912 Stockholm Olympics, winning a bronze medal in the 4 x 400 relay. Noted as the most daring of despatch riders, in 1916 he transferred to the RFC and on one mission was flying at a considerable height above the enemy lines with his observer, Hugh Cox, when their aircraft was attacked by two Fokker aeroplanes. However, Seedhouse manoeuvred so skilfully that the observer was able to get in 'some useful shooting,' and one of the planes was driven off. The second then attacked, and during the fight Cox noticed that his pilot had suffered a bullet wound in the back, yet he continued to outmanoeuvre the enemy machine until it broke off the action. By now Seedhouse was barely conscious, but he nevertheless managed to pilot the aircraft nearly 20 miles back to his aerodrome, where it was found to have suffered significant damage. The *North Bucks Times* of 21 March 1916 reported that he had now arrived at a hospital in England, and the RFC had 'expressed a deserved admiration for his example'. Seedhouse was 23 years old at the time of this encounter. The wound to his back was not too serious. It was a flesh wound, not too deep, the bullet having already spent itself on some metalwork. Once recovered, he was returned to military service as a flying instructor at Dundee. He died in Devon on 21 January 1966, but the emotional scars of his experiences never really healed.

Lieutenant Thomas Thornton Shipman of 87 Squadron the RAF was shot down in his Sopwith Dolphin by either Leutnant Wilhelm Neuenhofen or Vizefeldwebel Albert Lux of Jasta 27 on 10 August 1918. He was captured, news of which was reported on 18 September 1918:

> Amongst the airmen 'missing' in Friday's casualty list appears the name of Lieutenant T.T. Shipman RAF, who is well remembered in Leighton Buzzard for the remarkable exhibition of flying he gave over the town last spring, just before going to France. He joined the 8th Lincolns in the early days of the war, and when the Brigade came to Leighton Buzzard he was billeted with William and Edith Russwurm. The wounds he received at Thiepval made further service in the infantry quite impossible, and he then joined the Royal Flying Corps.

He spent the rest of the war in the officers' prisoner of war camp in Karlsruhe, later emigrating to Australia and dying there in 1976.

RAF Captain Harris Holberton Square was the son of a well-known local doctor, William Holberton Square, who treated the Prince of Wales after a hunting accident in which he broke his arm. Captain Square was 22 in 1914 when he became one of the first pilots of the war, serving as a flight sub-lieutenant in the RNAS. The *LBO* reported:

As airmen go he is quite an old flyer. Back in 1914 he was on seaplane patrol duty in the North Sea in connection with the detection of enemy submarines. Then in 1915 he took a hand in the defence of London against Zeppelin raids, and through no fault of his own had a bad crash with a Zeppelin, while night flying. He was in hospital for a long time and was discharged from service on medical grounds. But in 1917 he succeeded in persuading a medical board that he was fit for service again, and went out to France at once as a night bomber. Six months of this work caused a recurrence of his former illness and he was in hospital for three months, but at the conclusion of hostilities he was again in harness testing aeroplanes at an experimental station.

Captain Square married in Santander in 1921, and became the British Consul in Mexico, dying in Tampico in late December 1950.

CHAPTER 6

THE UNDERWATER MENACE

The invention of accurate torpedoes completely changed warfare at sea thirty years before the First World War and made the British Admiralty fear the Royal Navy would lose its supremacy. Bullivant and Co. Ltd, a company specialising in wire ropes, came to the rescue by inventing a torpedo net that could be hung like a skirt on booms round a ship. It would catch a torpedo and entangle it, preventing it striking the ship. Even if it did explode, damage would be limited. A measure of the urgency the navy had always felt at this threat is evident from an order made, remarkably, on the telephone in April 1885 only six years after the first telephone exchange was installed in London. The order was for 1,000 torpedo nets made of steel wire at the cost of £6 17s 6d each – all required to be sent to naval bases within ninety days. The first batch was to be delivered to Deptford where they 'are very urgently required'. and confirmation on paper followed the next day.

Although the nets proved adequate to protect ships from this fearful weapon for a few years, the respite did not last long. As happens with all arms races the torpedoes grew more sophisticated and powerful and had cutters fitted to the front to penetrate the nets. Bullivant's responded by patenting a device in April 1898 intended to defeat the cutters by placing steel rings round each joint in the net.

The company was in the forefront of making wire ropes and incredibly strong steel cables of all types both for the marine industry and for major construction projects like suspension bridges. They were used on the Royal Mail Steamer (RMS) *Titanic* to hold the main anchors, and pictures of the ship being launched were used in the company's sales brochure of the time. Bullivant's wire ropes were in demand all over the Empire, Europe and America.

Company headquarters was in Mark Lane near the Tower of London and they had a works at Millwall, but by 1912 Bullivant's decided that submarine nets were such an important part of the business that the company needed a factory dedicated solely to making this product. They set up a wire works for this in an old warehouse at the bottom of Lake Street, Leighton.

The rush order for torpedo nets from Bullivant's, showing the sudden fears for the battle fleet from this new kind of weapon that could be fired from a small boat and could sink a battleship. (Bridon Ropes, Doncaster Record Office.)

When war broke out in 1914 the technology had moved on again, and both Britain and Germany had developed even more powerful torpedoes. These could burst through the nets hung out to protect British warships. In the Admiralty there was again enormous alarm that the navy was not protected from these new weapons and there was no harbour safe from torpedoes or from the U-boats that fired them. A *Times* article on 20 October 1919, 'by our naval correspondent' reviewing the war, said:

Mr [Arthur] Balfour admitted, when First Lord, that there was no harbour on the east coast when war broke out which was adequately protected against the underwater menace, and Lord Jellicoe described in his book how the Grand Fleet

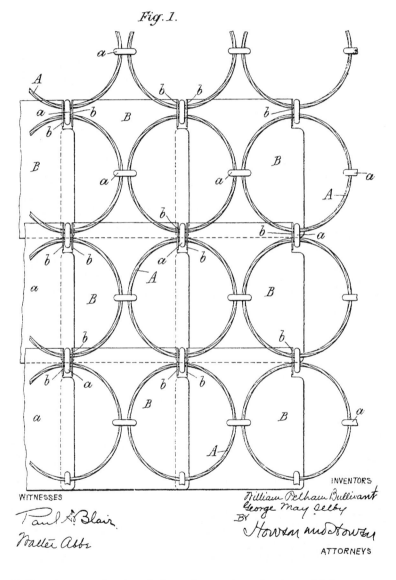

No. 804,704.

PATENTED NOV. 14, 1905.

W. P. BULLIVANT & G. M. SELBY.

TORPEDO NET.

APPLICATION FILED FEB. 28, 1905.

2 SHEETS—SHEET 1.

Fig. 1.

WITNESSES

INVENTORS

William Pelham Bullivant
George May Selby

BY

Howson and Howson

ATTORNEYS

Bullivant's patented various designs of net, as the technology of defence needed to keep pace both with the development of the U-boat and the increasing power of the torpedoes. The nets were supposed to be proof against both.

had to keep cruising almost continuously in the early days of hostilities, because, owing to the want of a secure anchorage, it was safer at sea than in harbour.

Again Bullivant's were asked to come to the rescue. *A History of the Wire Rope Industry of Great Britain* by E. R. Forestier Walker, written in 1952, says:

> On the outbreak of war in 1914 a tremendous demand arose, and the Admiralty leaned heavily on Bullivant's as the pioneers of such devices. Indeed it is the measure of their virtual monopoly in this matter that all harbour defences throughout the 1914-1918 war were supplied by Bullivant and Company.

At the outbreak of war Bullivant's kept on their original factory in Lake Street and built a new and much larger one in Grovebury Road, solely to produce the heavy-duty nets required. Boom defence nets were typically 200yds long and 48ft deep, and were made by splicing heavy greasy wires manually: difficult work. They were robust enough to be hung across the entrance to harbours, or supported on large buoys in a complete circle around a convoy at anchor. These were designed to protect the fleet in port from the U-boats entering the harbours or firing their torpedoes.

The company was brought under the control of the Ministry of Munitions although already subject to the Official Secrets Act. Years before, they had been barred from supplying any foreign power without permission. Because of the

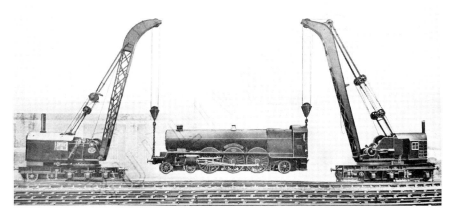

The Great Western Railway's 87-ton locomotive No. 111 *The Great Bear* being lifted on Bullivant's wire ropes: one of a number of illustrations in company brochures demonstrating just how strong their wire ropes were. (Bridon Ropes, Doncaster Record Office.)

importance of the work no one was allowed to report what was happening at the Leighton factory, thus precise details of what was made in the town are not known.

It must have been a large factory, however, and it is believed that up to 300 men, and boys who were too young to be called up, were employed there. Local tribunal hearings regularly exempted Bullivant's employees from military service. The first record of a tribunal sitting in the town was on 24 February 1916 when the case of nine wireworkers who were 'mostly young single men' was brought before the bench. All nine were granted exemptions without a hearing 'until the men leave their present employment'. There are also reports that when demand was very great in 1915, the basement of the Corn Exchange in Lake Street, also a large space, was taken over for making nets after it was no longer needed as a Red Cross hospital.

To give some idea of the importance of Bullivant's to the war effort, the company, which was already only a few yards from the railway, had its own siding built directly to the door of the Grovebury Road factory.

The map shows a siding running right up to the rear of the factory so that the heavy nets could be loaded directly into wagons.

The manager of the Leighton factory from its opening was Captain Thomas William Selby. His father and brother George had both been works managers of Bullivant's London operation but Thomas' early career had taken a different path. He had been an officer on the famous tea clipper *Cutty Sark* on its record-breaking trips from Australia to London. He joined the ship, aged 20, in 1886, first as a second mate and then as first mate. He was described as a 'highly regarded' officer although strict, and said to be 'a past master in the art of handling wire, in splicing it and knotting it'. He was given command of another clipper, the *Titania*, which regularly sailed between Vancouver in Canada and England.

When he retired from seafaring in 1908 he returned to England and Bullivant's where splicing wire was central to the business. His captaincy of ships had obviously made him a good leader, too, and in 1912 he was put in charge of the Leighton Buzzard operation, remaining in the post until 1923.

Perhaps the most extraordinary feat of Bullivant's and the torpedo nets made in Leighton was the continuous defensive net slung across the Channel to counter the U-boat menace. Torpedo nets weighing 8 tons and nearly 500ft long were supported by buoys and strung together in a continuous line across the Channel between England and France. The barrier was begun at Folkestone in 1915 and was intended to go all the way to Boulogne. Depending on the depths required, the nets were 48 to 96ft deep. In some places an additional net of 36ft was added to the 96ft deep type to make 132ft in all. To prevent the strong tidal currents from reducing the effectiveness of the nets, twenty-eight cast iron sinkers each weighing 370lbs were fastened to each net.

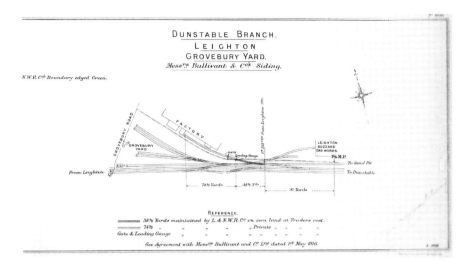

Drawing of the siding from the Leighton Buzzard to Dunstable line for the exclusive use of Bullivant's. The line went up to the entrance of their Grovebury Road factory. It also shows sidings to the gas works and Arnold's sandpit. The agreement with the L&NWR is dated 1 May 1916. (The London & North Western Railway Society.)

Laying and fixing the boom and net defences was mostly done by North Sea fishermen, pressed into service by the Admiralty. Many hundreds of trawlers and drifters were employed as supporting vessels, tenders and towing vessels. Most of the 6,000 people who crewed these various craft had been fishermen, who could no longer work because of the fear of enemy action. When the need for trawlers and drifters for minesweeping became urgent it was necessary to release some of these vessels from what was called the Boom Defence Service. To make good this loss, dumb barrage vessels without engines were designed and built, which could be towed into position and moored. These proved very successful. Fourteen such vessels, specially fitted, were utilised with good results to secure the last Dover Strait Barrage, in which they were moored permanently in two continuous lines across the Channel.

By 1916 most of the net was in place, but keeping it intact proved extremely difficult. There were not enough craft to police it, and as a result many Allied ships, not warned of its presence, blundered into it, fouling their propellers and punching holes in it. After a year it was officially abandoned, and there is still some dispute as to how successful it was. The Admiralty reported that all hostile enemy submarines had disappeared from the area, so frightened were they of being caught in the net. However, evidence later emerged that some German submarines had continued to slip through the Channel.

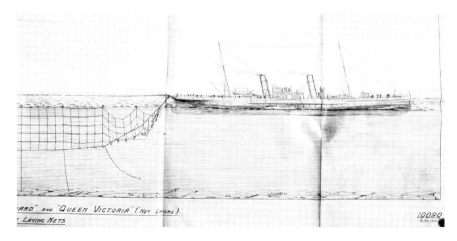

Sets of drawings, showing how submarine nets were slung below buoys and towed into position by ships. They lay folded up in the archives for nearly a century. Dozens of small craft were involved in the operation to protect British ports from U-boats. (Bridon Ropes, Doncaster Record Office.)

Bullivant's designed and built many types of ingenious nets. These included a net which sent up a flare when snagged by a submarine so that the craft could be tracked and attacked. Another, the mine-catching net, was originally designed to be towed through the Dardanelles to clear a safe passage for the warships before the invasion.

As well as providing nets for the defence of British ports, Bullivant's also, via the Admiralty, provided the French and the Italians with all their harbour netting. To help the Russians, an entire fleet of vessels with their personnel and nets was sent to the White Sea. Altogether 700 miles of boom defences were supplied for harbours in the UK, France, Russia, Canada and the Mediterranean. The United States, when it came into the war, copied the Admiralty boom defence handbook. This was a guide to using Bullivant's methods of defence and included the clips that the company had patented to prevent the nets being cut by submarines. Bullivant's supplied 750,000 of these clips to the Admiralty during the war.

Despite these enormous achievements, production in Leighton did not always run smoothly. Although there were restrictions under the 1911 Official Secrets Act against discussing anything that happened at the factory, a court case reported on 25 January 1916 allowed the *LBO* a mention of Bullivant's:

A scuffle which took place on 31st December landed a group of Leighton
Buzzard boys in court yesterday. William George Lake, Archibald Palmer, Fred

Gotzheim and Harry Tearle, all aged between 15 and 17, pleaded not guilty to obstructing 15-year-old Charles Weeks of Canal Bridge, Linslade. All the boys were employees at the wire works of Messrs. Bullivant and Company in Grovebury Road, a 'controlled establishment' under the Minister of Munitions. It appears that the boys, with Weeks as one of the ringleaders, had demanded a 50 per cent rise in their wages; when this demand was refused they had all gone on strike except Weeks and one other. As Weeks returned to work after his dinner break he was obstructed and molested by the defendants, causing him to arrive fifteen minutes late. He had first met thirty boys at the gate to the recreation ground near the church, who asked if he intended to return at the old rate of pay; he said that he did. They had let him pass, as had three other boys he met nearer the works. When he met Lake and Palmer, Lake pushed him into the hedge and struck him.

The company had previously experienced similar cases of intimidation and as a result had notified the police who kept watch on the boys. Police Sergeant Dennis stated that he had seen five boys make a rush for Weeks after one called out, 'Here comes Weeks,' with Lake hitting him and knocking him into the hedge. Weeks had then called out and Police Constable Cheshire ran after the other boys. To prevent any further incidents Lake and Palmer were arrested and detained overnight. The boys all pleaded not guilty. Lake claimed he had not struck Weeks; Palmer and Tearle denied touching him; and Gotzheim said they had only stopped to ask Weeks if he intended going to work.

While the company did not wish to press charges the military authorities had instructed the action to be taken to ensure there was no repetition of this behaviour. The boys had since returned to work and the firm was of the view that the publicity given to the case would be sufficient deterrent. The boys were told that interfering with the work of producing munitions was a very serious thing and that the maximum penalty for this offence was £100 fine or six months imprisonment. As it was a first offence they were fined only ten shillings, but were warned that if they came before the magistrates again they would be very seriously dealt with.

From the description of this incident, in which all the participants are described as boys, it appears that a large proportion of the workforce must have been school leavers too young to be called up to fight.

Another rare local report on Bullivant's was the following January 1917 when an inquest was held into the death of William Pantling, who acted as night watchman on Saturday nights. Pantling, also the landlord of the George and Dragon, Stanbridge, was described as a reliable person who worked as a casual labourer and relief night watchman at the company. William George Faulkner, the foreman

Bullivant's purpose-built factory in Grovebury Road was taken over in 1926 by Gossard's, who made women's undergarments. The offices were at the front. The large building at the back is where the submarine nets were made. The factory stretched down to the railway track to Dunstable.

at the works, said it was usual for Mr Pantling to ring his doorbell when he left in the morning. On this Sunday he had gone to the works and found him face down on the floor. The inquest concluded that Pantling had died of natural causes in the night.

As at Morgan's, the enormous contribution that Bullivant's workforce had made to saving Britain and its allies and shortening the war counted for nothing when peace was finally declared in 1918. The need for submarine netting disappeared and the company and its staff soon found themselves without work.

A clue to the size of the Grovebury Road factory came in the report in the *LBO* on 30 September 1919, when 650 soldiers and sailors from the town were entertained to a welcome home celebration. 'The dinner was served in the only building [in town] capable of seating so large a number of guests.' The report said that after every table in the north wing of the Bullivant's works was filled, the overspill sat at half a dozen tables in the eastern annexe and room was also made for the bandsmen.

By 1923, because of lack of orders, Bullivant's factory in Grovebury Road had closed. The company was a founder member of what was called British Ropes, part of a whole series of amalgamations and takeovers in the wire rope business designed to reduce capacity. Bullivant's eventually became part of Bridon Ltd, a company based in Doncaster, and still in the wire rope business.

CHAPTER 7

EVEN BOYS COULD FIGHT AT SEA

While not at the geographical centre of the country Leighton, Linslade and the surrounding villages are almost as far from the sea as it is possible to be. Despite this, from the early nineteenth century there had been a small but steady stream of sailors from this area.

One of the reasons for this was a supply of recruits from the Leighton Buzzard workhouse. How willing these boys were is not recorded, but it seemed to be a useful way of finding employment for growing lads and getting them off the books of the parish. The Leighton Buzzard Board of Guardians sponsored local boys, who were escorted to their training ship by the workhouse master. The Board received reports on their progress and continued to take an interest after they were launched on their naval careers.

However, there were many other ways of joining the navy, and during the course of the war over 120 local lads served in one capacity or another. Who were these men? And who were these boys required to fight like men? Some had been career sailors in peacetime, usually serving for twelve years, and had joined the Royal Fleet Reserve on being discharged. They were recalled to duty at the end of July 1914, a few days before war was officially declared.

Others had joined the navy before the war started and were already on active service. The navy maintained recruiting offices in Bedford and Aylesbury and regularly advertised in the local papers for fitters and turners, cooks, mates, shipwrights, sick berth staff and members of specialised crews. They also advertised for boys aged 15½ to 17 to become boy sailors, 2nd class. This was the age at which the workhouse boys were taken to join up.

The *LBO* of 19 June 1917 carried a notice from the Bedfordshire Education Committee stating that they were 'prepared to recommend one candidate for admission to His Majesty's Navy as a Boy Artificer [a plumber]. Candidate must be aged 15 on 1/1/1918. Full particulars and entry form available from the Director of Education.'

The Education Committee also offered scholarships, value £21 per annum, for training in seamanship, tenable on the training ship *Mercury*, which was moored on the River Hamble in Hampshire. After their training boys would be equipped to join the navy as boy sailors, with the prospect of a good career, possibly becoming warrant officers in due course and with the distinct possibility of obtaining a commissioned rank in their mid-20s.

This was in stark contrast to the many training ships moored in most major estuaries and on the tidal River Thames, which were run by local school boards, or by charities specifically for 'pauper boys', as the equivalent of children's homes. In the case of the scholarship the Education Committee went to great lengths to point out that the *Mercury* was not an industrial school for minor delinquents or boys in moral danger, but that only boys of exemplary character, with appropriate references, would be considered.

Thus there was a regular, if small, supply of local lads going to sea as boy sailors and, occasionally, as midshipmen, a commissioned rank but of a similar age. Unlike their comrades in the army, boy sailors aged between 15½ and 18 could serve on board ship overseas and fight, if required, with all the consequent dangers. Recruits in the army did not serve on the Front until they were nineteen.

Sadly, as a result of this policy, at the only major naval engagement of the war, the Battle of Jutland, which began on 31 May 1916, three boys with a local connection died.

Boy 1st class John 'Jack' Travers Cornwell was one of the most celebrated heroes of the war, and was just 16 when he died. He was awarded the Victoria Cross

The Stag Inn at the junction of Church Street, Plantation Road and Heath Road, before the First World War. Jack Cornwell's mother, Lily King, was born here when her parents ran the pub.

for outstanding bravery even when mortally wounded. His heroism caught the public imagination. Although his address was given as East Ham, his mother Lily King came from Leighton Buzzard where her parents and grandparents had been licensees of the Stag and the Falcon. The citation said: '1916: Mortally wounded early in the action, Boy, First Class, John Travers Cornwell remained standing alone at a most exposed post, quietly awaiting orders, until the end of the action, with the gun's crew dead and wounded all round him. His age was under sixteen and a half years.' The boy was brought ashore, and died three days later in hospital in Grimsby.

Boy 1st Class Reginald Thomas Varney was also 16 years old when his ship HMS *Black Prince* was sunk with all hands on the first day of the battle. Contact with the ship had been lost at '17.42h' and no positive sightings were made thereafter, but a German account suggests that at '23.35h' *Black Prince* had fired on SMS *Rheinland* and was soon in the searchlights of SMS *Thüringen*, after which she was bombarded by several German battleships, sinking within fifteen minutes. Reginald was born in Kentish Town but his mother Annie (Fookes) was from Leighton, his father Alfred a coach body maker from Ledburn and both families remained in the area.

Midshipman Cyril Henry Gerald Summers, aged 17, died when HMS *Indefatigable* was sunk with the loss of all but two hands. He was born in Leighton, the only son of Captain (later Lieutenant Colonel) Frank, DSO, DSC and Marjorie (née Prior) Summers of Padbury. He attended Wixenford School, Berkshire and then Osborne Naval College before joining his first ship, HMS *London*, in August 1914, aged only 15. He saw service with the Channel Fleet at Gallipoli in 1915, and then in the Adriatic. He was wounded in January 1916 and had only recovered sufficiently to join HMS *Indefatigable* on 22 May, nine days before the Battle of Jutland began.

Surface shipping was not only menaced by the U-boats of the Imperial German Navy. The RN had its own submarines. However, being a submariner came at a price: a one in three chance that you would die in service. Able Seaman

In honour of Jack Cornwell, a Scout before joining the RN, the movement created the Cornwell Scout Badge, awarded for 'pre-eminently high character and devotion to duty, together with great courage and endurance.' (Scout Association.)

The Falcon, on the corner of Stanbridge Road and Billington Road, now demolished, which Jack's grandparents Charlotte and George King moved to after they left the Stag. Their daughter Lily helped her mother to run the business after her father died.

Arthur William Page, described as a house boy from Linslade, had joined the navy, aged 16, as a boy sailor 2nd Class, becoming an ordinary seaman upon his 18th birthday. He transferred to the Submarine Service in July 1915 and after training at HMS *Dolphin*, the RN Submarine School, was posted to HMS *Maidstone*, the submarine depot ship at Harwich. His naval record states that on 6 July 1916 he was 'Lost on Duty', when HM Submarine *E26* failed to return from a patrol in the North Sea.

Alongside the sailors were the Royal Marines, who were essentially soldiers serving at sea. Since the early 1800s the marines had been divided into two units. The Royal Marine Artillery (RMA) had worn the blue jackets of the Royal Regiment of Artillery and were called the Blue Marines. Originally they manned the guns in much smaller vessels but subsequently they became responsible for the forward turrets of the battleships. The Red Marines were the Royal Marine Light Infantry (RMLI), so called because they originally wore red jackets like the British infantry. They were usually the first troops ashore and were the skirmishers of the British forces.

Gunner Frederick Arthur Paragreen, then a 19-year-old boot finisher from Heath and Reach, had joined the RMA in 1904. He served until October 1908, when he left and was transferred to the Royal Fleet Reserve. Back in civilian life he became a constable in the Metropolitan Police. In July 1914 he was mobilised and posted to HMS *Good Hope*. She had been in the Reserve Fleet but was re-commissioned in the so-called test mobilisation that took place shortly before the outbreak of war. HMS *Good Hope* was sent to be the flagship of the South American Squadron. Sailing into the Pacific Ocean the squadron was ambushed by Admiral Maximilian von Spee's cruiser squadron at the Battle of Coronel, off the coast of Chile. The *Good Hope* was sunk with the loss of all hands by the German cruisers *Scharnhorst* and *Gneisenau* on 1 November 1914, the first British naval defeat for over 100 years.

The Royal Naval Division (RND) was formed in August 1914. The Admiralty realised that with the mobilisation of the Reserve they would have between 20 and 30,000 men, for whom there would be no room on any ship of war. This surplus would be enough to form two naval brigades and one marine brigade, which would be available for home defence or for any special purpose. The marine battalions were named after RM home bases, and included an RMA battalion, and the naval ones after famous admirals. All three brigades were almost immediately sent to Europe, then to Gallipoli, and spent the rest of the war fighting in France and Belgium alongside their army comrades in the trenches. Because of heavy losses and the need to recall experienced sailors to go to sea, control of the RND had passed to the army in 1916.

Able Seaman (AB) Arthur James Galloway had entered service in May 1915 as an ordinary seaman and was promoted three months later. He was a member of Anson Battalion, and like many soldiers he suffered medical problems as a result of the awful conditions on the Western Front. He had periods in hospital in France, due to influenza, scabies and ulcers on his legs, serious enough to warrant a transfer to hospital in Brighton. Once fit again he returned to Anson Battalion and was recorded as wounded and missing in the fighting near Poelcapelle in Belgium on 26 October 1917, being officially declared killed in action the following year. He is buried in Poelcapelle British Cemetery, his body having been brought there from one of the surrounding battlefields after the Armistice.

On 1 July 1914 the Admiralty created the Royal Naval Air Service (RNAS), forming the naval wing of the RFC, part of the military branch of the RN. However, it did not officially come under the control of the navy until 1 August 1915. The RNAS operated aircraft, airships and balloons. Their main roles were fleet reconnaissance, patrolling coasts for enemy ships and submarines and attacking enemy coastal territory, and for some time they had responsibility for the defence of London. Later during the war several crack squadrons were sent to support the RFC on the Western Front. On 1 April 1918 the RNAS and RFC together formed the RAF.

The stories of two local naval flyers have been told in Chapter 5, but every pilot needed ground crew and it was reckoned that to keep one man in the air, forty were required on the ground. These men came from all backgrounds and from all sorts of trades.

Officer's Steward 2nd Class George Arthur Russell was born in Leighton and when he joined up in October 1915 he was a clerk in a printing works in Watford. He was posted to RNAS Seaplanes, Dunkirk and remained there until he was killed in an enemy bombardment of the town on 27 June 1917.

One rather surprising wing of the RNAS was the Royal Naval Armoured Car Division. Originally used for reconnaissance and for rescuing downed pilots, they were eventually seen as the replacement for cavalry. However, the increasingly static trench warfare of the Western Front proved unsuitable for these armoured Rolls-Royce greyhounds as they were known, so the squadrons were sent elsewhere, even to Russia. By mid-1915 the Admiralty had reviewed what was clearly a military function rather than a naval one, and the squadrons were transferred to the army, but they had been the pioneering motorised military units.

Petty Officer Mechanic John George Butcher was born in Leighton. He was a chauffeur in civilian life. The one thing that the Armoured Car Division needed was people with a knowledge of cars; drivers were relatively easy to train but those with mechanical knowledge were in very short supply. When he volunteered in October 1914 he was immediately made a petty officer and remained with the division until September 1915 when he was transferred to the Army Service Corps (ASC) MT (Mechanical Transport) and ultimately to 3rd Battery Light Armoured Car Brigade, sometimes called the Rolls-Royce Light Armoured Car Brigade. He saw service in France and Egypt, and at demobilisation held the rank of corporal and was a 1st Class Armoured Car Driver. Although Leighton and Linslade are far from the sea, ongoing research has identified almost 150 local men who served in various capacities in the navy during the war and the majority survived the conflict. The people of the two towns had a soft spot for these men and boys and national appeals for food to keep them healthy met with good local response.

'Will You Send Us Some Fruit and Fresh Vegetables &c. For the Fleet? This scheme has the approval of the Admiralty.' This was the slogan on a poster issued by the (National) Vegetable Products Committee, under the presidency of Admiral Lord Charles Beresford. This national committee had some 600 local committees all organising the collection and donation of fruit and vegetables for the Home Fleet. The first national appeal was made by Admiral Beresford in December 1914 for gifts of game, Christmas puddings, cakes and fruit for the Grand Fleet, the destroyer and torpedo flotillas, coastal submarines and mine-sweeping trawlers.

In his letter to the parishioners in the Linslade Parish Magazine of October 1915, the Revd Mahony wrote the following:

The Harvest Thanksgiving is of especial importance this year, and I have thought it right that we should observe it on a Sunday. The harvest of our own land has been plentiful, and all safely gathered in. The harvest of other lands, especially of our own great dominions, is available for our extra needs, thanks (under God) to the vigilant guard of our almost unseen navy. To mark our sense of what we owe to the navy in immunity from invasion, and a sufficient supply of food, I suggest that this year we shall send as much as possible of the fruit and vegetables used for the decoration of the church to the Vegetable Products Committee, which, under the presidency of Admiral Lord Charles Beresford, undertakes the forwarding and distribution of all such gifts direct to His Majesty's ships in home waters. I am pretty sure that I only have to mention this to secure a hearty response. I may mention that the committee states that potatoes are included in the ordinary rations of our seamen, but that for every other kind of vegetable and fruit they are dependent almost entirely upon voluntary gifts such as I suggest. Potatoes, therefore, will hardly be worth sending. Onions and similar vegetables which do not naturally lend themselves to the decoration of the church, will have to be kept out of the building, but will be sent off with the rest.

CHAPTER 8

THE SACRIFICE OF HORSES

In 1914 when war began the army had 250,000 horses and only eighty motor vehicles, so moving anything required horsepower. At the outbreak of hostilities the army decided it needed another 25,000 horses in the next six months. From the first day of the war the round-up of horses to be taken to the Front began. Linslade and Leighton Buzzard, being a centre for hunting and agriculture, were asked to give up their best mounts. In the first week of the war 500 had been rounded up, taken to Leighton station, and shipped south to be allocated to various army units. They were a mixture of draught horses, cobs and ponies, including the finest shire horses and the nobility's expensive hunters.

At the time nobody realised what terrible carnage there would be, involving both men and horses at the Front. In the four years of war Britain lost over 484,000 horses: one horse for every two men. In the beginning people were told the war would be over by Christmas and many probably believed their horses would be returned. Some were told that the finest hunters were needed as mounts for cavalry officers; apparently no one realised that in the trench warfare of the Western Front the cavalry would be as outdated as spears.

Gathering the horses was the responsibility of the Army Remounts Service. This was a very large organisation whose job it was to replace the horses injured or killed at the Front. By the end of 1918 nearly 19,000 men were serving in the Remount Department of the British Army, preparing horses to be sent to war. Many local men who had expertise with horses were recruited into this or into the Army Veterinary Corps (AVC). Their job was to look after the welfare of the horses and to save those that became sick or were wounded in order to return them to duty.

The War Department was not entirely without heart. Although the National Emergency Impressment Order issued under Section 115 of the Army Act enabled locally appointed purchasing officers to obtain horses, vehicles and equipment for the war effort, Lord Kitchener ordered that no horse under fifteen hands (60ins, 152cms) should be confiscated. This, he said, was at the request of many British children who were concerned about the welfare of their ponies.

RECRUITS REQUIRED for REMOUNT SQUADRONS, A.S.C.

AGE 25 to 40 years.
ENLISTMENT for the Duration of the War.
Must be organically sound, and may wear glasses.

Ordinary A.S.C. rates of pay, but if sent to the Expeditionary Force will receive

Corporal (Foreman)   ...   4/- daily.
Private (Rough-rider)   ...   3/6 daily.
Private (Groom)   ...   ...   3/- daily.

☞ APPLY TO NEAREST RECRUITER.

Many of the horses collected for the army were kept in stables locally and the Remount Service was keen to find recruits who had knowledge of handling them. This advertisement appeared in newspapers in Leighton Buzzard.

Collecting the horses and assessing which should be taken, and which left behind for essential work like ploughing, required expertise. The horses were bought at what the army's commissioners considered a fair price in order to obtain the co-operation of the people who owned them. The top price paid was not disclosed, but some horses must have been worth a lot more than the army was prepared to pay. For example, in Linslade there was more than one stud, where some of the horses were worth hundreds, possibly thousands, of pounds. Lord Rosebery at Mentmore Towers had bred three Derby winners locally in the previous twenty years.

Some of the best quality horses, including stud stallions, were left behind by the army, important blood stock to be preserved for the future, but many valuable horses were sent to the Front. The call to patriotism left some of the aristocracy feeling it was their responsibility to sell or even give their horses to the war effort.

How the process began was described in the *LBO* in the first week of the war:

Some half dozen parties, consisting of gentlemen who have been brought up to know the value of horse-flesh, and usually assisted by a veterinary surgeon, have been commissioned to take this task in hand throughout Bedfordshire, and as they are well-known residents in the county, with good local knowledge and animated by consideration for their neighbours' requirements in business, there is no reason to suppose that other than fair treatment, to the best of their judgement, has been meted out. In some cases, of course, tradesmen have lamented having to part with their best horses, but usually very fair prices have been given, and in some cases it is said that the involuntary vendors have rather shaken hands with themselves.

We may safely say that all concerned have recognised the emergencies of the situation and have resigned themselves to it loyally and with good grace. The horses are purchased at their assessed value, but, we believe, there is a maximum amount, which we have heard variously stated, but we have no wish to render a possible disservice by disclosing it. It is common knowledge that the general run of prices was from £35 to £45 but more for hunters and the best class of shire horse. The purchases have often involved a big sacrifice in the case of hunters, on which there has been a considerable raid, if it may be so described, seeing that some of the purchasing experts are themselves owners of hunters which they have willingly parted with, although some of these horses may have cost them, say, a hundred guineas or more. This class of horses is required for officers' chargers and some of the stables have been almost depleted. Two hundred were secured from Lord Rothschild's Stag Hounds.

The hunt gathering outside the Hare Inn at Southcott, a traditional start of the meet for nearly a century. Horses of this quality were said to be needed for cavalry officers.

Among the local owners of horses who showed great patriotism during the
collection of horses for the army is Dr (Sidney Morton Pearson) Roberts of
Linslade. When approached by the Honourable Artillery Company with which
he is connected and asked to sell his hunters, he at once presented the whole
of them – seven in number – as a free gift and declined to accept payment
of any kind.

The *Bedfordshire Times* reported on 14 August that before the war a census was
taken in each police division of all the horses, carts, motors and other vehicles, and
that once a year a military officer went round the country with the police and
noted those horses and vehicles that might be serviceable for military purposes.
The paper also said that the gentlemen who were buying for the military were
separated into three groups for cavalry, artillery and yeomanry. 'The purchasers
exercise discrimination and discretion, and take only a proportion of horses, in
order not to paralyse trade.'

This rather rosy picture of the collection of horses did not tell the whole story.
Since so many animals were being taken by the army there was some resentment,
as this article from the *LBO* published a few days later shows:

The Boxing Day hunt outside the Swan Hotel was one of the many pre-war local
traditions abandoned for the duration. Many of these fine horses probably ended up on
the Western Front.

William Simmons, who ran a mill in Leighton, used teams of horses to deliver his sacks of flour up to the start of the war. When his horses were requisitioned he had to buy a steam lorry to carry on his business.

> The fact that every suitable horse in this district has been commandeered for the army has meant a steady stream of horse boxes from Leighton Buzzard railway station during the past few days. Both dealers and hunting gentlemen in the district have been called upon to contribute to the supply in many cases to the disadvantage of the seller who, apart from the inconvenience of reducing his stock, has had to forfeit many animals at a price much below their estimated value. In all it is estimated that some 500 animals, including draught horses, hunters, cobs and ponies have been acquired from the Leighton Buzzard district.

Apart from not receiving the full sum they believed their horses were worth, some farmers and tradespeople were not happy to let their horses go because they needed them for their businesses. This feeling of injustice was compounded when people who appeared more privileged had managed to keep theirs.

This dissatisfaction came out in a letter which appeared in the *LBO* on 11 August 1914, only a week after war was declared. Ernest William Robinson who owned Liscombe Park Stud at Soulbury still had his horses when many others had been taken. Robinson's secretary, Francis John Holford explained to readers why his employer's horses had not gone:

> Sir – A rumour has been spread broadcast that Mr E. W. Robinson has refused to allow the government to take any of his horses for army purposes. I should be much obliged therefore if you would kindly publish the following facts. During Mr Robinson's absence from home I received notice to send as many horses as possible for army purposes, but the authorities were informed that there were several cases of strangles [equine mumps] on the estate, and Mr Robinson therefore considered it inadvisable to send any of his animals. My instructions, however, are that as soon as a veterinary surgeon gives a certificate to the effect that we are quite rid of the disease the whole stud is at the government disposal. The report that we sent sixteen horses up to London on Saturday last is quite correct but as this action might be misunderstood I should like to state that these came down from London for a month's rest (as in previous years) and were completely isolated.
>
> Owing to the firm to whom they belonged having supplied to the government eighty-one horses from their stables in London, I received instructions to return the sixteen horses referred to immediately.

Underneath the letter was a footnote which said: 'We are informed that since the above letter was written, ten horses have been sent to the Remount Staff, who have accepted all risks, Ed. *LBO*.'

The issue was not resolved, however, because in May 1915 an account of civil court arbitration appeared in the *LBO*. It was a case known as the Commandeered Horse, heard by Judge Thomas Whittenbury Wheeler KC at Linslade Court House and brought by Ernest Robinson of Liscombe, represented by Frank Dodd, for Messrs William Gravely Willis and Vivian Vere Willis, Solicitors, of Leighton Buzzard against the Army Council.

Robinson was asking for £460, the difference between the alleged market value of six horses commandeered on 14 August 1914, and the £240 paid for them. His horses had won many prizes but horses were bought and sold at different prices. The horses in question were one called Pale Ale, which he had bought from a Mr Worthington for £35, a brougham horse for pulling a carriage, £50, and four others, Perfect £200, Tango £125, Radium £250 and Duchess £40.

Dodd said this was a case of arbitration under the Army Act and Army (Amendment) Act, 1915. What his honour had to assess was 'the fair market value of the article requisitioned on the date on which it was required to be furnished as between a willing buyer and a willing seller'.

He said that on 3 August there was a state of war, and on 5 August Charles Claude Edmunds (land agent for Lord Rosebery at Mentmore Towers) was instructed to commandeer and purchase horses.

He communicated with Mr Robinson who was largely interested in horses and spent a great deal of time in breeding and keeping a stud of first class horses. Mr Robinson was away when the first message came and it was received by his secretary, Mr Holford. Mr Edmunds appeared to be somewhat brusque. At the time the message was received there was a horse on Mr Robinson's farm dying from septic pneumonia, following strangles. On being given notice to give up his horses Mr Robinson contacted Police Inspector Walker telling him he was afraid the horses were in an infected condition. He telephoned to Mr Prudames, the veterinary surgeon, who had attended the case, who certified that it was inadvisable to take the horses for army purchase. On August 10, in spite of that certificate, further notice came from the police that ten horses were to be sent down to be examined and six were taken for the army. That was the question of the dispute.

When the horses were taken Mr Holford went to see Mr Edmunds at a hotel, and Mr Edmunds, passing him a sealed envelope containing a cheque for £240 said: 'I don't want any more to do with you; if Mr Robinson isn't satisfied, let him go to the County Court.' After the horses were taken Mr Robinson wrote to Mr Edmunds that the way the horses had been taken was very unfair as they were being retained temporarily on veterinary advice for the safety of other horses. He was not paid a fair price and could not protest as he was away from home, the cheque had practically been thrown in his secretary's face and he was told: 'If Mr Robinson doesn't like it, write "under protest."'. He wrote at once to the Army Council asking them to inquire into his treatment at a suitable time, he was prepared to wait until after the war as he thought they would not want to inquire at once into a small claim like his.

The court was told that it would appear that no specific sum was given for each horse, just a bulk value. Mr Robinson said that Perfect was his favourite and he valued him at £200. He was willing to give them the other five horses if they would let him have Perfect back. Henry William Selby-Lowndes, Master of the Whaddon Chase Hunt, stated that the horse was worth at least £250, although a local dealer indicated he would give £175 for him to resell and make a profit. The value of the other horses that were taken was also discussed, and evidence under affidavit was given by both Selby-Lowndes and Captain Walter Charles Prudames, veterinary surgeon, neither of whom could attend the court as they were on military duties. Prudames was asked if the value would have been affected by the outbreak of strangles on the yard; he thought it would have done so. At that point the case came to a sudden halt because the government made an offer to settle the case and Robinson accepted.

Robinson told the judge he did not wish to make money out of the government, although he resented at the time the way he was treated. The offer amounted to something which would more than cover his disturbance in connection with these proceedings and he wanted to say that not one penny piece would go into his own pocket. The whole of the balance would be given to some military charity, so that it should not be said he came there to put money into his own pocket at the expense of his country.

Although little is known about Ernest Robinson he does not appear to have been taking the war as seriously as some. There is a curious news brief in the *Manchester Evening News* of 2 January 1915, five months after the war broke out. It said: 'A cavalry officer who returned to the Front this week took with him a pack of beagles for hare-hunting by the cavalry brigade to which he is attached. The pack has been lent by Mr Ernest Robinson of Liscombe, Leighton Buzzard.' The fate of these beagles is not known.

The commandeering of so many horses locally and across the country still left a large shortfall, so the government looked farther afield for fresh supplies. They went to the United States, where they arranged for another 500,000 horses to be sent. These were transported across the Atlantic in groups of ships called horse convoys. It was an immense undertaking; for the first three years of the war around 1,000 horses a day were sent. German saboteurs tried to poison the horses before they set off on the sea journey and the convoys became a target for naval attack; inevitably some were lost en route.

To help with the continual horse shortage as so many were being killed at the Front the army also purchased a large number of mules. Private Cyril Sayell from Linslade, who had joined the army as a teenager and been assigned to the AVC, had to look after some of them. In a letter addressed from the Church Army Recreation Hut in Woolwich and dated 17 September 1916, written to his friend Albert Edwin 'Ned' Tarbox, he describes his life:

> We are on Woolwich Common under canvas, and I don't mind it at all. There is one thing we get some good food and plenty of it and four meals a day. They don't half put us through it, six in the morning till five at night, drilling and cleaning these mules and some of the buggers kick like hell. I don't suppose I shall be here many more days so don't write back until I let you know where to write for certain. There are hundreds coming in here every day and you are only here for about four days before you are sent to the Front. There is a draft

off on Monday for France and they came here last Wednesday. I was put in it but when they ask for your age and I told them I wasn't 19 they've put me in the Reserve.

Later Cyril was posted to York, which he described as 'cushy' by comparison since they 'did not start work until 6.45 a.m. and lived in a barracks with four men to every room with gas, a fireplace and a good big cupboard to every man.' This time he was caring for horses. He survived the war and went on to become licensee of the Globe by the canal in Linslade.

Many of Linslade's stables, having lost most of their horses to the Front, became hosts to the Canadian Remount Service from November 1914. The livery stable run by Charles Downs at Castle House was one such. These were horses to replace those being used by the battalions of Canadian forces at the Front and must have included many horses sent on convoys from North America. They had to be broken and trained, and were kept in the various hunting stables in the district.

According to local reports: 'The long sea journey proved very trying for some of the animals, but the training they will undergo is expected to get them in good, hard condition in a few weeks. Other Canadian horses had also been sent for training to different hunting districts.'

Training these horses was difficult work. They were exercised by the local grooms and one of them, Matthew John Clarke, living at 12 Wing Road, sustained a compound fracture to his right leg which proved fatal. According to the inquest report his horse had shied and shot across the road while they were passing troops on the march, which led another Canadian remount to lash out and kick him making him fall from his horse. Although he was promptly attended by Dr Bernard Steadman and taken to Aylesbury Infirmary he did not improve, and the leg was amputated in an attempt to save his life. He died on 4 December, 1914, seventeen days after the accident. The jury returned a verdict of accidental death.

His death was one of a number of incidents involving the training of horses for the army that were reported during the conflict, showing that many animals must have been brought to the town as part of the constant endeavour to replace those killed at the Front.

As young local men volunteered to serve in different forces at the start of the war, businesses were short of labour, even in jobs that were considered essential war work. The situation became even more acute when the Military Service Act of January 1916 came into force, specifying that single men between the ages of 18 and 41 were liable to be called up for military service. Conscription started less than two months later on 2 March 1916, and in May was extended to married men. As more and more men died at the Front, the law saw several changes, casting the net ever wider for more recruits, and before the war ended the age limit was raised to 51.

Most businesses requiring the transport of goods needed horses, and men to tend and work them, but this was not always acknowledged in the tribunals. However, the exemption of those who were needed to keep the Army Remount Service going was considered more carefully. For example in the *Bucks Herald* of 22 April 1916 a Military Service Tribunal granted three months' exemption to a farrier, a Mr Meager of Linslade. He was single, aged 40 and due to be called up, but was said to be shoeing about 300 horses monthly for an Army Remount depot, in addition to his work for local farmers and tradesmen. There is no further evidence of this man's existence, however, and the newspaper account almost certainly applies to blacksmith Charles Tompkins of Leighton Road. A similar tribunal was being held regarding the exemption of 27-year-old Frederick Charles Meager, a farrier in New Road.

Other local businesses were affected. There was a detailed report about Southcourt Stud Farm at Linslade and Ascott House, Wing, both owned by the Rothschild family who had already sent many of their horses and staff to the Front. An account of the appeal of 'a single man of 26, passed for general service, who is employed at Southcourt Stud' appeared in the *LBO* on 12 December 1916. It gives an insight into the large numbers of people the Rothschild estates must have employed before the war to look after their horses, the stud and the pack of hounds used for hunting.

The grounds of the appeal by his employer were that many of the employees had enlisted, and there was such shortage of staff that they were already working under difficulties. It was important that the man should remain so that they could

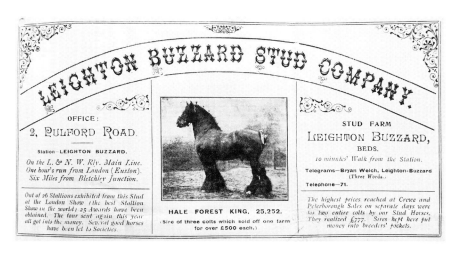

A number of studs around Leighton produced high quality horses. This letterhead boasts that the shire horses produced on this farm made more than £700 each at auction sales, far more than the army would expect to pay.

carry on this important breeding establishment, which was essential in the national interest. The man had a widowed mother to support and was the only son left out of four.

Mr Tarver, who appeared to support the appeal said he did so with diffidence, firstly because it was a principle on the Ascott Estate not to appeal for anyone if they could help it, and secondly because he was a military representative himself, and instead of appealing should be pressing men into the army. Occasionally there was a case like this where it was difficult to know what to do.

The stud farm employed nine men. There was a farm manager who was a qualified veterinary surgeon, the working foreman who had an exemption, four stallion men, one for each stallion, and four other general men who looked after the mares and the young stock. Three of the stallion men were aged 46, 57, and 58, and were really past the work. The only two young men were one aged 21 and the man now appealed for. Some of these horses were a very ticklish proposition, and now they were shorthanded one of the horses had to be left at home, whilst the others were being exercised. This year they had to foal eighty, and had fifty maidens and barren mares, four stallions and twenty yearlings, besides a few odd horses. From January to May two men had to sit up every night to attend to the mares foaling. All the animals were brought in at night, and that caused a lot of extra work. He would not appeal for the man for a moment if they could get anyone to take his place.

On the whole estate, out of 192 men before the war, eighty-two had joined the colours. Of men of military age in the building department they had only the clerk of the works left. He was so important that the military authorities had allowed him to remain. In the gardens they had only one man of military age who looked after the drains, the sewage and pumping. In the motor department they were left none. At the kennels the huntsman had gone, leaving in charge a man who was approaching 41, and the kennel man, aged 35, was only passed for home service. On the farm they had, in addition to the farm bailiff, only one man under 50 years of age. That left them with six men of military age on the estate. One of these would go directly they could get a substitute, leaving only the farm bailiff. Then there were the two men from the stud farm, one of whom was before them. Immediately substitutes were found he would be willing for these men to go.

Major Stewart William Jenney, for the army, said he recognised that it would be difficult to replace men of this kind. The advisory committee recommended that the appeal be dismissed, but in view of the value of the stud the appellant be not called up until 'a substitute was found by the military authorities'.

Another problem arose in food production because so many plough horses had been commandeered for the Front. Farmers were so short of horses that they were forced to hire some back from the authorities. This was done by applying to the Food Production Department, which caused considerable anger among the farmers who felt they had been deprived of their own animals and were reluctant

Tommy Mead and a pre-war ploughing team with farmer George Heley (left) on a farm near Stewkley showing that on heavy soil a team of three horses was needed to pull a plough. Tractors were introduced towards the end of the war but the shortage of horses must have caused severe problems.

to pay. An example was recorded in July 1918 when John James Clarke of 7 Church Square, Leighton Buzzard, applied to hire two horses and a man for a day. William Lathwell, the horse officer in charge of the depot at Leighton Buzzard, complained that while Mr Clarke had loaned the team for a day he had not paid for them and owed £1. Since he had refused to pay, legal proceedings would be taken against him.

With all these horses going off to war and the difficulty of finding replacements, horse welfare should have been paramount. New Zealander Bert Stoker recalled having been told in 1917, 'to lose a horse was worse than losing a man, because men were replaceable'. But the truth was the conditions were so bad after terrible winter rains that whole gun teams could be lost in the liquefied mud. The Royal Society for the Prevention of Cruelty to Animals (RSPCA) had been founded in 1824 and when war was declared they offered their services to help with the welfare of animals at the Front; typically, they were rebuffed by a ruling that the provisions set up by the AVC were enough. However, RSPCA members circumvented the problem by joining up, and in 1915 over half their inspectors and staff were serving in the army. Most had enlisted directly into the AVC and helped with the training of new recruits. Our Dumb Friends League launched another animal welfare organisation, the Blue Cross Fund, specifically for the relief of animals affected by war.

A threshing machine also needed a team of three horses to pull it – at least, so it would seem from this pre-war picture taken at Wing. There were a lot of protests from farmers when they lost both their able-bodied labourers and their horses to the war.

The plight of the horses at the Front touched the hearts of the people at home. On 14 September 1915, at the Tuesday market, a flag day was held in Leighton in aid of the RSPCA fund for wounded horses. The committee was asking the public to 'Buy a flag and help a horse'. Their leaflets claimed that 85 per cent of horses treated in RSPCA hospitals were cured. 'Those who contribute can therefore do so in the assurance that their money will be well spent both in preventing suffering and in helping our forces. This is the only fund of its type recognised by the Army Council and carries out work of national importance.'

To get some idea of the scale of the operation there were 1,300 officers serving as veterinary surgeons in the AVC across all the theatres of war. Their job was to look after all the animals used in the war including dogs and carrier pigeons, although horses were their major concern. One of the senior officers in the Corps was Lieutenant Colonel James MacArthur, a veterinary surgeon from Leighton Buzzard. Many horses were being killed or injured on a daily basis. During the conflict British AVC hospitals in France received 725,000 injured horses and successfully treated three-quarters of them. The horse hospitals could treat 2,000 animals at any one time.

The injured horses were brought to the hospitals in several forms of special ambulance. The horse trailer was first developed for use on the Western Front as an equine ambulance. Horses were also moved on foot, rail or barge. The barge was said to be the best way of moving those suffering from shell or bomb wounds. Feeding this number of horses presented an enormous logistical problem. Horse fodder was the single largest commodity shipped to the Front by some countries. The standard daily ration was 20lb of fodder, which was about 25 per cemt below what they would have been fed at home. However, because the gun horses pulled heavier loads their ration was 30lbs and they were allocated at least five hours a day eating time. On this basis the average battalion would need at least 7,840lb of oats and hay per week. Being fed less than their normal diet meant the horses were constantly hungry and would try to eat anything available including the wheels on the wagons. When food was really short the hungry horses would be fed sawdust cakes.

Poison gas was first used in 1915 and nose plugs were improvised to allow horses to breathe during the attacks; later on several gas masks were developed that looked like nosebags. The horses were sometimes driven so hard they would collapse with exhaustion, drowning in the mud because they were too tired to lift their heads enough to breathe.

Because of the appalling conditions for both men and horses the animals suffered a variety of different diseases. A major problem was 'debility' – a condition caused by exposure to the elements and hunger. There were also outbreaks of equine influenza, ringworm, sand colic and anthrax. In East Africa the highest death rates were caused by the tsetse fly.

Each battalion of 1,000 men had its own mules, riding horses and supply horses. A transport section of twenty men looked after them; cleaning mud off the animals and their equipment was a job that could take up to twelve hours.

Some of the local men who served in these transport units wrote about the horses in letters home. Trooper Arthur Charles Hull of 36 Dudley Street described a German retreat: 'Once when the shells got too thick I was detailed to take the horses back a bit, and you can take it from me that to ride your own horse and lead five more at a gallop under heavy fire is a pretty exciting job.'

However, not all the horses were on the Western Front. Trooper Thomas Chappin, of Vandyke Road was one of those sent to Egypt in a cavalry regiment. He recalled that the Bedouin Arabs were the finest horsemen he had ever seen. 'The horses we have out here are the finest to be had, all Arabs.' Edward Joseph Whiting of Heath and Reach, stationed with the Herts Yeomanry in Cairo, had a different opinion of the horses. He said in a letter home to his family:

The Arab horses we are riding are absolute devils. They bite and kick all day long. Yesterday I was out galloping along for about two miles on the Nubian Desert when the horse next to me grabbed my knee or the flesh just above it and would not let go. We galloped for about 100 yards with him gripping me and the man riding him could not pull him off. The horses are nearly all 'entire' and when they see the English mares the other regiments are riding, they go almost mad and rush after them kicking and biting. We get our own back quietly though and they are beginning to respect us a bit now.

Trooper Charles Harty Chandler, who had been a porter at Leighton Buzzard Workhouse before being posted to Egypt, wrote to the workhouse master, Charles Henry Swaffield, of his experiences. 'The worst of this country is we had a job to get water for the horses and men and several times we went all day without water (and the horses went so long as 56 hours without a drink or their saddles off).'

It is thought that by the end of the war eight million horses, mules and donkeys in total across all armies had lost their lives. Those that remained in service had a variety of fates. The British Army returned almost 70,000 surviving horses to Britain to be sold at auction but only those owned by officers were guaranteed a return passage. The fate of the rest depended on their age and fitness. The rest were either sold locally in the country where they were stationed as work horses or sent to slaughterhouses for meat. The Australian horses could not go home because of quarantine restrictions, so most of them went to India to be used as remounts by the British Army. New Zealanders' horses that were not required by the British or Egyptian Armies were shot to prevent maltreatment by purchasers.

Hugh Delafield, second from left, and his colleagues in the Bedfordshire Yeomanry at ease in Church Square. Standing opposite him in the foreground is George Garside, owner of Garside Sand and Delafield's uncle, who when he died left his nephew the business and the White House in Hockliffe Street.

CHAPTER 9

THE LINSLADE POSTMAN'S HORSE AND THE LAST GLORIOUS CAVALRY CHARGE

Arthur Sambrook spent a lifetime in uniform, starting as a telegram boy riding a bicycle in Leighton, promoted to mounted postman, then enlisting as a cavalryman in the First World War, and afterwards returning to be a postman. Later he became a special constable and served in that role in the Second World War. This is part of his story but also that of his faithful horse, Bluebell.

For a short time Arthur had been an errand boy, but joined the Post Office; he soon became a postman, and lived in Wing Road. When he graduated to mounted postman he needed somewhere larger to keep the horse, so he organised a move to Rosebery Avenue where he had a house built, now No. 7, with a stable at the rear and plenty of grazing in the fields nearby.

During those years before the First World War he and Bluebell delivered mail to surrounding villages, and part of their round was Mentmore Towers, home of the Rosebery family. Over the years he became friendly with the staff and was introduced into the Buckinghamshire Yeomanry through this connection. These were the volunteers, the local militia, who were part of an ancient tradition of local forces prepared to defend the country against foreign attack. For a man born in Old Road, Linslade, the youngest child of a large family, this must in itself have been an adventure. Arthur had been a pupil at the church school at St Barnabas, now Linslade Community Hall, and left when he was 12.

The Rosebery family, along with their relatives the Rothschilds at Ascott House in Wing, had considerable influence in the regiment which was also known as the Royal Bucks Hussars. Some of them were officers and encouraged their staff and local people to join. Of course, a qualification was that you had to own or have access to a horse, and Arthur had Bluebell.

For several years they trained with the local squadron and went to the annual training camps. The Yeomanry was a cavalry regiment with an archaic dress

The Buckinghamshire Yeomanry, also known as the Royal Bucks Hussars, at Wing in 1909 on their annual manoeuvres. The exercises lasted more than a week and involved Arthur Sambrook and Bluebell. They were camped in the field beyond the tollgate.

uniform, and the soldiers were equipped for the wars of the nineteenth century with a rifle and a sword. The sword was in a scabbard carried on the left side.

The day Britain declared war, 4 August 1914, the regiment was mustered. The regimental HQ was in Aylesbury, so, watched by the family, Arthur and Bluebell answered the call and set off down Rosebery Avenue. He met a comrade in Wing and together they rode the remaining 10 miles to join the rest of the regiment. The family never saw Bluebell again.

For a time the regiment was on routine training duties in East Anglia and the Midlands, as part of the 2nd Mounted Division of the British Army. In early 1915 it had already become clear that cavalry regiments were not going to be much use in trench warfare in France, and the whole division was sent to Egypt. After a long voyage they arrived on 8 April and were posted to Cairo.

In August that year the regiment was 'dismounted' – in other words, they left their horses behind and became an infantry regiment. Apart from 100 officers and men left in Egypt to look after the horses, the whole brigade was sent as infantry to take part in the Gallipoli campaign. This was the ill-fated attempt to take control of the straits of the Dardanelles, attack Constantinople (now Istanbul), the capital of the Ottoman Empire, and take the Turks out of the war, in order to open a new supply route via the Black Sea to Russia, then our allies.

Left: Arthur Sambrook in Royal Bucks Hussars dress uniform complete with cavalry sword, taken in a photographic studio in 1910. The uniform looks more in keeping with the Napoleonic Wars than the twentieth century.

Below: Arthur Sambrook on Bluebell in training after he had enlisted in 1914, now equipped with a rifle and khaki uniform ready to be sent to Egypt. The Hussars retained their swords.

This was a dark episode in the war, particularly for Empire troops from Australia, New Zealand and India. In appalling and exposed conditions they came under constant bombardment and were pinned down by the Turks, unable to press the attack. As part of a force of 20,000 men intended as reinforcements to secure victory, Arthur Sambrook landed at Suvla Bay in European Turkey on 20 August 1915. The plan was to link up with other forces hemmed in by the Turks.

As frequently occurs in the horror of warfare, the names of landscape features assumed enormous significance. In this case his regiment had to advance on the notorious Chocolate Hill, so called because of its colour, and then take part in the attack on Scimitar Hill, named because it was shaped like an Ottoman sword. The troops faced constant bombardment and machine gun fire, and many were cut down.

The unit's commanding officer, Brigadier-General Thomas Pakenham, Lord Longford, was among those killed in an unsuccessful charge on Scimitar Hill and the British suffered 5,300 casualties out of the 14,300 soldiers who participated.

As conditions worsened in constant rain and mud there was a stalemate, and the plan to seize the Dardanelles was clearly not going to succeed. On 31 October the remains of the brigade were evacuated to the nearby Greek port of Mudros, which the RN used as its base; when the Gallipoli Campaign was abandoned altogether in December, Arthur Sambrook returned to Egypt and, like the remaining members of the Bucks Yeomanry, was reunited with his horse.

Because of the losses suffered at the Battle of Scimitar Hill the remains of the Yeomanry were amalgamated into the 1st Composite Mounted Brigade. Arthur and Bluebell were attached to formations guarding Egypt until February 1917, when they were included in the Imperial Mounted Division, which was made up principally of Australian and British Cavalry units.

Among the officers of the Royal Bucks Yeomanry was Major Evelyn Achille de Rothschild, aged 31 and the second son of Leopold de Rothschild of Ascott House, Wing who, with Arthur Sambrook, had endured Gallipoli. Another officer was Neil James Archibald Primrose, aged 34 and the second son of Lord Rosebery. He was a Member of Parliament and had served in the Ministry of Munitions in 1915 before joining the Yeomanry in the field in 1916. These two were friends and had taken part in many hunts together at Ascott and Mentmore before the war. Evelyn de Rothschild owned half of the Southcott Stud. These were the two officers who had recruited their postman Arthur and his horse Bluebell to the Yeomanry.

The Imperial Mounted Division was deployed to Palestine to take on the Ottoman Army in one of the war's least reported but most successful campaigns. This theatre of war still had a use for cavalry, mainly because there were few roads and large areas with sparse vegetation where cavalry regiments could move fast. Watering the horses, however, was a major problem.

One of the key battles was for the strategic town of Beersheba in Palestine, which was being attacked by three British divisions. This was an important town because it controlled the only road and had one of the few water supplies. It was to be the scene of what was said to be the last successful cavalry charge in the history of warfare.

The charge was made in desperate circumstances. The cavalry, including Arthur on Bluebell with the Royal Bucks Yeomanry, had been deployed in the desert to the east of the town. Beersheba's eastern defences were held by 1,000 Turkish riflemen, nine machine guns and two aircraft, whose job it was to drop bombs on any advancing troops. The Turkish position was extended through a series of trenches and redoubts placed on commanding positions with good zones of fire. A decisive factor was that on the east and south the trenches were not protected by barbed wire. The Turkish forces were relying on the forbidding open terrain to deter attack and had not considered a cavalry charge.

To the west the three British divisions had been attacking heavily fortified Turkish positions since early morning on 31 October 1917. After a day's fighting the Turks had fallen back against the British onslaught but the vital wells needed for both men and horses to survive were still in the hands of the Turks. It was decided that the attack must be pressed home before dark and the cavalry were ordered to form up and prepare to charge.

We do not have Arthur's personal account of the battle, but there are many descriptions from other participants. The cavalry had ridden 36 miles through the desert to reach their positions. Their horses had not been watered for many hours and the dust was severe. They had waited out of sight, widely spread out as a precaution against being bombed.

Facing the new deadly weapons of modern warfare, including machine-guns, cavalry regiments' tactics in 1917 were to advance towards the enemy, dismount and, using the available cover, fight using their rifles. Here, however, there was no cover on the east so the cavalry first cantered towards the enemy then was ordered to make a full charge. The Australians had sharpened their bayonets to strike the enemy while the remnants of the Hussars riding with them still had their swords.

Although some horses were shot from under them, with the surviving troopers using their dead horses as cover, the rest of the cavalry continued at full gallop and overran the Turkish trenches. Many of the troopers' horses leaped over the trenches, and some were disembowelled from below in the process. Their riders, now unmounted, attacked the Turks' trenches from the rear while others carried on under sniper fire at full speed to the town centre where they took control, riding two abreast down the narrow streets.

The shock and speed of the attack obviously contributed to its success and more than 1,000 defenders surrendered. Crucially the wells and supplies of grain were captured intact, and the surviving horses, including Bluebell, gained a much-needed drink and good quality fodder.

In this major strategic victory against the Turks, thirty-one light horsemen were killed, thirty-six were wounded and at least seventy horses died, but no war correspondent was present, so it was neither recorded nor celebrated at the time. The Mounted Brigade, including Arthur and Bluebell, and the Bucks Yeomanry continued to take part in the bitterly fought campaign in which the Ottoman Army gradually retreated towards Jerusalem.

In the skirmishes and battles that followed, de Rothschild and Primrose died within days of each other.

On 13 November 1917 Evelyn de Rothschild was fatally wounded in another celebrated action: an attack on the El Mughar Ridge which was occupied by the Turks, barring the advance to Jerusalem. The cavalry of the Royal Bucks and the Queen's Own (Dorset) Regiment first trotted, then galloped almost 2 miles uphill

On his return to England and discharge from the Army, Arthur Sambrook acquired yet another public service role as a special constable.

In civilian clothes towards the end of a long life in uniform, Arthur Sambrook still sports one of the very impressive military moustaches much favoured by pre-war cavalrymen.

Arthur Sambrook's service brought him a rare set of medals, all bearing his name. On the left are two for service in the Bucks Yeomanry, one for 1914–15, and the second 1914-18 on which he is described as a horseman. Also a Victory Medal 1914–1919 and a Territorial Force Efficiency Medal. The final one on the right is post-war: 'For Faithful Service in the Special Constabulary.'

on to the crest of the ridge, forcing the Ottoman Army into retreat. The horses were completely exhausted and could not pursue the attack. The cost of this charge totalled sixteen killed and 114 wounded, and 265 horses dead.

Whether Primrose or Arthur, riding Bluebell, also took part in this action is unclear but it seems likely that both did, as this was their unit.

Just two days later on 15 November, the eve of his 35th birthday, Primrose died leading a squadron of his troops against the Turks at the Abu Shusheh Ridge. De Rothschild, who had barely survived the attack on El Mughar Ridge, died of his wounds on 17 November.

Despite the loss of two of their key officers in three days, the Yeomanry continued to harass the retreating army until eventually Jerusalem was captured.

After such a gruelling expedition, the cavalry might have expected to return to Britain to a hero's welcome. Sadly this did not happen. The soldiers came home but their unfortunate horses did not. The horses were left in Egypt and sold to the highest bidder, so Bluebell never did return to graze once more in Rosebery Avenue. Instead she probably ended her days pulling a horse-drawn cab, or a plough.

The reason these horses, the mounts of the remains of the twenty cavalry regiments originally sent to Egypt, were not repatriated was that the War

Department considered it not to be worth either trouble or cost. Battles in Europe had moved on to a new and even more brutal stage. Trench warfare, machine-guns, massed artillery and tanks meant there was no place for vulnerable cavalry horses.

The unhorsed regiments, on their return to the UK, were formed into cyclist battalions, or in the case of the Bucks Hussars, amalgamated with another regiment, the Berkshire Yeomanry; they were trained as C Battalion the Machine Gun Corps, later 101st (Bucks & Berks Yeomanry) Battalion, and sent to France in June 1918.

Arthur, already 39, was transferred to the Labour Corps (later the Royal Pioneer Corps) and discharged as a sergeant on 29 April 1919. He returned to the Leighton Post Office as a foot postman, for horses had been replaced here too; his public service continued and he would later volunteer as a special constable.

As a result of his extraordinary military career and his life in uniform, Arthur Sambrook was awarded five medals. Two are for service in the Bucks Yeomanry 1914–15 and 1914–18, on which he is described as a horseman. There is a victory medal 1914–1919, and a Territorial Force Efficiency Medal; and the final one (post-war) is for faithful service in the Special Constabulary.

CHAPTER 10

CRAMMING TWO TOWNS FULL OF SOLDIERS

Within a month of war being declared Leighton Buzzard and Linslade were asked to provide billets for more than 4,000 soldiers, mostly raw recruits into the British Army. For two small towns with a combined population of 9,000, many with large families, fitting in so many young men was a tall order.

At first, the request to open their homes to complete strangers came as a shock, and many local people resisted, but later the income that came with the soldiers in the form of board and lodging payments brought a welcome flow of money into the town. How did Leighton suddenly become an army town, when there were no previous military links? The answer lies in the massive recruitment drive for a new army which Lord Horatio Herbert Kitchener realised was going to be needed to fight the war.

It was a complete change in strategic thinking; prior to the beginning of the First World War the British Army was a professional army whose main role was the protection and the control of the dependencies of the British Empire. The soldiers were people who had enrolled voluntarily, unlike the huge armies of the continent, which were filled with conscripted men and officered by career soldiers.

Britain had dealt with the majority of the conflicts across the Empire by paying local allies to get their armies to fight for the British. A large army of native troops was stationed in India and commanded by officers from the British Isles. Smaller native military forces were maintained in other parts of the Empire, also commanded by officers from the British Isles.

During this period the primary roles of the Royal Navy were the defence of the British Isles and the maintenance of open sea routes for our huge Merchant Navy, which was trading across the British Empire and keeping Britain rich. The RN was at the forefront of the design and building of battleships, but was in direct competition with the German Imperial Navy, which supported the Kaiser's aim of developing a German colonial empire matching that of Great Britain.

By 1900, however, it was recognised that the army required major reform. The British Expeditionary Force (BEF) was created and the existing local Militia Volunteer Force and the Yeomanry organised into a new Territorial Force.

Men were enlisted into the Territorial Force by specific county associations, for example the Royal Bucks Hussars, and as part of a specific Army Corps. As well as regular drills in local barracks, recruits to the Territorial Force were to attend an annual training camp for a period of eight to fifteen days per year, or longer for cavalry units.

The Territorial Force formally came into existence on 1 April 1908 and its members were liable for service anywhere within the United Kingdom, but could not be ordered out of the country. However, it was stipulated that any part of the force, through its commanding officer, could offer to be liable for overseas service or to be called out for military service within the British Isles for defensive purposes.

By 1913 this Territorial Force had grown to 200,000 men. It was organised into 204 infantry battalions and fifty-six yeomanry regiments, all maintaining their local county connections. These were in turn part of fourteen divisions and fourteen cavalry brigades with support troops.

As the apparently uncontrolled rush to start the First World War gained momentum, the Prime Minister, Herbert Henry Asquith, quickly appointed Kitchener as Secretary of State for War. The following day at 11.00 a.m., 4 August 1914, Britain declared war on Germany, whereupon the BEF of the Regular Army was quickly assembled and transported across the Channel to France, while the Territorial Force was immediately called up for the defence of the Home Country.

Many completely untrained men also volunteered to join up to defend their country in the widely-held belief that it would 'all be over by Christmas' in 1914. Kitchener thought otherwise, and prepared for a long war with a significant number of casualties. He started a huge recruitment campaign, which soon featured the distinctive series of posters with the slogan 'Your Country Needs You'. Kitchener's picture was on many street corners pointing at every young man who passed by. The poster encouraged even more volunteers and has proven to be one of the most enduring images of the First World War. It is believed that Kitchener established these untrained recruits into 'New Armies' or separate army units, because he had a distrust of Territorial forces emanating from his experiences when attached to the French Army in the 1870 conflict with the Prussians. It was a seriously mistaken judgement, as the British Reservists of 1914 were younger and fitter than their French equivalents of a generation earlier.

By separating the New Armies from the Regular Army, Kitchener was unwittingly sowing the seeds of the disastrous campaigns fought by the British Army of 1915 and early 1916 when hundreds of thousands of inexperienced troops died. In 1914, however, the battalions of the New Armies, each containing 1,100 men, were quickly formed into their brigades and divisions. Large areas of land were immediately required to enable the construction of the barracks, the training facilities, the shooting ranges, the parade grounds and the support functions for such large numbers of men. Country landowners were approached, and many provided their estates to the War Office 'for the duration', an expression intended to cover the period of the war.

Only days after the start of the war in August 1914, Alfred de Rothschild, the owner of the Halton Park estate near Wendover, reached a gentlemen's agreement with Kitchener regarding the use of his estate by the British Army for the duration. The 63rd Brigade with 4,000 men, which formed a part of the 21st Division, was ordered to assemble at Halton Park early in September 1914.

The 21st Division was commanded by Lieutenant General Sir Edward Thomas Henry Hutton KCB, KCMG, FRGS, and the camp at Halton was to be the Brigade's training base, where the plan was to transform its battalions, officers

Halton House in Buckinghamshire as it was in 1914, when Alfred de Rothschild lent the army his estate 'for the duration' as a camp for training soldiers. In 2017 it was still in the hands of the RAF.

Soldiers of the 10th Battalion the York and Lancaster Regiment on parade in the recreation ground outside St Barnabas, Linslade. They were initially billeted in the town because Halton Park was not ready to receive them, and later returned when winter conditions meant that living in tents was bad for their health and morale.

and men into a cohesive and effective fighting force. The officers of both the Brigade and its battalions were drawn from the ranks of retired officers and newly commissioned officers, with only a small leavening of Regular Army officers. The latter, although experienced in colonial wars leading small forces of men, would lack some of the skills needed when fighting the large continental armies facing Britain and its allies across the trench systems of northern France and Belgium. Little information of the fighting conditions on the Western Front was passed by the War Office to the New Army's brigades, so it was hard to see how the officers or their men could be properly prepared for the terrible battles to come.

At Halton Park a huge tented encampment was established by late August 1914 to accommodate some of the units of the New Army's 63rd Brigade of the 21st Division. Orders were despatched to the local barracks of the Territorial Force in Lincoln, Pontefract, York and Taunton for the newly formed units of 8th Battalion the Lincolnshire Regiment, 10th Battalion the York and Lancaster Regiment, 12th Battalion the Prince of Wales's Own (West Yorkshire Regiment) and 8th Battalion the Prince Albert's (Somerset Light Infantry) to assemble at Halton Camp. These four battalions, each of 1,107 officers and men, would form the core of the 63rd Brigade's soldiery. Other military formations were ordered to transit through to railway stations to the west, east and south of Tring, which was the closest station to Halton Camp.

Leighton Buzzard railway station was designated to cater for the arrival of more than 4,000 soldiers, and a temporary platform was added to the station to accommodate the arriving troops. The War Office decided that the troops would be billeted on both Leighton and Linslade for only a few days prior to marching south to the tented encampment at Halton, and the householders of the two towns were told that overnight they had to make room immediately for these young men.

In preparation for their arrival, it was recorded in the Leighton Buzzard Urban District Council's minutes that the military would be charged one shilling per one 1,000 gallons for additional water pumped in consequence of the presence of troops in the town. In the minutes of 21 September 1914 the sanitary inspector was also instructed to make the necessary arrangements for dealing with additional scavenging (rubbish collection) and sewage in the event of troops coming to the town again.

However, despite the appeal to their patriotism and the orders of the army, not all the people of the two towns were willing to accept the billeted soldiers. The *LBO* of Tuesday 1 September 1914 reported thus:

> … the attitude of the householder, at the outset, is one of strenuous objection. Housewives who are careful of the comfort of their households deeply resent the interpolation of half a dozen or more strangers of unknown character and antecedents. Billeting officers have had the doors slammed in their face, infectious diseases have been imagined, and generally everything possible done to avoid having the troops. Only in a minority of cases did the officers find a cheerful willingness to co-operate with them.

A story circulated that a billeting officer was turned away by one housewife because all her children were suffering from measles, a serious infectious disease at the time. However, the next-door neighbour advised the billeting officer that no children lived there. The billeting officer returned to the first home and chalked a 6 on the door to indicate that six men would be billeted there. He reassured the housewife that she had no need to worry; all six men had already suffered from measles and would not be at risk from her children.

Army organisation, alas, was sometimes less than efficient. The householders were let down on a number of occasions during September 1914 when soldiers due to arrive did not appear. This was after residents had bought in additional foodstuffs in expectation of billeting the new arrivals. The *LBO* of 22 September 1914 said: 'If an adjutant had spent three minutes sending a telegram to the local police on Saturday, the weekend in some hundreds of homes in Leighton Buzzard would have been considerably more comfortable than it turned out to be.'

However, arrive they did and on 29 September 1914 the *LBO* reported that on 24 September:

A parade of about 1,100 men who enlisted in Lord Kitchener's Army, and at present billeted in Linslade, took place on Thursday afternoon and excited much interest among the townspeople. The men assembled in Linslade and shortly after their midday meal they marched to Leighton Buzzard Recreation Ground. Their appearance, allowing for the absence of khaki uniform, was smart and soldierly. Lieutenant-General Hutton wished to express his regret he felt that by some misunderstanding the townsfolk had prepared their hospitality for the whole of the soldiers with the result that some of them had been the loser.

As the men were marched back to their billets in Linslade, Hutton took the salute near the Leighton Buzzard Market Cross. The *LBO* continued by reporting a meeting conducted later that day between Hutton and local dignitaries in which the issue of compensation to be paid to the out-of-pocket householders was discussed:

No-one seems to know how the mistake arose. It is a matter of regret to all those in authority that the people, who were so ready to receive soldiers, should have been put to so much trouble and expense. It is felt that at a time like this, when

Troops billeted in Leighton and Linslade were supposed to be trained at Halton but much of their initial square bashing was done in local recreation grounds or in this case in Church Square. The lack of rifles shows the shortage of basic equipment.

our country is plunged into such a terrible war, we must all make sacrifices of one kind or another. Lord Kitchener himself has publicly asked that all mistakes, which must of necessity arise, should be forgiven and forgotten, and after the earlier patriotic address by General E. Hutton, it would seem to us that to offer compensation would be to doubt the loyalty of those whom we know to be the most loyal.

None was paid.

Luton suffered similar problems and in November 1914 the question of the payments to householders was resolved in a letter from Town Clerk William Smith:

Numerous complaints having been made to the Mayor and I and to the War Office as to the variation of the sums paid for billeting troops in houses in the borough, I think it well to state, for the information of the inhabitants, that the following are the rates which the military authorities are legally liable to pay:

Accommodation to be provided – lodging and attendance (in an occupied dwelling house) for soldiers, where meals furnished, price to be paid to occupier, 9d per night per man. (There is a specified scale of prices for meals).

Where no meals furnished, lodging and attendance (in an occupied dwelling house), and candles, vinegar, salt, and the use of fire and the necessary utensils for dressing and eating his meat, 9d per man per night.

For the 9d the military authorities can require the provision of a separate bed for each man (if a bed is available); but if they do not demand a bed they are still liable to pay the full rate of 9d per night for each man billeted in an occupied dwelling house.

For accommodation in an unoccupied dwelling house, or in a building not a dwelling house, the price to be paid is 3d per night for each man, and no bed or attendance can be required.

The letter added that any person who had received less than 9d per night per man should at once see the billeting officer and ask for payment of the arrears due. The accommodation cost of 9d per man was increased by the payment of 7½d for breakfast, 1s 7½d for dinner and 4½d for supper, a total of 3s 4½d per man per day billeted in a dwelling house. This payment is difficult to translate into twenty-first century values, but is about £14 per man per day, or the equivalent of two hours' work on the minimum wage. If there were three or more soldiers in the house this amounted to a lot of work and a significant income boost for a poor family.

Another report in the *LBO* of 29 September 1914 recorded:

The first detachment of three or four thousand troops who have been expected in Leighton Buzzard for some days arrived in the town at about three o'clock on Monday afternoon, and the police, assisted by a number of special constables, at once directed them to their billets. The new arrivals belong to the West Yorks Regiment and are expected to remain about a week but any alterations to military plans may prolong their stay to ten or eleven days or curtail it. Most of the men who arrived on Monday are without uniform although they were among the early recruits to Lord Kitchener's Army. A further 2,500 troops are expected to arrive on Wednesday or Thursday.

The expected arrivals on Wednesday got off their train in Leighton station for their billets, only to be ordered to get back on the train, which then took them down to Tring and a march to Halton Camp.

The following week the *LBO* said:

Two thousand men of the West Yorks and Lincolnshire Regiments who were billeted in Leighton Buzzard last week left on Saturday morning for a new training camp at Halton Park. With few exceptions they were without uniforms or arms but their time spent in Leighton Buzzard was not wasted. Every morning they paraded at 6.30 and spent the morning drilling in the Recreation Ground or at Page's Park.

The men marched off to Halton Camp. Still seemingly woefully short of equipment, and the majority still dressed in their civilian clothing and without a rifle, they arrived at Halton to find a tented camp where the necessary permanent accommodation had not been constructed. Although the men were fed and drill was undertaken there was very little military training for them or their officers.

By early November 1914 the weather was deteriorating, and the 63rd Brigade realised the men could not spend the winter under canvas in Halton Park, and it would be necessary to return them to billets in the local towns. Back to Leighton Buzzard marched the men of the 8th Lincolns, the 10th York and Lancasters, the 12th West Yorkshires and the 8th Somersets. It seems the attitude to the soldiers had now changed. The *LBO* commented on 17 November 1914: 'The return of the troops to Leighton Buzzard was generally welcomed. To traders and the poorer householders the presence of the men means a great deal. In fact, it will enable some provision to be made for possible trade depression in midwinter.'

With the influx of so many men, accommodation was very tight. It also caused some social problems.

On the evening of Saturday, 14 November 1914 the men were able to avail themselves of the many public houses in the town, a facility not available at Halton Camp, and a large number of men became drunk and disorderly. The *LBO* of 17 November 1914 blamed the few publicans who provided excessive amounts of drink for the drunken disorder, rather than the men. It also reported that it was

Billeting at
LEIGHTON BUZZARD.

One of a series of postcards made by enterprising local businesses for the soldiers to send to their families, making light of their cramped conditions. In the absence of telephones except for the very rich, sending postcards was the standard method for keeping the family informed of health and welfare. (Bedfordshire Archives.)

'bad for the householders who have faced considerable inconvenience to provide billets'. To try to stamp out this problem and restore discipline, Hutton issued an order on Monday, 23 November 1914 that all pubs in Linslade and Leighton within five miles of a billet were to be closed at 8.30 p.m.

During late November and December 1914 the churches, chapels and various associations began organising concerts, games and lessons for the men to join in during the evenings and the officers encouraged their men to participate. The benefit of regular billeting payments to the householders was quickly felt throughout Leighton Buzzard and Linslade, and the townspeople and the soldiers seemed to have had a good relationship.

By late November 1914 the Brigade had begun inoculating all the men in the battalions billeted in Leighton Buzzard. The *Bucks Herald* of 5 December 1914 reported under the headline 'Inoculating the Troops: Wild Rumours':

> The inoculation of troops billeted in the Leighton Buzzard district, which had been proceeding apace during the past few days, gave rise last weekend to a number of strange and unfounded rumours as to the condition of the men. It was asserted that serious illness was rife amongst the men since the inoculations,

and another was that three deaths had resulted. To allay these wild assertions the medical officers of the 63rd Brigade were interviewed on Monday and they definitely stated that no deaths whatever had resulted from the inoculation, and that there was no serious illness among the troops. They also pointed out that deaths from inoculation were practically unknown, and that all of the effects so far from the present inoculations were slight. The real reason for the inoculations were to protect the men from typhoid fever from which so many had died during the South African War.

However, the statement that there were no known deaths caused by inoculation may not have been the full truth. The *LBO of* 8 December 1914 reported that Private Harold Rodgers, of 10th Battalion the York and Lancaster Regiment, aged 19, had died in the early hours of Saturday, 28 November in his billet on Soulbury Road. Rodgers had been inoculated by his medical officer on Friday and had gone to bed unwell with a high temperature. An inquest was held on the Saturday and the medical officer certified that Rodgers was previously healthy and had died of heart failure. On Monday, 7 December, Rodgers' coffin was accompanied by a military escort of his friends and colleagues to Leighton railway station, destined for Rotherham and his home in Kilnhurst.

The inoculation of the troops must have caused some unpleasant side effects. The primitive medical equipment of the time and the size of the needles must have made it a painful business, even if the vaccines did not cause a reaction. The records of the Ministry of Munitions show that a company in Leighton Buzzard, Arthur Jackson, of Bassett Works, Bassett Road had a contract to provide the army with medical syringes. It does not record how many he made, but he employed nine men and five women on the work.

The officers and men settled into their winter billets and focused on their diet and regular exercise. Unfortunately rifles did not arrive for distribution to the men until late December 1914, and even then little ammunition was available for shooting practice. However, they were provided with uniforms and the men were seen regularly marching in formation around the district.

This certainly left its mark on the local parks. The Leisure Grounds Committee of the Leighton Urban Council which let Page's Park for sheep to keep the grass down gave the local farmer £8 of his annual rent back in March 1915 'for the damage done to the grazing by the troops'.

It was reported by the *LBO* that on Friday, 5 February 1915:

The commanding officer of the 12th Battalion of the West Yorkshire Regiment, which is now stationed in Leighton Buzzard, suffered a serious riding accident this morning. Colonel Lovebond was riding with his battalion between Billington

NOT WOUNDED–ONLY VACCINATED.

A Scene in Leighton Buzzard.

Another humorous postcard from Leighton Buzzard with a drawing of the Black Lion and the Cedars. Vaccination must have left people with some nasty after-effects, either as a reaction to the vaccine or from the marks of the needles. (Bedfordshire Archives.)

Leighton recreation ground before the war. Before the advent of the lawnmower, the parks and recreation grounds in Leighton and Linslade were regularly let to farmers who paid rent for the grazing to keep the grass down.

and Leighton Buzzard when his horse stumbled and threw him. His fellow officers put him in a carrier's cart and brought him to Leighton House, where he has been staying. Although he made light of the fall it appears he has suffered internal injuries and he has been transferred to a hospital for X-ray examination.

By the end of March 1915 rumours were circulating through Linslade and Leighton of the departure of the billeted men to Halton Camp. The *LBO* of 13 April 1915 reported:

The impending departure of the troops will terminate the sojourn before the guests have outstayed their welcome, and before many weeks are over most householders will wish their soldiers were back again. There is however little prospect of any more billeting except of a casual nature before the autumn, and it may be the last time that anyone now living will see English soldiers billeted in private homes.

As the 8th Lincolns paraded for the final time through Leighton Buzzard the salute was taken by Major John Young Storer.

Storer was born in Glasgow in 1880, son of the owner of a paint and varnish company supplying the ship construction companies of the Clyde. The business

The 8th Battalion the Lincolnshire Regiment on their final parade through Leighton Buzzard with Major John Young Storer on horseback, in the middle of the column. The soldiers are now equipped with rifles. (Imperial War Museum.)

expanded into the London docks and owned a site at Cubitts Wharf in Poplar, which became known as Storer's Wharf and the company also had offices in Leadenhall Street, then the centre of the British Empire's shipping industry. He quickly joined up in August 1914 and was commissioned as a temporary lieutenant with promotion to temporary captain on 2 October 1914, and finally temporary major on 25 January 1915, as second-in-command of 8th Battalion the Lincolns. Storer had spent the night before the parade in the Swan Hotel, Leighton Buzzard where he signed the visitors' book.

Once the parade was over, Storer marched his men to Halton Camp. The *LBO* of 20 April 1915 reported:

Two battalions of the 63rd Brigade left Leighton Buzzard for Halton Park last week. The men of the Lincolnshire Regiment were the first to leave. They paraded in Lake Street on Thursday [15 April 1915] with their mascot leading the way and marched out of town. The men made no secret of the fact that they were sorry to leave and the crowds of people who lined the roads gave them

The officers of the 8th Battalion stayed at the Swan Hotel for a last night of luxury before Halton Camp, and signed the visitor's book. The ditty in praise of the hotel in the comments column contains a tribute to Kitty Towers, who ran the hotel throughout the war.

a good send-off. The men of the Somerset Regiment left on Friday morning. They paraded in Church Square soon after 9 a.m. and marched off a few minutes later. The West Yorks battalion remain in billets in Leighton Buzzard and the York and Lancs men are still in Linslade; for how long is uncertain, but the order to leave billets is expected any day. The West Yorks billeted at Wing were marched into Leighton Buzzard yesterday [Monday] and now occupy the Lincolns' old billets.

At Halton Camp the business of converting the fit and healthy men into soldiers began, but these were not battled-hardened officers preparing their troops for the rigours of the Western Front. Many of the officers had no experience either and the first time they commanded troops was during exercises which attempted to prepare them and their troops for this type of new warfare. The men dug trenches at the camp as directed in the 1914 training manuals, but the carnage caused by artillery, machine guns and German assault tactics had already changed their design on the battlefield. Unfortunately, at Halton Camp the division and brigade staff officers

By this stage of the war the local people were clearly used to seeing troops marching through the town, but perhaps did not realise that this group were on their way to Halton Camp, then to the Western Front, and would never return. (Imperial War Museum.)

with battalion officers had few opportunities to train together and even fewer to absorb the lessons painfully learned by the Allied armies on the Western Front.

Notwithstanding, by early September 1915 the 63rd Brigade had left Halton, destination the Western Front. The 8th Lincolns arrived in France on 10 September 1915 and without resting marched off to the sound of the guns, towards what would become known as the Battle of Loos. It would result in terrible carnage.

The Battle of Loos was fought by the British with the intention of taking back from the Germans the coal-mining towns of Loos and Lens in north-eastern France. The proposed ground for the battle was unsuitable because the machine guns in the German front line could sweep across the level ground over which the British would attack. However, Field-Marshal Douglas Haig overrode his own instinct when it was suggested to him by Kitchener that co-operation with the French Army was essential and that 'we may suffer heavy losses'. Haig was provided with poison gas and elected to use it, a new tactic for the British Army and not an unmitigated success.

The gas was discharged at 5.50 a.m. on 25 September, but in the unsuitable wind conditions it drifted back into the British trenches, disabling troops who attempted to climb out at the start time of 6.30 a.m. Six divisions attacked, leaving in reserve and well to the rear of the battle the very recently arrived 21st Division containing the troops of the 63rd Brigade who had arrived tired, hungry and thirsty after their march across northern France. Although there was an opportunity to achieve a breakthrough with these reserves, they were neither close to the front line nor rested. More importantly, they were too new and inexperienced to mount a successful attack.

Major John Storer, with the 8th Battalion, accompanied his troops on horseback and took the salute as they marched down the High Street for the last time on their way to Halton Camp.

The battalion messengers were equipped with bicycles at this stage of the war. In the background are the new Leighton Buzzard and District Unionist Club and the spire of All Saints Church.

Disagreement between Haig and his commander-in-chief, Sir John French, about the release of the Reserve to Haig delayed their departure to the Front until mid-morning. As a result the first of the Reserve troops did not arrive at the start line until the evening.

The following day the Germans counter-attacked and the 21st Division was the focal point of the attack by artillery and experienced troops. This left the completely inexperienced 8th Lincolns, so recently billeted in Leighton Buzzard, occupying the most forward position of the Reserve force. They had no indication of where neighbouring troops were located and were without a compass bearing to take for their advance. It was recorded in a contemporary account that Major Storer commented on a number of occasions, 'If we were going to do any good we ought to have been here twelve hours ago.'

By 6.00 a.m. the 10th York and Lancasters, the 12th West Yorks and the 8th Somersets, the other members of the 63rd Brigade, were in their trenches near to the 8th Lincolns. It was planned that the 63rd Brigade would join other troops in an attack in an easterly direction at 11.00 a.m. However, half an hour earlier, the Germans attacked. They had brought up their reserves overnight, and mounted an intense artillery bombardment before attacking the troops of the 63rd Brigade in their trenches. Brigadier Norman Tom Nickalls, commanding officer of 63rd Brigade, and Lieutenant Colonel Harold Ernest Walter, commanding officer of 8th Battalion the Lincolns, were both killed during this action.

The casualty numbers among the 8th Lincolns were very high. Along with their commanding officer, all the company commanders were killed or wounded; all other officers were casualties. Of the 993 men who landed in France on 10 September 1915, only 522 were able to march off the battlefield.

Storer was killed on 26 September at the Battle of Loos, just five months after the 35-year-old officer had taken the salute at the parade in Leighton Buzzard. He has no known grave, but is commemorated on panels 31 to 34 of the Loos Memorial, in the Commonwealth War Graves Commission (CWGC) Dud Corner Cemetery. Along with his name are those of many of the men who had been billeted with him in Linslade and Leighton during that first winter of the war.

CHAPTER 11

OUR BOYS SIGN UP

After the initial rush of recruits in 1914 the government faced the serious problem of finding enough men to serve in the armed forces. At the start of hostilities almost half a million men volunteered as their 'patriotic duty' but within a year the numbers being recruited were never as many as the generals felt they needed to win the war.

As the war progressed the situation was not helped by the news from the Front; in Leighton and Linslade reports of local men killed, injured or missing in action were carried every week in the local papers.

At the start of the war no one could have known what was to come, so the government reacted to events as they happened. There was a standing army of 80,000 regular troops ready for war and a large number of reservists who had previously served in the army and were liable to recalled. The day war was officially declared, 4 August 1914, the reservists of Leighton and Linslade were called up from their civilian roles by mobilisation notice telegrams. The Leighton Reservists dashed off to the Town Hall before travelling to the Bedfordshire Regiment's Drill Hall, Bedford, where they filled gaps in the regular battalions; the remainder formed the initial cadre of the 3rd Battalion. As the BEF fought the Germans in France there was a feeling at home that the war would not be a long one, and many men who had no previous military experience volunteered to join their local regiments.

It is hard to understand the atmosphere of the time but there must have been considerable pressure on young men to enlist. An example is the attitude of the vicar of Linslade, William Stow Mahony. He used the parish magazine to keep a record of Linslade's young men who fought in the war:

I know there is a fairly long list of names hanging in the church porch of those Linslade men who are on active service, but it is not long enough for a place of this size. You may say that it is not my business to do the work of a recruiting sergeant. Perhaps it is not. But at least I shall not dissuade a single able-bodied man from enlisting, because I believe that the more men we can put into the field or set free to go into it, the sooner will our enemies realise that we are very much in earnest, and the sooner will the war be over.

In a later edition he wrote that recruitment had picked up: 'But yet there are many young men left who look strong and healthy enough to volunteer. We must suppose that they suffer from weak hearts or other invisible defects.' The pressure was increasing.

Elsewhere in the country there had been a movement to hand white feathers to apparently healthy young men who had not enlisted, suggesting that they were too cowardly to fight for their country. This led to the government issuing a Silver War Badge (see chapter 17) to all those engaged in vital war work so that they would be left alone by these vigilantes, many of whom were women. Those who were exempt from war service because they were carrying out 'essential duties' at home were given a certificate to produce to show who they were.

Daily from the beginning of the war until the signing of the Armistice in November 1918, St Barnabas Church offered prayers of intercession for those

S. 023.

MILITARY SERVICE ACTS 1916-18.

CERTIFICATE OF EXEMPTION.

I HEREBY CERTIFY, on behalf of the Secretary of State for the Home Department, that *Station Sergeant Harry White* a member of the Metropolitan Police Force, is exempted from the provisions of the Military Service Acts 1916-18, so long as he remains in that employment.

Commissioner of Police of the Metropolis.

Signature of holder: *Harry White*

(To be signed by the holder as soon as he receives this Certificate).

NOTE.—This certificate is liable to be reviewed at any time. If the holder leaves the Metropolitan Police Force the certificate must be given up.

Able-bodied men not in uniform were liable to be abused or treated with suspicion by the authorities, so those doing valuable war work at home were given Exemption Certificates. Issued to Harvey White, later publican of the Goat Inn in Old Road, Linslade, who served in the police during the war.

serving, and later in the war when the news of casualties began to mount the vicar toned down his calls for men to join up.

Nationally, after only a few months of enthusiastic patriotism the number of recruits began to dry up and by early 1915 the army was not enlisting enough volunteers to replace casualties. The government began to debate compulsory conscription but this was resisted by some coalition ministers, and a compromise suggested by Edward Stanley, Lord Derby, was reached. A new recruitment process based upon a National Register was launched in October 1915. The 'Derby Scheme' aimed to reconcile the demands of the army with the needs of industry by registering men for one day's service and then returning them to their civilian life. Men who were willing to do so were placed in the Reserve and called up when needed, with unmarried men first. However, insufficient numbers came forward and in January 1916 the government introduced compulsory conscription.

The Military Service Act of March 1916 had rendered liable for service all single men aged 18 to 41 years, but such was the need for recruits that this was extended to married men in May 1916, with exemptions for reserved occupations and conscientious objection. There was an initial promise that recruits would not be sent to the Front until they were 19, but this was later reduced to 18 years and 6 months. In April 1918 the call-up was extended again, to men aged up to 50. Before the introduction of conscription, the *LBO* had published a Roll of Honour – a list of men who were serving in the Royal Navy or the army, either as regular sailors or soldiers or as volunteers, with names listed alphabetically by town or village, with regiment or ship, if known. The list became too long to publish in full every week, so each place was listed in rotation. Even this became unwieldy and the last Roll of Honour lists in the *LBO* appeared in January 1916.

Hot on the heels of the Derby Scheme had come the Military Service Tribunals, held to protect any local occupations where expertise was required. In addition to the production of sand, nets and aircraft, looking after stud stallions, shoeing horses or running canal boats could also qualify as reserved occupations in Leighton and Linslade and, clearly, many skilled craftsmen had to be kept at home, otherwise the soldiers at the Front could not be properly supplied.

The issue was complicated by the fact that many women were recruited into jobs to replace men at the Front, and the question was often posed by tribunals about whether men could be sent to fight and replaced by women.

Across the country there was remarkable variation in the attitude of the tribunals to men seeking to avoid the call-up. In Leighton and Linslade there seems to have been a careful consideration of whether some men's skills were too valuable to be lost to the local community. Family circumstances were also considered. Curiously, there seems to have been a policy of naming some individuals who came before tribunals and keeping others confidential.

The fate of conscientious objectors, too, varied across the country. In Leighton Buzzard there does not seem to have been much sympathy for them. In one of the earliest local tribunals the *LBO* of 11 July 1916, reported the hearing of a self-employed married carpenter who claimed absolute exemption as a conscientious objector. He said that he belonged to the International Bible Student Association and produced voluminous documents in support of his claim, but the tribunal did not read them. The *LBO* reported:

> When the appellant was called, he claimed he accepted the principles of Christianity which were quite out of harmony with militarism and objected to any military service, although he was willing to give up his present occupation and work on the land. When asked how he reconciled enjoying the privileges of British citizenship with his refusal he responded that his hope was not in what the English nation was doing in the way of war, it was in Christ's Kingdom. When asked if he saw someone ill-using his wife would he not defend her he could not say what he would do, but that did not mean he would kill the man but try to keep to the principles of Christianity. He was unwilling to undertake any work for the army, even to save life. The applicant was held to serve and handed over to the military.

There was an altogether different atmosphere for other members of the community. For example the *LBO* of 20 March 1917 carried the hearing of George William Hedges of New Road, organist and choirmaster of St Barnabas Church, who appealed for further exemption after his previously granted three months had expired.

> Besides his own duties at St Barnabas Church, he performed the same role at All Saints Church. He also had work of national importance at Messrs Morgan's Aeroplane Works. The manager of the works employing the appellant as an assistant fitter manufacturing parts by hand also sat on the tribunal, and his foreman had said he would be sorry to lose the appellant. At present women were not as successful in the job and strangers had come into the works for employment. The works manager said there was no surplus labour and more men were wanted in this department and it would be hard lines to hold the appellant to serve whilst strangers were employed. The manager said the appellant was working from 6.00 a.m. to 6.00 p.m. and doing his musical work afterwards. The tribunal felt that his personal grounds had not changed and he had work of national importance. The appellant was given further exemption on condition that he was engaged on work of national importance.

The paper also reported on 20 February 1917 the arrest at the railway station at 7.15 a.m. of an alleged deserter, carrying a large amount of luggage. The magistrates heard that three call-up notices were sent to the defendant in January and February, each with an attached rail warrant, and then a final telegram. The defendant was carrying a rail ticket for Rugby and claimed that the call-up papers expired the next day and he was not an absentee because Morgan's had told him that they would resolve the matter during January. That morning he claimed to be taking home his wife and work tools before joining up tomorrow. The defendant was handed over to the military escort.

The decisions were sometimes difficult. For example the record of a tribunal appeal in the 20 March 1917 edition of the *LBO* stated that the appellant, a munitions worker in Morgan's, claimed that his certificates and badge provided by the Ministry of Munitions, exempting him from military service, had been wrongfully withdrawn. The badge was withdrawn after the appellant was called up and Morgan's provided no evidence that they wished to retain him. The case was deferred for him to be medically examined.

Private 3/7715 Ernest George Fathers of 1st Battalion the Bedfords, with his wife Emily (Coulson) and their children, Amy, James, Marion, Joyce, Gordon, Clement, Charles and Edith, in 1915. Ernest was a coach-painter and sign-writer, Emily a servant when they met in Linslade. He survived the war.

William John Dunnett and his children William, (Louis) Walter and Doris, in 1918. Fathers home on leave were frequently pictured in uniform with their children in their Sunday best. Dunnett's father, Maxwell had come from Caithness to Leighton to work for Baron Ferdinand de Rothschild. William, who survived the war, was a butcher.

In 1919 the *LBO* published a list of those who had served in the war but the record was incomplete, recording only 1,364 men serving from Leighton Buzzard. However, a further eighty-eight names are recorded on the List of Absent Voters, including two women serving in the Red Cross Voluntary Aid Detachment or VADs, with an additional eleven names which offer too little detail in the *LBO* list for any certainty whether they are included or not. It would therefore appear that at least 1,452 people served, more than one fifth of the population of the town. The record kept by the vicar of Linslade of the names of the men and women from Linslade who served is very difficult to read. Research has recorded the names of 400 who served including casualties, again around a fifth of the population.

With this number of men on active service and in harm's way, the impact of the war on the community in Leighton Buzzard was considerable. In 1914 Leighton was a close-knit community where, it seems, not only did everyone know everyone else, but may also have been related to them. In some areas, such as Mill Road and Vandyke Road, parents, children, cousins and grandparents lived within a few doors or streets of each other and the lives of neighbours were closely intertwined. This meant that bad news or a fatality in one household impacted on the whole community.

It is not possible to describe what happened to every family, but it seems that the areas of the two towns carrying a heavier burden were those where poorer people with larger families lived. Based on the lists of servicemen published in the *LBO* and the 1918 and 1919 Lists of Absent Voters, it appears that in Regent Street (which at the time had only fifty-four houses) at least fifty residents or sons of residents served in the war, of whom eight were killed. No. 40 (now 62 Regent Street) was home at different times to two families who each lost a son, Horace Andrews and Leonard Moore, while four separate families living at different times at No. 12 (now 22, Regent Street) supplied seven servicemen during the course of the war, including James Wernham who died.

In Vandyke Road, at least 120 residents or sons of residents served, and at least twelve died. In some parts of the road, nearly every house had at least one man, sometimes more, in the armed services at some time during the war. In the section of the road from Beaudesert to George Street, there were twenty-one houses on the odd-numbered side, of which at least thirteen had men serving. The even-numbered side of the street consisted of twenty-nine houses, but of the eleven houses with men serving, nine were in the ten houses numbered 12–30, including all three of the houses who lost a soldier. When extended families are taken into account, the stress endured must have been intolerable.

William and Maria Reeve, 84 Church Street

For William Benjamin Reeve and his wife Maria, of 84 Church Street, the war years must have been particularly difficult; a son, also William Benjamin, and his wife died in 1915, one grandson was wounded and another killed, and at least one son and four nephews were all serving in the armed forces, as well as their niece's husband and her five brothers-in-law.

The younger William was a drover and labourer, living at 8 Plantation Road with his wife, Harriett, and five of their six children. Their eldest child, Charles William Sapwell Reeve, Harriett's son from a previous relationship, was serving with the Bedfords.

On 5 July 1915, William junior had been out drinking all day with a friend. His last stop was at the Stag, where his father refused to buy him a drink, as he thought he had had plenty already. He went home to find his wife had returned from work and was in the house with their 15-year-old son (yet another William Benjamin Reeve) and one of his friends. Harriett sent the two boys to the cinema and half an hour later gunshots were heard, following which William was seen running across the road to his father's house, with serious wounds to his throat. The neighbours discovered Harriett shot dead, still sitting in her chair. William was taken to the workhouse infirmary to recover from his wounds and was charged with her murder in a case that came to be known as the Gun and Razor Tragedy. His trial lasted six hours and was held at Bedfordshire Assizes in October; he pleaded not guilty, stating that he loved his wife and that her death had been an accident, but the jury took just twelve minutes to find him guilty and he was sentenced to death. An appeal failed and he was hanged at Bedford Gaol on Tuesday, 16 November 1915. His parents, who had been in court for his trial, visited him the day before his execution.

Just over a month after Harriett's death and while William was awaiting trial, Harriett's son Charles was wounded in the action at Chocolate Hill in Gallipoli on 15 August, which ultimately led to his discharge from the army in 1916. Their son William Benjamin Reeve, who had been in the house just half an hour before his mother's death, moved to Harlesden to live with his married aunt, Jennie Tring. He was called up in May 1917 and by June 1918 was with the Royal Engineers (RE) at Haslar Barracks, Gosport. On 2 July 1918 he was admitted to hospital suffering from influenza. Pneumonia quickly set in and he died four days later in Queen Alexandra's Hospital, Cosham, a victim of the pandemic which was to ravage the world.

William and Maria's other son, George, a house decorator who lived next door to them at 82 Church Street with his wife Lily, enlisted under the Derby Scheme. This was due to end on 11 December 1915 and posters of the day advised young men to sign up to fulfil their national duty, warning that if they did not, they would become subject to the National Service Act due to come into force on 2 March 1916. With the deadline approaching, the number of men presenting themselves to attest became overwhelming; it seems likely that George Reeve was one of these, as his attestation is dated 10 December 1915. Men from the Scheme were called up in groups according to their age, and married men were promised that all eligible unmarried men would be called up first. As a result George was not called up until October 1916. In September 1918 he was assessed by the Medical Board as 'not likely to be fit' but he was not actually discharged until he was demobilised in 1919.

Sapper Thomas Reeve was William and Maria's nephew. He was brought up in Mill Road, but by 1911 his family were living on Vandyke Road at 'No. 1 Opposite

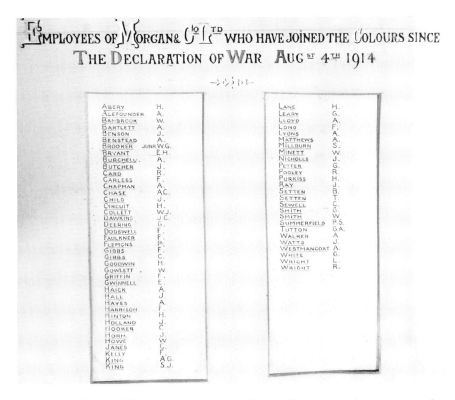

EMPLOYEES OF MORGAN & C⁰ L™ WHO HAVE JOINED THE COLOURS SINCE THE DECLARATION OF WAR AUG⁵ᵀ 4ᵀᴴ 1914

ABERY	H.
ALEFOUNDER	A.
BAMBROOK	W.
BARTLETT	A.
BENSON	J.
BENSTEAD	A.
BROOKER JUNR	W.G.
BRYANT	E.H.
BURCHELL	A.
BUTCHER	J.
CARD	R.
CARLESS	F.
CHAPMAN	A.
CHASE	A.C.
CHILD	J.
CIRCUIT	H.
COLLETT	W.J.
DAWKINS	J.C.
DEERING	G.
DODSWELL	F.
FAULKNER	F.
FLEMONS	P.
GIBBS	F.
GIBBS	C.
GOODWIN	H.
GOWLETT	W.
GRIFFIN	F.
GWINNELL	E.
HAICK	A.
HALL	J.
HAYES	A.
HARRISON	F.
HINTON	H.
HOLLAND	J.
HOOKER	C.
HORN	J.
HOWE	W.
JANES	C.
KELLY	F.
KING	A.G.
KING	S.J.

LANE	H.
LEARY	G.
LLOYD	A.
LONG	F.
LYONS	A.
MATTHEWS	A.
MILLBURN	S.
MINETT	W.
NICHOLLS	J.
PETTER	G.
POOLEY	R.
PURKISS	H.
RAY	J.
SETTEN	B.
SETTEN	T.
SEWELL	G.
SMITH	G.
SMITH	W.
SUMMERFIELD	P.S.
TUTTON	G.A.
WALKER	A.
WATTS	J.
WESTMANCOAT	A.
WHITE	G.
WRIGHT	L.
WRIGHT	R.

Morgan's workers could have gained exemption from military service, but sixty-one of the company's workforce volunteered to serve. This roll of honour was discovered in 2009, behind a wall in the Forster Institute, Linslade, during renovations.

Cemetery', while Thomas was working in Rugby as a butcher. By February 1915, he was a railway labourer in Leighton until he joined 260th Railway Company the RE. Thomas survived the war; he returned to Leighton to marry Alice Faulkner in 1919 and continued to work on the railway until 1926.

His cousins, Arthur, George and Alfred Cosby were also the nephews of William and Maria Reeve, being the sons of William's sister Emily of Baker Street, whose sand merchant husband, Frederick Cosby, had died in 1900. Alfred Cosby, a wire worker who had previously worked as a photographer's assistant, had tried to join up under the Derby Scheme on the same day as his cousin George Reeve but was rejected on health grounds. Despite this he was called up on 2 November 1916 and joined the Royal Field Artillery as a gunner, serving in India, Mesopotamia and Egypt and contracting malaria at some point during his service. His discharge papers record his civilian occupation as Secret Naval Defence Worker so he must have been working on the submarine netting produced at Bullivant's prior to joining the army. At least two of his brothers, Arthur, a house painter, and George, a greengrocer, also served.

Their sister Lizzie was married to William Linney, and lived next door to her parents at No. 2 Opposite Cemetery. William, a platelayer for the L&NWR, served in 277th Railway Company the RE. He was the eldest of twelve children, his father having married twice. Five of his six brothers also served: Frederick was gassed, and wounded twice; George was wounded twice; Alfred suffered multiple gunshot wounds and was discharged; Samuel was gassed and possibly wounded as well; and Albert Harry (known as Harry), having only joined up in 1918, did not see action but served in the Army of Occupation until 1920.

Maria Sear, 15 Vandyke Road

In 1914 Maria Sear was a 73-year-old widow, who might be considered to have done relatively well in life. She was born in Eaton Bray, the daughter of a shoemaker, while her husband Edmund, a bricklayer, started life as an agricultural labourer. By 1914 Maria owned three adjoining properties on Vandyke Road and was living at No. 15, with Nos 11 and 13 rented out to tenants. She had certainly had her difficulties, as Edmund died in 1901 aged only 59, but her seven children were all doing well and only the youngest, 28-year-old Fred, was still at home. Maria's eldest son, William, aged 44, a boot dealer, was living in Aylesbury with his wife and four children; 42-year-old James was married and lived in Battersea. Francis (37) was married with children and living in Watford, working for the L&NWR, and Thomas (32) had lived in Battersea before emigrating to Canada in 1906, where he was living with his wife and children. Maria's two daughters Sarah Puryer (40) and Lucy Digby (34) were both married with young children and living nearby in Albany Road and South Street.

She could have been forgiven for thinking that the days of worrying about her children were behind her, but the outbreak of war saw three of her sons and one of her grandsons serving in the army. James was already serving in 9th (County of London) Battalion the London Regiment, having joined up in 1910 for four years and re-engaged for a further four in March 1914. He was based in London, where he continued to serve until March 1916, when he was discharged due to his age and ill health. His brother Thomas joined the Canadian Expeditionary Force (CEF) in 1915, while Fred served first in the Middlesex Regiment and later in 1/13th (Kensington) Battalion the London Regiment. Both Thomas and Fred were wounded (Fred in October 1916 at the Battle of the Somme) although thankfully both survived the war and were demobilised in 1919. Maria's eldest son, William was too old to serve in the war, but his son Fred Inns Sear, who was just 17 at the outbreak of war, served in the Royal Army Medical Corps (RAMC).

Sarah Puryer's husband, Arthur, lost his nephew Ernest, who lived at 1 South Street. He was 24 when he died of wounds in France in 1917. The *Luton News* reported on 18 October that 'after being severely wounded in the thigh, [he] passed quietly away without being able to send any message to his sorrowing parents.' He was their only child.

Sarah Gaskin, 16 Vandyke Road

Across the road at 16 Vandyke Road lived Sarah Gaskin, a 54-year-old widow whose husband John Hillier Gaskin died in 1908. The couple had six children, one daughter and five sons, the youngest of whom, Stanley, was only 3 when his father died. His four older brothers all served in the army during the war. The youngest of the four, Harold, was already serving in the Bedfordshire Territorials when war broke out, having enlisted aged 17. He received the Territorial Force Medal reserved for existing territorial soldiers who volunteered to fight abroad, which is the rarest of the First World War medals. It was awarded to only five officers and twenty-three men of the Bedfords. He also received the Silver War Badge because of the effects his service had on his health.

The eldest of the brothers, Frederick, a butcher, was married and living with his wife and daughter in Hockliffe Road. As the advertised closing date for the Derby Scheme approached, 30-year-old Frederick was part of the rush to attest, enlisting at Luton on 10 December 1915. He was called up to serve in May 1917 and posted to the Reserve Battalion of the Royal Field Artillery (RFA) at Hemel Hempstead. During his service with the RFA, he was kicked by a horse and spent three months in hospital. He was transferred to the Tank Corps in August 1918 and was finally demobilised in March 1919. His younger brother, William, also served from 1916, while 24-year-old Ernest joined up in January 1915, serving in the RFA in a Trench Mortar Battery. On 27th April 1918, the *Bucks Herald* reported that he had been listed as missing and the following week published the news that 'Gunner E.J. Gaskin … who was reported gassed a week ago, has died and been buried at Rouen'. He had died on 18 April.

Wilfred Gaskin of Ravenstone, Hockliffe Road, was a distant cousin of the Vandyke Road family. He had been a railway clerk for the L&NWR at Euston and enlisted in 1917 aged 18, probably having been conscripted. He was transferred into the newly established RAF in 1918 but was injured in August that year in what was described as an 'aero accident'.

George Garside, the sandpit owner, his wife Annie and their nephew Hugh Frank Delafield in his Bedfordshire Yeomanry uniform in the doorway of the White House in Hockliffe Street, now the offices of the Town Council. The Garsides had no children and Hugh inherited the business and the house.

The Hack family, Ivy Cottage, [now 89] Vandyke Road

At Ivy Cottage, Daisy Hack was one of the twelve children (including two sets of twins) born to John Hack and his wife Mary Anne. The second son, William James, and one from each set of twins (Harry and Lillie) died within a year of their birth. Daisy's brother, Arthur (Harry's surviving twin), who was born in 1881, was married with children and when he enlisted on 20 January 1915, he was working as a bricklayer for Thomas Yirrell of Linslade. Daisy's youngest brother Henry John (usually known as John) enlisted in the RFA and arrived in France on 24 December 1915.

In 1916, Daisy married 24-year-old Joseph George Jordan of Wing (usually known as George), a lance corporal in the 15th Hussars (later attached to 16th Battalion the Royal Warwickshire Regiment). He was the youngest son of Henry and Mary Jordan of Prospect Place, Wing; their eldest son Edwin was also serving, and they had already lost their son Lionel, who was killed on 31 August 1915 aged 29. Daisy and George's son, born in October 1916, was named after him. A year later George was also killed in action, followed by Daisy's brother, John Hack on 27 April 1918, aged 25.

Daisy's elder brother Arthur survived the war, serving with the RE, but suffered deafness and serious ear infection as a result of exposure to gas, although this appears to have happened while on home service in North Wales in 1917 or 1918 rather than in the trenches. Before his arrival in France in October 1918, it was noted that he 'would not stand gas or gunfire. Not likely to improve' and it was recommended that he serve in a trench mortar battery. Prior to demobilisation in 1919, his deafness was assessed at 'less than 20%' but by 1920 his condition had worsened to 30 per cent disablement with an expectation that the condition was likely to last a further twelve months. He returned home to his wife Beatrice in Regent Street, and they had another child in 1919 but he died in 1924, aged only 43.

Mary Ann Horne, Long Row and Vandyke Road

Mary Ann Horne was the wife of Daniel Horne, a labourer. They married in 1905 and over the years lived at several houses in Vandyke Road including Nos 86 and 90, as well as 114 Long Row. All of these houses, which were in the area of Vandyke Road north-east of Regent Street, have since been demolished and the houses on Vandyke Road have been renumbered. In 1914, two of Mary Ann's three brothers, George and William Brandom (sometimes known as Brandon) were already in the Bedfords – in fact, they may even have enlisted on the same day. Her youngest brother, Levi Brandom, a blacksmith's striker at a motor works, enlisted in August 1914 and all were sent to France.

In July 1915, Levi, aged 21, was wounded, but worse news was to come when 24-year-old William was killed at Loos on 24 September 1915. His death was reported in the *North Bucks Times* on Tuesday, 12 October, quoting a letter from Private Frederick Chamberlain to his mother Matilda Chamberlain of 5 Mill Road. He wrote: 'It fills me with regret to tell you that poor Bill Brandom was killed on Thursday. He was shot clean through the heart and so did not suffer. Will you go and break the news gently to Sally.' William Brandom had a sister, Sarah Scutchings, but Sally may have been his sweetheart as the newspaper goes on to say that Private Chamberlain wrote to Corporal Brandom's sisters to tell them the news.

In 1916, Mary Ann's 31-year-old husband Daniel enlisted in the Royal Fusiliers and served in France and Belgium. He returned home after being discharged in September 1918 and a further six children were born. Levi Brandom served at Mons, Loos, Arras, Ypres, the Somme and Cambrai and was wounded four times. He was eventually discharged on 16 April 1919 and married in Fulham the same day.

Ellesmere Terrace families

Near Vandyke Road Cemetery stands Ellesmere Terrace, a group of seven houses now numbered 163 to 175 Vandyke Road. Two families living here were affected by the decision to extend conscription to men aged 41 to 50, which began on 10 April 1918. Arthur Forth of 1 Ellesmere Terrace (now 163 Vandyke Road), a

44-year-old stonemason with four children aged from 7 to 13, had been feeling unwell and was very worried about enlisting when he was conscripted into the RE for home service only on 20 June 1918. After just eight days he was admitted to hospital and on 16 September was discharged from the army, permanently medically unfit to serve.

His neighbour, William Freeman of 2 Ellesmere Terrace (now 165 Vandyke Road), was a 41-year-old market gardener and had been the caretaker at Vandyke Road Cemetery since 1906 when he had been promoted from grave-digger. William appealed unsuccessfully against his conscription and enlisted in the newly formed RAF on 3 June 1918, leaving behind his wife Lilian and two young children. He served until the end of the war and in 1919 returned to his post at the cemetery, which had been filled in his absence by the gravedigger, David Smith.

No. 7 Ellesmere Terrace (now 175 Vandyke Road) was the home at various times of three different men in the armed services. Albert Hall, a railway guard from Brighton had married a local girl, Harriett Butcher, at All Saints Church in June 1912 and served in the Mercantile Marine Reserve, while Harry Bierton served in the Bedfords. Both men were listed at 7 Ellesmere Terrace on the 1918 List of Absent Voters, as was Albert Reeve, a stonemason, who lived there in 1911 with his parents John Samuel Reeve, a monumental mason, his mother, Elizabeth, and four siblings, and who served as a sapper in the East Anglian RE.

David and Mary Ann Smith, 11 [now 27] Regent Street

In 1915, it is possible that David Smith, the Vandyke Road (Leighton-Linslade) Cemetery grave-digger, had the unenviable task of digging the grave for his own son. Twenty-five year old Private 13553 Joseph Smith had enlisted in the Bedfords in September 1914, following in the military footsteps of his father, who had served in the Royal Scots for twelve years, and his grandfather, who had served for twenty-one years in the 43rd Light Infantry.

On 16 June 1915, his parents received a telegram informing them that he had been seriously injured with gunshot wounds to the head, chest and arms, and was now in No. 11 General Hospital in Boulogne. By July, he had undergone surgery and been transferred to the military hospital at Woburn Abbey; he wrote to his parents assuring them that he was getting better and 'there will not be much the matter with me soon'. Sadly, he died on 20 July. On 8 September, his cousin, James Smith of St Andrew's Street (the son of Joseph's mother's brother William and his wife Agnes), died of wounds in France. James's elder brother, Robert, also died less than a month after the end of the war in the military hospital at Aylesbury, and was buried in Vandyke Road Cemetery.

Emma Clare, May Cottage, [now 5] Regent Street

Emma Clare's life had been difficult even before the war started. Born in Chalgrave in 1869, she had a daughter, Mabel, in 1888 and married carpenter Albert Theodore Clare in Hockliffe in 1891. Their eldest son Joseph, named after Albert's father, was born in April the following year, but died aged only 3 months. In the next six years, the couple had a further four children, two daughters, Florence Bertha and Eva Louisa, and two sons, Joseph Theodore and William Thomas, but before William was even 2 years old, his father died aged only 38.

In May 1916, Joseph enlisted in the Royal Fusiliers, transferring later to 10th Battalion the Queen's (Royal West Surrey) Regiment. He was followed into the army in January 1917 by William, a chauffeur, who enlisted in the ASC, as did his employer, Dr Claude Marriott Lovell Cowper. In August 1917, the *Luton News* reported that Joseph was in hospital in France, having been wounded in the left hand on the night of 31 July.

On Monday 17 September, William, 19, who by this time had transferred to 8th Battalion the Yorkshire Regiment (the Green Howards), died of wounds sustained at Passchendaele. On Friday of the same week, 20 September, as part of the same battle Joseph's battalion started an assault on an area known as Tower Hamlets Ridge, leaving their trenches at 5.40 a.m. They had only advanced 50 yards when, according to the battalion's war diary, 'they were met with heavy fire from two machine guns which did great havoc.' Joseph, 21 years old, was reported missing, presumed killed. His body was never found.

Annie Toe, 16 [now 26] Regent Street

Annie Toe was the wife of Frank, a Leighton Buzzard postman and former lamp-lighter, who had previously been in the Kings Royal Rifle Corps, having joined up when he was 17. She was fifteen years younger than her husband, whom she had married while he was still in the army, and they had eight children, six sons and two daughters. Their youngest son, (Walter) Dennis enlisted in the Bedfords on 6 January 1914, signing up for six years' service in the Reserves. He gave his age as '17 years 237 days' but given that his birth was registered between April and June 1897, he must actually have been 16 (and possibly 237 days!). After undertaking training, he was mobilised on 8 August 1914, serving initially in the UK. Over the course of the war all five of his brothers also enlisted, Ernest (21) and William (23) in 1914, followed by Albert Edward (22), usually known as Edward, in April 1915. A few months later, their father died, leaving just 26-year-old George and the couple's two daughters, Annie and Louisa, at home with their mother, as her eldest son, Francis, a hairdresser and confectioner, was married and living in Chingford.

In December 1915, both George and Francis enlisted under the Derby Scheme, George on 2 December and Francis on 4 December, five days before his 28th birthday. George was called up for service in May 1916 but in September it was reported that he had a long-standing heart condition, which meant that he was 'unable to march' and it was recommended that he be discharged as permanently unfit. In fact he continued to serve, in the Royal Defence Corps and ASC, until he was demobilised in September 1919. William also served at home, in the Labour and Tank Corps, and was demobbed in February 1919.

Ernest, a private in the Bedfords and later 1/4th Battalion the Essex Regiment, was sent to France in March 1915, and also served later in Egypt and Greece. Walter was posted to France in July 1916; Francis, who was called up to the RNAS in August 1916, was transferred to the army in November and embarked for France on 26 March 1917.

Edward, a postman in civilian life, also arrived in France in 1917 with 8th Battalion the London Regiment (Post Office Rifles). In April 1918, the *Bucks Herald* reported (in the same paragraph as that recording the death of Ernest

A picture of Vandyke Road taken at the beginning of the war and used as a postcard by Leonard Stenhouse, a soldier billeted in the road, to send to his family in Hull. In the distance, the chapel of rest in the cemetery.

Gaskin) that he had been gassed. Despite this, he was not discharged until March 1919 and in January 1920 was awarded the Silver War Badge.

Dennis was having a successful career in the army. In September 1916, he was transferred to 6th Battalion the Northamptonshires and in October was promoted in the field to sergeant. On 4 February 1917 he was appointed acting colour sergeant major (reverting to sergeant on 24 March). He was Mentioned in Despatches and in April 1917 was awarded the Military Medal for his part in the Miraumont Trench action of 17 and 18 February that year during the Battle of the Ancre. On 19 August of the same year he was wounded at Passchendaele and admitted to hospital at Boulogne six days later, suffering a penetrating gunshot wound to the left side of his head and a superficial wound above the knee of his left leg. He was sent back to England and admitted to King George's Hospital, London on 8 September, where surgery was performed to try to relieve the pressure on his brain, but he died of his wounds on 10 November and was buried in Leighton four days later. His brother, Francis, who had been transferred to the Northamptonshires in March, was granted seven days' special leave the following week.

Although all of Annie's other sons survived the war and married (Francis and William lived into their 90s and Ernest and George reached the ages of 85 and 79), she was to lose another son in her lifetime; Edward, who had been gassed in the war, died in 1931 aged 37.

In the much smaller town of Linslade each street had many men serving, and the sight of a telegram boy cycling into view must have chilled the heart of many a mother; but there were two inter-related families here from which an extraordinary number of menfolk were in the services.

Families with large numbers of men who volunteered in the early months of the war, before conscription was introduced, received a congratulatory letter from King George V thanking them for their patriotism, loyalty and devotion. They were known as Patriotic Families, and the Page family of 52 Springfield Road was one of these. Another was the Woolhead family, who lived at 48 and 50 Old Road. Each had six sons who volunteered.

George Page had married Rebecca Woolhead in 1869 in Wing, where the four eldest of their eleven surviving children, nine sons and two daughters, were born. In about 1879 they moved to Linslade, and lived in Southcott before settling in Springfield Road. George was a stableman at the Southcott stud farm and their children were born between 1871 and 1896.

One of the idiosyncrasies of large families is that sometimes nephews can be older than uncles. In the Page family, Charles, the eldest son married Mary Miller in 1893, and fathered a son, Arthur William, before his two youngest brothers, Lionel and Mark, were born.

Rebecca Page's younger brother Joseph Woolhead married Sarah Ann Hounslow in 1880, also in Wing, and they went on to raise ten children, one daughter and nine sons, born between 1880 and 1899. Joseph and Sarah Ann Woolhead moved to 4 Mentmore Road, Linslade, in about 1893, and then into Nos 48 and 50 Old Road. The move to Linslade may have been prompted by Joseph's new job with a grocer; he was previously a labourer.

The fact that Rebecca Page and Joseph Woolhead were brother and sister made their children cousins, and the link between the families was further strengthened in 1904 when Joseph and Sarah Ann Woolhead's only daughter Beatrice married her cousin Thomas Page, son of George and Rebecca.

Even after the Woolheads moved to Old Road living conditions for both families must have been very crowded, and like many young people in Linslade, the Pages and Woolheads were attracted by the idea of emigrating. In the early years of the twentieth century Canada was keen to increase its population, and advertisements appeared frequently in the *LBO* encouraging people to leave home for a new life. Land was available on the prairies and Canadian government agents also actively recruited young male agricultural workers and young women into domestic service.

The first to go was Joseph Woolhead, Beatrice's brother, who probably left soon after his sister's marriage; he married Anna Maria Rate in Scarborough, Toronto, Ontario in 1907 and must have written home encouraging the others, because in 1908 Beatrice and Thomas Page travelled with their year-old son Ernest Thomas to Toronto on RMS *Empress of Ireland*. They stayed for two years, came back to England but returned in 1912, Thomas first, then three months later Beatrice and Ernest Thomas; this time they made Canada their permanent home.

In 1913 four more of the cousins left for Canada. In March John Woolhead with his wife and three children departed, followed in May by Albert Page with his wife and their three sons, and finally in July Joseph Page with his wife and daughter and his brother John Page. They settled close to each other, in Agincourt and Scarborough, small townships which are now suburbs of Toronto.

Another route out of a crowded family home was to join the Royal Navy. Walter Woolhead joined in February 1908; his brother Albert Woolhead and George and Rebecca's grandson Arthur William Page joined together on 19 January 1910. All three of them later signed on for twelve years on their 18th birthdays. Albert Woolhead and Arthur William Page were almost the same age, although of different generations.

At the outbreak of war four of the Page brothers, Thomas, Albert, Joseph and John and two of the Woolheads, John and Joseph, were in Canada. Walter and Albert Woolhead and Arthur William Page were in the RN.

The first of the Page-Woolhead cousins to become a full-time soldier was Edward Woolhead, aged 18, who worked for a house decorator. He may have already been in the Territorial Force, following his brother Joseph's example; Edward's service in the Bedfords dates from August 1914. Joseph Woolhead,

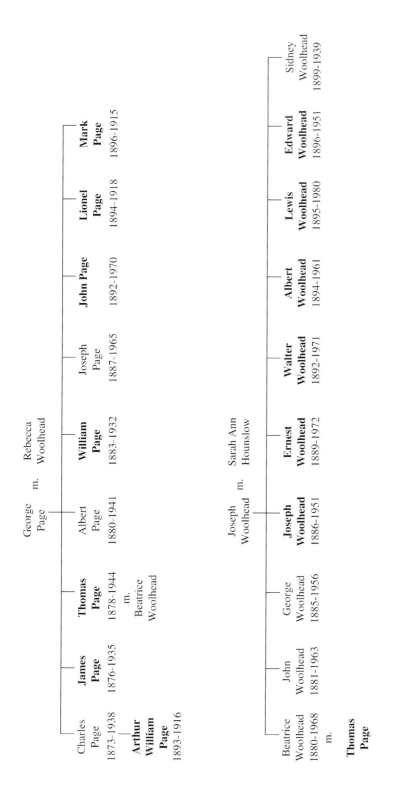

George   m.   Rebecca
Page   Woolhead

Charles | James | Thomas | Albert | William | Joseph | John Page | Lionel | Mark
Page | Page | Page | Page | Page | Page | 1892-1970 | Page | Page
1873-1938 | 1876-1935 | 1878-1944 | 1880-1941 | 1883-1932 | 1887-1965 | | 1894-1918 | 1896-1915
| | m. | | | | | |
Arthur | | Beatrice | | | | | |
William | | Woolhead | | | | | |
Page | | | | | | | |
1893-1916

Joseph   m.   Sarah Ann
Woolhead   Hounslow

Beatrice | John | George | **Joseph** | **Ernest** | **Walter** | **Albert** | **Lewis** | **Edward** | Sidney
Woolhead | Woolhead | Woolhead | **Woolhead** | **Woolhead** | **Woolhead** | **Woolhead** | **Woolhead** | **Woolhead** | Woolhead
1880-1968 | 1881-1963 | 1885-1956 | 1886-1951 | 1889-1972 | 1892-1971 | 1894-1961 | 1895-1980 | 1896-1951 | 1899-1939
m.
Thomas
Page

The extraordinary Linslade families of Page and Woolhead produced eighteen sons between them, most of whom volunteered to fight in the war. The two families inter-married and both sets of parents must have been in constant apprehension, fearing for the fate of their many offspring. The names of family members who served in the war are in bold type.

who enlisted later in Canada, had been a member of the 3rd (Reserve) Battalion the Bedfords for three years before leaving England, and was awarded a prize at the battalion annual dinner in 1904. Their brother, 19-year-old farrier Lewis Woolhead and his 20-year-old cousin Lionel Page, a draper's porter, soon followed, enlisting in the Oxfordshire and Buckinghamshire Light Infantry (O&BLI) in September 1914.

Next to enlist were two more of the Page brothers: Mark joined 4th Battalion the Seaforth Highlanders on 12 January 1915 and his older brother William followed on 1 March. Mark had needed to wait for his 18th birthday, but William was 31, a house painter and married since 1909 to Violet May Goodman. Mark had been a grocer's porter for several years, having almost certainly left school at 13 or 14. Leighton Buzzard did have an evening school for those who wished to continue their education, but there is no evidence that any of the cousins enrolled.

Many units of the Territorial Force were on summer training camp at the beginning of August 1914 and were immediately mobilised for home defence. Some battalions then travelled hundreds of miles to their pre-arranged war stations. Other men who were not 'Terriers' rushed to volunteer, perhaps through patriotism, or carried away by the excitement; there was an assumption that they should do so.

It seems odd that Mark and William Page should join the Seaforths, but the 4th, 5th and 6th Battalions, part of the Highland Division, were billeted in Bedford, their pre-arranged war station, between August 1914 and May 1915. Between 16 and 20,000 men came to Bedford immediately after mobilisation, bringing with them, amongst other things, twelve pipe bands. Bedford must have seemed very strange to the Highlanders, some of whom only spoke Gaelic, and the Highlanders must have seemed very exotic to their Bedfordshire hosts.

The families living in Canada kept up to date with news from their home town. In November 1914, the *Luton Times and Advertiser* reported that Mrs Gravely Willis, the wife of a Leighton Buzzard solicitor, who was assisting Belgian refugees, had received a letter, with a donation of eleven Canadian dollars and fifty cents from 'five Linslade boys' living in Ontario, who 'wished for the opportunity of helping in so noble a cause'. Their names were Tom, Albert, Joe and John Page and John Woolhead.

Men who had emigrated in recent years faced a dilemma: should they enlist in their new country or return to Britain? John Page, having lived in Canada for nearly two years returned to England in April 1915, and went with his older brother James to enlist in the O&BLI on 27 May. John was 22 years old and single but James was a 38-year-old house painter living with his wife and son at No. 21 Old Road. Their cousin Ernest Woolhead joined the ASC in June 1915; he had been a gardener, probably working for John Jeffery Martin at Linslade Nurseries, which was on land between Wing Road and the canal.

By the time John and James Page volunteered at the end of May 1915, their youngest brother Mark had been killed in action. Mark was in France for less than three months; he had been wounded on 13 April 1915, but returned to his regiment two weeks later and was reported missing, later presumed dead, on 9 May during the Battle of Aubers, an unsuccessful attempt to take Aubers Ridge, west of Lille. The Seaforths suffered particularly heavy casualties; none of them could advance beyond their own trench parapet because of the heavy enemy fire. Mark Page was 18 years old.

The *LBO* of 15 June 1915 published extracts from a letter written by Mark to a friend, giving his view of an infantryman's life and an insight into a remarkable character. He said he was thankful that his wound had healed, and that he was in good health. After explaining that he was on four days' rest after sixteen days in the trenches he said, 'The idea people in England have of us is one of constant trial and struggles, but believe me, I love being out here. It is not nearly so bad as people imagine.' He continued that he was getting enough to eat, although he acknowledged that some men were complaining. 'They would get on a lot better if they had made up their minds from the first to be satisfied with everything. That's what I did and I have no cause to complain yet.' Before proudly finishing with the news that they had been inspected by General Sir John French, he described playing hymns on his tin whistle for his comrades. Many of the Page-Woolhead cousins were members of the Methodist Church.

The last two of the cousins to volunteer did so in Canada: Joseph Woolhead joined the Canadian Expeditionary Force on 19 November 1915 and Thomas Page, Beatrice's husband, on 31 December. So at the start of 1916 Beatrice Page must have been worrying about her husband, six of her Woolhead brothers and four of her husband's Page brothers. Her brother-in-law and cousin Mark Page had already been killed, and 1916 brought the second loss to the Page family.

At the start of the year Lionel Page received a gunshot wound in the knee, but recovered. At the end of May, Walter Woolhead's ship HMS *Duke of Edinburgh* was involved in the Battle of Jutland. Walter served on this vessel, a cruiser, throughout the war. In the early months she was in the Middle East, and took part in an attack on Ottoman forces on Ras Sheikh Sayed, a promontory between the Red Sea and the Gulf of Aden, bombarding enemy positions from the sea and landing troops. Walter gave the impression in a letter published in the *LBO* on 15 December 1914 that he had crewed one of the boats used to land troops, and had come under fire. Later in the war HMS *Duke of Edinburgh* patrolled the area between Shetland and Norway, then performed escort duties in the North Atlantic. Walter's brother Albert Woolhead, a sailor since 1910, had first been posted to HMS *Dido*, a depot ship based at Harwich. HMS *Lightfoot*, a newly built flotilla leader which led the 1st Destroyer Flotilla, was also based there and he served on her before being transferred for the last few months of the war to HMS *Waterhen*.

Their nephew Able Seaman Arthur William Page was not so fortunate, and became the second of the Page family to die, having transferred from surface ships to submarines. His vessel, HMS *E 26*, built in Scotland, had originally been ordered by the Ottoman Navy in 1914. The E-class submarines were 180ft long, had a dive depth of 100ft and a speed of 15.25 knots, and were the backbone of the British submarine fleet throughout the war. Life on an E-class was very uncomfortable; the three officers had only one bunk between them and the twenty-seven ratings on board slept where they could.

E26 was lost on patrol off Terschelling, one of the Walden islands off the Dutch coast. On 2 July 1916, a German patrol boat reported seeing a trail of oil on the water, and attacked a submarine the next day. When *E26* did not return from patrol it was assumed that she had been sunk. There were no survivors, nor were any bodies recovered. Arthur was 22.

Also in July 1916, William Page, who had joined the Seaforths like his youngest brother Mark, was discharged from the army as unfit due to sickness, without having left England. He was awarded a Silver War Badge.

During 1917 two of the Pages received promotions and one of the Woolheads was seriously injured. John Page, serving with the CEF, was promoted to sergeant in September 1917 and his younger brother Lionel became an officer in October. Lionel Page had already been transferred from the O&BLI to the Royal Worcesters and promoted to lance corporal. He was commissioned as a second lieutenant in 1st Battalion the Worcesters on 30 October 1917, aged 23.

Lewis Woolhead, though seriously injured, survived the war. At Christmas 1917 he suffered a compound fracture of his left ankle while playing football for his battalion. Football tournaments were a common way to keep soldiers occupied during time away from the front line. After months in hospital he was left with a permanent limp and discharged from the army as unfit for military service on 10 September 1918. His disability might have made it difficult for him to return to work as a farrier, or perhaps there was less opportunity as the economy of Linslade moved away from horses. In later life he worked as a telephone switchboard operator.

By the beginning of 1918, ten of the twelve cousins who had volunteered were still on active service, five of them for more than three years. Second Lieutenant Lionel Page became the third member of the Page family to die, on 27 May 1918. That May, 1st Battalion the Worcesters was in the wrong place at the wrong time. At the beginning of the month they had been moved south from the Passchendaele Sector, near Amiens, to a quieter part of the Front, north-west of Rheims, but on 27 May they found themselves in the middle of the German attack at the start of the Battle of the Aisne. The Germans made significant advances and the battalion was almost wiped out. Lionel Page, who was 22 when he died, has no known grave.

When the Armistice was signed on 11 November 1918, eight of the serving Page and Woolhead cousins were still alive. The soldiers were demobilised during 1919, but Albert and Walter Woolhead had each signed on for twelve years in the navy. Albert's time had begun on his 18th birthday in 1912. His service record shows that he deserted in Greenwich in October 1919 but soon surrendered to the Metropolitan Police, and was discharged in January 1920 after serving twenty-seven days' imprisonment with hard labour. Walter completed his twelve years and resumed civilian life in April 1922. John Page, who had married Ida Emily Lewis in Cambridgeshire in 1917, and Thomas Page, who had left his wife Beattie in Ontario were repatriated to Canada, but John and Ida returned to Linslade some time later. James and William Page stayed in the Linslade area and both died in the 1930s.

Of the six Woolhead brothers, who all, remarkably, survived, Joseph Woolhead returned to Canada, and Ernest joined him there. Albert moved to Rugby, but Walter, Lewis and Edward stayed near Linslade.

George and Rebecca Page are buried in the churchyard at St Mary's, Old Linslade, as are their eldest son Charles and his wife, Mary. The names of Lionel Page, Mark Page and Arthur William Page appear on their parents' headstones, Lionel and Mark on George and Rebecca's and Arthur William on Charles and Mary's. All three are honoured on the Linslade and St Barnabas' Church First World War memorials.

CHAPTER 12

WOMEN ON THE FRONT LINE

As the war raged across Europe, the vast number of casualties meant a massive expansion of hospitals and a need for a large number of new nurses to tend the wounded. Many men with severe wounds died before they could reach hospitals, for these were sited out of harm's way. Seeing a need for forward treatment centres, many women made themselves available to help, sometimes with official approval but frequently without. Many of these independent women must have been involved in the women's suffrage movement, which at the start of the war suspended its campaign and turned members' energies to the war effort. All those who went to the Front were volunteers. Some were trained nurses; others acted as ambulance drivers, cooks and first-aiders. They worked in teams, setting up treatment centres close to the front line in order to give the injured a better chance of survival. Their extraordinary bravery led to many being decorated for showing great courage under fire. More than 2,000 volunteered in 1914, some refusing to be paid for their services, and many a wounded soldier would have died on the battlefield without them.

Alongside the regular trained nurses at the Front were two main bodies of volunteers, the Voluntary Aid Detachments (VADs) and the First Aid Nursing Yeomanry (FANYs).

The VADs were jointly run by the Red Cross and the Order of St John of Jerusalem, two organisations responsible for running hospitals, both in war zones and at home. Members were not trained nurses, but their role was to help medical authorities to care for the wounded. They had to be able to ride, using horse ambulances to take the wounded to hospital, and were trained to move, feed and tend the sick, including preparing splints and bandaging wounds. The preparation of sheds as temporary hospitals was another of their duties, as was cooking.

The FANY had been formed after the Boer Wars because so many soldiers had died in those campaigns from lack of first aid. However, the War Department bizarrely refused to recognise FANY nurses at the outbreak of hostilities. As a result the Belgians and French welcomed these volunteers who began working in their hospitals. Not until 1916 did the British War Office accept that the nursing yeomanry had a place, and women began to replace Red Cross men as ambulance drivers.

Leighton and Linslade provided a number of women who joined these groups and became volunteers behind the Front. All but one, who died of an illness, appear to have survived the conflict, despite being frequently under fire and in one case torpedoed. Some of the wounded men must have fallen in love with these 'angels of mercy' as they were regarded at the time, and at least one case is known in which the feelings were reciprocated. One nurse resigned her post when the war ended and travelled to Rhodesia to find her man and marry him.

Leighton opened its own hospitals for the war-wounded. The first was in the Corn Exchange and mostly treated soldiers who were injured in training locally or who became ill. Many of them were living in unheated buildings. The hospital closed after a few months when a military hospital opened in Aylesbury.

Perhaps the most remarkable story is that of two sisters, Edith Kate and Hilda May Dickinson, whose mother Adeline Fanny lived in Heath Cottage, Heath Road. They first served together in Belgium, and wrote letters home which make light of the horrors of the Front. Later Edith went on to take part in one of the most extraordinary feats of the war, an 800-mile trek across the mountains with

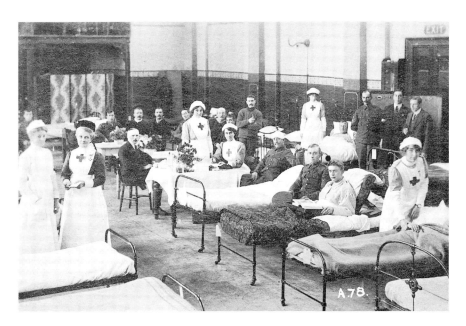

A postcard from 1914 of one of two hospital wards, totalling fifty beds, set up in the assembly rooms of the Corn Exchange in Lake Street for soldiers who had sustained injuries or become ill during in training. They were nursed by local members of the Red Cross, all volunteers.

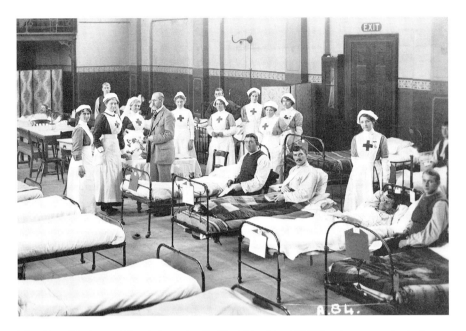

The Corn Exchange Hospital, run by Bedfordshire No. 18 VAD volunteers who had been called up at the outbreak of war. Some 200 soldiers were treated as outpatients as a result of injuries sustained during the vaccination programme.

the retreating Serbian Army during which she was close to starvation; she was awarded the Order of St Sava (5th Class). Hilda was decorated for her conspicuous bravery in Belgium.

A letter survives from one of the sisters dated 27 September 1914, less than two months after the start of the war, when they were with the British Field Hospital Corps in Belgium:

It is a great pity they had more nurses sent out here as now there is far too big a staff for the number of wounded. It was terrible to see the damage done (in Malines). The cathedral is riddled with cannon balls and every pane of glass in the glorious old windows is broken. Houses close to it are in ruins. We helped in the kitchen part of the hospital there, as there was very little fighting going on in the immediate neighbourhood and therefore few wounded were coming in. None of the wounded are kept there; they are just patched up and sent here as quickly as possible. From Malines we went out in an ambulance wagon to neighbouring villages close to the German lines. The Belgian cannon roared for hours but the replies were weak, owing, I understand, to the shortage of ammunition. At one village we visited (I had better mention no name) we could see some Germans only about 500 yards away moving about in a wood. The Belgians tried to fire the wood, but it was too damp to burn, so after several attempts they had to give it up. We watched the enemy from a railway bridge but had to be wary of stray bullets. The village where we stood had been in the hands of the enemy the day before, and they had totally destroyed it. Several of the houses were still burning. Most of the inhabitants had fled in time but there were sad tales told us of a handful who had not.

At a convent in this same village the whole place was sacked and fired, only the walls remaining, except the scullery which was intact. Here we found several small pieces of china and a quantity of copper cooking utensils which we transported to the Red Cross hospital at Malines which, by the way, is a seminary for priests in ordinary times, the hospital having been partly destroyed and rendered useless. It was most interesting to see the teams of dogs drawing the guns. They seem perfectly happy at their work and are well treated, as far I have seen. They are of the greatest use to the Belgians. They make a much smaller target than the horse, as they lie down the instant they stop and can be so easily screened from view. I hope to send you a snapshot of them taken by one of our ambulance men.

Yesterday we visited another village, or rather the outskirts, as the village was well within the German firing lines. There was a lovely old house, which had been sacked but not burnt. The graves of eight men, including two officers, were just within its gates, they had tried to defend the place. There were two cannon balls right through the walls, one *mitrailleuse* shell stuck in the wall beside the front door unexploded. I don't quite know what they will do with it as a tap would explode it. I expect it will have to be fired at from a distance. A case of wine glasses at the top of the house and a grand piano were the only things undamaged.

Four German Zeppelins have flown over during the last two days. I wonder they risk sending them when they are such good targets. Aeroplanes are far safer. Our hospital is some distance away from the cathedral and royal palace. We are not in much danger here.

A second letter is headed 29 September 1914, Antwerp:

We are getting very busy again, forty cases in yesterday and more expected at any moment. You will have seen by the papers that poor Malines is in flames. Some of our party had lucky escapes, but they moved every patient from the Malines Hospital during Sunday night, and got them through without a mishap, though both of the ambulance horses were killed. The patients were first taken to W----- Hospital but no sooner were they there than it was shelled, so they brought them on here.

I think almost the saddest thing we see is the constant stream of wretched, weary fugitives, each carrying a bundle. You will be pleased to hear that our hospital and one other had been selected for the most serious cases because they say we treat our men better than they are treated in any other hospital, and they are clamouring to come to *Les Anglais*.

Both the sisters were in Antwerp during the bombardment but, while in England for a few days before going back to the Front, one of them gave the following graphic account of their experience to the *LBO*:

We had just gone off to sleep when we heard a loud report followed by the scream of a shell. I cannot describe the effect of this sound, followed in due course by a terrific explosion. I lay and listened to three shells, each bursting nearer than the last and then I leapt up, and partly dressed ran across the courtyard to the hospital. For a minute or two I could not stop my teeth chattering. Almost as soon as I got over, the head doctor issued the order that all patients were to be carried to the ground floor and the cellars. That restored my equilibrium and the second I started to do anything I was quite happy again. I was quite thankful when, on talking the matter over with others, I found nearly everyone had experienced the same feeling.

Within an hour every one of the 113 patients had been carefully carried or helped down from the upper landings. The shots came at the rate of four per minute for several hours, a great many striking very near at hand. Few tried to sleep that night. We all sat up near the patients on the lower floors. For a time a few of us went out into the courtyard and watched the flash of the guns and the burning of some houses that had been struck.

When day broke the firing became less frequent. Then about 11.00 a.m. the firing became more concentrated. Our hospital appeared to be the centre. A shell struck the roof of a house almost opposite absolutely wrecking the front ground floor. The pavement had a big hole dug in it where I believe the shell struck from what I saw, shattering the bow window on its upward explosive journey and tearing out a beam from across the ceiling. No fewer than ten other houses were struck within twenty yards of the hospital but mercifully we all escaped unharmed. The patients were removed from the hospital in motor omnibuses and reached safety after an exciting journey. Just as they were about to start four more buses arrived with instructions to fill them right up and clear out, our hospital staff and all of us.

It was a very trying time packing everything we could that could be easily carried, both medical and household, and clothing. However, we had all ready and started the last bus off just after 3.00 p.m. It was certainly a curious coincidence that two shells came quicker and closer from the minute the first bus made its

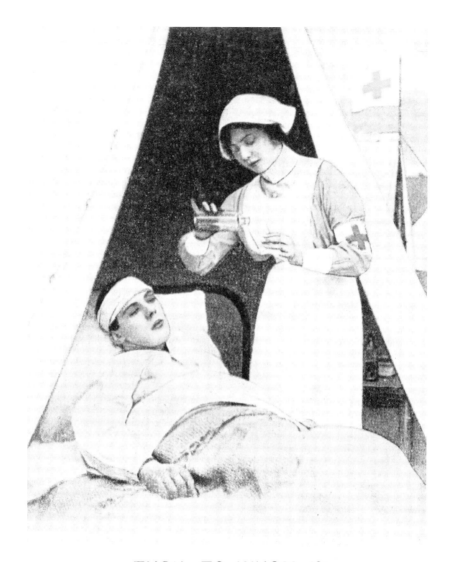

THOU, TO WHOM (2).
Still the weary, sick and dying,
Need a brother's, sister's care,
On Thy higher help relying
May we now their burden share,
Bringing all our offering meet,
Suppliants at Thy mercy-seat,

BAMFORTH (COPYRIGHT).

One of a series of postcards issued during the war giving a rather romantic image of the Angels of Mercy. It was an attempt to persuade more women to volunteer to help in France, at the field hospitals at the Front which were being overwhelmed with wounded.

appearance in front of the hospital, and just as we were about to start a shell exploded in our courtyard, luckily doing practically no damage. Then began a very exciting drive. Shells were bursting and houses burning on all sides. We drove through the town having to turn aside every few minutes on account of great holes made in the roadway by the bursting shells.

The two sisters afterwards separated. Edith Dickinson went with a friend, Annie Gertrude Holland, to Serbia and was attached as a chauffeur orderly to the first Serbian-English Field Hospital, near the Front in Belgrade. This was in the capable hands of Mabel St Clair Stobart. They had limited equipment, which comprised Ford motor ambulances, ox-wagons, horses, carts and a captured Austrian field kitchen.

On her return in January 1916, the *LBO* published Edith's account of her experiences, including an 800-mile journey to escape:

> The fall of Belgrade marked the opening of what proved to be several days of terrible hardships. Their hospital was inundated with maimed and wounded Serbians, and from these they learned that the fighting had been of the most terrible kind. The Serbian army was gallant enough, but the equipment was totally outclassed by that of the enemy, and they were soon overwhelmed. Fighting at close quarters in the streets of the capital was a commonplace, soldiers and civilians fought side by side, and the hand-to-hand nature of the struggles was proved by the fact that many of the wounds were gashes caused by sabres.
>
> When the retreat began, the wounded in the hospital were left in the charge of the Serbian doctors and Austrian orderlies. The party consisted of some fifty British doctors, nurses and orderlies, and as they were leaving an air raid by a fleet of German aeroplanes was actually taking place. The party entrained for Salonika, but hopes of covering much of the journey by rail were soon dashed to the ground, it being found that the rails had been torn up by the Bulgarians. The railway was accordingly abandoned and after proceeding some distance further by motorcar this also had to be left and the journey continued on foot. Wagons drawn by oxen and containing stores also had to be abandoned until the party had nothing beyond what they carried and what clothing they stood up in. The Austro-German army was then only a few miles away, and their big guns were in action.

Abandoning their original route over the mountains to the Adriatic because of Albanian hostility, they were forced to use a dangerous track:

> In some places the road was little more than a narrow ledge on the mountain side, and on more than one occasion vehicles were precipitated over the edge

and fell a distance of many feet, throwing out or either killing or injuring those who happened to be inside.

One of those who died was a nurse.

The food supply was very limited and rations had to be served out in gradually diminishing quantities. The prisoners who accompanied the party received food as far as possible. On many occasions these prisoners, who were Bulgarians and Austrians, had nothing to eat and many died of sheer starvation. Miss Dickinson saw officers of high rank in the Austrian army pick up cabbage stalks that had been dropped by the others, and bite at them ravenously. In the matter of food, the hospital party itself was better off than the bulk of the refugees, although the only bread they had was black bread and maize bread. The party had fortunately retained some of the hospital stores, of which Bovril and condensed milk came in very handy, and when a nurse discovered a tin of margarine and divided it, everyone who was fortunate enough to share it said it was delicious.

The cold grew intense as the party climbed high up into the mountains. In many places they had to wade through streams owing to the bridges being broken, and there was no chance of drying their clothes, which froze on the wearers and became as stiff as boards.

Some of the female nurses were wearing light summer dresses with totally unsuitable footwear. Edith was fortunate – she had breeches and top boots.

The lot of those not provided with anything like the proper clothing can be better imagined when it is stated that the track was frequently knee-deep in mud and slush in some places, and in others hard and slippery with a temperature of nearly forty degrees of frost.

Two of the mountains which the party had to ascend were 8,400 and 7,600 feet high respectively, and it was feared that the task of getting up the rugged paths would prove too formidable. Upon descending on the Adriatic side the atmosphere became warmer, however, and relieved their suffering somewhat. The hospital party sailed across the lake of Scutari, and a further tramp of two days enabled them to reach San Giovanni di Medua. From here they crossed to Brindisi in a small Italian vessel, which had arrived with food for the Serbian army.

At San Giovanni, however, they were told that the Austrian army was on the move, and unless they embarked on this ship they might have to remain. It was decided to risk the journey, and 300 people were packed into a small vessel, which had to combat heavy seas, as a result of which many of the voyagers were ill. The party of refugees presented a sorry spectacle when they arrived at Brindisi and there was some difficulty in getting sufficiently into the authorities' good books to be allowed to land. In fact, says Miss Dickinson: 'We looked simply wretched. Most of us were ragged, muddy and dirty, not having been in a bath for weeks. On top of this we were distressingly thin and our feet were showing through our boots.' The party entrained at Brindisi for Paris and thence to Le Havre and England.

The paper commented that since Miss Dickinson 'possesses a good constitution' she should recover after her 'terrible hardship' but that the 'horrors that accompanied the retreat are indelibly engraved upon her memory'.

At the time of this interview, Edith's sister Hilda was reported to be 'engaged in Belgian relief work in London.' However, by 1918 she had returned to the Front, having joined FANY and was part of the newly formed combined FANY/VAD unit based near the Front, the St Omer Convoy.

On 4 May 1918 this unit became part of the Second Army. This is an account of what happened to her next: 'The German spring counter-offensive in 1918 had the St Omer Convoy working day and night under heavy bombardment; on May 18 they came under fire during bombing raids on Arques.'

Beryl Hutchinson was second-in-command of the unit and describes their coolness under fire:

> At the veterinary hospital next to the station, they had just loaded up the victims of the first wave of bombs trying for the railway line when another raid came over. The men had their orders to shelter but the FANYs could not leave prostrate men unable to move so they put the ambulances in the deep shadow of one of the buildings and stayed with the men, chatting and smoking until the bombing was over. There was an army ambulance with its driving cab, complete with driver, blown right off and four stretcher cases left inside. They pulled up closely beside the wreck so the stretchers could be transferred. Noting that the spare wheel was still intact, they gave it shelter and ever after had two spare wheels for long runs.

For their coolness and courage under fire these women who stayed at their posts while the men sheltered were awarded a total of sixteen Military Medals and three Croix de Guerre. Beryl said that all decorations were questioned, as there were too many for one small unit; however, each one was so strongly supported by the British and French officers on the scene that all were allowed. The medals were presented to the FANYs and VADs in the field by General Sir Herbert Plummer, General Officer Commanding the 2nd Army.

News of Hilda's Military Medal was published in the *North Bucks Times* on 25 June. It reported that she had been awarded it for driving an ambulance at the

THOU, TO WHOM (3).
May each child of Thine be willing,
Willing both in hand and heart,
All the law of love fulfilling,
Ever comfort to impart;
Ever bringing offerings meet,
Suppliants to Thy mercy-seat.

BAMFORTH (COPYRIGHT).

An idealistic view of a nurse tending a soldier whose wounds look none too serious.
The postcards came complete with a poem, and are a long way from the harsh
reality of the terrible wounds the nurses at the Front dealt with.

Front and rescuing wounded under fire. The government's official notification in the *London Gazette Supplement* 30 July 1918 says:

> His Majesty the King has been pleased to approve the award of the Military Medal to the undermentioned ladies for distinguished services in the field. For conspicuous devotion to duty during a hostile air raid. All these lady drivers were out with their cars during the raid, picking up and in every way assisting the wounded and injured. They showed great bravery and coolness, and were an example to all ranks.

Another woman who narrowly escaped death was Edith Halford, who was born in Leighton Buzzard and joined the Red Cross as a nurse on 19 May 1915 when she was 26. Her parents were Edwin, a grocer, and Mary Ann; they lived at No. 22 Market Square. Her first posting was to the 1st Eastern General Hospital, Cambridge and while there she volunteered along with fifty-six other nurses for Foreign Service. HMHS *Transylvania*, bound for Salonika, left Marseilles for Alexandria on 3 May 1917 accompanied by two Japanese destroyers *Matsu* and *Sakaki*. The following day the ship was struck in the port engine room by a torpedo fired by the German U-boat U-63 under the command of Otto Schultze. The *Matsu* came alongside to take on troops before she sank, but twenty minutes later a torpedo was seen heading straight for the *Matsu* which managed to avoid it by going astern at full speed. Sadly the torpedo hit the *Transylvania* and she sank immediately with the loss of ten crew, twenty-nine army officers and 373 soldiers. Edith and the other nurses had managed to reach a lifeboat and spent about four hours on the open sea before being picked up by a tug. Undaunted, she continued her journey to Salonika, a formidable place to work. Many nurses suffered from malaria and dysentery and were invalided out; some asked to be transferred, but not Edith. She intended to stay, and on 3 September 1918 was Mentioned in Despatches, although details of what she did to achieve this distinction are not known.

It is possible that she knew another local woman, Florence Elizabeth Sayell, who was also posted as a nurse to Salonika. She was born in Horton in 1889 but moved to Springfield Road, Linslade with her family while still a child and attended Linslade Board School. Florence became a dressmaker like her mother Elizabeth, and her father Walter was a house decorator, but on 29 January 1912 she left for London and began her nurse's training at the Camberwell Infirmary. By 29 January 1915 she was a staff nurse and decided to join the Queen Alexandra's Imperial Military Nursing Service (QAIMNS). This was a bold decision because there were millions of soldiers, Regulars and Reservists, serving in Europe, India, East Africa, Palestine, Egypt, Mesopotamia, Salonika and Russia, about 10,000 in

France alone. None of these was a pleasant place to be in 1915 because of war, disease and hostile climate.

On 14 September 1916 Florence embarked on Royal Mail Steamer (RMS) *Carisbrooke Castle*, ultimately bound for Salonika, where she nursed at No. 29 Stationary Hospital. Her report from the matron said she had excellent nursing skills, was an especially good surgical sister and good at administration and ward management, 'most tactful and good at maintaining discipline'. She went on to work at No. 62 General Hospital, moving with it to Taranto in November 1917; once again the matron gave her a very good report. In August 1918 she extended her contract for another six months, but in the November resigned from the QAIMNS, citing family reasons. After the war she continued nursing at the Ministry of Pensions Hospital, Newcastle upon Tyne and at the Royal Sea Bathing Hospital, Margate. In 1923 she wrote and requested that her name be removed from the Roll of Reserves of the QAIMNS. In her reply, the matron wrote thanking Florence for her services and to convey best wishes for her happiness and success, perhaps already knowing what was behind the request because on 24 June 1924 Florence resigned, because of her forthcoming marriage.

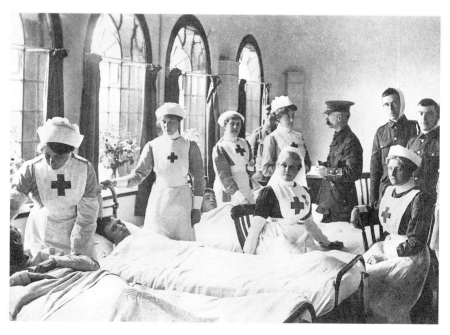

In August 1915 a new fifty-bed Red Cross Hospital was set up in the board room of the workhouse in Grovebury Road to treat patients injured at the Artillery Training School in Page's Park; other wounded soldiers were also admitted.

Lillie Louise Eames in her nursing uniform in 1914, when she arrived at the Leicester Royal Infirmary, where she worked in the operating theatre.

Work in any hospital must have been harrowing for nurses during the war. Apart from the physical injuries from bullets and shells there were the appalling effects of gas on lungs and eyes. Many men also suffered terrible but little understood mental and physical problems, generally classed as 'shell shock', which must have made them very difficult to care for.

Many nurses who had originally worked in France were recalled to England because their skills were better employed restoring to health the badly injured men who had been evacuated from the field hospitals nearer the Front.

One of those who stayed in England, at least at the start of the war, was Lillie Louisa Eames, a very experienced nurse. She was born in 1888, the daughter of William and Lucy Eames of Cheddington, and from 1908 was working at the City of London Hospital for Diseases of the Chest, Victoria Park. She transferred to the General Infirmary in Leicester on 11 January 1914, where from July she was the operating theatre sister.

By November 1915 she had been accepted for overseas service in the QAIMNS but was assigned to the Connaught Hospital, Aldershot, where she worked for two and a half years; the matron wrote in her report that her nursing skills were excellent and her management of the wards good. While she was there she nursed soldiers from the 2nd Rhodesia Regiment who had been fighting the Germans in East Africa but were sent to England to help in France. Many had contracted malaria, and by the time they reached Aldershot were so ill that they were immediately admitted to hospital.

Among them was Harry Marshall, whom Lillie nursed back to health. He and his colleagues were so weakened that they were sent back to Africa rather than to France. But Lillie herself left for France on 24 March 1918, posted to No. 4 General Hospital, Arques. These field hospitals moved closer to the Front as the Allies advanced, acting as reception centres and preparing the wounded for evacuation to England for further treatment. She was there for two months, receiving another excellent report from the matron before being moved to No. 10 Stationary Hospital in St Omer where, unfortunately, appendicitis meant a return to England. She was admitted to the Millbank Hospital, London on 26 June and her operation took place eight days later. In September Lillie travelled to the Huddersfield War Hospital for a medical check-up, at which she was declared unfit for duty and granted one month's extension to her sick leave.

Once able to resume her nursing duties she was sent to the Prisoner of War Hospital Camp, Oswestry, where injured enemy soldiers were treated. In her report the matron, Jessie Macqueen, said: 'Sister L.L. Eames has served under me since 1 November 1918. She was in charge of 200 beds and her duties were performed in an efficient manner. At present she is House Sister and her duties are carried out with ability and tact; she is a capable manager and interested in her work.'

Undeterred by being unable to get a job on a troopship, Lillie Eames paid for her own passage and set off from Southampton on RMS *Carisbrooke Castle*, bound for Cape Town. She travelled to Southern Rhodesia to marry Harry Marshall, the man she had nursed back to health in the Connaught Hospital after he contracted malaria.

All this time Lillie and her former patient Harry kept up a correspondence which became a romance, and on 3 January 1919 the matron wrote to the War Office on Lillie's behalf, forwarding her resignation and asking for her to be released on 28 February as she was proceeding to Rhodesia to get married. She pointed out that Lillie had been unable to make any arrangements for her travel, as the shipping agents required a copy of the War Office sanction that her resignation had been accepted. She also asked if it would possible, should any transport conveying repatriated troops to South Africa be available, for her to obtain an appointment and allow her contract to terminate in South Africa. Unfortunately the reply came back that there was no transport and Lillie should contact the office of the High Commission for South Africa at 34 Victoria Street in London. Lillie, apparently undeterred by this obstruction, left Oswestry and began her journey to Rhodesia on 28 March to find the soldier she was going to marry. Remarkably she left on the same ship that had once carried Florence Sayell to Salonika.

Another local nurse, Alice Dunleavy, was the daughter of Robert Anthony Dunleavy, station master at Leighton Buzzard, and his wife Annie; in 1911 the family were living at Ecila, Rosebery Avenue, and Alice was a schoolteacher. She

Alice Dunleavy lived in Linslade and served as a volunteer nurse in the Corn Exchange Hospital and two other military hospitals, but resigned in September 1916 when women were being recruited for work at Morgan's. She is working in their office in 1918. (Bryan Dunleavy.)

joined the Red Cross in November 1914 and served at various establishments: Aylesbury Auxiliary Military Hospital (at the Bifurcated and Tubular Rivet Co. factory) from November 1914 till 1 May 1915, and from that September at Leighton Buzzard Red Cross Temporary Hospital in the Corn Exchange in Lake Street. From here she went to the County of Middlesex Hospital, Hanworth Park, Feltham, but for some reason not recorded, left the Red Cross to work at Morgan's until they closed. After the war she stayed at home to look after her parents, living to the grand age of 95.

Nursing seems to have been a way for determined young women to break out from domestic duties and travel to exotic places. Annie Jane Weighall of Earls Gate, Stoke Road joined the VAD at Wing on 12 October 1913, and by the end of 1914 was sister-in-charge at the Officers' Military Hospital, Murree, Punjab, in what is now Pakistan. However, on 1 February 1915 she was ordered home, and because of her experience was made a sister at the Indian Military Hospital, Royal Pavilion, Brighton.

Later in 1915 she was transferred to the Royal Herbert Hospital, Woolwich; the following year she was promoted to sister-in-charge at the University VAD Section Hospital, Oxford, then appointed lecturer in first aid and home nursing by the Red Cross Society for the County of Buckinghamshire, giving lectures at Linslade, Stewkley, Wing and Aston Abbotts. By 1918 she was speaking at the Dobson War Relief Hospital, Blackheath, a Church Army recreation hut, the Prisoners of War Depot, the Royal Arsenal Barracks, Woolwich and at the Soldiers' and Munition Workers' Canteen at the Royal Arsenal.

People from all walks of life signed up to become nurses. Perhaps the most prominent locally was Marie, the wife of Leopold de Rothschild of Ascott House, Wing. As befitted her station, she was both commandant of the Wing VAD, involved with establishing, collecting equipment and arranging staffing at Aylesbury Military Hospital, and president of the County of Middlesex Red Cross Hospital, Hanworth Park, Feltham from January 1914 until February 1919. She was twice Mentioned in Despatches, and on 1 January 1920 was awarded the CBE for her work in Middlesex and for committee work for the Officers' Families Fund during the war.

Less is known about the careers of other nurses. Among them is Mrs Dorothy Ann Brown of Froxfield, 17 Billington Road who signed up for the Red Cross in October 1914 and served until February 1918. She performed commandant duties and worked at the Southwood VAD Hospital, Bickley and was awarded the MBE for her services.

Not all those who signed up for the Red Cross became nurses. Some were cooks or secretaries, and some performed cleaning or other duties. One of those with an unusual job was Mary Sophia Newman, of Perth House, Soulbury Road,

Ascott House, Wing, the home of Marie, wife of Leopold de Rothschild, who volunteered with the VAD in 1914 and served throughout the war. Her second son Evelyn, an officer in the Royal Bucks Hussars, was killed in Palestine in 1917.

She joined the Red Cross in January 1914, and until January 1919 is recorded as having worked for the War Library, Surrey House, at Marble Arch. This was part of an effort to provide free books and magazines for men at the Front. For example, the Admiralty requested that every sailor around the British Isles should have a free book. Among the things she was recorded as contributing for the troops were 320 Rudyard Kipling scrapbooks, although exactly what these were is not known.

Nor were they all women. Some men, too old or considered unfit for military service also volunteered. One of them was 38-year-old Frederick Hooper of 20 South Street, who was sent to the Red Cross Motor Ambulance Department at the Red Cross Hospital in Boulogne.

Some of those born in Leighton Buzzard but who had moved away were also volunteering. One of those was Tindall Harris, whose father Theodore was a banker at Bassetts in the High Street, now Barclays. Barred from military service because he was too old, he signed up for the Red Cross and was awarded the 1914 ribbon, becoming a voluntary ambulance driver at Étaples and St Omer and carrying over 5,000 wounded. While serving he wrote a book in which he said: 'In October 1914, I joined a Red Cross convoy for France as a voluntary driver. I was 52, lucky in that respect to be safe from the trenches.'

Another former resident was Mary Gertrude Tindall, whose father John had also been with Bassetts Bank. She was born in Leighton on 9 May 1880, and joined the Red Cross in 1910 as one of its first members. Suffering from a war-related illness, in August 1917 she returned to the family home in Sidmouth from No. 2 VAD Hospital, Exeter, where she was a Red Cross nurse, and on 20 September she died, aged 37. The *Sidmouth Observer* reported on her funeral: 'Despite the highest medical skill and best devoted attention Mary gradually became worse.' Her coffin was draped with the Union Flag and on it was a floral shield sent by the officers and staff of the Exeter hospital. Her name is on the Sidmouth War Memorial.

CHAPTER 13

THE CANARY GIRLS GET A RAW DEAL

In 1915 a large new workforce of women was recruited to work in munitions factories, mainly to prepare shells for the Front. Many Leighton and Linslade girls were employed in factories in Luton, and so important was their contribution that a special temporary halt was built on the Leighton Buzzard to Luton railway line at Chaul End so that these 'munitionettes' could alight directly at the gates of the National Fuse Filling factory, owned by George Kent Ltd.

Factories like this were converted from engineering works to meet what became known as the Shell Crisis of 1915, during which the government passed the Munitions of War Act to increase government oversight and regulation of the industry. David Lloyd George was made Minister for Munitions and his ministry regulated wages, hours and employment conditions at munitions factories. It forced the factories to admit more women as employees and by June 1917, 80 per cent of the weaponry used by the British Army during the war was being made by women. They were paid on average less than half the wages of men doing the same job. Factories treated them badly, particularly so, considering that the work was extremely dangerous and unpleasant. While they were officially known by the government as munitionettes, these women became dubbed the 'canary girls' because their skin turned bright yellow from constant exposure to liquid trinitrotoluene (TNT). It had been invented as a dye and was impossible to wash off, instantly identifying someone who worked in a munitions factory.

As a result of the munitions crisis a meeting was held on Wednesday 28 July 1915 at Shire Hall, Bedford, of engineering firms from Bedfordshire, Buckinghamshire, Cambridgeshire, Hertfordshire and Huntingdonshire. Samuel Whitbread, a brewer and the MP for Bedford, had called the meeting in response to a letter that had been received from the Ministry of Munitions. The location was chosen because Bedford and Luton were the two largest centres of engineering works, and Bedford had good railway links. A committee was elected and the twenty-two representatives made the decision to call themselves the South East Midlands Munitions Area.

Kent's was an established engineering firm, making meters in Biscot Road, Luton; they converted the site to making munitions shortly after war was declared. Their other site at Chaul End, where most of the Leighton girls were employed, became a filling works for fuses, detonators and gaines (tubes in the nose cone of a shell, filled with TNT to make sure the fuse successfully detonated the shell). The two factories produced many parts for aeroplanes including pistons and steering gear, but principally a dozen different types of fuse. A maximum output of 130,000 fuses a week was reached, and at its peak a workforce of 8,000, mostly women, were employed solely on the production and filling of fuses with explosives.

The actual filling was a simple process but very dangerous. One of the problems was TNT poisoning, which led to toxic jaundice as well as staining the skin. The women worked long hours, and some had to stand for the whole of their shift. They wore inadequate protective clothing and the required safety measures were not in place. There were also rules and regulations to be adhered to: they had to wear wooden clogs to avoid sparks, were not allowed hairpins or jewellery and no matches were permitted on their person.

The rows and rows of girls filling fuses with TNT in the George Kent factory at Chaul End, watched over by mainly male foremen, at the height of the shell crisis. Never previously published. (Bedfordshire Archives.)

Most of the Leighton and Linslade girls, men and boys who worked at Chaul End, filling fuses at Kent's. Although they wore overalls and were banned from carrying or wearing anything that might cause a spark, they were not offered facemasks or protective clothing.

These rules were strictly enforced because the risk of explosion was very real, and two Leighton boys who worked at the factory were brought before the magistrates in Luton for flouting them. Seventeen-year-old Joseph Alfred Charles Parrott of 51 Plantation Road, who had been found to have matches on him, was charged with contravening the Explosives Act. In court the works manager showed him a notice which had been posted at the entrance gate and elsewhere in the works, warning that matches or any other item likely to cause an explosion must be left with the gatekeeper and not taken into the works. He also produced a copy of the printed rules, showing that the penalty for infringement of this regulation was a fine of up to 40 shillings. The lad pleaded guilty to the charge. He said he had been at the works for just over six months and gave all his weekly earnings of £1 5s to his mother as there were five children in the family. The magistrate's clerk commented that he was too young to smoke, and he said he did not believe that all the lad's earnings went home. He was fined twenty shillings with a week for payment, with an alternative of fourteen days' imprisonment.

Another worker of the same age, John Norman of Lammas Close, was fined the same amount for taking a box of matches, tinder lighter and cigarette case within the boundaries. Bags were provided for such things, but Norman had the bag in his pocket along with the prohibited articles. These young men were lucky they were only fined. In the north of England a young woman found with matches in her possession was imprisoned for the same offence.

Although many of the women travelled by train to the factory, others cycled, presumably to save money because the wages were so low. This was a hazardous business, and there were reports of people being injured in accidents on the way home from the factory, and of four workers being fined for cycling without lights. Harry Marks and William Odell of Leighton Buzzard, and Alfred Downs of Linslade were each fined twelve shillings and Winnie Green of Leighton Buzzard five shillings. Presumably the fines reflected the fact that the men got paid more than twice as much as women.

The working hours were long and penalties for being late severe. These were some of the working conditions:

Hours of work: 8.00 a.m. to 7.00 p.m.; Saturdays, 8.00 a.m. to 12.45 p.m.

Time keeping: Employees will only be allowed to start at 8.00 a.m. or 8.30 a.m. The gates will be open from 7.45 until 8.00 a.m. and from 8.25 to 8.30 a.m. Any employee who fails to clock in by 5 minutes after 8.00 or 8.30 a.m. respectively will forfeit 15 minutes pay. Any employee who consistently starts at 8.30 a.m. will be liable to dismissal.

Breaks: 11.00 to 11.15 a.m., during which milk and biscuits will be served in the Mess Room free of charge; 12.45 to 1.45 p.m. for dinner; 4.40 to 5.00 p.m., during which tea will be served in the Mess Room free of charge.

Dinner: Any employee who wishes may have her dinner in the Mess Room, but she must either bring her dinner with her or make arrangements with the Mess Room attendant, who will in any case do any cooking that may be necessary.

Overtime: will be paid at the rate of time-and-a-quarter for all hours exceeding 52 per week.

Except at dinner time, no employee will be allowed to leave the works during working hours, without a pass from the head of her department.

Anyone found trespassing in a department to which she does not belong will be liable to instant dismissal.

An overall and cap will be provided for each girl. It is essential that the cap should be worn and in order to avoid accidents the hair should be completely covered thereby.

Even with the prevailing feeling that people had to do their patriotic duty it became apparent that the tough working conditions and low pay at Kent's were not acceptable to the female workforce, the highest rate being about 18s 10d for a 54-hour week, and an organised protest was held. This may also be an indication of the increasing confidence felt by the women of the period.

The Dunstable Dasher pulling into Leighton Station. The train the Canary Girls caught to reach Chaul End, where a special station was built for them to alight and walk straight into Kent's factory.

On Friday, 26 May 1916 at Chaul End, 427 out of the 467 women workers did not return after the midday meal. The firm's answer was to lock them out. The women remained in the works yard, noisily making their protest.

They went back to work on the following Tuesday but matters escalated and seventeen of them were singled out to appear before a government tribunal in Westminster, accused of being absent from work in contravention of government regulations on war work. The *Luton News* of 8 June 1916 reported:

Seventeen girls have appeared at a Tribunal at Westminster where they were charged with leaving their work at a firm under government control without leave on Friday May 26th and Monday May 29th.

Edward Bolton, the manager of the department in which the girls were employed, appeared for the company, but to little effect. He stated that the company employed 467 girls, who were engaged entirely in manufacturing items for the government. He complained that on Friday 26 May, 427 girls had stayed in the works yard after the midday meal, singing, booing and demonstrating. On the following Monday only 86 had come in to work; the rest had stayed outside the works entrance.

After questioning, Bolton admitted that on the Friday the girls were effectively sent home until Monday morning when they had not returned to work after ten minutes' grace. He also admitted that a number of the girls had wished to see him on Monday morning, but denied that they were turned out by policemen. A union representative had tried to get to the works early on Monday morning to meet the girls before they went in, but his train was late and he did not arrive in time to do anything before the gates were shut. He thought if he had more time he would have been able to get the girls back to work. Bolton had told him that the girls were suspended for two days and notices were put up to this effect. A meeting was held between the girls and the labour representatives and they returned to work at 7.30 a.m. on Tuesday 30 May.

After some prevarication Bolton admitted that he had heard from a foreman that the girls intended to come out on strike unless they received a halfpenny an hour pay rise. The union representative complained of lack of tact and breach of faith by Bolton, and suggested that the strike was the result of a genuine misunderstanding by the girls, who had only wanted to discuss their grievance, whereas instead of doing so he had sent the girls home. When asked the amount earned by the girls Bolton gave unusually high figures which were the exception rather than the norm. The chairman of the tribunal agreed that the girls had a grievance, and felt their wages were not very high for the work they were doing. The employer had acted arbitrarily in shutting the girls out on Saturday, and with a little tact most of the girls would have returned to work on Monday morning. He therefore did not regard the failure to go back to work on Monday as an offence. The refusal to work on Friday did clearly constitute an offence against the regulations. However, in view of the blame which should attach to their employer, their low wages, the cost of their fares, and their loss of income over the two days, he proposed to fine them only one shilling each. In any future dispute he urged them to rely on a union leader to settle the matter in a proper way. The tribunal judge, while recognising that the women's strike was illegal, strongly criticised the management, especially Bolton, and only fined the girls one shilling instead of a possible £5 a day which he was capable of imposing.

The paper later reported:

> As a result of the strike at Luton, a conference has been held in London to consider their rate of pay, attended by the Beds Engineering Employers' Association, three of the girls, and Mr Harry White of the Workers' Union. An increase of a penny an hour had been under consideration, but the firm concerned has now received the agreement of the Ministry of Munitions to a new wage scale under which the bonus system has been withdrawn and the following flat rates of pay introduced: 3¼d to 4d per hour for girls under 16; 3½d to 5¼d per hour for those ages between 16 and 17; 4d to 5¼d per hour for those between 17 and 18, and 4½d to 6d for those aged over 18. However there was still dissatisfaction and the original application for a penny per hour increase was submitted to the Employers' Association.

It was argued that these girls were still being paid less than at other works in the town, that many came from a distance and had to pay for expensive lodgings or for rail fares. The firm was still not prepared to make any concessions, and refused to consider paying a bonus in addition to the current rates. 'The Workers' Union now intends to send the application to the Central Conference due to be held at York in September.'

The outcome of the dispute is not recorded, but the danger of the work resulted in both individual injuries and deaths. One example which made the news was the injury to Violet Gladys Golding of Cross Street, Dunstable, who was only 16. A detonator exploded as she was taking it from the press and the tops of her thumb and a finger from her left hand had to be amputated. She became the youngest recipient of the newly established Medal of the Order of the British Empire, awarded to her for her bravery in returning to work in the same department. Kent's were so impressed by her courage that they gave her £50, and when King George V visited the factory on 13 November 1917, he spoke to Violet congratulating her upon her pluck and inquired if her hand was better.

There were other accidents and explosions, and a total of ten workers were killed. Among them was 17-year-old Nora Tomkins of Lanes End, Heath and Reach, one of four women working in the detonator room during an explosion on 1 March 1918 who all died of burns shortly after. The rest of the factory was protected from this room by thick concrete blast walls because it was so dangerous.

On 9 March Nora was buried in her village. A hundred of her workmates, dressed in their munition workers' uniforms, led the coffin from her home in

Seven of the Canary Girls from Leighton, with a couple of shells. Most of the girls look very young to undertake such dangerous work with toxic chemicals.

The works also had poetry competitions, presumably intended to raise morale. This poem, *Verses on the War*, by Edith Page from Shop B, won a prize on 7 December 1917.

```
Buck up the 80 Fuze girls,

And work with all your might,

No matter what your job is,

Just strive to do the right.


Think of the lads in khaki,

And our brave boys in blue,

Just show them what we're made of,

To win this battle through.


No matter what the bonus is,

Just work with might and main,

And our brave lads will thank us,

When they come home again.
```

Lane's End to the parish church, and lined up on each side of the entrance as the cortège passed through. There is no record of her precise burial place, but Nora's name appears on the Heath and Reach war memorial, the only woman to be so remembered on any in the Leighton area. Thomas William Janes, a young Leighton man, had also died as the result of an explosion at the factory. The explosion was on 21 February 1917, and his death on 1 March, a year to the day before that of Nora.

In addition to the long hours and hazardous conditions, the work was boring. To relieve it one worker placed a note in a fuse, rather like placing a message in a bottle. The *North Bucks Times* of 10 October 1916 reported:

Miss M. Underwood, of 19, Friday Street, Leighton Buzzard, is a munitions worker, and one day put her name and address inside the top of a fuse. She has now received a letter from the sergeant who fired the shell at the Huns, telling how proud the army is of the work the girls at home are doing.

Dear Miss Underwood, Please excuse the liberty I am taking in writing to you, but finding your address inside a fuse, thought I would let you know that it arrived out here. I cannot say where it is now, as it was fired into the Hun lines a few hours ago. The battery has been out here since the war first began, so we have been through the mill a little bit, and nothing gives us greater pleasure than to send souvenirs over to Fritz with the compliments of our munition workers at home, and I can assure you that we are not giving them much rest at present. All of us out here are very proud of the way our girls at home are keeping us going, but we can still do with millions more rounds of ammunition. At present we are paying back what we owe them from the days of Mons, Marne, and Aisne, and I think we are doing it fairly well. I mustn't forget to thank you for the good wishes; next time I fire I will send a few compliments over to Fritz for you. I must finish now, wishing you the best of luck and hoping you will make thousands of more rounds, and remain, yours truly, G. Randall (Sergt.), RFA, BEF.

Despite the long hours of tedious work the young women obviously felt they were doing their duty to support their men at the Front. For many it was also the first paid work they had ever had.

By the end of the war the women workers at the Chaul End factory had filled 11 million fuses, 30 million detonators and 6 million gaines with explosives. but in the same way as at other factories working at full pelt to fulfil government contracts, the peace brought an end to new orders and thus to the jobs of the canary girls.

CHAPTER 14

BANDAGES, PNEUMONIA JACKETS AND REFUGEES

Since so many local men were at the Front, and news regularly arrived of fierce battles and many wounded, the people of the district answered the call from the Red Cross to provide essential hospital equipment such as bandages, splints, swabs and clothing. Although war hospital supply depots were established in every major town, it appeared that the Leighton area was particularly active, and produced a remarkable number of items. The Leighton Buzzard Detachment of the Red

3963. 8. High Street, Market Day, Leighton Buzzard.

The High Street on Tuesday market day, just before the war. Halfway along on the right is Leighton House, an imposing building once lived in by Baron Ferdinand de Rothschild while he was building Waddesden Manor. It was demolished after the Second World War and is now a shop.

Cross Society placed an advertisement in the *LBO* on 18 August 1914, two weeks after the start of the war, seeking 'ladies to volunteer who were willing to assist in making garments for sick, wounded and convalescent sailors and sailors.' They were asked to apply to Mrs Mary Swire at Leighton House, High Street, who would supply materials ready cut out for the purpose.

Just outside the town at Grove, a Red Cross working party was formed. By 15 August 1915 they had sent to the Buckinghamshire branch: twenty-one day shirts, six flannel nightshirts, four pairs of pyjamas, thirty-one handkerchiefs, twenty pairs of socks, two scarves, one helmet, two pairs of mittens, twelve bed jackets, nine pillows and nine pillow slips.

The Leighton Buzzard and District branch of the war hospital supply depots, however, was on an altogether different scale. It opened in March 1916 with seventy workers at the first meeting, and by the end of the first month they had sent out 647 items to hospitals, including pneumonia jackets, and had 100 regular volunteer workers. They were looking for volunteers to make bed rests, bed tables and crutches for wounded soldiers, which were said to be particularly needed by the French.

To raise money, local people donated goods for auction for what had become known as the Leighton War Hospital Supply Depot. A pen of seven bantams was put up for sale, and the first successful bidder donated them again. In all they were sold thirty-two times. A clutch of eggs was sold the same way raising more than £5 for the depot. Businesses contributed too; the Victoria Picture Palace donated one day's takings to the Grove Depot.

To raise funds for materials a garden party was held in September 1916 at Harcourt, Stoke Road, Linslade, 'by kind permission of Sir Edward Oswald Every'. By 6.00 p.m. more than 1,000 people had paid for admission, and the lucky 500th entrant, Trooper Frank Conquest of Soulbury, won a watch. The *LBO* said:

> There was an extensive programme of events; a particular popular feature was a sketching exhibition by artist Captain Bruce Bairnsfather, famous for his humorous cartoons of trench life. Three sketches were donated to be auctioned or raffled in aid of the Supply Depot fund. Other attractions included performances by Lieutenant Brent Smith, a well-known pianist, an Australian soprano Miss Thelma Peterson, a demonstration of bird whistling by a Belgian army officer, and war stories from Mr W.V. Robinson, a Canadian entertainer. In the evening there was entertainment from the Dunstable Dazzlers, and the band of the Royal Engineers played during the afternoon. During the evening, an auction gift sale raised around £45 from eighty-six lots, with seventy shillings paid for one fat sheep. Other items for the sale included an umbrella stand, a violin, grapes, tennis balls, a fox skin muff and some guinea pigs.

Linslade Red Cross Working Party was also active; Mrs Johnstone Harris gave an account of the funds raised and the items made during 1916. A total of 632 garments had been sent off, 145 from January to June, 487 from July to December, and many letters of appreciation had been received from the Front. They had also collected £18 for men from Linslade who were prisoners of war, who had been sent food and clothing parcels.

By October 1916 Leighton's war hospital supply depot had 130 workers producing items for English and Allied hospitals. This letter from Hôpital Chaptal, Paris, was typical of many received by the depot:

Very many thanks in the name of my numerous sons for your ever-welcome present. Today I distributed the slippers, shirts and vests, and you would have been amused and happy to see them; it was quite like a fair; and to hear their remarks of English generosity. I assure you, those who are working so generously for the French 'Tommies' would understand how much good they are doing for them. Poor fellows, they are so brave in suffering, and it takes very little to bring a smile even to those who are blind. If you would continue, when you have time, to send some more slippers, and please, some smaller sizes among them as my boys have little feet. Shirts, vests and socks are always welcome; also some toothbrushes, and if you have some more counterpanes ready, as the other wards are a wee bit jealous; so amusing to hear them.

The Military Hospital, Belfast, wrote:

The consignment of supplies which is periodically received from your depot is above criticism, as regards both quality and workmanship. We and the patients are delighted. It saves the nurses an immense amount of work to have surgical dressings so skilfully and carefully prepared.

No. 11 Casualty Clearing Station of the BEF in France, where many consignments had been sent, wrote:

Many thanks for the hospital requisites received, which deserve nothing but praise. You are doing a noble work in a noble way. I trust you will continue to do so as long as this awful war lasts. Without your splendid help I fear that our patients would have been obliged to forego some of those comforts which count for so much under the trying conditions of this campaign. May Providence help you to continue to carry on this self-imposed task.

The Leighton Deport reported that in September and October 1916 alone, 2,239 items had been supplied to hospitals, including ninety-two pairs of mittens in response to a rush order from Mesopotamia.

One of the key organisers was Mrs Mary Bourne Cowper, wife of one of the town's doctors. She reported on the depot's first year, operating at Hoddesdon Villa, Lake Street, lent free by Mrs Ada Louise Procter of Lake House. The UDC had excused all rates and the expense of heating the depot was limited to one small gas bill, as the coal merchants of Leighton Buzzard kept them entirely in coal for the winter months. Money had been raised through entertainments, and furniture was donated by Leighton traders.

The depot had made and sent to hospitals 1,900 garments and 10,800 surgical dressings and bandages. In addition they had received ninety-four articles from the League of Honour Working Party, sixty from Moreton House School, Dunstable, forty-eight from William David Cook's carpentry workers, 342 from the boys of Beaudesert School and 200 sundry presents, making a grand total of over 13,500

Hoddesdon Villas in 2017, virtually unchanged since the First World War when they were turned into a factory to provide bandages, clothing and wooden items such as crutches for the comfort and help of the wounded soldiers in hospital at the Front.

articles. The cost of the wood needed at Beaudesert, for items like crutches for the wounded, had been met by Bedfordshire Education Committee.

Each room in Hoddesdon Villa was used by a different team, each organised by a 'head of room', most of whom were the wives of local businessmen.

Ada Louisa Procter of Lake House, 24 Lake Street and Alice Letitia Bassett of the Hatch, Heath, ran the garment room; Abigail Letitia Till of the Union Workhouse (with Miss E. Brown), bandages; Annie Henrietta Grimmett of 20 Grove Road and Mrs Gilbert, surgical dressings and swabs; Miss Clara Fossey of The Heath Lodge and Sarah Catherine Thornley, slippers; Annie Charlotte Phillips of Hillesden, 27 Lake Street and Mary Jane Aveline of Fair Field, 23a Grove Road, teas; Miss Maud Mary Pease, knitting and packing. Sixty workers had won the War Office Voluntary Workers' Badge. Henry Edward Grimmett had audited the books. The amount of material cut up during the year was 9,176 yards or 5½ miles. That quantity of material would stretch from Leighton to Stanbridge by way of Eggington and back again, Mrs Cowper claimed.

The Leighton depot continued to get larger and went on to produce even greater quantities of materials for the Front; in May 1917 the *LBO* reported: 'Since the depot opened the work has carried on continuously by a patriotic band of workers who have given of their service ungrudgingly in the cause of the wounded.'

By then they had sent to hospitals in France 20,625 garments, dressings and bandages. But the depot was running out of funds. Money was short mostly because of the increased price of their main raw materials, wool and cottons. However, the need for work at the depot was even greater because of the numbers of wounded and a Depot Day had been organised to raise funds. The *LBO* reported:

This was a great success; the programme included two concerts and a dance at the Corn Exchange. A quite extraordinary number of subscriptions had been collected, and concert tickets sold in advance, and the crowded audiences listened to the two performances. The concert programme was of the usual type, and it remained to Lady Ivy Linton Every and her helpers to provide the most startling innovation – a sale of fashionable and model hats. It included a marvellous collection of what, for want of another word, are 'creations' which had been presented by local and other well-wishers. Mrs Howe, The Knolls, and Mrs Richardson, of Wayside, had charge of the sale, and as many of the hats were returned after being bought at higher figures to be raffled for, eventually the hat sale proved a very profitable innovation. There was also a well-patronised flower stall in the vestibule, arranged by Mrs Annie Garside, and a refreshment stall arranged by Mrs Phillips who, with a band of Depot workers, also provided the teas.

The contributors to the concert programme were Mr W. V. Robinson, a Canadian entertainer who is popular in the London Halls, and somehow managed to get real music out of a mouthorgan; Mrs Leaf, the well-known pianist, who played two solo's [sic]; Capt. H.H. Cobb, who specialises in coster impersonations; and a party of pierrots known as the Follies, including Mrs P.C.E. Lovett, Mr E. Robinson, Mr A.Q. Roberts, Mr Aldwick, Mr L.W. Yeoman and Sergt. [sic] Green. Mr Robinson's services at the evening service were given free. Alfred Sutro's duologue, *A Marriage Has Been Arranged*, was played in a very appropriate setting by Capt. J.O. Murphy and Miss Mollie Ronan, whose dramatic abilities are already known to local audiences.

The stage had been beautifully decorated by Mrs Clarke. A military orchestra from Bletchley provided, by permission of Col. Lister, an excellent programme of dances after the evening concert. Also at the end of the evening bouquets were presented to ladies who took part in the entertainment by Mr Bassett, Mr Lovett, Sir Edward Oswald Every and Mr Richardson, and to Lady Every, who organised the whole affair, by the Depot.

It is recorded that, during the three-and-a-half years of its existence, 300 people worked at the depot.

Although the work of these supply depots provided a means for many people in the two towns to support the war effort voluntarily, there were many other ways to help people who had suffered because of the conflict.

There was an urgent need to find accommodation for some families from the large influx of Belgian refugees to Britain. Widespread sympathy was felt for the Belgians, whose country had been neutral at the start of the war but had been invaded and pillaged by the German army. The remnants of the Belgian army fought with the Allies, and many of the civilians fled. Leighton and Linslade provided a safe haven for some of them.

By October 1914, 16,000 Belgians refugees had arrived in Britain and the government was already appealing for temporary homes for them. Soon the numbers had swelled to 25,000. The government asked that whole families should be kept together, and special arrangements made for the protection of women and young girls.

Leighton Buzzard responded to this, and Mrs Gertrude Emma Gravely Willis of Hockliffe Street, a member of a well-known family of solicitors in the town, set up a small group who began looking for accommodation and suitable furniture. Local businesses and people offered their help and donations soon started coming in.

The *LBO* reported:

Dr. Lewis Worts placed at the disposal of Mrs Gravely Willis his house The Hollies in North Street, rent free. The lady's appeal for furniture has been met with a sympathetic response – so much so that all requirements have been met except perhaps a few more minor accessories. The necessary sum for the maintenance of the exiles has not yet been guaranteed, but a number of offers has already been received, and it is hoped that more will be forthcoming. It should be noted that the whole of the money will be spent locally.

With the preparations in place:

... a Belgian family was selected and the intention is to offer them, quiet, unobtrusive hospitality, with as little publicity as possible – in fact to treat them as well-bred Belgians would treat an English family under similar circumstances. Their arrival had been kept low key; they came direct from London accompanied by Mr and Mrs Gravely Willis. The Belgian national flag was flying from the portico of The Hollies and there were many other little surprises to make their homecoming as agreeable as possible.

The family are a distinguished Belgian professor and his wife and a family of nine children, ranging in age eight to twenty. Professor Joseph J.E. Gillet is a well-known Belgian scholar, a Doctor of Science of the University of Liège, Professor at the Athenée Royale, Brussels and at L'École Normale de L'État à

Holly Lodge (left), a large and very old house in North Street made available for a large family of Belgian refugees for the duration of the war. It was demolished to make way for West Street in the 1970s.

Nivelles; he has still wider claims to national repute as a specialist in mathematics and entomology.

The paper then carried a long interview with the professor about his trials while fleeing from the German army, and being bombed by Zeppelins in Ostend, an experience which led him to escape with his large family to England.

Mrs Gravely Willis was not the only person setting up houses for the Belgians. The following week the number of refugees had risen to twenty-six. The Wesleyan Methodists had found a house in Beaudesert, No. 29, which was offered rent free for as long as required by Joseph Richard Labrum, a local coal merchant, who had also provided free coal. Karel de Hulsters and his family from Ostend made this their home. Arrangements were made for collectors to call upon members of the church and congregation for donations or weekly subscriptions from a penny a week upwards or loans of furniture, household utensils and fittings for the house. Soon a family of twelve, including grandparents and grandchildren, was scheduled to arrive, so another house at the corner of Clarence Road and Heath Road was found where all could be accommodated.

The paper listed all the names of the new Belgian residents, where they were living and the names of the local residents who had donated houses. Again the Belgians, who were clearly very grateful for the generosity of local people told the paper of their experiences while escaping from the German invasion.

Linslade was also taking in Belgian refugees. A house in Rothschild Road had been given by Gordon and Mabel Thomas of the Martins and a second was found in Old Road. The members of the Ladies' Sewing Meeting at the Hockliffe Street Baptist Church took on responsibility for making this suitable for housing another six refugees. 'If possible, the refugees will all be one family of the humbler classes.'

Linslade Nursing Association brought another Belgian family to the town and housed them in Wing Road Terrace, collecting furniture and other donations locally including from Morgan's.

It was not only the local community which wanted to help the Belgian refugees. Letters appeared in the *LBO* from other parts of the country, and one from Canada, offering their support. This last was from members of the Page and Woolhead families of Linslade (see also Chapter 11). In 1914 they wrote:

> Agincourt, Ontario, 24 October 1914.
> I was pleased to learn that in Leighton Buzzard something is being done for the relief of the Belgian refugees. We are five Linslade boys and I am enclosing an order for 11 dollars and 50 cents from Thomas Page, Albert Page, Joe Page, John Page, John Woolhead and the Rev. J Anthony. Our minister is willing, if you are favourable, to arrange a concert or lecture to assist your funds from which a good

sum could be raised, and if you would send me a letter authorising me to collect funds on your behalf I would do my best. Wishing you every success.

Yours truly T. Page (formerly of Rose Cottage, Springfield, Linslade.)

The Belgian community, many of whom had lost all their possessions in escaping their country, clearly found a welcome in the town. In 1915, Linslade Infants' School admitted a Belgian girl. To show their gratitude the refugees joined in with all manner of fundraising events in the town for the war effort. When a concert was given for the soldiers in February 1915, the Belgians contributed nearly every item on the programme. There were 'songs by Mlle Paula de Hulsters, M. Jules Deruelle and M. Gasseo, duets by Mme Vanacker and Mme Sys, cello solos by M. Nicholas Wedemeyer; the National Anthem of the Allies (the *Hymne des Alliés* by Albert Grossaint) by a chorus of Belgians'.

Another Belgian who was to delight audiences in the town was Charles Piron, who arrived after fleeing his homeland in 1916. He had narrowly escaped execution, for the day after he fled to the Netherlands seven of his friends were shot as spies. He appealed to the town through the *LBO* for a waterproof for a friend who was fighting in the trenches. The waterproof was duly donated and he wrote in thanks to the paper:

> We Belgians, particularly those from Wallonie, knew nothing of, or rather did not understand, Great Britain. Since the early days of my stay in England I have had reason to appreciate, at its true worth, the generosity of the British people, and especially of British ladies – a generosity which is characterised by the sincerity, the discretion, and the great delicacy with which it is dispensed.

There was also sadness among the families who had become part of life in the town. In February 1916 Madame Celine de Hulsters died of pleurisy at her home in Beaudesert. Her large family and other refugees attended the funeral along 'with many friends from Leighton', and she was buried in the cemetery in Vandyke Road.

Although the Belgian refugees received a warm welcome from the British government at the beginning of the war, the official attitude changed at the Armistice. The authorities wanted returning British soldiers to be welcomed and homes made available for them to live in. The refugees had to leave. Many Belgians who had found work to help the Allied war effort had their employment contracts terminated, and the government offered free one-way tickets back to Belgium. This was offered for a limited time to encourage a swift response. To many it seemed their new friends were being pushed out of the country, but the policy appeared to suit the Belgian government, which needed its citizens back to help rebuild their own country.

CHAPTER 15

ALL HUMAN LIFE IS HERE

Within weeks of war being declared, Leightonians fell back upon trusted strategies to meet new challenges – to solve almost any problem, form a committee. The *LBO* of 25 September 1914 informed readers that: 'A committee representing all the interests in the town has been appointed to deal with distress in Leighton Buzzard.' When the government appealed for the people to invest in war bonds, a scheme to prevent the country going bankrupt, a local war loan committee was immediately formed.

Leighton and Linslade in wartime, as in peace, were by no means home to a population who were all of exemplary character and intent on pulling together. There were a few less savoury aspects of life in the town, as there had been before and as there would be after.

Most of the hundreds of cases at military service tribunals were men seeking exemption legitimately and for good reason. A few, however, involved people who seemed to the authorities to be trying to avoid conscription through simple cowardice. These were unceremoniously handed over to the military at the end of the hearings.

Meanwhile, magistrates at the Leighton Buzzard Petty Sessions were busy with incidences of fighting, irregular school attendance, using obscene language on the highway, thefts of fowls and cigarettes, driving vehicles without lights and dangerous stone-throwing. There were also cases of profiteering on foodstuffs. In April 1917 John Stevens, aged 50 and a market gardener of Heath, was one of several dealers summoned for the offence of selling potatoes at a price 'exceeding the rate set down by the food controller'. He was fined £1 for two offences of supplying local grocers. The shopkeepers were willing to pay the extra because otherwise they would have had no potatoes to sell.

While some local traders were being fined for illegally watering down milk, the government was officially watering down the beer, because intoxication was thought to be reducing productivity. New government restrictions on public house opening hours also kept the magistrates busy.

Pubs were a major part of social life and the two towns had forty licensed premises between them at the start of the war. However, income was badly hit by the campaign by the government to reduce drinking. Lloyd George even succeeded in April 1915 in persuading the King to pledge that no alcohol would be consumed at royal palaces until the end of the war.

The pubs had previously been open all day from 5.00 a.m. until a half hour after midnight, but the government cut this from noon to 2.30 p.m. and 6.30 p.m. to 9.30 p.m. Taxes were increased, and beer consumption dropped steadily during the war, along with convictions for drunkenness.

These new restrictions were not popular, and led to several cases of police keeping watch on pubs and arresting people seen leaving outside normal hours with milk jugs and other containers full of beer.

The 71-year-old landlady of the Crown Inn at 72 North Street, Mrs Margaret Gotzheim, was one of those prosecuted. She appeared at the Leighton Police Court following a raid on the Crown and an adjacent cottage, charged with selling intoxicating liquors during prohibited hours, and for selling a child beer which was not in a sealed container. Her case was heard, together with those of two men and

A group of soldiers outside the Traveller's Rest in Heath Road, taken from a postcard sent by one of the soldiers saying that all leave had been cancelled; no clue to their unit offered. Dated November 1914, so it is likely that they were billeted in the town before being sent to France.

a woman who were charged with being on licensed premises during prohibited hours and with sending a child for beer. Two of these co-defendants were Henry James Dover and his wife Amelia, a daughter of Mrs Gotzheim, who lived next door to the Crown at 2 Bedford Street.

Evidence was given by the police to the effect that jugs full of beer were being taken from the back door of the Crown into the Dovers' house next door, where they were being consumed or passed on to others. The situation was complicated by the reluctance of family members to give evidence that might support the police case. One of Mrs Gotzheim's forty grandchildren, Henry Charles Samuel, admitted seeing his aunt, Mrs Dover, drink a half-pint, but said he had never seen any beer sold before opening hours on a Sunday. Another co-defendant, Mr George Short, was found in the Crown Inn, but said he was delivering papers, as he had done regularly for several years; he denied having been served with anything although police said there were drops of beer hanging on his moustache. No beer was found by the police in the Dovers' house and the magistrates dismissed the case for lack of evidence.

Food and its distribution caused increasing problems and there was a number of cases of people breaking into houses simply to steal food. There were also strict regulations about what could be fed to animals. A long test case was heard against George van den Poele, of Castle Stables, Linslade for feeding hunters with cereal foodstuffs and for using wheat straw for other purposes than feeding livestock. His defence was that the horses were to be sold for remounts for the army and needed to be in top condition. Despite evidence from the army on his behalf, saying that government horses were allowed oats, the magistrates decided that, since they were not at the time owned by the army, van den Poele should be fined ten shillings.

Occasionally, a court case which the town would probably not wish to have broadcast to a wider public was faithfully recorded by the *LBO*. The headline from 30 May 1916 was 'The Friday Street Brothel'. There followed a detailed account of the proceedings:

Mrs Rose Phillips of 25 Friday Street, Leighton Buzzard, has appeared at the Leighton Buzzard Police Court charged with permitting the premises to be used as a brothel. The defendant, a tall, smart-looking woman aged 23, whose husband is a soldier at the Front, was allowed to be seated during the hearing. All women were asked to leave the court.

Police Sergeant Dennis stated that he had known Mrs Philips for some months and had kept observation on the house from 25 March. At various times he had seen men and women enter the house between 11.00 and 12.00 p.m., both in couples and singly. Another girl lived with Mrs Phillips, although her parents lived in the town. He gave the names of a soldier and other men he had seen visiting the house, but admitted he never actually saw anything wrong between the parties who went there. Two other policemen had seen men entering the house and observed Mrs Phillips associating with men in the street. One had seen her behaving familiarly with two men at the corner of Friday Street and had heard her say to them, 'Let us come to business.'

Mary Adcock, the wife of the licensee of the Royal Oak next door to the defendant's house, said Mrs Phillips had been in the public house with men, left by the back way and gone with them to her own house. On the day after Good Friday she had two girls and two men with her. They went into 25 Friday Street at 3.30 p.m. but she did not see them come out. On Easter Monday another man bought some sandwiches at the pub then went to Mrs Phillips's house; again she did not see him leave. She had occasionally been into her neighbour's house but had never seen any 'impropriety'.

Thomas Underwood of 6 Friday Street lived opposite Mrs Phillips. He had also seen men visit the house; some came out drunk and he once saw a man leave at 4.45 a.m. He had given Mrs Phillips his opinion of her character and told her she should be ashamed of herself. He did, however, admit that despite claiming to have a 'pretty good character' himself he had been convicted about thirty times for poaching and drinking. His wife Emily Underwood stated that two other women were living with Mrs Phillips, and she had often seen men coming out at about one in the morning. There seemed to be some suspicion that Thomas Underwood had himself wished to 'visit' Mrs Phillips but had been refused.

A police sergeant from Winslow (Bucks) told the court he had known Mrs Phillips for 4½ years. Her husband had been a respectable farm labourer before he was called up. At the end of 1914 he had warned her to behave herself. She had told him she was doing nothing wrong and 'there was no harm in talking to soldiers'. In December 1915 her house had been placed out of bounds for the men of the 2/5th Norfolks stationed at Winslow. She moved to another address, but soldiers used to stay with her for weekends and the landlord gave her notice to quit. She had then moved to Leighton Buzzard.

Mrs Phillips' solicitor submitted that all the evidence was circumstantial and there was no case to answer; nobody had proved that anything wrong had happened at 25 Friday Street. The magistrates disagreed. Mrs Phillips was convicted and sentenced to one month's imprisonment with hard labour. An appeal was made for a fine as an alternative as Mrs Phillips had four children aged under five, but the magistrates refused. When told her fate Mrs Phillips laughed and said she did not mind, but then broke down and sobbed bitterly.

Not everything reported in the *LBO* involved lawlessness. Among the regular agricultural features by 'Rusticus', sports fixtures, updates on the progress of the war and deaths on active service (which were reported with sad regularity), other poignant human tragedies unfolded. In 1917 Leighton-born Harriett Maude Watson had brought her 12-year-old son Arthur from London for a country holiday, only for him to fall into one of the Billington Road sandpits and drown. And who knows what was behind the story of an apparently well cared for 3-week-old baby boy found abandoned in 1916 in a shrubbery at Mile Bush on Soulbury Road? The baby appeared to have been left by a middle-aged man and a young woman who had arrived by train then left again. The baby was taken to the workhouse and later adopted.

On a more positive note, business was much as usual for most small local firms, many of whom were able to adapt and cater for a less affluent wartime market. Robinson's made protective casings for shells; Malcolm George Carter, a motor engineer operating from 35 Soulbury Road, guaranteed extra mileage when he retreaded old motor tyres by the steel rubber process; Brown's 'new patent light plough' advertised in 1916 could be drawn by a pony or cob, invaluable for anyone whose heavy horses had been requisitioned.

Where possible, employers gave work to soldiers returning from the Front. Some who had lost a leg were trained as basket weavers by Robinson's and early in 1920

Robinson's basket works in Lake Street was taken over to make protective cases for the shells being delivered to the Front. The company is recorded in the council minutes as buying up all the available willow from the osier beds along the Ouzel water meadows to increase production.

Post Office staff posing in about 1916 in the grounds of The Cedars, Church Square. They were forced to take on female postmen to cope with both the increased workload caused by the war and the loss of men to the armed services.

the Bedfordshire Agricultural Executive Committee received a letter from Agnes Jemima Pain of Heath Park House, enquiring as to the possibility of being sent an ex-soldier as a pupil in poultry-breeding, one area of farming where the work was lighter.

War both changed society and speeded up development. The vast influx of billeted soldiers and the disappearance of many local men to the Front caused a dramatic increase in the volume of letters handled by the Royal Mail. At the start of the war the Post Office in Leighton was open all night so that reservists could cash their postal orders in order to have the money to join their units. From November 1914 to March 1915, when the highest number of billeted soldiers were lodged in the two towns, the number of items handled weekly by the Post Office doubled to 146,000 incoming and outgoing letters, newspapers and postcards.

Eventually, because so many postmen had volunteered for the services, army orderlies were called in to help distribute the mail. By September 1915 the Post Office made the decision to employ women, and the two new 'lady postmen' were to be seen delivering letters to business houses in the principal streets of Leighton. Even so, because of the pressure of work, deliveries were reduced to twice a day.

TOBACCO AND CIGARETTES

FOR YOUR FRIENDS AT THE FRONT.

For 26 we can send

Your Friend in the EXPEDITIONARY FORCE on the Continent

Postage (costing 1 -) included

8 ozs Mitcham Shag. Mild, Medium or Full strength ; or

8 ozs. Rutter's Cricket Green Mixture; or

200 Rutter's " Tens" Cigarettes (weight 8 ozs) ;

DOUBLE THE QUANTITIES FOR 4 -.

Give your friend's name, number and Regiment to your Tobacconist
and we will forward direct. Tobacco and Cigarettes for the use of
British Forces are admitted into France. Duty free.

COMFORTS for your FRIENDS at the FRONT

r24

One of many advertisements in the *LBO* inviting people to send presents to friends at the Front. Many small charities were set up to buy warm clothing, chocolate and other items of luxury food for the men in the trenches.

The workload was also increased by parcels containing both food and clothing that were dispatched to soldiers serving at the Front. Later, prisoners of war needed extra rations, and were allowed to receive parcels via the Red Cross. Several local charities were set up to send these gifts. Most of the items, including tins of cigarettes, were sent through the post.

In December 1916 Hockliffe Street Wesleyan Methodist Church sent a Christmas parcel to every former member of its Sunday school now serving in the armed forces. Over 100 parcels were sent, containing chocolate, butterscotch, soap and other useful items. This had increased from seventy the previous Christmas.

Other fast-expanding services were telegrams and the telephone. Telegrams were sent not only to notify families of casualties but also to give news of home leave, and also used by the services to contact individuals and units to give them orders.

The use of telephones was rapidly accelerated by the war, but the total number of telephones was so low that the *LBO,* as a service to readers, was able to print the entire telephone 'list' for the town and district. Only businesses and the wealthy had a telephone. In September 1916, the Leighton Buzzard directory contained just 121 numbers and took up less than two columns of one page. At that time each telephone apparatus needed its own individual line to the exchange, hence the multiple lines seen attached to telegraph poles in old photographs of the towns.

The Post Office had the No. 1 line, the removal firm of Aveline and Phillips No. 2, Brantom and Co. No. 4. George Garside, the sandpit owner was No. 9, and Leopold de Rothschild No. 26. All of the factories fulfilling government orders had their own lines, as did the Union workhouse, the railway station, the police station and the waterworks. Heath and Reach had its own sub-exchange with ten numbers, Hockliffe had eight and Soulbury just two, of which one was the Post Office.

Wartime brought many restrictions. Gas pressure was reduced because the Ministry of Munitions needed more locally 'to provide the government with materials for high explosives'. The Leighton Gas Company hoped that, in a 'patriotic spirit', householders would replace flat flame burners with incandescent mantles that gave a brighter light but used less gas.

Street lamps, also lit by gas, were turned off altogether as a result of a Home Office order that was rigorously enforced. The *LBO* reported:

> While the great majority of tradesmen have cheerfully complied with the instruction that no window may show more than a 'dull subdued light' there have been difficulties with reflected light, where light bouncing off a mirror or polished metal has sent escaping beams into the street. Blind makers are extremely busy and struggling to meet the large number of orders they have received. While most people are very willing to co-operate with the order, many are still forgetting to close the shutters or draw the blinds before the gas is lit. So far a gentle reminder has been thought sufficient. Leighton Buzzard market is being closed at 6.00 p.m. and evening services at All Saints Church have been moved to the afternoon as it is impossible effectively to screen the church windows.
>
> While Leighton has been plunged into darkness, Linslade, being in a different county, is not subject to the same regulations. The anomaly has been partly dealt with by Linslade Urban District Council abolishing street lighting; however, traders are still burning gas lights and motorists are still using their headlights. Linslade Council are believed to have applied for an order which will bring their town in line with its neighbour. In the meantime Leighton's inhabitants must hope that they will not be the victims of bad German marksmanship if a bomb aimed at Linslade misses and hits the darkened streets of Leighton Buzzard.

Troops frequently passed through Leighton Buzzard and for short periods were billeted here. These five characters pictured in Church Square all appear to be motorcycle messengers, but no one can identify them. From a local family album.

Linslade soon followed Leighton's example, however, and the St Barnabas church magazine reported that it had shaded its outside lights, painted the windows and put screens over the chancel lights. In addition there were no lights in the aisles and the windows into the vestry and the belfry had been curtained.

While the blackout was being strictly enforced Leighton magistrates were happily fining Miss Mabel Bosence of Heath and Reach ten shillings for riding a bicycle without a light on 14 November. She said the wick on her oil lamp needed trimming and it had gone out while she was cycling along.

Within two months new rules had come in prohibiting the use of headlights on motor vehicles. Anyone showing more than a 12 watt bulb or an acetylene and or oil lamp would be prosecuted.

The blackout had been imposed because of a fear of German air attacks. Although bombing was rare inland in the war there was widespread fear that it might happen after much publicity had been given to Zeppelin raids in London. With trench warfare at a stalemate, Germany developed super-Zeppelins capable of flying at 13,000ft and cruising at 100mph. These were able to fly higher than aircraft and avoid attack while being able to travel over Britain and drop bombs to strike terror into the civilian population.

A column of advice was published on 16 October 1917 in the *LBO* about what to do in an air raid. This included taking cover in the nearest building or behind a strong wall or tree. If there was no cover 'get into a ditch or a hole in the ground. Horses should be secured sufficiently to stop them running away.'

It turned out to be timely advice, because three days later a Zeppelin attacked Heath and Reach. It was one of eleven airships of the Imperial German Navy which had set out to raid the industrial areas of Middle England, the largest fleet of airships ever to attack Great Britain.

The Zeppelins flew too high to be heard from the ground, and could only be identified by listening posts equipped with the new mechanical acoustical 'ears' called orthophones.

As the raid progressed it became clear to the pilots that headwinds would make it difficult for any of the airships to reach their intended targets. The fleet split up, but individual airships carried on as best they could. The available evidence points to the airship which came over Leighton being L53, commanded by Kapitänleutnant der Reserve Eduard Prölss, the pre-war fire chief at Magdeburg. The airship had taken off from Nordholz, near Bremerhaven in Lower Saxony, just after noon and had come inland over the Wash at 8.30 p.m. It was driven south by the strong winds above 20,000ft and by 10.00 p.m. was over Bedford. Here an engineering works and a military school were showing lights, which attracted a string of 110lb (50 kg) bombs from the airship. It then swung south-east, and at 10.40 p.m. the crew spotted faint lights in Heath and Reach and dropped a magnesium flare. Apparently they could not see Leighton as mist obscured the town centre.

Freak winds gusting up to 60 knots (69mph), and its high altitude, meant that the Zeppelin could not be heard from the ground. But the flare or a signal from a listening post caused a 'take cover' warning to be sounded: three blasts on the hooter at Brown's factory in Lake Street. To observers in Leighton the flare seemed to be over the town, but in fact it was nearly 2 miles away. Before the flare had reached the ground there was the loud whistle of falling bombs and eleven explosions followed in quick succession.

At Heath and Reach next morning, it was found that the bombs, including a 660-pounder (300kg), had all fallen in open fields between Overend Green Farm and Shenley Hill Road. The wide spread of the bombs showed the high speed of the Zeppelin, as there was only the briefest period between the explosions. Fragments of one bomb had fallen near houses but the only damage was the shattering of several windowpanes. Seven craters were found in the fields more than 7ft (2.1m) deep and 10ft (3m) wide, indicating what might have happened if the bombs had been dropped thirty seconds later and fallen directly on Leighton Buzzard town centre. A crowd of souvenir hunters appeared in the fields and the tenant of one of the fields, Mr Ralph Dancer, found the only casualty of the raid – a rabbit.

The weather that saved the Midlands from the Zeppelin raid also hampered the war effort at home. In February 1917 a prolonged frost completely stopped traffic on the Grand Junction Canal. The ice was from 4 to 7in (10 to 18cm) thick, and all the boats were held up for more than two weeks. Over a dozen boats, most of them owned by local sand merchants, were frozen in near Linslade bridge laden with sand for munitions and agricultural implements. The *LBO* reported:

> A powerful ice boat has been at work, drawn by eighteen horses, breaking ice from Grovebury sand pits to Fenny Stratford, but the larger lumps of floating ice constituted a danger to cargo boats, and made the work too hard for the horses. Even the steamers, which of course are more powerful than horse boats, were unable to travel. Two steamers made a start on Thursday morning from Linslade bridge, but were held up again after proceeding about 2 miles. Besides having an effect on the sand traffic, the stoppage has a serious effect on the boatmen. Their horses, although standing idle, have to be fed regularly, and at the present prices of horse fodder, the cost is about £1 per week. In addition, many of the boatmen have to pay 16s. weekly for boat hire. A few of the boats were able to leave yesterday.

A year later the abnormal rains that caused such havoc in the trenches in France because of deep mud also resulted in flooding in Lake Street. The street originally derived its name from the constant overflowing of the Clipstone Brook. On this occasion it stopped workers from Bullivant's reaching the wire works, and they lost pay as a result. The council promised to provide a ferry service to prevent it from happening again.

There were complaints about the sanitary conditions in some parts of the town. The General Officer Commanding of the 63rd Brigade said he feared for the health of his troops billeted in the town. The council blamed 'abnormally wet weather', but said 'steps will be taken'. They later received a letter from the same officer thanking them for the 'billeting arrangements and the reception of troops by the civil inhabitants'.

The council did its best to keep the normal services of the town going, and to look after its finances. During an outbreak of scarlet fever in 1914 the council charged the military £1 11s 6d for each case cared for in its isolation hospital in Union Street (now Grovebury Road) and increased the wages of the nurse by 2s a week to look after them. They had billeted fifty soldiers in the Union workhouse at the beginning of the war, and later, when the board room was turned over as a hospital, they tried to recoup costs by charging the Royal Field Artillery 9d a night per patient for their accommodation.

Other extra demands for services were made on the council because of the war effort. In July 1915 a new 3in water main had to be connected to the Bullivant's factory under construction in Union Street, and they had to accommodate a military guard on the waterworks because they were regarded as of strategic importance and might be a target of sabotage.

Much later, in May 1918, the town's water supply was extended down Billington Road to Morgan's new aerodrome at Scott's Field.

Keeping the peace with residents was an ongoing task for the council, whether over the damage to roads by the sand industry or the noise from football games. Various streets, including Friday Street, were closed to 'locomotive traffic' so that local people could still get about town, and a ban was imposed on football being played by the troops in the recreation ground on Sundays.

Football did not cease, however. Although the ban also meant that no games were to be played at any time in the lower parts of the recreation ground, the *LBO* reported on the 'Munitions Final' in March 1918:

> A huge and very excited crowd watched the deciding match of the Luton Munitions League on Saturday between Bullivant's and Morgan's (Leighton Buzzard) and Vauxhall (Luton). The game was played on the Leighton ground and was very evenly contested, but the crowd keenly resented the frequency with which the local men were penalised by the referee, Mr George Rowe, of Toddington, and he had to be escorted off the field by the police at the end of the game. Both sides scored twice, but both teams having won an equal number of points during the season, the Vauxhall men took the cup on their better goal average.

As the war progressed the shortage of food became a major issue, and by 1917, because of the U-boat blockade, major efforts were made to control prices, conserve supplies and grow more grain. Regulations were brought in to prevent wholesalers from charging shops extra for basic commodities like milk, butter and potatoes.

This led to a milk strike in December 1917, when Leighton milk retailers refused to sell any of their produce at the government price of 6d a quart because they were making a loss; they demanded 7d. The Traders Association of the two towns supported the milk dealers, and agreement was reached with the County Food Control Committees on a new price.

Among the more bizarre schemes to save grain for food was the collection of horse chestnuts to make acetone for the production of high explosives. The

Ministry of Munitions claimed that a ton of conkers saved 10cwt of barley, and 250,000 tons would be required in 1917. These would be collected by lorry, sent by the Ministry. Nationwide the scheme proved so successful that the munitions factories were swamped with conkers.

One of the biggest issues was the government's desire to plough up pasture to grow crops. This met with a lot of resistance, not least from Leighton Buzzard UDC who decided not to plough up parks and recreation grounds for allotments. This caused a row with the Duke of Bedford, one of the government's appointees to oversee the programme, because Frederick George Woodman, vice-chairman of the council, suggested that the walled estate at Woburn should be ploughed up rather than used for grazing deer, raising pheasants and fox cover. Woodman was a poultry keeper and bemoaned the loss of many fowl to marauding foxes.

This criticism may have spurred an act of altruism from the Duke of Bedford, who had a large collection of different species of deer on his estate. To help feed the hungry population he ordered a cull of the deer, and it was recorded that in the three months up to March 1918 he had distributed free 46,000lbs (20,865kg) of venison.

The government continued to be seriously alarmed by the country's inability to grow enough food to feed the its citizens, and soldiers were drafted in to help farmers who had lost all their farmhands to the draft. As early as July 1917 it was reported that 1,500 soldiers had been brought into Buckinghamshire to help with the hay and corn harvests. Along with them a total of twenty-one new Titan tractors had been delivered and the Buckinghamshire War Agriculture Committee was pressing for more, as well as ploughs and cultivators so that more grassland could be turned into arable.

A survey of land had been made and an extra 40,000 acres (16,187 hectares) in Buckinghamshire were to be ploughed for the 1918 harvest. They would all be sown with cereals. If farmers did not co-operate, compulsory powers would be exercised.

This scheme also applied to Bedfordshire but there were many failures, partly because some farmers had never grown cereals and had no idea how to do so. Another reason was that much of the land was not suitable. This led in Bedfordshire alone to 148 farmers claiming compensation for losses suffered when the crops they were growing failed.

Expertise was in short supply. A notice appeared in March 1917 in the *LBO* titled 'Ploughing before Munitions', saying that the ministry wished it to be known that skilled ploughmen should return wherever possible to the land for the ploughing season. Employers should do everything in their power to facilitate the return of these men for a few weeks and reinstate them when ploughing was finished.

In addition to munitions workers and soldiers, German prisoners of war were used to help on farms and women's war agricultural committees were formed to organise the Land Army girls. Women were recruited from towns and given efficiency tests in agricultural work before being given uniforms and allocated to farms to replace men who had been called up. In January 1918 German prisoners of war were brought to Leighton and the Bridge Street stables of the Cedars were converted for their accommodation. A month later, it was reported that forty 'healthy looking' German prisoners had arrived and had been set to work hedging and ditching in Vandyke Road.

Belts were tightened, the old ways were changing and Linslade and Leighton had begun to think that life would never return to normal when it was suddenly all over.

CHAPTER 16

THE MOST MOMENTOUS DAY IN HISTORY

Contrary to what we might expect, Armistice Day in Leighton and Linslade met with muted celebrations and a sense of bewilderment; after such a long ordeal, people seemed almost afraid to believe that peace had finally come.

At least that was the verdict of the *LBO,* which said: 'It was difficult to realise that drizzling November day was the most momentous in history, and would ever be celebrated as the day on which human liberty triumphed over despotism, not only in this country but throughout the world.'

While the Morgan's band played cheerful music and the Boy's Brigade Bugle Band 'thundered and blared through the streets after dark', the chief feeling was one of relief and thankfulness, the paper reported.

It was the remembrance of the heavy toll of hundreds of Leighton and Linslade men and women who died during the conflict that prevented the people coming on to the streets to celebrate. Instead, the most striking factor was the huge proportion of the population that went to churches to the hurriedly arranged services of thanksgiving. Congregations were said to be the largest seen since the war began, and townsfolk had come 'to express in sincerity their thanks for deliverance from the horrors of the past four years'.

All Saints, St Barnabas, Hockliffe Street Baptist and Methodist Churches were all said to be full, and there were additional special services. One of these at All Saints, on Christmas Eve 1918, was of thanksgiving for the workers at the Leighton War Hospital Supply Depot. Afterwards the workers returned to the depot and formally closed it. Mary Cowper, the principal organiser, later received an MBE for her services.

Wartime restrictions imposed by the 1914 Defence of the Realm Act, or DORA as it was affectionately known, were removed the moment the Armistice came into force. The people of the town experienced 'mild shock' on hearing the clocks on the town hall and All Saints Church chime the hour for the first time in four years.

Every church in the neighbourhood also rang its previously silenced bells with the joyful news. 'The night was so calm that the sounds could be heard in Leighton Buzzard even from Stanbridge.' So many regular ringers had gone off to war that in some places women had to be brought in to ring the bells, and in others novices. 'Some of the novices were well meaning, but not very effective.'

The rescinding of DORA also ended the strictly imposed blackout. Shopkeepers and householders in the two towns drew back their blinds so that people in the street had no longer to 'grope for the edge of the pavement or jostle other people' to find their way home.

Despite the shortage of coal to make gas, arrangements had been made to light half the street lamps. This would begin immediately in Linslade where the council had been paying to maintain the lamps during the war, but would take some time in Leighton because the council had been refusing to pay the gas company and the dispute needed to be resolved.

This sense of relief that the end of the war brought to the towns, and the family celebrations as men discharged from the forces began to come home from the Front, lasted for months. Over the same period the industries that made the towns' roles so vital in the war effort began to be wound down. They faced cancelled contracts and an uncertain future, which caused the disappearance of the jobs which some of the soldiers expected to find on their return.

A temporary cenotaph was erected in front of the market cross while committees were formed in the two towns and surrounding villages to organise the erection of permanent memorials to the fallen.

Yet more committees were formed to welcome home and provide a special day for all the men who had survived the conflict and returned.

The first was in January 1919, for sixty men who had been prisoners of war and were now repatriated. Any former POW living within 5 miles of Leighton Town Hall qualified, and was entertained to dinner at the Corn Exchange. Theodore Bromhead Bassett presented every man with a silver-plated cigarette case as a souvenir. Much larger and more lavish events were held months later when all the demobbed soldiers and sailors could be assembled.

In Leighton the town was hung with bunting and 'even dogs and donkeys' obeyed the order to decorate. The celebration was on 15 September 1919, a Thursday, and by common consent early closing day had been brought forward an hour; all shops closed at midday to enable the celebrations to begin in earnest.

The *LBO* began its report by saying that the town 'in proportion to its population provided more fighting men for the Great War than the great mass of industrial towns.'

With the band of the Bedfordshire and Hertfordshire Regiment at their head, the 650 men who had returned to Leighton after serving in the army and navy marched down the High Street. There were large crowds but no cheering. 'Most

The first temporary war memorial, guarded by Scouts, placed by the Market Cross; the focal point for the first Armistice anniversary in 1919. It was taken down when the monolith was erected in Church Square a year later.

minds and hearts were perhaps a little too full of the thoughts of the grim tragedies that these men had lived through.'When they passed the temporary cenotaph 'there was an eyes left and a salute' to the fallen.

The marchers, mostly in civilian clothes, continued down Lake Street to Bullivant's factory in Grovebury Road, described as the only room in the town large enough to host such a gathering. These men sat down to a sumptuous dinner in a wire works decorated with 800 flags. Soup was followed by joints of beef, mutton and pork along with a great variety of vegetables.

After the meal there were speeches and toasts before the men went to the town's recreation ground for sports. A crowd of 3,000 watched the games, which lasted until 6.30 p.m. The paper reported that some competitors failed to finish races; three collapsed, but were none the worse for their experience, implying that the ex-soldiers might have had too good a lunch.

In Linslade the celebrations were held on a Saturday, again declared a half-day. On this occasion the sports were held in Stoke Road playing field in the afternoon and the celebration dinner followed. This time 220 sat down to dinner at the Gables, the home of Dr Roberts.

The paper reported:

> Some idea of the catering can be gathered from the fact that it included 40lbs of salmon, 140lbs of beef, 40lbs of pork, 40lbs of ham, 48 rabbit and beef steak pies and four bushels of potatoes and other vegetables. On the liquor side there were 72 bottles of whiskey and port and double this quantity of beer and mineral waters. Cigars and cigarettes were also plentiful. The festivities went on until midnight, when the National Anthem was sung.

Despite these celebrations it was clear that, as well as the many families still grieving, there was considerable dissatisfaction among the returning soldiers. This was mostly because of the lack of jobs, and a number of public meetings were called by trades unions, at which men aired their grievances. This loss of jobs had begun soon after the Armistice. Before most of the men had arrived home the 'canary girls' were all out of work as the government began to cancel contracts for armaments.

Among the first to suffer in Leighton and Linslade was the sand industry. When the Ministry of Munitions ended their commitment to pay for road repairs, the resourceful sand quarry owners, with a full order book for their specialist sands, needed to move fast.

With the co-operation of the local councils, who were only too keen to get the sand traffic off the roads as well, the decision was made to set up a narrow-gauge railway to run between the pits and the canal.

By April 1919 plans were prepared for laying a railway track, and on 14 May the survey was complete, quotations were to hand, a contract was let for £11,220

The first party for returned soldiers was held in the Corn Exchange in January 1919. These sixty men who had all been prisoners of war wore their uniforms; at later welcome home parties soldiers turned out in civilian clothes because they had already left the services.

and an application was made to the county highways committee for permission to construct nine level crossings across Leighton roads between the quarries and the canal. In parallel with the construction of the line, a company was set up to be responsible for it.

A meeting on 3 June 1919 at the Swan Hotel heard the proposals to build a line to carry sand. The company would be known as Leighton Buzzard Light Railway Ltd. The sand merchants guaranteed a minimum annual traffic of 70,000 cubic yards (53,518m³) for ten years. Rights of way for thirty years over most of the route had already been obtained. Most of the £20,000 capital had already been promised at the meeting; the balance was soon subscribed, about a third of it contributed by the sand merchants. The company was incorporated on 26 July 1919 with its registered office at 20 Bridge Street, Leighton Buzzard.

Four months later, on 20 November 1919, a year after the war ended, the railway was opened and the need to transport sand by road disappeared. It brought an end to a local trade that had existed for more than a century since the sand quarries started exporting their heavy loads all over the country via the canal and railways.

The armour cladding on this train to protect the driver on the Western Front proved impossible to remove when it was brought to Leighton by the sand quarry owners. It was a regular sight driving through Leighton on its way to the canal for the next thirty years.

On the opening day a special train of hastily-built rolling stock took all those who had invested in the line on a tour from one end to the other.

Most of the equipment for the railway had come from army surplus stock from the Western Front, and for thirty-four years the railway used four of the First World War 40hp (30kw) locomotives to haul the sand trains over the mainline, some complete with the armour originally fitted to withstand enemy fire. Unknowingly they left a legacy which has become a modern-day tourist attraction.

Two more of the armoured engines and the sand quarry workers who had to drive them. They must have been extremely hot to drive in summer with only a slit to look through to see where you were going.

Other smaller industries which had served the country well during the war were also able to adapt and survive. Brown's the agriculture machinery merchant continued to serve local farmers, and the shortage of horses gave rise to a brand new best seller – tractors. Robinson's basket works went back to weaving traditional baskets from the osier beds on the water meadows.

However, two of the largest factories in the towns would disappear. Bullivant's was the most obvious candidate to lose its market because it produced very specialised products, and there was no longer a threat from Germany's U-boats. By the time of the coming-home party for the servicemen it was clear that the main part of the factory had ceased production; it could not otherwise have been made available to seat so many for a grand luncheon.

Bullivant's had already begun consultation with other wire rope manufacturers, all of whom realised that there was surplus capacity in the business, and eight companies amalgamated into one, British Ropes. This gave Bullivant's the freedom to close its factories and sell their Leighton plant. As part of the sale, the freehold buildings of the Grovebury Works were valued in 1923 at £8,224 and the land they stood on at £600. The whole property including furnishings was said to be worth a grand total of £10,444.

For a while the factory stood empty, but soon another company took over – Gossard Ltd, makers of ladies' undergarments, and in the 1990s the famous Wonderbra. The role of Bullivant's in the First World War was soon forgotten.

Perhaps the most painful decline was that of Morgan's. After the Armistice the building of some aeroplanes, mainly the Vimy bomber, was briefly continued for the Ministry of Munitions, although the workforce was reduced. There was no gradual winding down of the supply of the smaller planes, simply a complete halt, and Morgan's was left with incomplete aircraft and large supplies of wood, wire, canvas and instruments. By early 1919, in response to the decline in business volumes, they began to lay off 500 women and men. There were 800 people working at the plant at the time and the 500 were immediately given notice with a fortnight's wages. There was a threat of strike action, and most of the workforce retired to the Victoria Hall in Hockliffe Street after work at the beginning of March 1919 to consider what to do.

After a three-hour meeting, the call to strike was abandoned after it was pointed out that all over the area people were losing their jobs and there was a surplus of labour. There was also concern about the effect on the town of a strike.

One of the ordinary diesel locomotives brought from the Front in 1918, towing sand out of an Arnold's quarry. These were the first diesel engines to be used on any railway line in Britain.

Trains were not the only ex-army equipment to come in useful immediately after the war. This ex-WD Commer truck was adapted by Lake Street company Aveline & Phillips as a removal van.

After working so hard night and day, the workforce must have been distressed to read in the *LBO* of 28 May 1919:

> At Henlow aerodrome near Bedford, many machines, including Sopwith Camels, FE2Bs, RESs, De Havilands (6s and 9As), and Bristol Fighters have been delivered from the makers complete (with the exception of the engines), and mechanics and women workers, armed with hammers and hatchets, have under orders broken them to pieces. The pieces, except the metal work, which has been sorted and stored, have been mostly gathered into bags, taken away and used as firewood.

Former members of the workforce who had volunteered to fight at the Front were now returning from their period of service and seeking their old jobs in Morgan's, and by August there was considerable ill feeling in the town. Richard Arthur Wheatley, the works manager, addressed a large meeting of the Leighton Federation of Discharged and Demobilised Sailors and Soldiers to answer charges that ex-servicemen were being discriminated against on unemployment and other subjects. The *LBO* reported that he dealt with 'the various charges which had been made against the works as to there being a refuge for shirkers during the war, and that they were now showing an unsympathetic attitude towards returned fighting men. To show how incorrect the charges were, Mr Wheatley stated that at present 160 ex-service men were employed by them.' Later: 'Mr Wheatley said that the only way the works could keep be kept running was by the employment of a certain percentage of female labour.' This was presumably because they earned far less than men for doing the same job.

A month after this meeting the government cancelled all remaining contracts. Morgan's had already begun their attempt to re-direct their business into a post-war world, but first had to dispose of raw materials and equipment needed for aeroplane building. In January 1920 an advert in the *Bucks Herald* addressed 'To Whom It May Concern' suggested cartage contractors could remove large quantities of unwanted stock between 14 and 20 January 1920 and they should apply to the works manager for details.

The company launched a large range of new motor cars, offering to do as they had done before the war – build vehicles of the highest quality to the specification of the purchaser. It was to no avail. They could not compete with the production line methods being developed by Ford, and the company faced bankruptcy. It was bought in mid-1920 for £203,000, (about £12 million in 2017), by R.E. Jones Ltd, a Welsh catering business with aspirations to expand into London. Morgan's was purchased primarily to obtain the company's two London showrooms, which were in prime sites and were used by Jones Ltd for the sale of cars. The vast works in Linslade were disposed of by being split and sold as smaller units.

The loss of so many jobs so quickly after the war gave rise to much discontent in the town. In Luton on Peace Day, 19 July 1919, a riot broke out, policemen and firemen were attacked and injured in the streets and the town hall was burnt down. Nothing of this magnitude occurred in Leighton but this serious disorder was only 12 miles away. Locally there were many reports of trades unions being formed and defending the wages and rights of workers. The railway strike of September 1919 stopped all trains through Leighton station, and the supplies of milk for London delivered by local farmers were left uncollected on the platforms.

Food continued to be in short supply. The rationing of commodities such as sugar, introduced towards the latter stages of the war, showed no sign of abating. Even in 1919 government inspectors were intent on ploughing up more and more land, and the obviously unsuitable water meadows behind All Saints Church were earmarked to grow wheat, even though the ground was clearly too wet. Claims for compensation for unsuitable land ploughed up continued until well after 1920.

Undoubtedly, though, the most difficult and emotionally-charged issue of all was how to commemorate the dead. None of the bodies of those who had fallen in the war had been repatriated, by order of the Imperial War Graves Commission.

Taken on 19 October 19 1920. It took three days to erect the Leighton war memorial. A lead tube with copper and silver coins of the period was placed beneath a bolt at the bottom of the monument.

Almost all organisations of any size had lost men in the war, and many wanted to put up their own memorials to ensure they were not forgotten. In the two towns and surrounding villages there are still twenty-six memorials surviving containing 440 different names of those who lost their lives. Another eighty-four men who died are not on any memorial. Some were simply forgotten because they had no relatives to put their names forward, but some families deliberately opted not to have their names included. The reasons for this are difficult to understand at this distance in time but in 1919 there was widespread disillusionment with the war, and the belief that many brave men had died needlessly.

For others there was an urgent need for memorials. Each village had its own discussion and both Leighton and Linslade had committees that commissioned and put up one central memorial for each town. Perhaps the most elaborate for a single organisation was for the Old Boys of Beaudesert School. Ninety-four former pupils had died. Other lists of the fallen were at the London and Middlesex Bank (in 2017 the NatWest), the Post Office, the Scout Hut and the Salvation Army Citadel in Leighton; in Linslade there were two memorials for members of the congregation in St Barnabas Church, one of which was specifically for bell ringers.

Soldiers stand in silent salute to their fallen comrades in Linslade Square next to the canal bridge after the dedication ceremony on Armistice Day in 1920.

Crowds gather round the Linslade War Memorial after its unveiling on 11 November 1920. The cross was moved in 1955 to the Memorial Gardens in Mentmore Road because it was regarded as a traffic hazard.

The Faith Press in Wing Road, a publishing house, put up a shield displaying the names of those staff it had lost.

By far the largest in the district was the monolith erected in Church Square, Leighton. This is the largest single block of granite ever mined in Britain. An all-male committee included Robert Richmond, a local magistrate, who had lost two of his three sons on the Somme and Lieutenant Colonel James Macarthur, from the Royal Veterinary Corps. Not a single woman was consulted about what kind of memorial she would like, and it was Mr Richmond who located the piece of granite lying unused in a builder's yard from before the war. The committee approved his choice without any public consultation.

Controversy abounded in both towns and surrounding villages about the location of the memorials. Most people wanted the most prominent position possible to ensure that the dead would never be forgotten. The memorial to Linslade's casualties was set in the middle of the road in Linslade Square, on a site that is now a mini-roundabout near the canal bridge at the junction of Stoke Road and Wing Road. After the Second World War it was moved to Memorial Gardens in Mentmore Road because it was a traffic obstruction.

The relatives of those named on the war memorial were invited to stand in the front of the crowd when the war memorial was unveiled. Almost the entire population of Leighton turned out for this Armistice Day in 1920.

The Leighton memorial was originally to be put in the middle of Bridge Street, but the Rev. George Frederick Hills, Vicar of All Saints and a member of the war memorial committee, offered a site at the end of the vicarage garden. The committee declared that the memorial would be large enough that everyone entering the town would see it without obstructing the traffic.

It took three days to erect the monolith with hoists and pulleys. The *LBO* concluded that:

> Leightonians of a thousand years hence, when perhaps tramways run on either side of the monument into distant suburbs of a large city, will probably look with reverence upon this rugged mass of granite, with the names still legible on its panels, and think kindly of these rugged fighters whose granite courage saved Britain in her hour of need.

Despite these stirring words, everyone knew there was widespread discontent with the situation in the country a year after the end of the war. Many ex-servicemen, some physically or mentally maimed by their experiences, could not find work

After the opening ceremony in Church Square the crowds part to allow a march past by the army to salute their fallen comrades.

and begged on the streets. The government set up many schemes for them to find employment, such as retraining them to keep chickens or other jobs on farms, but many could not be placed and were left without jobs or homes.

Sir Arthur Oliver Villiers Russell, Lord Ampthill, who unveiled the Leighton memorial on Armistice Day 1920 clearly felt he needed to address the problem. 'Everywhere we see discontent, mutual distrust, cruel selfishness and ruthless self-seeking. Worst of all, we see the soldier begging his bread in the street because the doors of employment are closed to him.' His speech goes on to question the cause of the war, the purpose of it and why so many men lost their lives. But he justified the sacrifice by saying: 'We fought for freedom, justice and right against the peoples who had been nurtured in the creed that might is right and sought to subjugate and dominate the rest of the world.'

The fact that he needed to make such a powerful speech shows the degree of unrest and disquiet about the sacrifices of the soldiers, sailors and airmen and about the aftermath of the war – unemployment, lack of housing and food shortages.

CHAPTER 17

FOR VALOUR

The fortitude and bravery of those in both armed forces and non-combatant services was acknowledged in various ways during and immediately after the war. Countless medals were struck, the most numerous received by men and women from Leighton and district being the British War Medal for all who had served overseas between 5 August 1914 and 11 November 1918, and the Inter-Allied Victory Medal, issued to most who were awarded the British War Medal and to all recipients of the 1914 or 1914-15 Stars; the Stars were campaign medals for the Old Contemptibles of the BEF.

The first two medals worn together gained the nickname Mutt and Jeff, after the eponymous popular American first strip cartoon. When displayed in conjunction with either of the Stars, the trio was often known as Pip, Squeak and Wilfred, three *Daily Mirror* cartoon characters from the 1920s.

The bronze 1914 Star was for those who had served during the first sixteen weeks of the war, from 5 August 1914 until midnight on 22 November 1914; an additional clasp indicated their having served under enemy fire. Recipients had helped the French to hold back the German army during the training and equipping of new recruits. The Battle of Mons, the Retreat to the Seine, the Battles of Le Cateau, the Marne, the Aisne and the 1st Battle of Ypres all took place in this period of less than four months. The bronze 1914-15 Star was for any who had served during that period in any theatre of war against Germany.

To those who were discharged as a result of sickness or wounds the Silver War Badge was presented, only to be worn with civilian clothes, to show that a man had done his duty.

Awards were also given for conspicuous valour and for distinguished service. Of these, people connected with Leighton Buzzard are known to have received one Victoria Cross (VC), three Distinguished Service Orders (DSO), one Distinguished Service Cross (DSC), nine Military Crosses (MC), fourteen Distinguished Conduct Medals (DCM), forty Military Medals (MM), three Meritorious Service Medals (MSM) and several Silver War Badges; in addition there are sixteen instances of being Mentioned in Despatches, these being detailed official reports from commanders in the field.

The VC remains the highest award for gallantry, awarded to members of the armed forces for an act of outstanding courage or devotion to duty in the presence of the enemy.

The DSO was awarded to army officers for an act of meritorious or distinguished service in wartime and usually when under fire or in the presence of the enemy. It was also made available for officers at the equivalent rank in the Royal Navy and, from 1 April 1918, the Royal Air Force.

The DSC was awarded to naval officers below the rank of Lieutenant Commander for gallantry at sea in the presence of the enemy.

The MC, the British Army equivalent of the DSC, was for gallantry during active operations in the presence of the enemy.

The DCM recognised an act of gallantry in the field by a member of the armed forces below the rank of officer, the other ranks' equivalent of the DSO.

The MM was awarded to other ranks of the British Army and Commonwealth Forces for gallantry and devotion to duty when under fire in battle on land.

The MSM had different criteria for eligibility for each service. Awarded in the army, it was for meritorious service by non-commissioned officers (NCOs).

Mentioned in Despatches (MiD) means that an individual is mentioned by name and commended for having carried out a noteworthy act of gallantry or service; a Despatch being an official report by the senior commander of an army in the field which gives details of the military operations being carried out.

In addition to these, several non-British awards were bestowed on people from this area.

Where the recipient of a gallantry award died while serving, more information will be found in Chapter 18. Entries in both have been asterisked.

Despite thorough research, it is possible that there have been omissions and for this we apologise wholeheartedly. It has been thought appropriate to follow alphabetical order of surname of the recipients:

Private 43003 **Herbert Ashby MM** of 6th Battalion the Northamptonshire Regiment, Billington, 'for gallant conduct and devotion to duty' (*LBO* 1 May 1917).

Private 80513 **James Baker MM★** of the Royal Army Medical Corps (RAMC), Sandy Lane, Heath Road, Leighton Buzzard, 'for gallantry in the field, this being for disregarding the advice of his officer, which was to go to the dressing station after being wounded, and instead attend to his comrades.' (Possibly May 1917)

Major **Francis Marshall Bassett Croix de Guerre (French)** of the Bedfords, Ampthill, formerly of The Knolls, Plantation Road, Leighton Buzzard. (18 March 1919)

Major (Temporary Lieutenant Colonel) **John Retallack Bassett DSO** of the Royal Berkshire Regiment, The Heath, Plantation Road, Leighton Buzzard, 'for distinguished service in connection with Military Operations in Egypt and Hedjaz'. (4 September 1918)

> **MiD** (may have been pre-war)
>
> **Osmaniah Medal (4th Class)** possibly 1914
>
> **Order of the Nile (3rd Class)** possibly 1916
>
> **Légion d'Honneur Croix de Chevalier** awarded 10 October 1918
>
> **Order of El Nahda (2nd Class)** conferred 27 October 1919 by His

Majesty King Hussein Bin Ali of Hedjaz.

Second Lieutenant 548255 **William Herbert Baumbrough MM** of 22nd Battalion the City of London Royal Engineers, Canada, formerly of Market Square, Leighton Buzzard, 'for devotion to duty, bridge building at the Battle of Cambrai'. (Possibly October 1917)

Private 41614 **William Ernest Bond MM★** of the RAMC, attached to 88th Battery the RFA, Mentmore. (*Gazette* 1 September 1916)

Lance Corporal 9387 **Frederick Boyce DCM★, MM★** of 2nd Battalion the Bedfords, 33 Friday Street, Leighton Buzzard, 'for gallantry on the Somme'. (DCM possibly August 1916; MM posthumously)

Private 18769 **Albert William Brandom Medal of St George (4th Class)** of 2nd Battalion the Bedfords, Great Billington, 'for conspicuous gallantry at Trônes Wood. In taking a message to Headquarters, Private Brandon discovered that the enemy were working round his party; he immediately returned with the information, and then set out again with the message, although four previous runners had either been killed or wounded.'

Private (later Second Lieutenant) 2658 **William Harpur Brantom DCM★** of the Civil Service Rifles, Ivydene, Stoke Road, 'for running up to the German trenches and throwing in bombs from the edge at Festubert'. (25 May 1915; *LBO* 21 September)

Private Stk/918 **Henry Gerald Briggs MM** of 10th (Stockbrokers) Battalion the Royal Fusiliers, Wing Road. 'During the attack on the 23rd, he located and effectively dealt with two enemy snipers who were proving very troublesome during a temporary hold-up. When the objective was reached he undertook and carried through very valuable patrol work at great personal risk.' (*Gazette* 11 July 1917)

Major **Charles Noel Frank Broad DSO** of the Royal Artillery, Cheddington, 'for valuable and distinguished services in the field'. (*LBO* June 1917)

Company Quartermaster Sergeant **Alexander Brown DCM** of the Middlesex Regiment, Old Road, 'for his services in the Somme battle, taking reinforcements through the German barrage and taking a trench with two machine guns'. (*LBO* January 1917)

Sergeant **Arthur Brown MiD** of 11th Battalion the Middlesex Regiment, late of Mill Road. (April 1916)

Sergeant 9136 **William George Bull MM** of the O&BLI, Crafton, 'for bravery in the field'. (*Gazette* 10 September 1918)

Private 23352 **George Bunyan MM and Bar** of the Bedfords, Mill Road, 'for bravery in the field'. (November 1916 – newspaper of 27 February 1917 cites *Gazette* 19 February 1917.)
    Bar to MM (14 April 1918, reported *Bucks Herald* 22 June 1918)

Private 2765, later 200040, **William Bunyan MM** of 5th Battalion the Bedfords, Mill Road, 'for gallantry during aggressive patrols around Umbrella Hill and Fischer Hill during the night of 3rd–4th October 1917 in Gaza'. (War Diary 9 October 1917)

Private M2/120788 **John George Butcher MM, MiD** of the ASC, formerly Petty Officer Mechanic F1112 of the Royal Naval Division, 29 Soulbury Road, 'for bravery in the field' in Alexandria (awarded 12 February 1917; *Gazette* 17 April 1917)
    MiD (*Gazette* 6 July 1917)

Second Lieutenant **John Carter MiD★** of 10th Kite Ballon, Section the RAF, Vicarage Lane, Ivinghoe. (8 November 1918)

Lance Corporal 10515 **Charles Chandler DCM** of 6th Battalion the Bedfords, Harlington, formerly of Heath and Reach, 'for conspicuous gallantry and devotion to duty when in charge of a section of pack mules carrying rations to the front line. When wounded in the eye, side and leg, he had himself placed on a mule, reorganised the pack team under fire, and brought them safely back to the transport lines, remaining on duty for two and a half hours after being wounded.' (28 March 1918)

Corporal 89437 **Fred Cheshire MM and Bar** of the RE, Ascott. (*NBT* July 1917)

Lieutenant **Bernard Talbott Chick DSC** of HMML *263* the RNVR, Bank House, 'for action whilst in command of HM Armed Motor Launch 263, against an enemy Submarine, which resulted in the sinking of the U boat in North Sea, July 1918'. (11 January 1919)

Second Lieutenant 3497 **Walter James Collett Croix de Guerre (Belgian)** of the RFC/RAF, 47 Hockliffe Street, 'for distinguished services rendered during the course of the campaign'. (*Gazette* 15 April 1918)

Boy First Class **John 'Jack' Travers Cornwell VC★** of HMS *Chester,* East Ham. (Jack's mother, Lily King, was from Leighton Buzzard, where her parents and grandparents had been licensees of The Stag and The Falcon.) During the Battle of Jutland 31 May–1 June 1916, 'Mortally wounded early in the action, Boy First Class John Travers Cornwell remained standing alone at a most exposed post, quietly awaiting orders, until the end of the action, with the gun's crew dead and wounded all round him. His age was under sixteen and a half years.' (Posthumous)

Second Lieutenant 16375 **Frank Croxford MM** of the Bedfords, North Street and Rosemary Glen, Heath and Reach, 'for action East of Ypres where the 8th Middlesex suffered heavy losses'. (*Gazette* 27 October 1916)

Captain **Alfred Christopher Dancer MC★** of 5th Battalion the Dorsets, Rammamere Farm, Great Brickhill, 'at the Fighting for Mouquet Farm'. (July–September 1916).

Private 266352 **William Dickens MM** of 1/1st Buckinghamshire Battalion the O&BLI, Lane's End, Heath and Reach, 'for devotion to duty on the Italian Front, when carrying badly wounded men to safety under very heavy shell fire'. (*NBT* 8 October 1918; *Gazette* 21 January 1919)

Miss **Edith Kate Dickinson** of 1st Serbian–English Field Hospital, Heath Cottage and Moulton. Order of St Sava (5th Class). (See also Chapter 12)

Orderly **Hilda May Dickinson MM** of the FANY, Heath and Reach. (31 July 1918) (See also Chapter 12)

Second Lieutenant **Vernon Gilbert Dixon MC** of 17th Battalion the King's Royal Rifle Corps, Whitefriars, Leighton Buzzard. 'While at Festubert, together with another officer he carried out a raid on the enemy trenches, successfully cutting the first line of barbed wire and blowing a way through the second line of wire until stopped at the third line by heavy small arms fire and forced to retire. It was reported that, although wounded, he behaved in a cool and gallant manner throughout.' (July 1916; *Gazette* 29 December 1916; *LBO* 17 April 1917).

Temporary Lieutenant **Vivian William Herbert Dixon MC** of 13th Battalion the King's Royal Rifle Corps, Whitefriars, Leighton Buzzard, 'for having carried out successful raids and aggressive patrolling in No Man's Land during 1917 and 1918'. (*Gazette* 2 April 1919)

Lieutenant **George F. Douglas MC** of the Canadian Machine Gun Company, Whiteley House, Hockliffe, 'for bravery and devotion to duty on the battlefield'. (*LBO* December 1917)

Captain **Charles Bryan Draper MiD** of the Bedfords, Grove and Dudley Street, 'for services in connection with the Egyptian Expeditionary Force'. (1918 and 1919; reported *Bucks Herald* 22 June 1918)

Quartermaster Sergeant 285563 **Thomas Haldane Facer MSM** of 2/1st Battalion the Oxfordshire Yeomanry, Crescent House, Ashwell Street. (*Gazette* 3 June 1919)

Private 16999 **Arthur William Foster MM★** of the MGC, formerly 9778 1st Battalion Northamptonshires, Billington.

Private 41671 **William Stanley Galloway Croix de Guerre (French)** of 4th Machine Gun Section/Squadron, 19 Billington Road, 'for good work at the re-taking of Hangard Wood, on the Amiens Front'. (March 1918)

Driver 2656 **Cyril Giltrow MM** of 24th Australian Field Artillery (Howitzer) Brigade, Hockliffe. 'On the nights of 4th and 5th July, 1918, as he was driving his team of mules attached to a GS wagon loaded with trench mortar bombs in the rear of Hamel, the enemy placed a heavy barrage on all roads in the vicinity. A wagon immediately in front of him was blown off the road, drivers and horses being casualties. With great coolness and presence of mind Driver Cyril Giltrow drove his team a little off the road and remained standing by his mules for 1½ hours under heavy fire, awaiting instructions from a guide, who had gone forward to receive instructions from an officer.' (*Gazette* 21 October 1918)

Lance Corporal 10494 **Alfred Green MM** of 6th Battalion the Bedfords, Prospect Place, Wing, 'for brave and arduous work on the battlefield as a stretcher bearer'. (*Gazette* 13 December 1917)

Lieutenant 13039 **Henry/Harry Guess DCM, MC** of the Royal West Kent Regiment, 18 Back Lane.

DCM 'for heroically rushing to the rescue of his fallen officer and carrying him (minus a leg) 700 yards on his back under heavy fire to safety'. (*Luton News* of 22 February 1917 quotes mother, 'It was on 27th July.')

MC 'for conspicuous gallantry and devotion to duty. He displayed great courage in controlling his men during a determined hostile attack, and later, when the enemy penetrated the line, he organised his platoon to cover the portion that was broken, and then, counter-attacking, regained all lost ground. His services were of the utmost value to his company commander.' (29 July 1918)

MiD for bravery while fighting at Hill 60

Private (Acting Sergeant) 16589 **Walter Guess MM, MiD** of 8th Battalion the Bedfords, 18 Back Lane. 'The destination was a well concealed point, but although several men offered to go, they proved unable to find their way. Private Guess then said that he would "have a go", and after starting off had to hide in pot-holes several times, and cross, at the double, several bullet-swept open places. He finally arrived on the point of collapse, and was barely able to tell where the paper [*sic*] was concealed.' (*Gazette* 27 October 1916) At Loos.

MiD for 28 December 1915, near Ypres (letter dated 28 March 1916)

Nurse **Edith Halford MiD** of the VAD, 22 Market Square, Salonika. (3 September 1919) (See also Chapter 12)

Private G/37101 **Sidney Hazzard** (cited as Haggard) **MM** of the Queen's (Royal West Surrey) Regiment, Summerleys, Eaton Bray. (*Luton News* 14 June 1917; Edinburgh *Gazette* 11 July 1917)

Corporal G/60813 **William Henley DCM** of 24th Battalion the Royal Fusiliers, School Lane, Eaton Bray. 'In the operations against the enemy's trench system east of the Canal-du-Nord, on the 12th September 1918, he led the bombing attack along the support line by which the enemy were driven out of their positions. The fighting at close quarters lasted for twelve hours, when the trenches were cleared and twelve machine guns captured.' (*Gazette* 9 January 1920)

    MiD (*Gazette* 14 February 1919)

Second Lieutenant **Hamilton Elliott 'Tim' Hervey MC and Bar** of the RFC, Billington. 'For conspicuous gallantry in action. He displayed great courage and skill on several occasions as machine gunner, and materially assisted in several successful flights.' (Both in *Gazette* 10 January 1917)

    MiD (by Churchill for his many attempts to escape from prisoner of war camps).

Private 5358, later 200938 **Edward Holmes MM** of the Bedfords, 58 Hockliffe Street, 'for his part in the raids on Umbrella Hill in July 1917'. (*Gazette* 18 October 1917)

Sergeant 19255 **George Howlett DCM** of the Bedfords, Eaton Bray, 'for conspicuous gallantry in action. Although wounded, he stuck to his post for two days. When his officers had become casualties, he took command of his company, displaying great courage and initiative.' (*Gazette* 16 November 1916)

Sergeant 8172 **Leonard William Hubbocks DCM** of the Bedfordshire and Hertfordshire Regiments, The Stag, 69 Church Street, 'for conspicuous gallantry and devotion to duty. When in command of a platoon he showed the greatest coolness in reconnoitring a position for the defensive flank he had been ordered to form, and in getting the men into position, though the enemy's fire was very heavy. Later, he led his men forward in daylight under machine gun and rifle fire, to reinforce the front line, and, being uncertain of the position and strength of the enemy, he went out with another NCO to reconnoitre at great risk. Having been successful in his object, he returned with information of the greatest value.' (3 September 1918)

Private 4781, later 40114, **Frank Janes MM** of 1st Battalion the Bedfords, 42 South Street.

Private 536442 **Harold Janes MM** of the RAMC, Queen Street, 'for bravery in the field'. (*Gazette* 14 March 1918)

Private 32139 **Herbert Kent MM★** of 4th Battalion the Bedfords, Ledburn.

Private 14327, later 201287, **Walter Kingham MM** of 5th Battalion the Bedfords, Hockliffe, 'for his part in the 3rd Battle of Gaza in November 1917'. (*Gazette* 2 April 1918)

Lance Corporal/Private 9678 **Robert Lake DCM Croix de Guerre (Belgian)** of the Essex Regiment, 14 South Street. (*Gazette* 12 July 1918)

Sergeant Major **E.C. Landsberger DCM** of the RFA. Son of Mrs Creed, of 41 Hockliffe Road, 'for gallantry and devotion to duty at Ypres on July 25th, 1917'.

Lieutenant Colonel **James Macarthur MiD** of the Army Veterinary Corps, 16–18 North Street.

Company Sergeant Major 18379 or 8030 **Ernest Rufus Matthews MM★** of 2nd Battalion the Suffolks, Ipswich, formerly Chapel Path.

Corporal 202020 **Rupert Henry Ebenezer Matthews MSM** of the Royal Garrison Artillery (Clerks Section), 21 Hockliffe Road. (*LBO* 13 July 1917; *Gazette* 30 May 1919)

Sergeant 956139 **Kenneth McCubbin DCM** of 460 Battery 216th Brigade the RFA, Lake Street. 'On the night of the 7th/8th October 1918 the battery wagon lines near Becalaere were heavily shelled. One shell burst in the tent where he was sleeping, killing four men and wounding him in two places. Nevertheless, he forthwith rendered first aid to the survivors and afterwards gave assistance to other wounded men. He next saw his subsection horses safely away, and then was one of the foremost in a party extinguishing some burning ammunition wagons, after which he reported his wounds. He showed conspicuous gallantry and devotion to duty.' (October 1918)

Private 18379 **Frederick James Millins MM★** of No. 4 Company, 2nd Battalion the Grenadier Guards, Park Lodge, Mentmore (before KIA November 1917).

Nurse **Annie Cecilia Mabel Newman MiD** of the VAD, Perth House, Soulbury Road.

Private **Alfred Norman MM** of the Canadian Contingent, Canada, formerly of Hockliffe, 'for bravery in taking four wounded men under heavy fire to a place of safety'. (*Luton News* 27 December 1917)

Nurse **Mary Page MiD** of the 12th Buckinghamshire VAD, Ascott.

Second Lieutenant 755 **Arthur John Pearson MC★** of the MGC, formerly 8th (Reserve) Battalion the Northamptonshires, later 29 Squadron the RFC, Shenley House, Heath and Reach. 'For conspicuous gallantry during operations. When held up by the enemy's fire after an advance through heavy fire, he established himself in a shell hole and held on for five hours. He then withdrew, bringing back his gun and a wounded man.' (*Gazette* 19 August 1916 when in MGC)

Captain **William Reginald Guy Pearson MiD★** of the RFC, formerly of The Cedars. (MiD by General Haig on 20 May 1918)

Private 18314 **Arthur Charles Pilgrim MM★** of 14th Battalion the Royal Warwickshires, formerly 22952 of the Somerset Light Infantry, 5 Stoke Road, 'for his actions as a stretcher bearer under fire during the Battle of Bucquoy in late August 1918'.

Lieutenant 2159 **John 'Jack' Auguste Pouchot DCM★** of the Queen's Westminster Rifles, London, formerly of the Bell Hotel, Market Square/High Street, Leighton Buzzard, 'for conspicuous gallantry on 8 January 1915, in going, in the face of heavy fire, to the assistance of Corporal (409 Richard De Roupe) Roche and Private (2304 Philip Henry) Tibbs, who had both been mortally wounded.' (*Gazette* 30 June 1915 – aged 15 and first in the Regiment)

Private 19149 **Edwin George Randall MC** of 4th Battalion the Grenadier Guards, Wing. (Diocesan newsletter December 1916)

Private M2/178158 **William John Randall MM★** of 13th Siege Battery, Ammunition Column the RASC, Ledburn. (*Luton News* 28 August 1919)

Captain **George William Richmond DSO, MiD** of the RE Special Reserve, Heathwood, Heath Road, 'for conspicuous gallantry and determination while forcing a passage of the river (*Tigris and Dialah Crossings)*. His coolness and resource were mainly responsible for the successful launching of the pontoons which effected the crossing, and his attitude was an inspiring example to all under his command. He has previously done fine work.' (20 June 1917)
  MiD (August 1917)

Sapper WR/270169 **Albert George Robinson MSM★** of 18th Light Railway Company the RE, Soulbury. (Awarded posthumously 17 June 1919; amended 1 April 1920)

Private M2/074969 **Stanley Rolls MM** of Motor Transport, ASC, attached Ammunition Column, Sandy Corner, Heath and Reach. (*Gazette* 2 August 1918)

Sergeant G/2186 **Augustus Housden Roser DCM★** of 8th Battalion the East Surrey Regiment, 55 North Street, 'for an act of conspicuous gallantry during the battle of Albert'. (22 August 1918)

Marie de Rothschild CBE MiD of the VAD, Ascott. (On two occasions) (See also Chapter 12)

Private 19878 **Henry Charles Samuels MM** of the MGC, Burcott, 'for carrying messages through shellfire and carrying his wounded officer to safety'. (*LBO* January 1917)

Sergeant 833 **Harry Sharp MM** of 10th Battalion the Lincolnshires, formerly of 10 North Street, 'for taking charge of a platoon of men when his officer had been put out of action and capturing a machine gun crew'. (26 August 1917)

Private 242005 **Wilfred John Sharp MM** of 1/5th Battalion the Border Regiment, Hockliffe, 'for carrying 29 messages under heavy shellfire'. (December 1917; *Luton News* January 1918 'of Beds Regiment')

Sapper 142595 **Lawrence Bertram Arthur Smith MM** of the RE, 40 Hockliffe Street. (*Gazette* 23 October 1918)

Major **Alwyn Holberton Square MC** of the RFA, Bridge House, Bridge Street, 'for conspicuous gallantry with his battery in action, under heavy barrage fire.' (*Gazette* 7 November 1918)

   MiD *Luton News* 20 Dec 1917

Private 28784 **George Stevens MM** of the Royal Welsh Fusiliers, St Andrew's Street. 'During operations against the enemy on 21st April 1917, Private Stephens showed unfailing courage and devotion to duty as a stretcher bearer, and was seen to dash from one man to another under heavy fire. Undoubtedly he saved many lives.' (*LBO* 12 June 1917)

Major (Temporary Lieutenant Colonel) **Alfred Joseph Elton Sunderland MiD★** of 2nd Battalion the Devonshires, Eggington Vicarage.

   MiD three times. (*Gazette* 11 December 1917)

Nurse **Hester Mary Tatham MiD** of the VAD, Wing Vicarage**.** (November 1918)

Sergeant 43254 **Walter Dennis Toe MM★ MiD** of the Northamptonshires, 16 Regent Street, 'for great gallantry and devotion to duty during the fighting for Miraumont Trench'. (*Gazette* 17 April 1917)

Sergeant PS/2275 **Hubert Grainger Towers MM** of 4th Battalion the Middlesex Regiment, the Swan Hotel, High Street, 'for gallantry and devotion to duty'. (*Gazette* 19 June 1919)

Lance Corporal 60102 **Walter Munday Vigor MM, MiD** of the Royal Fusiliers, Bridge Street, 'for his courage and fine example as a company stretcher-bearer; also his untiring rendering of first aid to the wounded and carrying casualties over most difficult ground under heavy shell and machine gun fire'. (*Luton News* 27 September 1917)

Private 15252 **Robert Watson MM, DCM** of 12th Battalion the Prince of Wales's Own (West Yorkshire) Regiment, later 312843 the Royal Engineers, St Andrew's Street, 'for laying telephone lines under fire'.

   DCM 'for capturing a number of German prisoners' (anecdotal, no documentary evidence).

   Private 18348 **Charles West MM** of 4th Battalion the Bedfords, 130 Heath Road. (*Gazette* 23 July 1919)

Sergeant 12835 **Ernest George Willis MM** of 7th Battalion the Norfolks, George Street, Wing. 'After his officer had been badly wounded, Sergeant Willis carried on holding the trench with his men and consolidated the position, thereby saving many lives.' (*North Bucks Times* July 1917)

CHAPTER 18

LADS IN THEIR HUNDREDS

The name of this chapter is from a poem by A.E. Housman, lamenting the boys and men who had gone from a different part of Britain to fight another war. From the towns and villages within Leighton Buzzard Poor Law Union, more than 500 of those who set off for the war did not return.

The original aim of this chapter was to research and record the life stories of those named on the various war memorials and rolls of honour within the Union. By 1914 the area had a population of 18,206 and comprised in Bedfordshire: Billington, Chalgrave, Eaton Bray, Eggington, Heath and Reach, Hockliffe, Stanbridge, Tilsworth; and in Buckinghamshire: Cheddington, Edlesborough, Grove, Ivinghoe, Leighton Buzzard, Linslade, Mentmore, Slapton, Soulbury, Stoke Hammond, Wing. Because of the mobility of the local population, those from Battlesden, Ledburn, Northall, Potsgrove and Pitstone (the latter joined the Union in 1923) have also been included.

In the first instance, names were collected from war memorials, rolls of honour and burial grounds. These were then matched where possible to records kept by the Commonwealth War Graves Commission (CWGC), household schedules presented for the census of 1911, service records, war diaries, newspaper archives and parish records. Biographies were compiled, each concluding with the location of the war grave or memorial. Appendix C is a guide to additional references on memorials and rolls of honour within the Leighton area.

It soon became apparent, however, that there were many more casualties than are named on the local memorials. Recognition of those whom work or military service had brought here or taken away was sometimes to be found in towns and villages elsewhere in the British Isles, and in a few instances even further afield. At least one man was buried locally after dying while billeted here. Several of the names appear on more than one memorial; some have seemingly been remembered only on the gravestones of relatives; the existence and fate of others is known only because their deaths were mentioned in local newspapers.

The place names throughout are as used in England at the time – Menin, Passchendaele, Poelcapelle, Ypres – but even exact dates and countries of death for many men could not be identified. Entries in the Registers of Soldiers' Effects often give a date followed by 'on or since, presumed dead' or 'in France or Belgium'. These servicemen, having no known graves, are commemorated on memorials located near the sites of the main areas of conflict.

Commonwealth War Graves Commission details have been simplified: only the cemetery or memorial name with grave or panel references are given. For burials with a three-part reference, the Roman numeral indicates the plot, the letter indicates the row, the number indicates the grave itself: Plot IX Row F Grave 27 is written IX F 27. For most memorials, numbers refer to panels or bays; for the Thiepval Memorial, numbers refer to piers and letters refer to the faces of those piers.

The efficiency of military record-keeping during these conflicts was astonishing but in some cases there would inevitably only ever be the sparsest of details. Additional information has occasionally come to light where letters home from soldiers have survived, describing their friends' deaths. Consequently, although the following biographies are the result of intensive research, it is impossible to know if all casualties have been identified.

1914 Monday 14 September: Private 7729 **Albert Bolton** aged 30 of 2nd Battalion the Worcesters died of wounds received during the Battle of the Aisne. Born in Wing, he and his family later lived in Bassett Road and at the age of 17 he was a stableman in Bridge Street. He enlisted in the Reserve in 1903 and in 1911 was working in a colliery, living in Wales with his wife and children. Husband of Mildred (Roberts) of 31 Friday Street; son of Henry and Elizabeth (Walter) Bolton of Wing. La Ferté-Sous-Jouarre Memorial.

1914 Monday 14 September: Lance Corporal 7673 **Jim Paxton** aged 30 of 2nd Battalion the Worcesters died during the Battle of the Aisne. He enlisted in 1903 and was recalled from the Reserve at the outbreak of war. In 1911 he was in Littleworth with his first wife Polly (Favell) and their sons, a carter on the Ascott Estate, but was widowed in 1912. Husband of Elsie Louise (Jeffs); son of William and Sarah (Pease) Paxton of High Street, Wing. La Ferté-sous-Jouarre Memorial.

1914 Monday 21 September: Shoeing Smith 12516 **Frederick Nicker** aged 36 of P Battery the Royal Horse Artillery died in Woolwich. Born George Frederick Lilliston, the son of George Edgar and Sarah (Forsdike) Lilliston, in Suffolk, he took the surname Nicklin when his widowed mother married James Nicklin. He enlisted as Frederick Nicker in 1895 as a shoeing smith, his previous occupation, and worked as a labourer at the Army Ordnance

Depot at Weedon between leaving the army and rejoining. Husband of Beatrice (Butcher) of 20 Soulbury Road. Woolwich Cemetery Plot II Grave 318.

1914 Tuesday 22 September: AB 203733 **Leopold Charles Burrows** aged 31 of the RN was one of the forty-eight crew who died when HMS *Hogue*, a Cressy-class armoured cruiser, was sunk with two of her sister ships 18 sea miles north-west of the Hook of Holland by the German submarine *U-9*. Originally a boy sailor, he had completed a twelve-year engagement by 1913, joined the Royal Fleet Reserve and was mobilised on the day war was declared. Husband of Alice Amelia (Tanner) of Brixton; son of William and Louisa (Curtis) Burrows of Hackney, formerly of South Street. Chatham Naval Memorial.

1914 Wednesday 14 October: Company Sergeant Major 6462 **Levi John Kimble** aged 32 of 1st Battalion the Bedfords died at No. 8 General Hospital, Rouen, of wounds probably received at Givenchy during the Battle of La Bassée. A regular soldier since 6 January 1899, he had served in South Africa, India and Ireland. Born in Loughton, Buckinghamshire, and registered as John, he used the name Levi in the army and married as Levi John Kimble. Husband of Ethel Kate (Ward) of Leighton; son of George and Mary Ann (Harris) of Shenley Brook End. Bois-Guillaume Communal Cemetery I A 13A.

1914 Wednesday 14 October: Private 9021 **Bert Turney** aged 27 of 1st Battalion the Kings Own (Royal Lancaster) Regiment died at 10th Field Ambulance, probably wounded during the Battle of Messines. A farm labourer before enlisting in Banbury in July 1906, he was in India in 1911 and went to France with the British Expeditionary Force in August 1914. Brother of **Alfred Henry Turney**; son of Robert and Ellen (Fiddler) Turney of Soulbury. Ploegsteert Memorial 2.

1914 Tuesday 20 October: Private 7670 **George Wells** aged 29 of 1st Battalion the Bedfords died at No. 2 London General Hospital, St Mark's College, Chelsea after surgery to amputate a leg damaged by shrapnel at the Battle of the Aisne. Born in Ivinghoe, by 1901 he had left the village for Hill Farm, Water Stratford where he was a groom. Husband of Gertrude Delphiner (Belfall) of Ivinghoe, formerly of Colchester; son of Arthur and Mary Ann (Windmill) Wells of Ivinghoe. Ivinghoe (St Mary), south of church.

1914 Monday 26 October: Private 8142 **Lewis Dyer** aged 31 of 1st Battalion the Bedfords died in action near Festubert. At the age of 2, he was with his mother and two siblings in Leighton Buzzard Workhouse; ten years later he was loading wagons at the lime works in Totternhoe and living with his grandmother, his younger sister and an uncle. By 1911 he had enlisted and was in 'Bermuda and Jamaica' with his regiment, but left the Reserve to live with his sister in Luton, where he worked for John Leon Frenay-Pirotte, appropriately enough a straw-hat dyer. Brother of **Sidney Dyer**; son of Sarah Dyer, late of Eaton Bray. Le Touret Memorial 10, 11.

1914 Monday 26 October: Private 9456 **William Robinson** aged 30 or 31 of 2nd Battalion the Bedfords died in action near Becelaere during the 1st Battle of Ypres. Born in Overstone, Northampton, he was living in Linslade soon afterwards. He was a regular soldier, enlisting in 1909 and seeing service in Bermuda and South Africa before arriving in France three weeks before his death. Son of Henry Levi and Emma Elizabeth (Murby) Robinson, stepson of Eunice (Pantling, formerly Kent) of 74 Old Road. Ypres (Menin Gate) Memorial 31, 33.

1914 Wednesday 28 October: Private 9377 **William Albert Hurkett** aged 18 of 2nd Battalion the South Staffords died near Frezenberg. He and his mother were both born in Leighton. Son of William and Ada Ann (Lancaster) Hurkett of Kensington. Ypres (Menin Gate) Memorial 35, 37.

1914 Wednesday 28 October: Private 8249 **Frank Charles Philips** aged 20 of 2nd Battalion the Scots Guards died in action near Gheluvelt. Born in his mother's birthplace of Leighton, his father a house-painter and vocalist from Antwerp, he was living in Camberwell by 1901 but was back by 30 June 1902 when he was admitted to Beaudesert School. They moved to Yorkshire shortly before 1911; Frank became an apprentice wool sorter, but he was a box maker when he enlisted. Son of Cornelius Leopold and Mary Agnes (Makepeace) Philips of Stanningley. Ypres (Menin Gate) Memorial 11.

1914 Wednesday 28 October: Private 8109 **Edward John Tew (Two)** aged 30 of 1st Battalion the Bedfords died while his battalion was supporting the front line at Festubert. By 1911 he was already serving abroad (enumerated in the census as Bermuda and Jamaica) with the 2nd Bedfords. Of 45 Vandyke Road; brother of **William Henry Tew (Two)**; son of Henry and Emma (Pilgrim) Two of Billington Crossing. Le Touret Memorial 10, 11.

1914 Sunday 1 November: Gunner 10860 **Frederick Arthur Paragreen** aged 29 of the Royal Marine Artillery died at the Battle of Coronel. Born in Heath and Reach, he was a baker's assistant at the age of 15. Husband of Mabel (Deveson) of Fulham; son of Hezekiah and Harriett Whetstone (Stevens, later Bierton) Paragreen of Gig Lane, Heath and Reach. Portsmouth Naval Memorial 5. (See also Chapter 7).

1914 Sunday 8 November: Private 3/7286 **George Pratt** aged 25 of 2nd Battalion the Bedfords died in action at Mons. Born in Leighton, he attended Beaudesert School and worked as a railway labourer before enlisting. Son of James and Jane (Timms, later Woolhead) Pratt and stepson of Albert Woolhead of 42 Mill Road. Ploegsteert Memorial 4.

1914 Sunday 8 November: Private 9519 **Jack Walker** aged 23 of 2nd Battalion the Bedfords was reported missing, death presumed. The 2nd Battalion were near Ploegsteert on 8 November with no casualties reported, but some men had been buried on 4 November. Born in Linslade, he was a regular soldier before the outbreak of the war. Son of John and Letitia (Oakes) of 38 New Road. Ploegsteert Memorial 4.

1914 Friday 20 November: Private 13577 **George Walter Holmes** aged 22 of 10th Battalion the Bedfords died at the Isolation Hospital, Harwich. Born in Heath and Reach, he was a farm labourer in the village until he enlisted. Son of John and Sarah Ann (Constable) Holmes of Lane's End, Heath and Reach. Dovercourt (All Saints) churchyard III E 10.

1914 Tuesday 24 November: Private 13750 **John William Crabb** aged 32 of B Company, 8th Battalion the East Yorkshires died at the Red Cross Hospital at the Corn Exchange, Leighton of pneumonia and malarial fever; his was the first death there. Husband of Mary Jane (Aitchison) and son of William and Theresa Thompson (Aire) Crabb, all of Hull. Hull (Hedon Road) Cemetery.

1914 Saturday 28 November: Private 15824 **Harold Rodgers** aged 19 of 10th Battalion the York and Lancasters died suddenly in his billet, 2a Soulbury Road. Born in Mexborough, he was a steel worker before enlisting. Son of Arthur and Fanny (Biggs) Rodgers of Kilnhurst, Yorkshire. Kilnhurst (St Thomas) Cemetery Extension B 8. (See also Chapter 10.)

1914 Thursday 3 December: Private 3/6053 **William James Dawson** aged 25 of 1st Battalion the Bedfords died in action in Belgium. Born in Leighton, he had attended Beaudesert School and was a bricklayer before enlisting. He had completed ten years' service, being called up as a reservist shortly after the outbreak of war. Husband of Rosie R (Smith); son of William Alfred and Sarah Ann (Webster) Dawson of 4 Chapel Path. Ypres (Menin Gate) Memorial 31, 3.

1914 Sunday 20 December: Second Lieutenant **Harold Augustus Rupert Tooley MM★** aged 35 of 1st Battalion the Royal Guernsey Light Infantry, attached to 2nd Battalion the Leicestershires, died in action at Givenchy. He was born in Leighton, where his father was a corn dealer. In 1901 he was working as a clerk, presumably in the family forage business, and by 1911 was manager of Town Mills in St Peter Port, Guernsey. He enlisted in the RGLI in November 1914 and left Guernsey for Le Havre a month later with 2nd Battalion the Duke of Cornwall's Light Infantry. Husband of Zelie Laine (Hocart) of 1 George Place, Union Street, Guernsey; son of Alfred William and Caroline (Simmons) Tooley of The Osiers, Linslade. Le Touret Memorial 47. (See also Chapter 16.)

1915 Friday 1 January: Ordinary Seaman SS/4976 **John Ashby** aged 18 of HMS *Formidable* was lost when the vessel was torpedoed during an exercise in the English Channel. Born in Streatley, he enlisted on 28 May 1914, having previously worked as a sand carter. Son of Charles Samuel and Sarah (Peck) Ashby of Potsgrove. Chatham Naval Memorial 10.

1915 Saturday 9 January: Private 4878 **Richard James Hyde** aged 21 of 5th Battalion the Bedfords died while training in Newmarket, 'a sufferer from fits and it was in one of these that death took place'. Born in Leighton, he attended Beaudesert School and was a few miles away in Water Eaton in 1911, a 'farm labourer, do anything', before returning to enlist. The date of death on his burial record is 10 January, the address 26 Regent Street. Son of Benjamin and Ellen (Campkin) Hyde of 28 Vandyke Road. Leighton-Linslade Cemetery A 215.

1915 Wednesday 27 January: Private 8617 **Henry 'Harry' Dickens** aged 18 of 3rd Battalion the O&BLI died at the Alexandra Hospital, Cosham after being wounded. He was born in the Tower Hamlets of Stewkley parents who had returned to the village by 1901 and had a connection with Soulbury. Son of John and Emily (Dickens) Dickens of Dunton Road Stewkley. Stewkley (St Michael) churchyard.

1915 Wednesday 10 February: Second Lieutenant **William Crabtree** aged 18 of 8th Battalion the Lincolns died at Tring Military Hospital after a road accident in the early hours of the morning between Startops and Tring Ford reservoirs; he was a passenger in a taxi which overturned after a tyre burst. While stationed with his regiment in Linslade, he had been billeted at Castle House. Son of William Henry Robinson and Helen (Blagbrough) Crabtree of Doncaster. Doncaster Hyde Park Cemetery.

1915 Friday 5 March: Private 10594 **Samuel George Coker** aged 21 of 1st Battalion the Welsh Regiment died at 15th Field Ambulance in Belgium after being wounded. Born in Pitstone, he was a farm worker. Of Tring; brother of **Alfred Coker**; son of James Thomas and Sarah (Shillingford) Coker of Town Houses, Pitstone formerly of Pitstone Church End Cottages. Dranouter Churchyard II B 8.

1915 Friday 12 March: Second Lieutenant **Robert Harold Strong** aged 29 of 2nd Battalion the East Surreys died in action at Neuve Chapelle. His captain wrote: 'He was walking round the billets when the enemy started shelling and was observing the results of the bursting shells when one pitched close to him and mortally wounded him.' His parents having separated by 1899, he enlisted at the age of 15, attended the Royal Military School of Music at Twickenham and was Acting Bandmaster with his regiment in Burma. Brother of **Benjamin Clarence Strong** and **Francis William Cooper Strong** (alias **John Stewart**); son of Robert Bennett and Linda Elizabeth (Cooper, later Turner) Strong of Hampstead, formerly of Heath and Reach. Loker Churchyard II C 20.

1915 Saturday 27 March: Private L/7532 **John Freeman** aged 30 of 16th (The Queen's) Lancers died of pneumonia at the Military Hospital, Curragh Camp in County Kildare. Born in Mentmore, he was working on his father's farm in 1911. Son of William and Frances Elizabeth (Woodman) Freeman of Checkley Wood Farm, Hockliffe. Curragh Military Cemetery, County Kildare Grave 1210.

1915 Tuesday 20 April: Private 3/7465 **Cyril Samuel Meakins** aged 20 of 1st Battalion the Bedfords died at No. 3 Casualty Clearing Station (CCS), Poperinghe after being wounded defending Hill 60 (17 April–7 May) during the 2nd Battle of Ypres. He attended Eaton Bray school and worked at the lime works in Totternhoe, the first man from the village to die in the war. Son of Arthur William and Emma (Fountain, later Ward, later Pratt) Meakins, stepson of George Pratt of Bower Lane, Eaton Bray. Poperinghe Old Military Cemetery II M 43.

1915 Wednesday 21 April: Private 14315 **Henry Hagger Wood** aged 27 of 1st Battalion the Bedfords died in action at Hill 60. Born in Sandon, Hertfordshire, he moved to Heath and Reach, following brother William, and later enlisted there. A court case against him for the theft of beer in Heath in 1912 was dismissed on the grounds that he had been teetotal for many years, but another the following year left him with the choice of fourteen days' hard labour or a 10s fine for trespass and poaching. Considering the nature of his crime, he was unlikely to have been able to pay. His surname is sometimes hyphenated. Son of Joseph and Rebecca (Manning) Hagger Wood of Sandon. Ypres (Menin Gate) Memorial 31, 33.

1915 Wednesday 21 April: Private 3/6054 **John 'Jack' Lawson** aged 25 of 1st Battalion the Bedfords died in action at Hill 60. Born in Leighton, he attended Beaudesert School and was a general labourer at a sand pit before enlisting. Husband of Sarah (Brandon) of 55 Church Street; son of William and Jane (Hubbins) Lawson of 50 St Andrew's Street. Ypres (Menin Gate) Memorial 31, 33.

1915 Wednesday 21 April: Private 13852 **Thomas Underwood** aged 27 of 1st Battalion the Bedfords died in action at Hill 60. A hawker of fruit and flowers, he was a reservist in the Bedfords for eight years, and was mobilised at the outbreak of war, reaching France in November 1914. Husband of Ethel (Smith, later Povey) of Kent, formerly of 16 Baker Street; son of David and Mary (Cotching) Underwood of 23 Soulbury Road, formerly of 104 St Andrew's Street. Ypres (Menin Gate) Memorial 31, 33.

1915 Thursday 22 April: Sergeant 7001 **Ernest John Rowe** aged 31 of No. 2 Company, 1st Battalion the Canadian Infantry, formerly of 29th Waterloo Regiment, died near Vlamertinghe during the 2nd Battle of Ypres on the first day that chlorine gas was used by the Germans. His family, all of them born in Leighton, had settled in Aldershot by 1891. Already in Canada, he was a machinist and had enlisted in the militia before the outbreak of war. Husband of Frances Emma (Docksey) of Ontario; son of John William and Mary (Scott) Rowe of Aldershot; grandson of George and Ann (Pratt) Rowe, late of 6 Back Lane. Ypres (Menin Gate) Memorial 10, 26-28.

1915 Friday 23 April: Lance Corporal 3/3333 **Samuel White** aged 38 of 1st Battalion the York and Lancasters, formerly 4182 of 3rd Battalion the Scots Guards, was reported missing, death presumed, during the Battle of Gravenstafel Ridge. He volunteered soon after war was declared, having previously served for eight years. He was born in Linslade but moved to Nottinghamshire, was a labourer in a glue factory in 1911 and a miner when he enlisted. Son of Andrew and Ann White (Quick) of 14 Soulbury Road. Ypres (Menin Gate) Memorial 36, 55.

1915 Sunday 25 April: Private 511 **Alexander McCubbin** aged 21 of 10th Battalion the Australian Infantry died on the Gallipoli Peninsula. Born in Leighton, he had attended Beaudesert School and was apprenticed to a wholesale hosier before he boarded the P&O liner *Beltana* on 9 July 1912, leaving Liverpool for Melbourne, Australia via the Cape. The passenger list shows him listed as a clerk, and intending his future permanent residence to be Australia. He settled in Broken Hill, mining until he enlisted. Son of James George and Harriette (Lambert) McCubbin of Lake Street, formerly of 35 High Street. Lone Pine Memorial 32.

1915 Tuesday 27 April: Private 937 **George Lewis Holland** aged 28 of 1st Battalion the Lancashire Fusiliers died of wounds sustained on 25 April in the storming of W Beach during the landing at Cape Helles. Already in the regular army, he was in India at the outbreak of war. Son of Ambrose and Mary Ann (Jelley) Holland of 40 Springfield Road. Helles Memorial 66A.

1915 Wednesday 5 May: Private 13035 **Henry John King** aged 30 of 1st Battalion the Bedfords died in action at Hill 60. Born in Tilsworth, he was already married by 1911 and was a lime burner, probably at Totternhoe. Husband of Ethel Emily (Perry, later Kesteven) of Dunstable; brother of **Archie William King**; son of Alfred and Sarah Ann (Timms) King of Tilsworth. Bedford House Cemetery Enclosure No. 4 XI D 7.

1915 Wednesday 5 May: Private 29216 **George Potts** aged 53 of the RAMC died at the Royal Victoria Hospital, Netley after being wounded. Born in Billington, he was a foreman house painter on the Earl of Rosebery's estate in Mentmore. Husband of Selina Annie (James); son of James and Jemima (Seabrook) Potts of Billington. Netley Military Cemetery CE 1685.

1915 Sunday 9 May: Private 2669 **Mark Page** aged 18 of 1/4th Battalion the Seaforth Highlanders died in action near Aubers. Brother of **Lionel Page**;

uncle of **Arthur William Page**; son of George and Rebecca (Woolhead) Page of 52 Springfield Road. Le Touret Memorial 38, 39.

1915 Tuesday 11 May: Private 8002 **William George Holme**s aged 22 of 1st Battalion the Suffolks died after being wounded in action. Born in Islington, he attended Beaudesert School, enlisted in Leighton and by 1911 was already with his regiment in Aldershot. Only child of Police Constable William John Holmes and Sarah Matilda (Richley) of 6 Fern Cottages, 6 George Street. Tyne Cot Cemetery LXII C 13.

1915 Sunday 16 May: Second Lieutenant **William Godfrey Willoughby Garforth** aged 32 of 2nd Battalion the Scots Guards, formerly the Special Reserve of Officers, died in action during the Battle of Festubert. His mother was a daughter of the 8th Baron Middleton and he was born in Yorkshire and educated at Charterhouse School, Godalming before living in Burcott where he was well known as the land agent of the Ascott Estate: he opened the batting for Ascott cricket team, hunted with Lord Rothschild's staghounds and served on the committee of Buckinghamshire County Cricket Club. Of Ascott; son of William Henry and the Honourable Hylda Maria Madeline (Willoughby) Garforth. Pont-Du-Hem Military Cemetery X C 12.

1915 Thursday 27 May: Stoker Petty Officer 170472 **John Orchard** aged 48 of the Royal Navy was one of 352 people killed when HMS *Princess Irene* exploded while being loaded with mines in the Medway Estuary. Born and brought up in Soulbury, he was a farm labourer before enlisting in November 1892 and had risen to the rank of petty officer before the war. By 1911 he had already apparently been married to Alice Maud Mary for three years and was living in Rainham. Son of Joseph and Martha (Foskett) Orchard late of Soulbury. Chatham Naval Memorial 11.

1915 Saturday 29 May: Private 2900 **Charles Arthur Howe** aged 19 of 1st Buckinghamshire Battalion the O&BLI died of gunshot wounds received in trenches at Ploegsteert. He was born in Rugby, but moved with his family to Linslade in 1903 where he was a bell ringer at St Barnabas Church, and worked for the L&NWR until enlisting soon after war was declared. Son of Alfred and Sarah Ann (Farmer) Howe of 49 New Road. Boulogne Eastern Cemetery VIII A 54.

1915 Tuesday 20 July: Private 13553 **Joseph Smith** aged 25 of 1st Battalion the Bedfords, formerly of 4th Battalion, died at the Abbey Hospital Woburn.

A journeyman carpenter born in Leighton, he trained at Dovercourt after enlisting and was drafted to 1st Battalion on 27 April 1915. While in action at the Battle for Hill 60, he had escaped injury when shrapnel shattered his rifle butt. Only son of David and Mary Ann (Smith) Smith of 11 Regent Street. Leighton-Linslade Cemetery B 588.

1915 Saturday 7 August: Trooper 325 **Arthur Albert Pearson** aged 25 of B Squadron Original the 10th Australian Light Horse Regiment died in action during the assault on the Nek at Walkers Ridge. Born in Leighton, he worked for Mary Bates at Hill Farm, Whipsnade before leaving for Perth, Western Australia some time after 1911 and was again a farm hand when he enlisted in Guildford, Perth in the Australian Imperial Force on 23 October 1914. On 8 February 1915 he embarked from Fremantle on HMAT *Mashobra*. Son of William and Emma (Millis) Pearson of 12 Dudley Street. Ari Burnu Cemetery F 38.

1915 Sunday 15 August: Private 2846 **Frederick Ernest Perry** aged 21 of 1/5th Battalion the Bedfords died in action in Gallipoli. From a letter to his mother from Lieutenant Colonel Edgar William Brighten, commanding his battalion: 'He was known to be hit badly, and I imagine... that he was hit again and killed as he lay on the ground or while he was trying to get away... and I am only sorry that I can give you no further details. As you know, he was one of my own Headquarters Section, and he had been sent to Brigade Headquarters with a message from me. From this errand he never returned.' Born in Newton Longville, he had moved with his family to Leighton by 1911 where he worked for Thomas Brantom & Co., cattle cake manufacturers, later enlisting there. Son of David and Mary Jane (Horne) Perry of 11 Queen Street. Helles Memorial 54, 218.

1915 Monday 16 August: Private 5037 **George Robert Farnham** aged 20 of 5th Battalion the Bedfords died at Suvla Bay, Gallipoli in his first battle. Born in Orpington, he was a farm labourer, and arrived in Eaton Bray with his family after the 1911 census was taken. Son of John and Fanny (Brigden) Farnham of Dunstable, late of Eaton Bray. Helles Memorial 55, 218.

1915 Friday 20 August: Private 2269 **Lionel Jordan** aged 29 of 4th Battalion the Yorkshires died when hit by an enemy shell in a trench near Armentières. Born in Wing, he became first footman to Sir Hugh Bell Bt, the Lord Lieutenant of North Yorkshire, and enlisted in Northallerton. He had been in France for four months when he died. Brother of **Joseph George Jordan**; son of Henry and Mary (Brown) Jordan of Prospect Place, Wing. Chapelle-D'Armentières Old Military Cemetery D.

1915 Saturday 21 August: Private 1745 **Dennis Arthur Horne** aged 23 of the Royal Bucks Hussars (1/1st Buckinghamshire Yeomanry) was presumed to have died during the Battle of Scimitar Hill on the Gallipoli peninsula. Having enlisted in October 1914, he was in Egypt in April 1915 and moved from there to fight unmounted at Gallipoli. Born in Stewkley, he worked on the family farm. Youngest son of Edwin and Sarah Ann (Coleman) Horne of South Cottesloe Farm, Wing. Helles Memorial 17.

1915 Saturday 21 August: Private 1775 **Harry Archibald Thorpe** aged 19 of the 1/1st Berkshire Yeomanry presumed to have died fighting dismounted, during the Battle of Scimitar Hill. Born in Leicester, he had worked as a baker's assistant and moved to the Leighton area shortly before WW1. Son of Charles William and Emily Elizabeth (Bridger) Thorpe. Helles Memorial 18 and 19.

1915 Sunday 22 August: Private 15557 **Albert Bird** aged 36 of 9th Battalion the West Yorkshire Regiment (Prince of Wales's Own) died in action in Gallipoli. He was born in Houghton Regis where his parents kept the Crown, but his father then turned poultry dealer and the family settled in Chalgrave. By 1901 he had moved to Luton to work as a straw-plait dyer in the hat trade. Son of Daniel and Sarah (Pratt) Bird of Tebworth. Helles Memorial Panels 47-51.

1915 Sunday 29 August: Private 6325 **Herbert Hodge** aged 19 of 10th Battalion the Royal Warwickshires died in action in France. Born in Rhayader, Radnorshire, he and his family moved around the country with his father's labouring jobs, eventually arriving in Heath and Reach. Son of William and Eliza Jane (White) Hodge of the Axe and Compass, Heath and Reach. Le Touret Memorial 6.

1915 Sunday 29 August: Trooper 889 **George Thomas Rose** aged 23 of 4th Reinforcements the 10th Light Horse Regiment, Australian Imperial Force, died during the assault on Hill 60 Anzac. Born in Fenny Stratford, he was a baker's assistant and a bandsman and songster in the Salvation Army. On 22 November 1912 he was aboard *Orsova* of the Orient Line, leaving London for Fremantle, Australia. On 7 January 1915 he enlisted in the AIF in Perth and on 13 April that year embarked with the 3rd Light Horse Brigade from Fremantle on HMAT A8 *Argyllshire*. The address he gave was that of a Mr Culling of

Walywin, Wickepin. Son of Henry and Amelia (Woolhead, later Bates) Rose of 46 Union Street. Lone Pine Memorial 10.

1915 Tuesday 31 August: Private 4327 **Alec Joseph Faulkner** aged 20 of 5th Battalion the Bedfords died of wounds in Gallipoli a few weeks after arriving there. Born in Leighton, he attended Ashton Grammar School in Dunstable and was a solicitor's clerk for Messrs Pettit, Walton and Co. before enlisting. He had been in one of the first drafts sent to the Dardanelles. Son of William and Sarah Ann (Timpson) Faulkner of Pear Tree Cottage, Heath Road. Helles Memorial 54, 218.

1915 Monday 6 September: Private 4735 **Harold Arthur Quick** aged 19 of A Company, 1/5th Battalion the Bedfords died after being wounded in Gallipoli. Born in Leighton, he had been a captain at Beaudesert School and was a Salvation Army bandsman, playing tenor horn and cornet. He was apprenticed as as carpenter with Albert Edward Sear when he enlisted. Son of Alfred James and Clara (Hobbs) Quick of 70 Hockliffe Road. Helles Memorial 54, 218.

1915 Wednesday 8 September: Private 13550 **James Smith** aged 20 of 1st Battalion the Bedfords died at No. 5 CCS in Corbie, having been wounded in the neck three days earlier. Born in Leighton, he worked for the local building firm of David Cook and Sons. He enlisted in August 1914 and was posted to France in March 1915. Brother of **Robert Smith**; son of William and Agnes (Ellaway) Smith of 70 St Andrew's Street. Corbie Communal Cemetery I A 28.

1915 Thursday 23 September: Private 13034 **Archie William King** aged 28 of 2nd Battalion the Bedfords died of wounds in France. Born in Tilsworth, he first worked on a farm but later dyed straw-plait at home; for several years a member of Stanbridge and Tilsworth Cricket Club, he had been in France since February. Brother of **Henry John King**; son of Alfred and Sarah Ann (Timms) King of Tilsworth. Chocques Military Cemetery I D 117.

1915 Saturday 25 September: Lance Sergeant 9434 **William John Brandom** aged 24 of 2nd Battalion the Bedfords died after being shot through the heart during the Battle of Loos. Born in Leighton, he was already with the Regiment at Maida Barracks in Aldershot by 1911. Son of Joseph and Sarah Jane (Scrivener) Brandom formerly of 17 Mill Road. Loos Memorial 41.

1915 Saturday 25 September: Private 18591 **Baron Percy Gale** aged 16 of 5th Battalion the O&BLI died during an assault on the ruins of Bellewaarde Farm. Born on 27 October 1898 in Cheddington, he almost certainly lied about his age when he enlisted at Watford soon after the outbreak of war; he was the first and the youngest casualty from the village. Son of Arthur and Agnes (Thompson, later Fitzroy) Gale of Aylesbury, formerly of Cheddington. Ypres (Menin Gate) Memorial 37, 39.

1915 Saturday 25 September: Private 3/6845 **John Major** aged 22 of A Company, 2nd Battalion the Bedfords, formerly of 3rd Battalion, died after being shot in the head at Loos, having already been wounded twice. Born in Leighton, he was a bricklayer's labourer and had already served for six years in the Bedfordshire Territorials Special Reserve when war broke out. He was transferred to 2nd Battalion when they returned from South Africa and fought in several actions. Son of George and Mary Jane (Sturman) Major and stepson of Beatrice Florence (Fountain) Major of 32 Bedford Street. Loos Memorial 41.

1915 Sunday 26 September: Private 7771 **James Bull** aged 31 of 2nd Battalion the Worcesters died in action at Loos. A cowman on a farm, he enlisted in 1903 and was recalled from the Reserve in August 1914. Son of Joseph and Sarah (Woolhead) Bull of Crafton. Loos Memorial 64, 65.

1915 Sunday 26 September: Private 13632 **James Henry Holland** aged 27 of 10th Battalion the York and Lancasters was reported missing, presumed dead, during the Battle of Loos. A cutler before enlisting in September 1914, he was billeted in Linslade during the winter of 1914-1915. Husband of Eva May (Millins) Holland of 21 Waterloo Road; son of John and Elizabeth (Hurt) Holland of Sheffield. Loos Memorial 105, 106.

1915 Sunday 26 September: Private G/3748 **Horace Sidney Tompkins** aged 20 of 8th Battalion the Queen's Own Royal West Kent Regiment was reported missing, death presumed, near Loos. He had been apprenticed to a carpenter, probably his father, before enlisting in Willesden, where his mother had relatives. Son of Ernest John and Matilda Emma (Allison) Tompkins of High Street, Cheddington. Loos Memorial 95-97.

1915 Tuesday 28 September: CSM L/7619 **Edwin White** aged 33 of 2nd Battalion the Buffs (East Kent Regiment), formerly 5740 of 3rd Battalion, died in action leading his men in an attack on Fosse 8 near the Hohenzollern

Redoubt. He first enlisted in 1899 while working in a hotel in Ramsgate and served in the Boer War before buying himself out and returning to his family home. He was a postman before re-enlisting in 1903 in the 2nd Battalion, then served in South Africa, Hong Kong, Singapore and India before his posting to France in January 1915; he was promoted to Company Sergeant Major in July that year. Son of Edwin and Bessie (Guess) White of 24 Wing Road. Loos Memorial 15-19.

1915 Thursday 30 September: Private 18252 **George Jenkins** aged 21 of 2nd Battalion the Bedfords died a day after being wounded during the Battle of Loos. Born in Ramsbury, near Marlborough, he came to Clipstone with his family in the late 1880s and by 1911 was a farm worker in Hockliffe. At Woburn Sessions in October 1913 he was ordered to pay costs of 7s 6d for riding a bicycle without a light at 11.30 p.m. He enlisted in November 1914 and trained at Ampthill. Husband of Florence Rose (Bleaney) of Hockliffe; son of George and Harriet (Miller) Jenkins of Reads Farm, Hockliffe. Étaples Military Cemetery IV H 9.

1915 Thursday 30 September: Private L/15481 **Edward John Randall** aged 18 of 4th Battalion the Middlesex Regiment died in action during a counter-attack on the enemy near Sanctuary Wood; he had been in France for two months. A labourer like his father, he was the son of Robert and Elizabeth (Smith) Randall of Rose Terrace, Littleworth. Ypres (Menin Gate) Memorial 49, 51.

1915 Thursday 30 September: Private 2720 **Thomas Rogers** aged 31 of 1/4th Battalion the Northamptonshires died at sea, on HMHS *Glenart Castle*, after being wounded at Gallipoli. He was born in Dunstable but was with his parents in Chicheley in 1901, marrying and remaining there as horsekeeper on a farm in Eakley Lanes when they moved to Pitstone. Husband of Bertha Rose (Ellis, later Umney), of Chicheley; son of Edwin and Eliza (Kempston) Rogers of Town House, Pitstone. Helles Memorial Panel 156.

1915 Friday 8 October: Private 74104 **Robert Joseph Turney** aged 23 of 28th Battalion the Canadian Infantry (Saskatchewan Regiment) died in Belgium. Born in Slapton, he worked on the family farm until leaving for Canada some time after the census was taken in England in 1911. On his attestation papers he gave his forenames as Robert James. Son of Joseph and Maria (Turney) Turney of Church Farm, Slapton. Ypres (Menin Gate) Memorial 18, 26, 28.

1915 Wednesday 13 October: Second Lieutenant **John Trude Fripp** aged 28 of 4th Battalion the Lincolnshires died in action in the front-line trenches at Bois Grenier, shortly after the Battle of Loos. Born in Willesden, he had moved to Leighton with his Leighton-born mother by 1901; he was a member of Bees House at Berkhamsted School 1900–02 and is commemorated on their memorial website. Like his father, he became a dental surgeon. Son of John Trude and Elizabeth Flemons (Emery) Fripp of 10 Church Square. Loos Memorial 31–34.

1915 Saturday 16 October: Private 12576 **Frederick Joseph Tofield** aged 21 of 6th Battalion the O&BLI died in a front line trench south-west of Armentières. Born in Soulbury, a farm labourer, he volunteered soon after war was declared and had been in France for about three months when he died. Son of William Francis and Sarah (Tearle) Tofield of Brook Cottages, Soulbury. Rue-Du-Bacquerot No. 1 Military Cemetery II D 26.

1915 Wednesday 27 October: Private G/4869 **Edward George Adams** aged 25 of 13th Battalion the Duke of Cambridge's Own (Middlesex) Regiment died at No. 10 CCS at Remy Sidings (Lijssenthoek) soon after being shot in the throat. Born in Leighton, he was an underman for the L&NWR at Willesden Depot and in May 1915 had married a Leighton girl whose family were also living there; her father, too, worked for the L&NWR. After enlisting in Willesden while living in Harlesden, he was sent to the Front with the Regiment on 1 September 1915. Son of **Frederick Adams**; husband of Lily Louisa (Baines) of 117 Vandyke Road; one of four serving sons of Frederick and Edith (Toms) Adams of 31 Mill Road. Lijssenthoek Military Cemetery I B 34.

1915 Thursday 28 October: Sapper **Joseph Rickard** aged 42 of 1/3rd Kent Field Company the RE died when HMS *Hythe*, en route from Mudros, sank 50 miles off Cape Helles in Gallipoli, following a collision. Born and brought up in Wingrave, he was a bricklayer, like his father. Husband of Martha (Mardell) of 8 Plumtree Cottages, Pitstone; son of George and Ellen (Gurney) Rickard of Wingrave. Helles Memorial 24–26 or 325–328.

1915 Sunday 14 November: Lance Corporal 1482 **Edwin Joseph Whiting** aged 26 of 1/1st Battalion the Hertfordshire Yeomanry, the Household Cavalry and the Cavalry of the Line, died in hospital in Malta. He was born in Heath and Reach and moved to Watford with his family, later working as a clerk with the L&NWR. Son of Edwin and Alice Sarah (Roberts) Whiting of Watford, formerly of Heath Green, Heath and Reach. Pietà Military Cemetery D VI 6.

1915 Tuesday 28 December: Private 16389 **Leonard George Whitbread** aged 26 of 8th Battalion the Bedfords died after being hit by shrapnel near Poperinghe. He was born in New Bradwell where his father was a tailor but had moved via Chalgrave to Leighton with his family between 1901 and 1911 and had attended Beaudesert School, being a well-known local footballer. By the time he enlisted in Leighton he was a tinsmith with Messrs Cooper and Co., ironmongers, of Market Square. Husband of Clara (Rolls) formerly of Queen Street; son of George and Clara Emily (Cockerell) Whitbread of 30 St Andrew's Street. Ypres (Menin Gate) Memorial 31, 33.

1916 Saturday 11 January: Private T/969 **Arthur John Beckett** aged 30 of 1/5th Battalion (Territorial Force) the West Surreys, attached to 2nd Battalion the Norfolk Regiment, died in the action to break the siege by the Turks of the British-Indian garrison at Kut Al Amara, Mesopotamia. Son of Thomas Roberts and Emily (Cox) Beckett of Cublington. Kut War Cemetery H 13.

1916 Sunday 23 January: Private 406381 **Percival Rose** aged 24 of 19th Battalion the Canadian Infantry (Central Ontario Regiment) died after being struck by a bomb in the trenches in Belgium. Born in Heath and Reach, he was an assistant to grocer Thomas Albert Jeffery at 13-15 Market Square before emigrating to Canada. On 11 April 1913 he was on board *Virginia* of the Allen Line at Liverpool, bound for Halifax, Nova Scotia. Son of John and Louisa (Goldney) Rose of Heath Green, Heath and Reach. Ridge Wood Military Cemetery I M 3.

1916 Friday 4 February: Private 18481 **James Adams** aged 35 of 2nd Battalion the Bedfords, formerly of 3rd Battalion, died in shellfire in the trenches at Suzanne, near Maricourt. Born in Billington, by 1891 he and his family were in Leighton where he attended Beaudesert School and was a sandpit labourer for George Garside, his father being a foreman there. After military training for eight months at Ampthill, he went with his regiment to France in 1915. He had enlisted in the militia in 1901 for six years but had purchased his discharge for £1 in August 1904. Husband of Alice (Dawson) and one of several serving sons of Josiah and Alice (Lee) Adams, all of 72 Plantation Road. Cerisy-Gailly Military Cemetery II E 2.

1916 Thursday 10 February: Private 2720 **Percy Thomas Bodsworth** aged 20 of 1/1st Buckinghamshire Battalion the O&BLI died in shellfire in a trench near Hébuterne, leading a party of stretcher bearers. Born in Linslade, he was a clerk on the L&NWR before enlisting and a member of the St Barnabas's Church Lads' Brigade. Youngest child of George and Rebecca (Stevens) Bodsworth of 28 Old Road. Hébuterne Military Cemetery I A 6.

1916 Tuesday 28 March: Private 4092 **Arthur Wadelin** aged 40 of 1/1st Buckinghamshire Battalion the O&BLI died in shellfire in a trench at Hébuterne. Born in Warrington, when he enlisted he was at Liscombe Park, Soulbury in his fourth post as butler, having previously worked in Essex, Birmingham, Lancashire and Yorkshire. Husband of Alice Jessie (Broad) of Liscombe Park, later of St Faith's, Ashwell Street; son of Samuel and Hannah (Birch) Wadelin, late of Warrington. Hébuterne Military Cemetery I A 2.

1916 Friday 31 March: Private 12527 **Sidney Guess** aged 22 of 6th Battalion the O&BLI died in shellfire in a trench at Essex Farm, north of Ypres. Born in Wing, he worked on a farm before enlisting. Son of George Guess and Jane (Woolhead) Guess of Rothschild Road, Wing. Essex Farm Cemetery I J 5.

1916 Tuesday 11 April: Private 22216 **Edward Joseph 'Ted' Plummer** aged 19 of 4th Battalion the Grenadier Guards died on patrol duty in Ypres. Nephew of **Alfred George Plumme**r; son of Hattil James and Kate (Viccars) Plummer of Towcester; grandson of John and Ann (Hyde) Plummer of High Street, formerly of Mill Road. Potijze Burial Ground Cemetery D.

1916 Monday 24 April: Gunner 69821 **William Charles Meager** aged 35 of 32nd Company the Royal Garrison Artillery (RGA) died at Parkhurst Hospital, Isle of Wight, having sustained a severe head injury in a diving accident. Born in Leighton, he had been a steward on the P&O liner *Salsette*. He had enlisted only a few months before his death and was on duty as an officers' servant. Husband of Annie Augusta Brockless (Hobbs) of 26 Waterloo Road; son of William and Annie (Wilmore) Meager of Wing. Parkhurst Military Cemetery XI A 92.

1916 Tuesday 25 April: Private 13874 **Charles Hall** aged 27 of 5th Battalion the Duke of Edinburgh's (Wiltshire) Regiment, formerly 14147 the O&BLI, died in action in Mesopotamia. Born in Leighton, he attended Beaudesert School, and while living in Stony Stratford and working in the family greengrocery business, he enlisted in Wolverton. Of Watford; son of Amos and

Emma Jane (Atkins) Hall of Stony Stratford, formerly of 5 Summer Street. Amara War Cemetery XX D 8.

1916 Thursday 4 May: Private 12033 **George Keen** aged 20 of 6th Battalion the Bedfords died of wounds near Monchy-au-Bois. Born in Linslade, he attended Beaudesert School and left to be an errand boy in Leighton until he enlisted in Watford. Son of Thomas and Mary (Morris) Keen and stepson of Mary Ann (Ellingham) Keen of 4 Ashwell Street. St Amand British Cemetery I A 3.

1916 Friday 5 May: Private 23496 **Albert Edward Saunders** aged 33 of 7th Battalion the Princess Victoria's (Royal Irish Fusiliers) died near Loos. He was born in Leighton but had moved to Watford with his family after his mother's death in 1895. Husband of Alice Eleanor (Child); son of Alfred and Jane (Bodsworth) Saunders of Watford, formerly of Plantation Road. Loos Memorial 124.

1916 Sunday 7 May: Private 401702 **Ernest Brazier** aged 21 of 49th Battalion the Canadian Infantry, a stretcher bearer, died in shellfire trying to reach a wounded comrade in a trench near Hooge. Born in Linslade, after working as a farm labourer and at the Faith Press in Wing Road he emigrated to Canada in 1912 and enlisted in London, Ontario in March 1915. Son of Harry and Elizabeth (Halsey) Brazier of 30 Wing Road. His grave was destroyed in a later battle. Special Memorial, Sanctuary Wood Cemetery.

1916 Wednesday 10 May: Sapper 158742 **Amos Thompson** aged 27 of 4th Provisional Company the Royal Engineers died of pneumonia in Kent. He was born in Heath and Reach where he and his father were carpenters. Husband of Mabel Florence (Cowley) of Lane's End, Heath and Reach; son of Alfred John and Maria (Dancer) Thompson of Pear Tree Cottage, Heath and Reach. Heath and Reach Cemetery Grave B 47.

1916 Wednesday 31 May: Private 3255 **Lawrence Braham Claridge** aged 34 of 1/4th (City of London) Battalion (Royal Fusiliers) died at No. 19 CCS, Doullens. He had already served in Malta, Egypt and the trenches of the Dardanelles. Born in Surrey, he still lived there in 1901 with his parents but by 1911 was a clerk at the Anglo-South American Bank in Chile before enlisting in October 1914. His father came from Stony Stratford, his mother from Somerset. Son of George Frederick and Frances (Pitt) Claridge of 6 Grove Road. Doullens Communal Cemetery Extension No.1 I C 14.

1916 Wednesday 31 May: Able Seaman J/16898 **George Arthur King** aged 21 of HMS *Defence* died with the rest of the ship's complement at the Battle of Jutland. The *Defence* was escorting the Grand Fleet and was hit by two salvoes from a German battlecruiser. The rear magazine was detonated and fire spread to the secondary magazines, which also exploded. Born in Plymouth, after his parents died in 1904 and 1908 he was adopted by his uncle and aunt Henry John and Mary Agnes (Meacham) King of Market Square with whom he lived at 14 Grove Road while attending Beaudesert School and working first for his uncle and then for Cecil Roberts as a hairdresser's assistant until he joined the navy in 1912. Son of George and Emma Blanche Johns (Nicholson) King, late of Wolvercote. Plymouth Naval Memorial 12.

1916 Wednesday 31 May: Midshipman **Cyril Henry Gerald Summers** aged 17 of HMS *Defatigable* died at the Battle of Jutland. Son of Frank and Marjorie (Pryor) Summers of Padbury, formerly of Leighton. Plymouth Naval Memorial. (See also Chapter 7)

1916 Wednesday 31 May: Boy 1st Class J/38258 **Reginald Thomas Varney** aged 16 of HMS *Black Prince* died during the Battle of Jutland. Son of Alfred and Annie (Fookes) Varney of Newport Pagnell, formerly of Ledburn; grandson of Henry and Maria (Green) Varney of Ledburn. Portsmouth Naval Memorial 14. (See also Chapter 7)

1916 Friday 2 June: Boy 1st Class J/42563 **John 'Jack' Travers Cornwell VC★** aged 16 of the Royal Navy died after being wounded on HMS *Chester* during the Battle of Jutland. Born in Leyton, Essex, he was one of several children from his father's long partnership with Lily King, late of the Falcon, Billington Road. Son of Eli Cornwell and Lily King of Commercial Road, Stepney. Manor Park Cemetery. (See also Chapter 7)

1916 Saturday 3 June: Officer's Steward 3rd Class L\7460 **Alfred Cooper** aged 21 of shore base HMS *Victory I* died of wounds received in action on 31 May on board HMS *Malaya* during the Battle of Jutland. He was a baker's assistant before enlisting. Son of James and Rachael (Stevens) Cooper of Cheddington. Rosskeen Parish Churchyard Extensions or Burial Ground C 378.

1916 Monday 5 June: Private 112095 **Harry Money** aged 22 of 5th Canadian Mounted Rifles (Quebec Regiment) died at St John Ambulance Brigade Hospital, Étaples. He was evacuated there after being wounded by shrapnel as he was moving from a dugout to a trench at Maple Copse on 2 June probably during the Battle for Mount Sorrel. On 9 February 1911 he had been in Avonmouth, on board Royal Canadian Northern Steamships Ltd *Royal Edward*, bound for Halifax, Nova Scotia, where he worked first as a farmhand and then as an oxyacetylene welder and mechanic. Youngest son of Amos and Emma (Hines) Money of Woburn Road, Heath and Reach. Camiers Road Cemetery 5 D 44/21.

1916 Sunday 11 June: Private **Sidney John Pantling** aged 28, believed to have been in the Bedfords, died at 24 Mill Road. Son of Eli and Naomi (Sturman) Pantling of 24 Mill Road. Leighton-Linslade Cemetery F 23 General Grave.

1916 Tuesday 13 June: Private 53937 **Stanley Wallace Bake**r aged 26, formerly of 52nd Field Ambulance the RAMC, died from pleurisy at the County Hospital, Bedford. He had enlisted in Cirencester on 20 January 1915 but had served in Torquay for only 117 days before being discharged on medical grounds. His burial record gives his occupation as furniture salesman. Son of Harry William and Mary Grace (Williams) Baker of 4 Market Square. Leighton-Linslade Cemetery BB384.

1916 Monday 19 June: Capt **Horace Edmund Martin** aged 24 of 1/8th Battalion the Middlesex Regiment died of wounds three weeks after being wounded while supervising his men digging trenches in front of the front line near Hébuterne. A keen sportsman and army cadet since attending Aylesbury Grammar School, he graduated in history at Cambridge and was a teacher before his commission into the Middlesex Regiment at the outbreak of war. He was promoted to captain in December 1915. Only son of John Jeffery and Katherine Wells (Jeffery) Martin of Rothschild Road. Le Tréport Military Cemetery 2 O 14.

1916 Saturday 1 July: Rifleman 550230, formerly 1810, **Reginald Alfred Cornish** aged 21 of 1/16th Battalion the London Regiment (Queen's Westminster Rifles) died in a diversionary attack at Gommecourt. Born in Leighton but brought up in Linslade, he studied drapery at evening school before working in London and volunteered immediately at the outbreak of war, arriving in France before the end of 1914 and witnessing the Christmas Day Truce. Son of Herbert Stockbridge and Ellen Eliza (Roadnight) Cornish of 6 Wing Road Terrace. Thiepval Memorial 13 C.

1916 Saturday 1 July: Sergeant 19820 **Joseph Ginger** aged 30 of C Company, 7th (Service) Battalion the Bedfords died during the early hours of the 1st Battle of the Somme. Born in Leighton, where his father kept the Golden Bell, Church Square for over twenty years, he was a carpenter in 1911. Son of Joseph and Rosina (Bailey) Ginger of 31 Dudley Street. Thiepval Memorial 2 C.

1916 Saturday 1 July: Sergeant 16200 **Reginald William Missenden** aged 26 of C Company, 7th (Service) Battalion the Bedfords was reported missing, death presumed, attacking the Pommiers Redoubt near Montauban. Born in Whaddon, he was a blacksmith farrier in New Road when he enlisted. One of five serving sons of Joseph Mayo and Elizabeth (Gaskin) Missenden of Whaddon. Thiepval Memorial 2 C.

1916 Saturday 1 July: Corporal 16998 **Frederick Charles Ruffhead** aged 32 of B Company, 7th (Service) Battalion the Bedfords died in action as the 1st Battle of the Somme began. Born in Leighton, he attended Beaudesert School and was a carpenter at Brown's foundry until enlisting in September 1914. Brother-in-law of **Richmond Lawrence**; son of Thomas Henry and Eliza (Smith) Ruffhead of 28 Hockliffe Road. Thiepval Memorial 2 C.

1916 Saturday 1 July: Corporal 15254 **Samuel Smith** aged 34 of 11th Battalion the East Lancashires (Accrington Pals) died in action near Serre. Born in Rishton, Lancashire, he worked as a carter before enlisting. Husband of Florrie (Ainsworth) of Accrington; son of Harry and Harriet (Garrett) Smith of Wing. Euston Road Cemetery I D 7.

1916 Sunday 2 July: Lance Corporal 13648 **John Chevens** aged 27 of 10th Battalion the York and Lancasters died of wounds in No. 36 CCS, Heilly. Born in Bamford, Derbyshire, he had been a railway labourer before enlisting and was billeted in the Leighton area during the winter of 1914–1915. Husband of Nora Beatrice (Russell) of Birds Hill, Heath and Reach; son of Benjamin and Elizabeth (Broomhead) Chevens of Derbyshire. Heilly Station Cemetery, Méricourt-L'Abbé I B 18.

1916 Sunday 2 July: Private 19265 **Albert Frederick Lugsden** aged 29 of 2nd Battalion the Bedfords died in action during the 1st Battle of the Somme. He was a horsekeeper on a farm and later worked at William Edmund Wallace's nurseries. Husband of Ada (Gadsden) Lugsden of St Giles Yard, Eaton Bray; brother of **Amos Lugsden**, **Arthur Joseph Lugsden** and **Frederick**

Lugsden; eldest son of David and Sarah Ann (Rollings) Lugsden of High Street, Eaton Bray. Thiepval Memorial 2 C.

1916 Monday 3 July: Private (Signaller) 12098 **Albert John Cook** aged 27 of 7th Battalion the Suffolks died in action during the 1st Battle of the Somme. Born in Leighton he attended Beaudesert School and was a picture framer in Fenny Stratford when he enlisted in Lowestoft. Son of Charles James and Ann (Peverill) Cook of 42 Ashwell Street. Thiepval Memorial 1 C, 2 A.

1916 Tuesday 4 July: Second Lieutenant **William Harper Brantom DCM★** aged 27 of 15th (County of London) Battalion the London Regiment (Prince of Wales's Own Civil Service Rifles), formerly 2658, died when hit by a shell fragment in a trench near Souchez, north of Arras. He enlisted in September 1914, was wounded during the action in which he won his DCM and commissioned in the same regiment on 11 October 1915. Educated at Dunstable Grammar School, he was a keen sportsman and a member of the St Barnabas's Church Lads' Brigade. Only child of William and Emily Florence (Harper) Brantom of Ivydene, 27 Stoke Road. Bois-De-Noulette British Cemetery I E 9. (See also Chapter 17.)

1916 Thursday 6 July: Able Seaman J/6798 **Arthur William Page** aged 23 of HM Submarine E26 was lost at sea. Born in Linslade, he had enlisted in the Royal Navy as a boy sailor. Nephew of **Mark Page** and **Lionel Page**; son of Charles and Mary (Miller) Page of 28 Wing Road, grandson of George and Rebecca (Woolhead) Page of 52 Springfield Road. Portsmouth Naval Memorial 13. (See Chapters 7 and 11)

1916 Friday 7 July: Lance Corporal 24345 **John Henry Chaundy** aged 30 of 12th Battalion the Manchesters died in France. He was born in Hockliffe, son of a schoolmaster, and was an assistant journalist in Elmore, Gloucestershire in 1901 but by 1911 was married with a son and was a railway stoker in Openshaw, Manchester. Son of James Elias and Emma Margaret Ruth (Johnson) Chaundy formerly of Hockliffe. Thiepval Memorial 13 A, 14 C.

1916 Saturday 8 July: Lance Corporal 12974 **George Charles Halsey** aged 21 of 7th Battalion the Bedfords died when a shell dropped into his section of a British-held trench. Born in Bushey, he was a billiard marker in Watford, where he enlisted. Husband of Elizabeth (Quick) of Bassett Road; son of George Alfred and Elizabeth Mary (Cottrill) Halsey of Watford. Thiepval Memorial 2 C.

1916 Monday 10 July: Private 22385 **Frederick Chase** aged 19 or 20 of 6th Battalion the Bedfords died when struck by a shell on the Somme. Born in Chalgrave, he worked on a farm and in March 1915 narrowly escaped conviction for 'gaming with cards' under a hedge. Son of William and Sarah Ann (Giltrow) Chase of Watling Street, Hockliffe. Thiepval Memorial 2 C.

1916 Tuesday 11 July: Private 13317 **Henry Charles Elliott Bunke**r aged 28 of 2nd Battalion the Bedfords died after being badly wounded by shrapnel at Trônes Wood; he was last seen being placed, unconscious, on a stretcher. Born in Tilsworth, by 1911 he was a paper-cutter at Waterlow & Sons Ltd, a printing works in Dunstable, and had been a member of Tilsworth Cricket Club. Son of Henry and Annie (Elliott) Bunker of Tilsworth. Thiepval Memorial 2 C.

1916 Tuesday 11 July: Private 18772 **John Deeley** aged 19 of 2nd Battalion the Bedfords died at Trônes Wood. Born in Eaton Bray he was a hewer at the lime and stone works in Totternhoe. Son of William and Elizabeth (Holland) Deeley of High Street, Eaton Bray. Thiepval Memorial 2 C.

1916 Tuesday 11 July: Lance Corporal 19196 **William Freeman** aged 20 of 2nd Battalion the Bedfords died at Trônes Wood. Born in Heath and Reach, he enlisted in Ampthill. Son of Edward Woodman and Louisa (Kent) Freeman of 1 Thomas Street, Heath and Reach. Thiepval Memorial 2 C.

1916 Wednesday 12 July: Sapper 67628 **Leonard Pantling** aged 42 of 126th Field Company the Royal Engineers died at Mermetz Wood. Born in Leighton, as was his wife, he was a bricklayer, and lived for some years in Hammersmith and Willesden. Husband of Emily Ann (White) of 41 Hockliffe Road; son of William and Catherine (Hack, formerly Washington) Pantling of 20 Plantation Road. Thiepval Memorial 8 A, D.

1916 Friday 14 July: Private 26125 **Harold Woodall** aged 25 of 9th Battalion the Loyal North Lancashire Regiment, formerly 26068 the Bedfords, died in action in France. Born in March, Cambridgeshire, he was a carnation grower who was boarding with William Bates in Leighton in 1911, and enlisted in Luton. Husband of Lily (Feary) of 4 Clarence Road; son of Harry and Eliza (Crofts) Woodall of March. Thiepval Memorial 11 A.

1916 Saturday 15 July: Private 14960 **William Peppiatt** aged 21 of 6th Battalion the Bedfords died in action in France. Born in Edlesborough, he and several brothers were farm labourers in the village. Son of David and Hannah (Dyer) Peppiatt of 24 Northall Road, Edlesborough. Thiepval Memorial 2 C.

1916 Saturday 15 July: Rifleman C/1600 **Frank Pickering** aged 21 of 16th Battalion the King's Royal Rifle Corps was presumed to have died attacking High Wood. Born in Littleworth, in 1911 he was a gas fitter, lived with his uncle in Surrey and later enlisted there. Only child of Merrishaw and Frances (Stockton) Pickering of Littleworth. Thiepval Memorial 13 A, B.

1916 Monday 17 July: Acting Bombardier 95 **Henry John Staines** aged 24 of 126th Siege Battery, the RGA died at 22nd Field Ambulance of wounds received during the Battle of the Somme. He was a carman when he enlisted in May 1915. Husband of Mary Elizabeth (Meager) of George Street, Wing; brother-in-law of **William Charles Meager**; son of Henry and Annie Elizabeth (Pursell) Staines of 12 New End, Hampstead. Dartmoor Cemetery, Becordel-Becourt I F 53.

1916 Wednesday 19 July: Private 4331 **Benjamin William Green Warr** aged 22 of 2/1st Battalion the O&BLI died almost certainly at the Battle of Fromelles, an unsuccessful distraction attack to keep enemy troops away from the Battle of the Somme. He was born in Gayton but the family moved to Fenny Stratford when he was a child and by 1911 he was apprenticed to a plumber and living at 59 Vandyke Road. Son of Thomas and Sarah J. (Green) Warr of Fenny Stratford. Loos Memorial Panels 83-85.

1916 Sunday 23 July: Private 1950 **Sydney James Fountaine** aged 29 or 30 of 9th Battalion the Australian Infantry, the Australian Imperial Force (AIF) died at the Capture of Pozières. Born in Wing, he and a brother had sailed for Australia on 16 September 1910, living near Brisbane, Queensland where he was a labourer before enlisting in February 1915; he sailed for France two months later. Son of Joseph and Sarah (Staples) Fountaine of New Road, Wing. Villers-Bretonneux Memorial.

1916 Sunday 23 July: Private 11509 **Charles Hill** aged 29 of 105th Company the MGC formerly 16110 of the Duke of Cornwall's Light Infantry and later 15229 of 8th Battalion the Somerset Light Infantry, died after being wounded in the Bernafay and Trônes Woods area. Immediately war was declared he enlisted in Birmingham but was transferred to the Somersets before they were billeted in Leighton and Linslade during the winter of 1914–15 where he met his future wife, whom he married on his final leave before going to France.

Husband of Lilian May (Woolhead) of 10 Ship Road. La Neuville British Cemetery I D 42.

1916 Tuesday 25 July: 3226 Private **Francis John Vasey** aged 25 of 11th Battalion the Australian Infantry, AIF died during the Battle of the Dunes at Pozières. Born in Wing, he worked as a clerk for Messrs Brantom & Co., coal and corn merchants of Leighton, and served in the Bedfordshire Yeomanry for two years before leaving for Australia via Cape Town on *Commonwealth* in January 1911. In the summer of 1915 he was working in Wickepin, in the wheat belt area of Western Australia, but gave an address in Boulder when he enlisted on 29 June 1915 with the AIF at Blackboy Hill, Perth, a large training camp. Son of Robert and Emma (Woods) Vasey of Wing. Villers-Bretonneux Memorial.

1916 Thursday 27 July: Private 3/7032 **Leopold Francis Harold Going** aged 21 of 1st Battalion the Bedfords died after being buried by a shell during the 1st Battle of the Somme. Born in Woburn Sands, he worked in Leighton as a coal carter before enlisting. Brother of **Herbert Going** and **William John Going**; son of Frederick and Harriet Salt (Perry) Going of 29 Mill Road. Thiepval Memorial 2 C.

1916 Thursday 27 July: Private 19893 **Francis John 'Jack' King** aged 23 of 1st Battalion the Bedfords died at Delville Wood. Born in Leighton, he had been a labourer in an iron foundry and volunteered in his home town in September 1914. He fought at Loos and the Somme. Brother of **Joseph King**; son of John and Mary Ann (Pratt) King of 24 St Andrew's Street. Thiepval Memorial 2 C.

1916 Friday 28 July: Private 20072 **Sidney Charles Shepherd** aged 32 of 8th Battalion the Bedfords died in action in Belgium. Born in Leighton, he attended Beaudesert School and was apprenticed to a draper. Son of Alfred and Eunice (Holiman) Shepherd of 12 St Andrew's Street. Potijze Chateau Wood Cemetery C 23.

1916 Sunday 30 July: Lance Sergeant 3/7041 **William Thomas Eggleton** aged 21 of 2nd Battalion the Bedfords died at Trônes Wood. Born in Leighton, he seems to have remained in the town, attending Beaudesert School, working on a farm and at the wire works before being posted to France. Son of John and Sarah (Stevens) Eggleton of 69 Heath Road. Thiepval Memorial 2 C.

1916 Sunday 30 July: Private 3/7428 **Thomas George Kempster** aged 21 of 2nd Battalion the Bedfords died in action in France. Born in Leighton, he had been a Boy Scout and a well-known local football player, and enlisted in Bedford in the Special Reserves prior to the war. When hostilities began he was in the service of Viscount Duncannon, probably at 17 Cavendish Square, London W. While on active service he had been admitted to hospital with rheumatic fever. Son of William and Catherine Matilda (Holmes) Kempster of 28 North Street. Thiepval Memorial 2 C.

1916 Sunday 30 July: Private 29602 **George Edgar Willis** aged 28 of 20th Battalion the King's (Liverpool) Regiment died in an attack on Guillemont, which was unsuccessful due to thick fog, gas shells and machine gun fire. He was born in Linslade and, his mother dying when he was a year old, was brought up by his father, a stud groom. Youngest child of William and Charlotte (Roome) Willis of 29 New Road. Thiepval Memorial 1 D, 8 B, 8 C.

1916 Monday 31 July: Lance Corporal 8027 **William John Going** aged 28 of 1st Battalion the Bedfords died of wounds at No. 38 CCS, Heilly. Born in Woburn Sands, he worked for a while in Essex before marrying. Brother of **Leopold Francis Harold Going** and **Herbert Going**; husband of Annie (Humbles, later Shackleton) of 7 Barrow Path; brother-in-law of **George Humbles** and **William Humbles**; son of Frederick and Harriet Salt (Perry) Going of 29 Mill Road. Heilly Station Cemetery II E 58.

1916 Tuesday 1 August: Private G1487 **Reginald George Humphrey** aged 26 of 17th Battalion the Duke of Cambridgeshire's Own (Middlesex) Regiment died in France. Born in Grove, by 1911 he had moved with his widowed mother to Brentford, where he was a builder's labourer. Son of William James and Ruth (Saunders) Humphrey of Brentford, late of Grove Locks and of 17 Ship Road. Quarry Cemetery III E G5.

1916 Saturday 5 August: Private 4131 **Frederick Bernard Hankin** aged 25 of 25th Battalion the Australian Infantry died in action on the Somme. From the *Edmonton Bulletin* of 1 March 1930:

Missing Soldier's Body Identified After Many Years

After a silence of nearly eleven years Mr and Mrs Charles Hankin, of Heath, Bedfordshire, have been informed of the finding and identification of their elder son Frederick, who was reported missing on August 5, 1918 (sic), while serving with the Australian contingent in France. Articles in his possession which led to his identification were a gold ring on his finger bearing his name, and the photograph of a girl living at Brisbane. These and several letters have been sent to his mother.

Born in Sussex, he grew up in Heath and Reach along with his younger brother, their three siblings having died as children. Brother of **Robert Hayes Hankin**; son of Charles Frederick and Mary Ann Frances (Van Baars) Hankin of Thomas Street, Heath and Reach, formerly of Islington. Serre Road Cemetery No. 2 XXIX B 5.

1916 Tuesday 8 August: Private 18773 **Theodore John Pratt** aged 22 of 2nd Battalion the Bedfords died after being wounded in France. Born in Eaton Bray, he had worked on the family farm before enlisting. Son of Frederick George and Bethia (Gadsden) Pratt of Ley Farm, Eaton Bray. Abbeville Communal Cemetery VI K 12.

1916 Tuesday 8 August: Private 23063 **Albert Edward Whitbread** aged 28 of 2nd Battalion the O&BLI, was posted as missing, death presumed, near Guillemont. Born in Linslade, he was a gardener before enlisting in late 1915. Son of William and Mary (Woolhead) Whitbread of 2 Soulbury Road. Thiepval Memorial 10 A, D.

1916 Friday 11 August: Lance Corporal 9387 **Frederick Boyce MM★ posthumously, DCM★** aged 28 of 2nd Battalion the Bedfords died of wounds in hospital in Rouen. Born in Bragenham, he joined the Bedfords as a regular soldier, serving in Bermuda and South Africa. Son of William and Rebecca Ellen (Cooper) Boyce and stepson of Minnie (Vickers) Boyce of 33 Friday Street, formerly of Heath and Reach. St Sever Cemetery B 28 2. (see also Chapter 17.)

1916 Monday 14 August: Private 5957 **William James Pease** aged 31 of 1/4th Battalion the O&BLI died in an enemy counter-attack near Pozières. Born in Wing, he was a miller's carter when he enlisted in March 1916 and had been in France for only about three months. Son of James and Jane (Mead) Pease of Church Road, Wing. Thiepval Memorial 10 A, D.

1916 Tuesday 22 August: Private 7269 **William Nash** aged 37 of 3/5th Battalion the Bedfords died at Aylesbury Military Hospital. He was born in Stewkley but his parents had moved to 31 South Street by 1901, whereas he was living and working as a grocer's assistant in High Wycombe. In 1911 he, his wife and their son were visiting her parents in Wing and had moved to Leighton by the time he enlisted in Luton. His burial record has his age as 36. Husband of Annie Louise (Page) of 52 Hockliffe Road; son of William and Sarah (Harding) Nash late of South Street. Leighton-Linslade Cemetery DD 12A.

1916 Thursday 24 August: Temporary Captain **Harold Stedman Richmond** aged 26 of 9th Battalion the King's Royal Rifle Corps died on the Somme, hit by a rifle bullet as he led his company on a successful assault on the German trenches under heavy shell and machine gun fire. Educated at Berkhamsted and at Brasenose College, Oxford, he entered the Malay Civil Service, and was at Batu Gagah when war was declared. With the KRRC he went to France in May 1915 and was severely wounded in the jaw on 31 July that year. Returning to France on 17 February 1916, he was gazetted captain in June. Brother of **Frederick Robert Richmond**; son of Robert and Fanny (Green) Richmond of Heathwood, Heath Road; cousin of **Cecil Henry Green**. Thiepval Memorial 13 A, B.

1916 Thursday 24 August: Private 17725 **Albert Rogers** aged 30 of 5th Battalion the O&BLI died in France. Born in Edlesborough, he was first a ploughboy and then, by 1911, a shepherd living in the village at Mount Pleasant. Husband of Alice (Clarke) of Ashton Cottages, Edlesborough; son of Jesse and Jane (Hull) Rogers of 3 Pebblemoor, Edlesborough. Delville Wood Cemetery XIII H 10.

1916 Thursday 24 August: Corporal 10669 **Arthur Sturman** aged 27 of 5th Battalion the O&BLI died in France. Born in Eggington, he was a footman for the Leon family at Bletchley Park in 1911 and then became a groom, latterly at Moreton Hall, Moreton Morrell, Warwickshire. Son of William and Annie Maria (Cox) Sturman of Eggington. Thiepval Memorial 10 A, D.

1916 Sunday 3 September: Private 469349 **William George Hall** aged 17 of 2nd Battalion (Eastern Ontario Regiment) the Canadian Infantry died on the Somme. Born in Leighton, he attended Beaudesert School before his mother took the children to Canada on the *Carthaginian* in July 1909 a year after his father's death; his parents had met and married there in the early 1890s and his elder sister was born there. William, a labourer, enlisted on 23 August 1915, in Sussex, New Brunswick, giving his date of birth as 24 January 1897 and obviously passed for 18 years and 7 months. Son of George and Eliza (Hodgson) Hall late of 3 Summer Street, stepson of Arthur C. Giffen of Goldboro, Nova Scotia. 2nd Canadian Cemetery C 8.

1916 Tuesday 5 September: Private 9219 **Joseph Benjamin Shackleton** (served as **Joseph Benjamin Wise**) aged 28 of 1st Battalion the Bedfords died in action in France. The family alternated between the two surnames, the reason being unclear, and in 1911 he was with the regiment in 'Bermuda and Jamaica'. One of six serving sons of John William and Sophia (King) Shackleton of 16 Friday Street. Thiepval Memorial 2 C.

1916 Thursday 7 September: Private 426521 **Hayward James Luck** aged 30 of 3rd Battalion the Canadian Infantry (Central Ontario Regiment) died in action on the Somme. Born in Leighton, he lived there with his family before leaving Liverpool for Quebec on 1 May 1908 on *Emperor of Butan* of the Canadian Pacific Line. Once in Canada, he homesteaded in the Serath district before working as a clerk at Regina, as he had done in England, until he enlisted. Cousin of **Edward Lewis Luck** and **Sidney James Luck**; son of Thomas James and Harriet (Wells) Luck of Hendon, formerly of 53-59 High Street. Sunken Road Cemetery I C 9.

1916 Saturday 9 September: Private G/14503 **Bertie Frank Brown** aged 20 of 2nd Battalion the Royal Sussex Regiment died in action with the BEF in France. Born in Leighton, he attended Beaudesert School and was a farm labourer when he enlisted in Dunstable. Son of Charles and Emma (Alcock) Brown of Rose Villas, Barrow Path. Thiepval Memorial 7 C.

1916 Tuesday 12 September: Rifleman 5725 **(Richard Edward) Thomas Phillips** aged 37 of 1/16th Battalion the London Regiment (Queen's Westminster Rifles) died in action in France. Born in Far Cotton, he was living with his paternal grandmother in Bridge Street in 1891 and was a travelling furnishing salesman, temporarily in Rugby in 1901 and boarding in Brighton in 1911. Son of William and Julia J. (Byrns) Phillips late of Rutland, formerly of Leighton. Thiepval Memorial 13 C.

1916 Friday 15 September: Private 20744 **Arthur Janes** aged 19 of 8th Battalion the Bedfords died in France. He was a leather cutter, living with his cousin Philip Fountain in Kings Langley in 1911. In the index to the civil registration of births his mother's maiden name is Emmerton but a marriage has yet to be found and his parents' precise names are not known. Cousin of **Ernest Fountain**. Nephew of Edward and Sarah (Emmerton) Fountain of Bower Lane, Eaton Bray. Thiepval Memorial 2 C.

1916 Friday 15 September: Rifleman S/10558 **Alfred Henry Turney** aged 18 of 8th Battalion the Rifle Brigade died in an attack on Delville Wood near Longueval. A farm labourer, he added two years to his age when he enlisted in May 1915 just after his 17th birthday and had been with the Battalion in France for nine months when he was killed. Brother of **Bert Turney**; son of Robert and Ellen (Fiddler) Turney of Soulbury and Thiepval Memorial 16 B, C.

1916 Friday 15 September: Private 15580 **Frederick George Webb** aged 21 of D Company, 8th Battalion the Bedfords died in action in France. Born in Heath and Reach, he was living there with his paternal grandparents at Fox Corner in 1901 and 1911 and was a carpenter's labourer when he enlisted. Son of John Holmes and Lizzie (Kempster) Webb of Thomas Street, Heath and Reach, formerly of Picket Lodge, Rushmere; grandson of Thomas and Hannah (Holmes) Webb of Woburn Road, Heath. Thiepval Monument 2 C.

1916 Friday 22 September: Gunner 33526 **Frederick James Hardy** aged 34 of 129th Brigade HQ the RFA died in Salonika from appendicitis. He had been wounded in November 1914, necessitating his transfer to 1st Southern General Hospital, Edgbaston. Born in Dunstable he had served his apprenticeship as a machine printer in Houghton Regis before enlisting in the Royal Regiment of Artillery in Dunstable in 1904. Husband of Florence (Groom) of 12 Bower Lane, Eaton Bray; son of James and Charlotte Anne (Arnold) Hardy. Salonika (Lembet Road) Military Cemetery 444.

1916 Sunday 24 September: Lance Corporal 21034 **James Wernham** aged 26 of 9 Platoon, 2nd Battalion the Border Regiment, formerly 7146 the Bedfords, died near Armentières when hit by a sniper while going on sentry duty. Born in Newbury, he was living in Leighton by 1901, was a member of the Baptist church and attended Beaudesert School before serving an apprenticeship with James Mims, stonemason. Only son of William and Harriet (Booker) Wernham of 12 Regent Street. Tancrez Farm Cemetery I J 25.

1916 Tuesday 26 September: Private 27504 **Edward Lewis Luck** aged 22 of 15th Battalion the Canadian Infantry (Central Ontario Regiment) died in France. Brother of **Sidney James Luck** and cousin of **Hayward James Luck**; son of John and Annie (Webster) Luck of Toronto, late of Henley; nephew of Thomas James Luck, late of 53–59 High Street. Vimy Memorial.

1916 Wednesday 27 September: Private 3/6920 **John Horne** aged 23 of 1st Battalion the Bedfords died when a German bomb exploded after he had been relieved from the trenches. Born in Leighton, he attended Beaudesert School and later worked as a sandpit labourer. Son of George and Sarah Ann (Fenn) Horne of 94 Vandyke Road. Citadel New Military Cemetery V A 11.

1916 Thursday 28 September: Lance Corporal G14800 **Cyril Frederick Gibbs** aged 19 of 2nd Battalion the Royal Sussex Regiment, formerly 6823 the Essex Regiment, died in action in France. Born in Leighton, he was a coach body builder and attended the evening school, enlisting in July 1914 at Bury St Edmunds with the Bedfords. Son of George William and Minnie Elizabeth (Yirrell) Gibbs of Norwood, South Street. Thiepval Memorial 7 C.

1916 Thursday 28 September: Private 15292 **Arthur John Kingham** aged 26 of 7th Battalion the Bedfords died in action during the capture of the Schwaben Redoubt. Born in Wingfield, he was a farm labourer before enlisting in Toddington. Son of James Joseph and Sarah Ann (Armsden) Kingham of Wingfield. Thiepval Memorial 2 C.

1916 Thursday 28 September: Private 18202 **Frank Charles Robinson** aged 28 of 7th Battalion the Bedfords died during the capture of the Schwaben Redoubt. Born in Linslade, he was a farm labourer living in Stanbridge before enlisting. Husband of Grace Lily (Cox) of Stanbridge; son of Robert and Sarah Ann (Turvey) Robinson of 15 Church Road. Connaught Cemetery XI H 7.

1916 Friday 29 September: Lance Corporal 15743 **Thomas John Heley** aged 33 of 7th Battalion the Bedfords died of wounds in France. Born in Leighton, he had attended Beaudesert School and had worked as a carpenter but was living with his family in Luton in 1911. Husband of Elizabeth (Simpson) of Luton; son of Fred and Eliza Ann (Roberts) Heley of Luton, formerly of 68 North Street. Puchevillers British Cemetery III D 44.

1916 Saturday 30 September: Private 11959 **Gilbert Tom Bogg** aged 20 or 21 of 11th Battalion the Royal Fusiliers died after being wounded during the Battle of Thiepval Ridge. Born in Hampshire, he was a gamekeeper like his father, working in Derbyshire, before enlisting. Brother of **Harry Stanley Bogg**; son of Jonathan and Agnes Louisa (Harvey) Bogg of Liscombe. Puchevillers British Cemetery V B 33.

1916 Saturday 30 September: Private 28135 **Noel Stephen Samuel** aged 21 of 8th Battalion the East Surreys, formerly 9228 the Royal Sussex Regiment, disappeared, death presumed, during an attack on the Schwaben Redoubt. Born and brought up in Linslade, he moved to Lewisham before 1911 where he was a paper merchant's clerk. Son of George Henry and Kate (Croxford) Samuel of Hove, late of Waterloo Road. Thiepval Memorial 6 B, C.

1916 Tuesday 3 October: Rifleman 7714 **Ernest Edward Richards** aged 25 of 9th Battalion the London Regiment (Queen Victoria's Rifles), formerly 5200 of 20th Battalion the London Regiment, died of wounds sustained during the Battle of the Somme. His mother was from Cheddington but he was born and brought up in Lewisham and was a milkman before enlisting. Son of Edward and Sarah Ann (Cutler) Richards. Bronfay Farm Military Cemetery, Bray-Sur-Somme I C 2.

1916 Thursday 5 October: Private 10866 **Ernest Weedon** aged 23 of 4th Battalion the Royal Welsh Fusiliers, formerly 2559 the Bedfords, died of wounds in France. He was born in Eaton Bray, where he and his family were farm workers. Brother of **Frederick William Weedon**; son of William and Hannah (Oakins) Weedon of Prentice Lane, Eaton Bray. Dernancour Communal Cemetery Extension III E 16.

1916 Saturday 7 October: Private 32811 **John Thomas Hammerton** aged 28 of 6th Battalion the O&BLI, formerly 3414 the 2/1st Queen's Own Oxfordshire Hussars, is presumed to have died in an assault near Gueudecourt. Born in Wing, he was a bricklayer on the Ascott Estate. Husband of Nellie (Taylor); son of Charles Henry and Elizabeth (Pollard) Hammerton of Bay Cottages, Wing. Thiepval Memorial 10 A, D.

1916 Sunday 8 October: Lance Sergeant G/15875 **George Alma Janes** aged 28 of 20th Battalion the Duke of Cambridge's Own (Middlesex) Regiment died in action in France. An earlier injury had resulted in the loss of an eye. He was a carman for a corn chandler, living in St Pancras in 1911. Husband of Alice (Goacher) of Chalk Farm; brother of **Charles John Janes** and **Harry Janes**; son of David and Sarah Jane (Emerson) Janes of Kentish Town, formerly of Bassett Road. Philosophe British Cemetery I G 34.

1916 Monday 9 October: Temporary Second Lieutenant 407 **Cecil Henry Green** aged 29 of 6th Battalion the O&BLI, formerly 10th (Public School) Battalion the Royal Fusiliers, died at No. 38 CCS, Heilly, a day after being seriously wounded. Born in Leighton where his father was a master maltster, he attended school in Berkhamsted and later worked for a corn dealer. He had previously escaped injury when buried by a shell while in his dugout. Cousin of **Frederick Robert Richmond** and **Harold Stedman Richmond**; son of William Sparrey and Anne (Sargeant) Green of Horwood, 16 Grove Road. Grove Town Cemetery Grave I J 16.

1916 Monday 9 October: Private 32854 **Oscar Rimington** aged 23 or 24 of 6th Battalion the O&BLI, formerly 2502 the 2/1st Queen's Own Oxfordshire Hussars, died when shot through the head while on a reconnoitring expedition near Bernafay Wood and the Bray–Albert road; his wife's brother was with him when he died. Previously a telegraph clerk at Ascott House, he had married only a few weeks before his death. Husband of Sarah Emily May (Pitchford) of Wing; son of Charles Hardy and Grace Amelia (Earp) Rimington of Littleworth. Thiepval Memorial 10 A, D.

1916 Monday 9 October: Private 11908 **Joseph Rogers** aged 24 of 6th Battalion the O&BLI died of wounds probably received in the attack on Rainbow Trench near Gueudecourt on 7 October during the Battle of Le Transloy; he had previously been wounded. Born in Wing, he was a labourer before enlisting in October 1914. Son of Edmund Joseph and Annie (Randall) Rogers of The Fields, Ascott, Wing. Carnoy Military Cemetery V 10.

1916 Thursday 12 October: Acting Corporal/Private 18205 **John William Clarke** aged 22 of 2nd Battalion the Bedfords was posted as missing, presumed dead, during the Battle of Le Transloy. He was born in Willesden but by 1901 was living with his paternal grandparents in Battlesden and working on a farm. Son of John William Clarke of Notting Hill; grandson of John and Eliza (Godfrey) Clark of Battlesden. Thiepval Memorial 2 C.

1916 Thursday 12 October: Private 13619 **William John Ruffett** aged 20 of 2nd Battalion the Bedfords died when the trench where he was a machine gunner was shelled. He was born in Hertford, but his father was a gamekeeper and this kept the family on the move; by 1911 they were farming in Ivinghoe Aston. Son of William and Susan Jane (Cross) Ruffett of Vine Farm, Ivinghoe. Thiepval Memorial 2 C.

1916 Friday 13 October: Sergeant 16384 **Frederick Charles Leach** aged 24 of 8th Battalion the Bedfords was acting CSM when he died of wounds at 14 Corps Main Dressing Station. He was born in Eggington and worked in the village as a gardener. Husband of Maud (Horn, later Ellingham) of Dunstable; only son of Charles and Sarah (Pantling) Leach of Eggington. Thiepval Memorial 2 C.

1916 Sunday 15 October: Private 17875 **William Hart** aged 24 of 2nd Battalion the Bedfords died after being wounded on the Somme. Born in Leighton, he attended Beaudesert School and had been a hairdresser's assistant prior to his enlistment in Bedford. Son of Frederick William and Annie (Holtom) Hart of St Andrew's Street. Heilly Station Cemetery III C 41.

1916 Thursday 19 October: Corporal 2699 **Stanley Harold Dunham** aged 26 of 1st Battalion the Hertfordshires died of wounds in France. He was born in Leighton, his father working there for some years as a railway timekeeper. Son of Sam and Ellen Jane (Hewlett) Dunham of Watford, formerly of Dudley Street. St Sever Cemetery B 13 16.

1916 Thursday 19 October: Private 460180 **Arthur Seabrook (alias Arthur John Smith)** aged 37 of the New Brunswick Regiment the Canadian Infantry died in France. In 1901 he was a bricklayer's labourer, still living with his parents in Cheddington but by 1911 appears both to have changed his name to Smith and left for Canada. Son of George and Charlotte (Stevens) Seabrook of Cheddington. Étaples Military Cemetery XII A 10A.

1916 Sunday 23 October: Private 18132 **Albert Horley** aged 21 of 7th Battalion the Bedfords died in action in France. Born in Heath and Reach, he worked on his father's farm before enlisting in Bedford. Youngest son of William Benjamin and Anne (Coles) Horley of Town Farm, Heath and Reach. Pozières British Cemetery I D 12.

1916 Thursday 26 October: Private 32729 **Alfred Bonham** aged 22 of 2nd Battalion the O&BLI, formerly 5859 4th Battalion (Reserve), died in action in France. In 1911 he was working at a brewery. Son of Joseph and Elizabeth (Norris) Bonham of Ivinghoe. Euston Road Cemetery III M 7.

1916 Tuesday 14 November: Private 5/4052 **Robert Joseph Seddon** aged 21 of 5th Battalion the Royal Sussex Regiment died instantly when hit by a shell while working on infrastructure at Bazentin-Le-Grand Wood. He was twice turned down as unfit, before being conscripted into a pioneer battalion. Born in Heath and Reach, he was a gardener and a bell ringer at St Barnabas Church. Son of Frederick and Elizabeth (Plumb) Seddon of Pear Tree Cottage, Linslade. Martinpuich British Cemetery E 26.

1916 Thursday 16 November: Private 45153 **John Charles Boon** aged 21 of 99 Company the MGC (Infantry), formerly 2887 of 5th Battalion the City of London Rifles, died during the Battle of the Ancre. Born in Aspley Guise, he had worked at the Leighton Buzzard Gas Company and had already been in the Territorial Army for four years when he enlisted at Bunhill Row, London. Son of Henry and Margaret Elizabeth (Adams) Boon of Aspley Guise. Frankfurt Trench British Cemetery Row B Grave 14.

1916 Thursday 23 November: Private 4484 **Thomas Frederick Lionel Alldritt** aged 23 of 13th Battalion the Royal Fusiliers (City of London Regiment) died of wounds at No. 22 General Hospital, Camiers. Born in Lancashire, he came to Linslade in the mid-1890s and was initially a pupil at Linslade Infants' School, his father taking up a post as elementary schoolmaster at Beaudesert Boys' School. After attending this school for four years, he moved to Shefford with his family, where his father was to become a head teacher. He became apprenticed to a plumber in Bedford before enlisting in London and embarking for France in December 1914. In March 1915 he contracted enteric fever after being wounded at Ypres. Son of George Frederick and Clara (Potter) Alldritt of Shefford, formerly of 25 Waterloo Road. Étaples Military Cemetery XX B 10A.

1916 Sunday 31 December: Sergeant 1646 **Albert Edward Kennett** aged 29 of No. 2 Australian General Hospital the Australian Army Medical Corps died of pneumonia. The family emigrated in 1893 and he became superintendent of the Ambulance Brigade in Cairns, Queensland; his father, superintendent of the Warwick Ambulance Brigade there for fourteen years, had died a week earlier. Son of James Dalton Kennett and Eleanor (Ball) Kennett, of Wooloowin, Queensland, formerly of the North Street Institute, Leighton. St Sever Cemetery Extension O IV E 1.

1917 Friday 12 January: Driver 52727 **James Smith** aged 26 of 19th Signals Company the RE died at No. 3 Australian CCS, Gézaincourt of broncho-pneumonia. He was a cowman at Mead Farm, Stanbridge before enlisting. Son of George and Sarah (Lee) Smith of Chichester, formerly of Billington. Gézaincourt Communal Cemetery and Extension II E 12.

1917 Thursday 1 February: Private 6217 **Percy Charles Archer** aged 26 of 3/4th Battalion the O&BLI died at Endell Street Military Hospital, London. Born in Ivinghoe, he was an egg merchant and already married by 1911. Husband of Emily (Harrowell) of Cheddington; son of Edwin John and Emily (Turner) Archer of Garsington, formerly of New Street, Cheddington. Cheddington (St Giles), north-east of church.

1917 Thursday 1 February: Sergeant 14284 **Henry William Gordon** aged 25 of 3rd Battalion the Grenadier Guards died at a bombing school in France. As a police sergeant he had served under Superintendent Thomas Babbington Woods in Leighton. Husband of Annie Louise (Fosbrook); son of Richard William and Clara Annie (Richardson) Gordon of Westgate-on-Sea, formerly of Bedford. Heilly Station Cemetery V G 30.

1917 Friday 2 February: Corporal/Acting Sergeant 52388 **James Henry Parker** aged 25 of 7th Battalion the Prince of Wales's Leinster Regiment (Royal Canadians), formerly 14841 the Bedfords, died in action in Belgium. He had attended Pulford School and had completed his apprenticeship as a baker in Stanbridge. Son of John Alfred and Louisa Ann (Rice) Parker of 105 Prospect Place, Heath Road. Pond Farm Cemetery Grave J 17.

1917 Monday 5 February: Private GS/27949 **Harry Dennis Gutteridge** aged 26 of 7th Battalion the Royal Fusiliers was posted as missing, presumed dead, in France. He was born in Leighton and, after the death of his father, moved to Luton where he lived in his mother's boarding-house and worked in a straw-hat factory. Husband of Martha Ann Charlotte (Preece) of Luton; son of Dennis and Mary Ann Isabella (Cheney, formerly Cook) Gutteridge of Luton, late of the Curriers' Arms, Middle Row. Thiepval Memorial 8 C, 9 A, 16 A.

1917 Monday 5 February: Lance Corporal 23134 **James Norman** aged 25 of 1st Battalion the Bedfords died in the trenches in France after being hit in the head by a machine gun bullet. Born in Beeston Green, he had been stationed as a police constable at Leighton some time between 1911 and his enlistment. Of 81 South Street; son of Jesse John and Jane Hannah (Braybrook) Norman of Beeston Green. Le Touret Military Cemetery, Richebourg-L'Avoué IV C 10.

1917 Tuesday 6 February: Private GS/60156 **Edward Tucker** aged 34 of the Royal Fusiliers, formerly 23401 the Bedfords, died when a trench mortar exploded in his dugout in France. Born in Hockliffe, he had first worked on farms and later for Arnold's. He had been a bell ringer for eighteen years. Son of Frederick Charles and Emma (Frost) Tucker of Hockliffe. Klein-Vierstraat British Cemetery I B 13.

1917 Thursday 8 February: Private 3923 **Walter Hollingsworth Ostler** aged 26 of 1st Battalion the Honourable Artillery Company (HAC) died during an attack on Baillescourt Farm in a sunken lane on the north bank of the Ancre, opposite Grandcourt. Born in Dunstable, he attended Ashton Grammar

School and was an auctioneer in Leighton before enlisting on 23 June 1915 in Finsbury. Son of William Walter and Adeline Patti (Hewett, latterly Fenn) Ostler of Dunstable; stepson of Patrick James Fenn. Thiepval Memorial 8 A.

1917 Saturday 10 February: Stoker 2nd Class K/39110 **Archibald James Payne** aged 31 of HMS *Pembroke II* died of empyema at the Royal Naval Hospital, Gillingham, despite surgery. Born in Leighton, he had worked in the family grocery business at 52-54 North Street and had been a Special Constable before joining up on 20 December 1916. His burial record gives his occupation as grocer. Brother of **Leslie Payne**; husband of Ada (Olney) of 21 Stanbridge Road, formerly of 36 Lake Street; son of George and Mary Ann (Turney) Payne of Harley House, 54 North Street. Leighton-Linslade Cemetery Grave B 52.

1917 Wednesday 14 February: Private 30910 **James Henry Collins** aged 36 of 4th Battalion the Bedfords died after being wounded during fighting along the Somme. He was born and grew up in Hertfordshire, where he worked on farms. Husband of Rose (Moran) of Woburn Road, Heath and Reach; son of William and Susan (Lewis) Collins of Little Heath, Hertfordshire. Varennes Military Cemetery I D 30.

1917 Wednesday 14 February: Air Mechanic 1st Class 45071 **Percy Edward Knightley** aged 26 of 46 Squadron the Royal Flying Corps (RFC) died near Poperinghe. Born in Haggerston, he was apprenticed to a chair-maker but was in Linslade by 1914, enlisting under the Derby Scheme and being transferred into Section B to await call-up. Husband of Mabel (Keen) of 35 Waterloo Road; son of George Edward and Alice Maria (Day) Knightley of Hackney. Poperinghe New Military Cemetery II C 11.

1917 Friday 16 February: Private G/44026 **Harry Woodcraft** aged 27 of the Middlesex Regiment died in action in France. It is unclear from military records if he served in the 17th (1st Football) or the 19th (Public Works) Battalion. Born in Eaton Bray, he worked on farms and possibly at the lime works in Totternhoe. Brother of **Ernest Woodcraft**; son of John and Elizabeth (Fountain) Woodcraft of Bower Lane, Eaton Bray. Courcelette British Cemetery I E 7.

1917 Saturday 17 February: Lance Corporal F/3439 **Joseph Bierton** aged 32 of 4th Battalion the Duke of Cambridge's Own (Middlesex) Regiment died in action on the Loos Salient. Born in Leighton, he was a sand merchant's bookkeeper and clerk when he enlisted in January 1916. Husband of Alice

Elizabeth (Yea) of 9 George Street; son of David and Leah (Chandler) Bierton of 33 Lake Street. Philosophe British Cemetery I M 19.

1917 Monday 19 February: Private 41486 **William Edward Dean** aged 29 of 13th Battalion the Essex Regiment, formerly of 8th Battalion the Northamptonshires, died in action at Miraumont. Born in Luton, he was a master butcher, his parents having moved to Leighton when he was young, and had played in the Leighton Thursday football team. Husband of Gertrude (Deeley) of 89 Church Street; son of William and Maria (Simpson) Dean of Silverdale, 22 Hockliffe Road. Thiepval Memorial 10 D.

1917 Sunday 25 February: Gnr 132591 **William John Cooper** aged 41 of 73rd Company the RGA died in Lahore from illness. He was born in Leighton but worked for a straw-hat manufacturer in Islington before moving to Eccleshill, where he was a goods porter until he enlisted in Bradford. Son of John Thomas and Sarah (Duncombe) Cooper, late of Gig Lane, Heath and Reach. Karachi 1914–1918 War Memorial.

1917 Saturday 3 March: munitions worker **Thomas William Janes** aged 17 died at Bute Hospital, Luton ten days after an accident 'at a Luton works'. He received 'injuries to the face, body and left arm'. His burial record has his date of death as 2 March. Son of Frederick and Elizabeth 'Betsey' (Major) Janes of 12 St Andrew's Street. Leighton-Linslade Cemetery B 466A. (See also Chapter 13)

1917 Tuesday 6 March: Private 13746 **Francis 'Frank' William Bryant** aged 35 of 1st Battalion the Northamptonshires died in action in a raid on the German front line near Barleux; he had previously been wounded three times. He was born in Bermondsey where his father was a shipping clerk and had been a gardener at Ascott House, but was living and working in Peterborough when he enlisted soon after war was declared. Husband of Amy (Lovell) of Littleworth, Wing; son of William and Caroline (Bush) Bryant. Ennemain Communal Cemetery Extension I D 2.

1917 Friday 9 March: Second Lieutenant Pilot **Arthur John Pearson MC★** aged 29 of 29 Squadron the RFC, formerly of 8th (Reserve) Battalion the Northamptonshire Regiment and the MGC, died in action. Educated at the Royal Latin School, Buckingham and the City & Guilds Institute, London, he had been employed by Western Electric Co., Woolwich and worked on the installation of telephone exchanges in China (including the Imperial Court at Peking) and in South Africa, Australia and Belgium. Son of George and

Henrietta Sarah Ann Roads (Brinkler) Pearson of Shenley House, Heath and Reach. Arras Flying Services Memorial. (See also Chapters 5 and 16)

1917 Saturday 10 March: Private 265681 **William James Pope** aged 22 of 1/1st Bucks Battalion the O&BLI died when a gas shell exploded, probably in a front-line trench near Barleux. Born and brought up in Sussex, he was an under gardener at Ascott House when he enlisted 2348 of 1/1st Bucks Battalion soon after the outbreak of war. Son of Charles and Elizabeth Ann (Stephens) Pope of Crawley, Sussex. Hem Farm Military Cemetery I L 18.

1917 Sunday 11 March: Private 23406 **Albert Edward Birch** aged 30 of C Company, 4th Battalion the Bedfords died at Highfield Hospital, Liverpool after being wounded in the face and eye a month earlier. Septic poisoning had followed successful surgery. He had been Augustus Charles Prynne's gardener at Leedon before enlisting under the Derby Scheme, training at Ampthill and arriving in France in mid-1916. Son of David and Caroline (Foster) Birch of the Square, Hockliffe. Hockliffe (St Nicholas), near north-west corner.

1917 Tuesday 13 March: Second Lieutenant **Frederick Robert Richmond** aged 34 of 22nd Battalion the Durham Light Infantry was killed by a shell about a mile north of Bouchavesnes while making his way up the trenches with a working party. On the outbreak of war he joined the Public School Battalion as a private and, after initially refusing any promotion, was made sergeant and then company sergeant before the battalion went to France in November 1915. In March 1916 after much active service he returned to England to train at Oxford before joining the Durham Light Infantry as second lieutenant. In September he returned to the Front to join a Pioneer Battalion. Born in Leighton, he attended Berkhamsted School and was an auctioneer for Messrs Cumberland & Hopkins, becoming a partner on the retirement of Samuel Hopkins. He was 'the moving spirit of the Leighton Buzzard Tennis Club and one of the founders of the Leighton Buzzard Amateur Operatic Society'. Brother of **Harold Stedman Richmond**; son of Robert and Fanny (Green) Richmond of Heathwood, Heath Road; cousin of **Cecil Henry Green**. Delville Wood Cemetery XXVI R 3.

1917 Wednesday 14 March: Private 169 **Joseph Chandler** aged 25 of 44th Battalion the Australian Infantry AIF died in action near Armentières. While working as a bricklayer in Australia, he enlisted on 28 February 1916 and embarked a month later on His Majesty's Australian Transport (HMAT) *Suevic* for Plymouth whence, on 4 November, the battalion left for the Western

Front. Of Highgate Hill, Western Australia; son of James and Maria (Messenger) Chandler of Cheddington. Cité Bonjean Military Cemetery V A 14.

1917 Thursday 22 March: Private G/37096 **Edward Groom** aged 31 of 1st Battalion the West Surreys died in France. Born in Water End, he was a nurseryman in Eaton Bray and was married by 1911. Husband of Alice Rosa (Scott) of Church Lane, Eaton Bray; son of Charles Edward and Emily Maria (Colyer) Groom of Water End, Hemel Hempstead. La Neuville Communal Cemetery B 93.

1917 Thursday 22 March: Private 71234 **Hortensius Stephen Smith** aged 28 of 89 Company the MGC, formerly 20781 the Bedfords, died of wounds in France. Born in Kings Langley, he spent much of his childhood in Kennington, coming to Linslade to live with his maternal grandmother by 1901 and enlisting in Aylesbury. Latterly of Aston Clinton; only brother of **Arthur James Smith**; son of James and Catherine Elizabeth (Thompson), formerly of 37 Old Road. St Hilaire Cemetery, Frevent II E 2.

1917 Tuesday 27 March: Private 201158 **Ernest Edward Cornish** aged 20 of D Company, 4th Battalion the Essex Regiment, formerly 20542 the Bedfords, died in action in Palestine. Born in Leighton, he was working as an errand boy in a boot shop before enlisting in Luton. Son of Stephen Ernest and Catherine Annie (Croxford) Cornish of 36 Baker Street. Jerusalem Memorial 33-39.

1917 Tuesday 27 March: Lance Corporal 252485 **Mervyn Cecil Crook** aged 27 or 28 of 2/3rd Battalion the London Regiment, formerly 20542 the Bedfords, was posted as missing, death presumed. Born in Leighton, where his family lived for over two decades, he was a baker in Ealing in 1911. Husband of Mabel Florence (Heath); son of George Charles and Mary Anne (Lister) Crook, formerly of 83 South Street. Tyne Cot Memorial 148-50.

1917 Tuesday 27 March: Private 201140 **Fred Lugsden** aged 22 of 4th Battalion the Essex Regiment died in action. In 1911 he was working at Wallace's nurseries in Eaton Bray. A news item of December 1914 mentions that four Lugsden brothers had enlisted; more were to follow them. Brother of **Albert Lugsden**, **Amos Lugsden** and **Arthur Joseph Lugsden**; son of David and Sarah Ann (Rollings) Lugsden of High Street, Eaton Bray. Jerusalem Memorial 32-38.

1917 Saturday 2 April: Private 265789 **William Mead** aged 25 of 2/1st Bucks Battalion the O&BLI, formerly 2516, died in action, possibly from friendly fire, in an attack near Soyecourt north-west of Saint-Quentin. An agricultural worker like his father, William was born in Stewkley, but the family lived in Soulbury for many years, then in Wolverton, before moving to Slapton around the start of the war, where they remained. Son of George and Sarah (Beasley) Mead. Vadencourt British Cemetery V A 2.

1917 Monday 2 April: Private 3123 **Harry Smith** aged 20 of 21st Company the MGC (Infantry), formerly 10945 the Bedfords, died after his company had attacked and captured the village of Henin. Already under heavy fire from snipers, he had dug an emplacement for his gun and begun firing at the retreating enemy when a rifle bullet killed him. He was born in Olney and was still a child when his family moved to Leighton, his mother's birthplace. There he attended Beaudesert School and was a Scout leader; he served an apprenticeship at Faith Press in Linslade before enlisting. Son of Arthur and Alice (Webster) Smith, of Bulbrook, Bracknell, formerly of 26 Vandyke Road. Arras Memorial 10.

1917 Monday 2 April: Private 19651 **George Woolhead** aged 32 or 33 of 1st Battalion the Dorsetshires, formerly 8365 the Bedfords, died in action. He was born in Ridge Hill, Hertfordshire, his parents having moved there from Stewkley a few years before his birth; he was in Sheep Lane, Battlesden by 1911, married for five years but alone in the house, and his wife was with their son at her parents' home in the village. Husband of Miriam Maud (Clark) of 4 Battlesden; son of Charles and Martha (Smith) Woolhead of 23 Potsgrove. Chapelle British Cemetery IV B 11.

1917 Monday 9 April: Private G/15861 **George Garnett** aged 35 of 6th Battalion the Queen's Own (Royal West Kent) Regiment died at Arras. Born in Aylesbury, he had worked as a basket maker until he enlisted in Peterborough, Huntingdonshire. In 1908 he and his wife had twin boys, both of whom died shortly after their birth. Husband of Ada Louisa (Ridgway) of 46 Hockliffe Street; son of George and Mercy (Humphrey) Garnett of Aylesbury. Ste Catherine British Cemetery Grave F 11.

1917 Monday 9 April: Private 475292 **Sidney James Luck** aged 27 of Princess Patricia's Canadian Light Infantry (Eastern Ontario Regiment) died in France. Brother of **Edward Lewis Luck**; cousin of **Hayward James Luck**; son of John and Annie (Webster) Luck of Toronto, late of Henley; nephew of

Thomas James Luck late of 53-59 High Street. Bruay Communal Cemetery Extension D 23.

1917 Monday 9 April: Private 43510 **Percy Thomas Miles** aged 24 of 10th Battalion the Lincolnshires died of wounds in France. He was born in Edlesborough and worked on farms both there and in Horton. Son of Richard and Mary (Slatter) Miles of Horton, formerly of Main Road, Edlesborough. Arras Memorial 3, 4.

1917 Monday 9 April: Second Lieutenant **William Francis Paddock** aged 22 of 4th Battalion the Royal Fusiliers, formerly Private 6667 of 18th Battalion, died at No. 19 CCS after being wounded south of the Arras–Cambrai road. Born in Wing, he first attended Eaton Bray school, then Dunstable Grammar School. Eldest son of William Peters and Katharine Louisa (List) Paddock of School House, Eaton Bray. Duisans British Cemetery III C 2.

1917 Monday 9 April: Private 871056 **John Noel Steadman** aged 21 of 78th Battalion the Canadian Infantry (Manitoba Regiment) died in action on Vimy Ridge. Born in Thornborough, he was a farm labourer when he enlisted at Winnipeg on 4 February 1916 with the Manitoba Infantry. He was transferred to the 108th Battalion the Canadian Expeditionary Force and arrived in France in December 1916. Of St Boniface, Winnipeg; brother of **William Niven Steadma**n; son of the Reverend William and Frances Sophia Anne (Niven) Steadman of 53 Dudley Street. Vimy Memorial.

1917 Wednesday 11 April: Private 15856 **Joseph Meggison** aged 25 of 8th Battalion the Somerset Light Infantry, formerly 14314 the Northumberland Fusiliers, died in France. Born in Blyth, Northumberland, he was a shipyard labourer in 1911. Husband of Olive Harriet (Edwins) of 26 Lake Street; son of Ralph and Frances (Payne) Meggison of Howdon, Northumberland. Arras Memorial 4.

1917 Thursday 11 April: Private GS/3751 **Frederick Waring** aged 25 of 8th Battalion the Queen's Own (Royal West Kent Regiment) died in action in France. He was born in Aston Clinton, moved with his family to Pitstone and worked there on farms until he enlisted in Willesden. His widowed father married Caroline Hill in 1896, and she is named as his mother in military records. Son of Philip and Ellen Eliza (Bligh) Waring of 2 Church End, Pitstone. Maroc British Cemetery I Q 20.

1917 Friday 13 April: Gnr 9529 **Joseph Brand** aged 40 of 125th Siege Battery the RGA died of wounds at No. 12 General Hospital, Rouen. Born in Wing, he was a telegraph messenger and boot repairer before enlisting 2806 in the Royal Artillery in 1894, serving in India before being discharged in 1906, and then a gardener before re-enlisting. Husband of Mary Jane (Mead) of George Street, Wing; brother of **Albert Brand**; son of Joseph and Ann Brand (Rogers) Brand; stepson of Sarah Ann (Culverhouse) Brand of High Street, Wing. St Sever Cemetery Extension O VIII J 2.

1917 Friday 13 April: Corporal 32181 **Frederick William Weedon** aged 20 of 6th Battalion the Bedfords died at No. 19 CCS. Military records state that the casualty station had left Agnes-Les-Duisans on 4 March and reopened on 15 April in Frévent; however, a detachment had been sent to open a CCS for walking wounded at Avesnes-le-Comte, and on 2 April this was converted into an advanced operating theatre. Born in Eaton Bray, in 1911 he worked on a farm before enlisting. Brother of **Ernest Weedon**; son of William and Hannah (Oakins) Weedon of Prentice Lane, Eaton Bray. Duisans British Cemetery III J 3.

1917 Monday 16 April: Tpr 920 **George Leonard Girling** aged 24 of 2/1st Corps the Bedfordshire Yeomanry died of tuberculosis at his parents' home in Leigh-on-Sea, Essex after being invalided out of the army with bronchial pneumonia contracted while training at Hatfield Peverel in December 1915. Born in Dunstable, he and his family were already living in Leighton in 1901 when his father was manager of Barclay's Bank. Son of Frederick and Elizabeth Sarah (Smalley) Girling of Leigh on Sea, formerly of the Bank House, 2 Market Square. (Burial place unknown).

1917 Thursday 19 April: Sergeant 201257 **John Herbert Carey** aged 32 of C Company, 1/4th Battalion the Norfolks, formerly 8179 of 3/4th Battalion, was posted as missing, death presumed, in Gaza. A cycle maker when he enlisted aged 19 in Leighton in 1905, he had previously served in 3rd and 1st Battalion the Bedfords; in 1911 he was at Longmoor Camp, East Liss. Son of John and Henrietta Louisa (Bennett) Carey of Bushey, formerly of 38 St Andrew's Street. Gaza War Cemetery XXIII D 1.

1917 Friday 20 April: Corporal 22879 **Joseph Clarke** aged 34 of 4th Battalion the Bedfords died in action near Gavrelle. In 1911 he was a farm labourer, living with his wife and daughter at 44 Pinfold, Woburn. Husband of Minnie (Whiting) of School House, Leighton Street, Woburn; son of

Thomas and Alice (Staniford) Clarke of Sheep Lane, Potsgrove. Arras Memorial Bay 5.

1917 Friday 20 April: Lance Corporal 29512 **Thomas Edmund Redding** aged 33 of 8th Battalion the Bedfords died at Loos. Born in Leighton, he attended Beaudesert School and had managed Elizabeth Janes's milk round for the seventeen years before he enlisted in Luton. After training at Ampthill, he was transferred to Felixstowe before being drafted to the Western Front a few months before his death. Husband of Lizzie Kate (Nash) of 44 Church Street; son of Jabez and Emma Elizabeth (Purton) Redding of 42 Union Street. Loos Memorial 41.

1917 Monday 23 April: Second Lieutenant **Ernest Thubron Dunford** aged 24 of 13 Squadron the RFC died of wounds received twelve days earlier near Arras. He was born in Newcastle upon Tyne and was a clerk when he enlisted in Canada on 23 September 1914. Son of Errington and Gertrude Ann (Thubron, later Freeman) Dunford; stepson of Edward George Freeman of Woburn Lodge, Linslade. Douai Communal Cemetery Row D Grave 12. (See also Chapter 5.)

1917 Monday 23 April: Private 41823 **Albert Oliver Emerton** aged 21 of 16th Battalion the Manchesters, formerly 144506 the RFA, died in action at Chérisy. Known in the family as Oliver, he was born in Chalgrave and lived there until enlisting. Son of Levi and Deborah (Tearle) Emerton of Tebworth. Arras Memorial Bay 7.

1917 Monday 23 April: Private 13119 **Arthur Jackson** aged 20 of 1st Battalion the Bedfords died in action in France, one of seven officers and 230 other ranks from his regiment who died on that day. Born in Eaton Bray, in 1911 he was a coal dealer's labourer. Son of Jeffrey and Mary (Henley) Jackson of the Green, Eaton Bray. Arras Memorial 5.

1917 Monday 23 April: Private 22011 **Sidney Roberts** aged 21 of 1st Battalion the Bedfords died 'while gallantly fighting in the first wave' in France. Born in Leighton, he worked with his father as a shoeing smith before enlisting in the ASC in Bedford on 3 June 1915. Son of George and Alice (Woodwards) Roberts of 4 Bedford Street. Arras Memorial 5.

1917 Tuesday 24 April: Private 787076 **Alfred Horn** aged 24 of 3rd Battalion the Canadian Infantry (Central Ontario Regiment) died at the Canadian

Base Hospital in Boulogne, having been shot in the thigh. He had worked in Leighton as a net maker but was in Canada by July 1915 and enlisted in Perth, Ontario. Son of Walter William and Eunice (Dimmock) Horn of Mill Road. Wimereux Communal Cemetery I I 10.

1917 Friday 27 April: Second Lieutenant **Kenneth Healing** aged 23 of 6th Battalion (Territorial) the Sherwood Foresters (Nottinghamshire and Derbyshire) Regiment, formerly 1585 the Royal Bucks Hussars, died after being shot by a sniper in France. He was born in Kensworth, attended Ashton Grammar School in Dunstable as a boarder and later worked at the London County and Westminster Bank in Leighton. Son of John and Emmeline (Reynolds) Healing of Dunstable. Templeux-Le-Guerard British Cemetery I A 48.

1917 Saturday 28 April: Private 31786 **Fred Costin** aged 23 of 6th Battalion the Bedfords died in action during the Battle of Arras. He was born in Edlesborough and later lived in Eaton Bray, working as a nurseryman. Husband of Mary (Rollings) of Sparrow Hall Cottages, Edlesborough; son of John and Emma (Janes) Costin of Summerleys, Eaton Bray. Arras Memorial 4.

1917 Saturday 28 April: Private 21350 **Sidney Frederick Lovell** aged 23 of 2nd Battalion the O&BLI is presumed to have died in the first wave of the attack at the Battle of Arleux. He was born in Burcott and was a farm labourer before enlisting. Son of John and Elizabeth Jane (Cutler) Lovell of Burcott. Arras Memorial 6, 7.

1917 Saturday 28 April: Private 26196 **Frank Mead** aged 22 of 2nd Battalion the O&BLI, formerly of 6th Battalion, died during the dawn attack at Oppy Wood. This took place under the support of a creeping artillery barrage and there were heavy casualties. Born in Littlecote, between Dunton and Stewkley, he and his family had moved to Leighton between 1911 and 11 October 1915 when he enlisted in Aylesbury. Son of William and Selina Jane (Clements) Mead of 18 South Street, formerly of Stewkley. Arras Memorial 6, 7.

1917 Saturday 28 April: Private 35888 **Horace James Pantling** aged 24 of 10th Battalion the Loyal North Lancashires, formerly of the Royal Fusiliers, died in the attack on Greenland Hill during the 2nd Battle of the Scarpe. He had sailed from Folkestone on 6 January 1917 and arrived in Étaples the following day. Born in Leighton, after leaving Beaudesert School he was first a grocer's errand boy but a labourer when he enlisted at Luton on 24 May 1916, and was a member of the Salvation Army. Son of Arthur William and Mary Jane (Samuel) Pantling of 48 Plantation Road. Arras Memorial 7.

1917 Saturday 28 April: Private 202654 **Ernest Roff** aged 20 of 2/4th Battalion the O&BLI, formerly 6473, died in Belgium. He was born in Billington and in 1911 was working on a farm, as was his older brother Fred, lodging with and presumably helping to support financially his widowed paternal grandmother, Mary Ann. Son of George and Sarah Jane (Pheasant) Roff of Whaddon Farm, Slapton. Thiepval Memorial Pier 10 Faces A, D.

1917 Sunday 29 April: Private 32112 **Alfred John Dawson** aged 21 of 6th Battalion the Bedfords died of wounds in France. Born in Leighton, he attended Beaudesert School, was a Scout and served his apprenticeship as a printer with Faith Bros Printers in Wing Road before enlisting in Leighton. Son of Alfred George and Jane (Finch) Dawson of 50 Mill Road and stepson of Eliza (Hogg) Dawson. Aubigny Communal Cemetery Extension II G 65.

1917 Sunday 29 April: Private 26133 **John Piggott** aged 20 of 6th Battalion the Bedfords died in action in France. The only one of seven children to be born in Stanbridge, he grew up in Tilsworth and was a grocer's errand boy before enlisting. Son of Frederick and Caroline (Darby) Piggott of the Green, Tilsworth. Arras Memorial 5.

1917 Thursday 3 May: Sergeant 17156 **William Banwell** aged 33 of 7th Battalion the Bedfords died in the 3rd Battle of the Scarpe. He was born in Tilsworth but his family had moved to Heath and Reach by 1901 where he worked as a carpenter in the family business. Son of William and Lydia (Rowe) Banwell of Woburn Road, Heath and Reach. Arras Memorial 5.

1917 Thursday 3 May: Private 40784 **Charles Cook** aged 32 of 9th Battalion the Essex Regiment, formerly 46603 the Royal Fusiliers, died while a prisoner of war after being wounded. Born in Chalgrave, he always lived and worked on farms in the area. In 1910 he was discovered trespassing with several other men and a sheepdog on the Duke of Bedford's land, and was given a fine of 5s with 12s 6d costs or fourteen days' imprisonment; they all received a warning from the Bench about 'Sunday morning strolls'. Husband of Olive Maud (Garner) and son of Alfred and Sarah Louisa (Tucker) Cook, all of Watling Street, Hockliffe. Douai Communal Cemetery Joint Grave H 15.

1917 Thursday 3 May: Lance Sergeant 33039 **Charles Harris** aged 41 of 1st Battalion the Princess Charlotte of Wales's (Royal Berkshire) Regiment, formerly 19727 the Ox&BLI, died in action in France. Born in Little Billington, he originally joined the army aged 18 and served in South Africa; he re-enlisted although no longer liable for being called up. Husband of Minnie Emily (Crawley) of 36 Bassett Road, late of 8 Water Lane; son of William Clarke and Catherine (Adams) Harris of Wolverton. Arras Memorial 7.

1917 Thursday 3 May: Private 26398 **Albert Victor Howe** aged 20 of 5th Battalion the O&BLI, formerly of 2nd Battalion, was posted as missing, death presumed, during the 3rd Battle of the Scarpe. He was a clerk and attended Leighton Buzzard Evening School before being called up. Brother of **Sidney Ernest Howe**; son of Philip Robert William and Kate (Field) Howe of 24 Waterloo Road, later of 12 Southcourt Avenue. Arras Memorial 6, 7.

1917 Thursday 3 May: Rifleman S/28379 **Charles John Janes** aged 31 of 9th Battalion the Rifle Brigade died in action in France. In 1911 he had married and was a coffee-house keeper in Kentish Town, but was a pastry packer when he enlisted in May 1916, disembarking at Le Havre seven months later. Brother of **George Alma Janes** and **Harry Janes**, Husband of Maud (Skinner) of Kentish Town; son of David and Sarah Jane (Emmerson) Janes of Kentish Town, formerly of Bassett Road. Arras Memorial 9.

1917 Thursday 3 May: Private 265935 **Claud Janes** aged 19 of 5th Battalion the O&BLI, formerly of 4th Battalion, was missing, wounded while crawling between shell holes in an unsuccessful attack during the 3rd Battle of the Scarpe. He enlisted as 2749 of 2/1st Battalion at the outbreak of war aged 17. Born in Leighton, but brought up in Linslade, he had two older brothers who emigrated to Australia, both serving and surviving. Son of Edward Foll and Rosa (Chitham) Janes of Southcourt Avenue. Arras Memorial 6, 7.

1917 Thursday 3 May: G/13095 Lance Corporal **Reuben Jeffery** aged 23 of A Company, 6th Battalion the Buffs (East Kent Regiment), formerly 14590 of 4th Battalion the East Surreys, was missing, death presumed, during the 3rd Battle of the Scarpe. He was born in Suffolk but the family moved to Crafton when his father became a groom at the stud. Having moved to Epsom, he was a motor driver when he enlisted at Kingston. Only child of Frederick William and Thurza (Crane) Jeffery of Hamilton Stud, Newmarket, late of Crafton. Arras Memorial Bay 2.

1917 Thursday 3 May: Lance Corporal G/22795 **Cuthbert Pratt** aged 19 of 6th Battalion the West Surreys died of wounds in France. Son of Edward and Susannah (Mead) Pratt of Great Billington. Duisans British Cemetery II Q 29.

1917 Thursday 3 May: Gunner 106626 **George Sayell** aged 25 of D Battery, 36th Brigade the Royal Horse Artillery (RHA) and RFA died in shellfire near Arras. Born and living in Cheddington, in 1911 he was a yard porter for the L&NWR. Son of Andrew Humphrey and Ellen (Hemley) Sayell of High Street, Cheddington. Roclincourt Military Cemetery II B 18.

1917 Thursday 3 May: Private 266531 **Frank Whitaker** aged 20 of 5th Battalion the O&BLI died in France. Born in Brixton, he came to Cublington with his mother in the early 1900s after the death of his father; before marrying, she had lived at the Bell with Mary Pullen, her sister. He had left school by 1911 and was a house boy. Son of Frank and Elizabeth (Brazier) Whitaker of Post Office, Cublington. Arras Memorial 6, 7.

1917 Saturday 5 May: Private **Harry George Pratt** aged 24 of 5th Battalion the O&BLI died of wounds probably sustained during the attack on Hillside Works, Vis-en-Artois. Known as Bobadee to his family, he worked in the building department of the Ascott Estate and played football for Wing, his birthplace, before enlisting at the beginning of the war. Son of Joseph and Ada (Langston) Pratt of Leighton Road, Wing. Bucquoy Road Cemetery I F 1.

1917 Saturday 5 May: Lance Corporal G/19267 **Bernard Frank Whitman** aged 27 of 7th Battalion the Queen's Own (Royal West Kent) Regiment died after being wounded in France. Born in Kildare, Ireland, he was the son of a carpenter with the Royal Engineers, living in Aldershot by 1891. He was a railway porter in Leighton when he enlisted there in the 3/1st Kent Cyclists Battalion. Son of William and Emily (Wood, later Wilson) Whitman of Johannesburg, South Africa; brother of William Henry Whitman of 15 Billington Road. Warlincourt Halte British Cemetery IX G 10.

1917 Sunday 6 May: Gunner 315376 **Frederick Charles Mead** aged 23 of Wessex (Hampshire) Heavy Battery the RGA died without regaining consciousness half an hour after being hit in the head by a shell. He was born in Leighton where he attended Beaudesert School. Son of William and Fanny (Makepeace) Mead of Luton formerly of 2 Church Street. Vlamertinghe Military Cemetery VI K 7.

1917 Monday 7 May: Private 198209 **Frederick William Cleaver** aged 32 of 28th Battalion the Canadian Infantry (Saskatchewan Regiment) died in action after the capture of Vimy Ridge during the Battle of Arras. Born in Leighton, he had been a hay binder before emigrating to Canada. Once there he worked as a waiter, signing his attestation papers on 18 November 1915, having served for six months in the Volunteer Corps. Of Fort William, Quebec; son of Alfred and Elizabeth (Gower) Cleaver of 53 Lake Street. Vimy Memorial.

1917 Friday 11 May: Private 115 **Henry Bransom**, a railway service guard of the 23rd Canadian Infantry Brigade, died of septic bronchitis at the General Hospital, Vancouver, having been admitted a month earlier, and was buried with military honours. He was born in Leighton and was a corn miller and dealer; he still lived and worked there in 1911. Of Vancouver Island, formerly of 7 Plantation Road; son of James and Mary (Rickard) Bransom, late of Plantation Road; brother of Martha Bransom of Stechford. Vancouver (Mountain View) Cemetery, British Columbia Block 38 Plot 4 Lot 2 Grave C9194.

1917 Saturday 12 May: Private 907743 **Richmond Lawrence** aged 31 of 102nd Battalion the Canadian Infantry died when a grenade landed in a front line trench near Liévin; his grave was subsequently lost. Born in Essex, he was brought up in Linslade where his father was landlord of the Elephant and Castle Hotel. He was a carpenter when he emigrated to Imperial, Saskatchewan in 1908, coming home to marry in 1914 and returning before his son was born in Canada in 1916, around the time he enlisted. Brother-in-law of **Frederick Charles Ruffhead**; husband of Agnes Selina (Ruffhead); son of Edward and Emily (Burgh) Lawrence of Romford. Vimy Memorial.

1917 Sunday 13 May: Private G/65269 **Thomas Elmer** aged 32 of 4th Battalion the London Regiment, formerly 11839 the Royal Fusiliers, died in action in France. Born in Hoggeston, he grew up in Swanbourne and worked on farms. Husband of Eleanor Balaclava (Roads) of 21 Ashwell Street; son of Daniel and Mary Ann (Pitkin) Elmer of Nearton End, Swanbourne. Arras Memorial 3.

1917 Wednesday 16 May: Lance Corporal/Private 33071 **William Albert Charles Page** aged 19 of 6th Battalion the Bedfords died of wounds in France. He was born in Leighton. Son of Albert Charles and Annie Elizabeth (Turney) Page of Newport Pagnell, late of Clarence Road. Étaples Military Cemetery XVIII N 19.

1917 Monday 21 May: Private 41614 **William Ernest Bond MM★** aged 28 of the RAMC, attached to 88th Battery the RFA, died of wounds in France. He was a carpenter, born and living in Mentmore, where his father was a coachman. Son of Albert and Charlotte (Green) Bond of Mentmore. Fosse No. 10 Communal Cemetery Extension I C 11. (See also Chapter 17).

1917 Monday 21 May: Rifleman 323790 **Alfred George Plummer** aged 40 of 2/6th Battalion the London Regiment (City of London Rifles) died in action after going over the top with the rest of his section. Born in Leighton, he was living in Fulham, assistant to an ironmonger by 1911, and enlisted in London. Uncle of **Edward Joseph 'Ted' Plummer**; son of John and Ann (Hyde) Plummer of High Street, formerly of Mill Road. Arras Memorial 9, 10.

1917 Monday 28 May: Private 33076 **Mark Rollings** aged 19 or 20 of 6th Battalion the Bedfords died of wounds in No. 41 CCS, Agnez-Les-Duisans. Born in Eaton Bray, he worked on a farm after leaving school. Son of George and Jane (Horn) Rollings of 14 Victoria Terrace, Bower Lane, Eaton Bray. Duisans British Cemetery IV M 26.

1917 Wednesday 6 June: Driver M2/047095 **James Frederick Brown** aged 42 of 9th Divisional Supply Column the ASC died at No. 2 Canadian General Hospital, Le Tréport, having slipped from a lorry which then ran over him. Born in Leighton, he was working as an asylum attendant in Bow, London in 1901 and it was likely that during this period he met his future wife, a nurse at another asylum in that area. By 1911 he was a tramway driver with four children. Husband of Rosa Ann (Brown) of Hanwell; son of James and Elizabeth (Fletcher) Brown of 2 Queen Street. Mont Huon Military Cemetery III G 10B.

1917 Saturday 16 June: Sergeant 231132 **Herbert Stanley Briggs** aged 25 of 2/2nd Battalion the London Regiment (Royal Fusiliers) was missing, presumed killed by shellfire, working on front-line trenches near Arras. He served an apprenticeship as a printer before leaving Linslade to work in London and then emigrate to Canada in March 1914, returning immediately after the outbreak of war to enlist. Husband of Alice Louisa (Dubbins) of Stanbridge Road; son of Edward and Rachel Annie (Emery) Briggs of 1 New Road. Arras Memorial 9.

1917 Saturday 16 June: Private 27085 **Thomas Woolhead** aged 35 of 2nd Battalion the Suffolks died in action in France. He was born in Heath and was a sand carter there. Son of William and Sarah Ann (Dickins) Woolhead of 8 Bryant's Row, Heath and Reach. Monchy British Cemetery I F 14.

1917 Saturday 23 June: Private 26614 **Albert Knight** aged 26 of 13th (Service) Battalion the Forest of Dean Pioneers (Gloucestershire Regiment) died in action in Belgium. Born in Edlesborough, he worked on a farm in Northall before enlisting. Son of George and Sarah Ann (Smith) Knight of Church End, Edlesborough. Vlamertinghe New Military Cemetery IV D 5.

1917 Sunday 24 June: Sergeant 33777 **Robert James Beaumont** aged 28 of 8th Battalion the Bedfords died in action during raids and attacks on Hill 70 during the Loos Salient. Born in Norwich, he and his family were in Leighton by 1901 where he attended Beaudesert School. He had already enlisted in the Bedfordshire Territorials and been discharged 'time expired' in 1916, but rejoined in December that year. Husband of Beatrice Esther (Bellamy, later Newman) of Kempston; son of William and Minnie (Clements) Beaumont of Heath Road, formerly of 12 Chapel Path. Philosophe British Cemetery II R 7.

1917 Wednesday 27 June: Officer's Steward 2nd Class L7598 **George Arthur Russell** aged 27 of RN Seaplane Base Dunkirk, the RNAS, died during an enemy bombardment. Son of Henry Frederick and Catherine (Street) Russell of Watford, formerly of Edward Street. Dunkirk Town Cemetery I D 8. (See also Chapter 7).

1917 Tuesday 10 July: Private 80513 **James Baker MM★** aged 23 of 7th Field Ambulance the RAMC died in the General Infirmary, Leeds. Despite several operations, including amputation of a leg, septicaemia in his right thigh followed gunshot wounds received seven weeks earlier. Born in Linslade, he had attended school in Eggington and then Beaudesert School in Leighton and was working as a gardener when he enlisted in Bedford on 2 November 1915. He left Southampton for Rouen with the BEF on 2 August 1916 and returned home only after being wounded in May 1917. Only son of George and Hannah Sarah (Lowe) Baker of Sandy Lane, Heath Road. Heath and Reach Cemetery Grave A 100. (See also Chapter 17)

1917 Thursday 12 July: Bombardier L/31058 **Claude Cheshire** aged 21 of B (202nd Siege) Battery, 177th Brigade the RFA, formerly 77541 the RGA, died after being wounded in action near Vlamertinghe. His father, a police sergeant, had been stationed in Leighton for several years between February

1906 and April 1911 and Claude had been a member of the newly-formed Buzzard Scout Troop. When the family moved to Eaton Socon, Claude joined the Scout troop there, becoming a King's Scout. Son of Frederick Charles and Jane (Edwards) Cheshire of Shefford. Vlamertinghe New Military Cemetery I F 32.

1917 Wednesday 17 July: Private GS/49685 **Samuel Sayell** aged 33 of 32nd Battalion the Royal Fusiliers died in Belgium. Born in Cheddington, he grew up in Mentmore where he was a carter on a farm. Husband of Frances Annie (Harmsworth); son of Henry and Elizabeth (Foxon) Sayell of Crafton, formerly of Mentmore. Lijssenthoek Military Cemetery XVI F 20.

1917 Sunday 22 July: Private 98039 **Thomas William Kiteley** aged 21 of 69th Company the MGC (Infantry), formerly G/52281 the Royal Fusiliers, died in action in Belgium. Born in Leighton, he attended Beaudesert School and worked as an upholsterer for Aveline and Phillips before enlisting in Luton. Son of John Henry and Emily Jane (Clarke) Kiteley, of Wayside, Grovebury Road. Ypres (Menin Gate) Memorial 56.

1917 Thursday 26 July: Private 201524 **Joseph Henry Creamer** aged 25 of 2nd Battalion the Bedfords died in shellfire near Zillebeke while burying a comrade. Born in Heath and Reach, he worked on farms before enlisting. Son of John and Alice Jane (Fleckney) of Hockliffe. Bedford House Cemetery Enclosure No. 4 II CI 5.

1917 Thursday 26 July: Private 271609 **Frederick Charles Groom** aged 27 of 1st Battalion the Hertfordshires, attached 234th Field Company the RE, died of wounds at No. 4 CCS, Dozinghem. Born in Stanbridge, where his father farmed, he had moved with his family to Leighton by 1911 and was working as a moulder in an iron foundry. He was a bandsman and songster in the Salvation Army. Son of Joseph and Deborah (Chandler) Groom of 71 Lake Street. Dozinghem Military Cemetery I H 4.

1917 Thursday 26 July: Private 29628 **Ernest Oliver Tompkins** aged 45 of 2nd Battalion the Bedfords died when a shell exploded, returning from front-line trenches at Zillebeke. Born in Ship Road, he had served as 693 with the the Royal Horseguards in the Boer War. He later deserted but re-enlisted in the Bedfords, probably in 1915. Husband of Minnie (Botsworth); son of Thomas and Susan (Halsey) Tompkins of Watford, formerly of the Hare Inn. Bedford House Cemetery Enclosure No. 4 II CI 2.

1917 Sunday 29 July: 9597 Private **Francis William Cooper Strong (alias John Stewart)** aged 29 of 2nd Battalion the Duke of Edinburgh's (Wiltshire) Regiment died in Belgium after being hit by a shell. He had enlisted in 1906, and when war broke out was drafted from India to France. Injured at the Battle of the Marne, he recovered but was wounded in the leg during the landing at Suvla Bay, after which he was transferred to Egypt, where he suffered a haemorrhage from the wound. Back in France, he recovered from being wounded on the Somme, but was killed when he returned to active service. It is unclear why he served as John Stewart. His parents having separated by 1899, he was boarding with a grocer in Rothersfield, Sussex by 1901. Brother of **Benjamin Clarence Strong** and **Robert Harold Strong**. Son of Robert Bennett and Linda Elizabeth (Cooper, later Turner) Strong of Hampstead, formerly of Heath and Reach. Ypres (Menin Gate) Memorial 53.

1917 Tuesday 31 July: Private 41713 **Robert Henry Fallick** aged 35 of 8th Battalion the Lincolnshires died in action in Belgium. Born in Ardingbourne, he and his wife and son moved to Soulbury soon after 1911. Husband of Annie Lavinia (Harmer), of Council Houses, Soulbury; son of Silas and Mary Rachael (Foote) Fallick, Aldingbourne. Ypres (Menin Gate) Memorial 21.

1917 Tuesday 31 July: Gunner **Harold Victor Randall** aged 20 of B Battery 71 Brigade the RFA died during the Battle of Picklem Ridge, the opening engagement of the Battle of Passchendaele. Born in Islington, he was a gardener in Wing in 1911. Son of James and Annie (Sawyer, later Blanchard) Randall of Islington, formerly of Wing and Stewkley; grandson of George and Jane (Brand) Randall of Church Street, Wing. Ypres (Menin Gate) Memorial 5 and 9.

1917 Tuesday 31 July: Private 205660 **Thomas Stibbon** aged 36 of 10th Battalion the Queen's Own (Royal West Kent) Regiment died in Belgium. He was born in Long Sutton, Lincolnshire and in 1911 was a farm worker, living with his family in Swaffham. Husband of Maud (Griffiths) of Grove Place; son of John and Sarah Alice (Vickers) Stibbon of Swaffham. Ypres (Menin Gate) Memorial Panels 45 and 47.

1917 Tuesday 31 July: Lieutenant Colonel **Alfred Joseph Elton Sunderland MID★** aged 42 of 2nd Battalion the Devonshires died during an offensive which started at 0350 near Railway Wood, Zillebeke. He had been invalided for ten months in 1916 (17 February to 15 December). A career soldier since 1895, he saw action with the Devonshires in South Africa, receiving the Queen's Medal with three clasps and the King's with two, was a captain with the regiment in Malta in 1911, was gazetted major in September 1915 and fought on the Somme. Son of Reverend James and Florence Margaret (Elton) Sunderland of Eggington Vicarage. Belgian Battery Corner Cemetery I F 2. (See also Chapter 17).

1917 Tuesday 31 July: Private G/14427 **Frank Thomas Weaver** aged 39 of 8th Battalion the West Surreys was reported missing, death presumed. He was born and grew up in Aylesbury, living two doors away from his future wife. In 1911 he was a journeyman basket maker in Somersham but had moved to Leighton by 1916. Husband of Isa Miranda (Figg); son of Joseph and Blanche (Hardy) Weaver of Aylesbury. Ypres (Menin Gate) Memorial 11-13, 14.

1917 Wednesday 1 August: Private 220024 **William John Rowland** aged 19 of 2nd Battalion the Wiltshires died in action in Belgium. Son of William and Minnie (Horne) Rowland of Stank Lane, Pitstone. Ypres (Menin Gate) Memorial 53.

1917 Thursday 2 August: Private G/8348 **James Joseph Mead** aged 26 of C Company, 9th Battalion the East Surreys, formerly 15715 the Bedfords, died in action in Belgium. He was a joiner and carpenter when he enlisted and after transfer was posted to France with the BEF on 5 October 1915, receiving the 1914-15 Star. Son of James Joseph and Mary Ann (Thornton) Mead of 68 North Street. Ypres (Menin Gate) Memorial 34.

1917 Sunday 5 August: Sergeant 18251 **Herbert Henry North** aged 47 of the Bedfords died at home after an accident near the Milton Bryan turning off the Woburn to Hockliffe road. Despite warnings, he jumped from 'a motor car in motion' driven by Ernest Alfred Heady and concussed himself by falling on his head while attempting to retrieve two partridges which had been struck by the vehicle. With service totalling thirty years, he had fought in India and the Boer War, afterwards working at Totternhoe Lime Works and then taking over the licence of the Bell Inn, Hockliffe before enlisting once again to be posted to Kempston Barracks where he trained new volunteers and conscripts. Husband of Lizzie (Bonwick) of Hockliffe; son of Harry and Elizabeth (Foxley) North of Tilsworth. Tilsworth (All Saints), near south boundary.

1917 Sunday 5 August: 235092 Private **William Stevens** aged 19 of 2nd Battalion the Prince of Wales's Volunteers (South Lancashire Regiment), formerly 3215 the Bedfords, died in action in Belgium. Son of Samuel and

Emily (Dawson, later Watts) Stevens of 66 Church Street. Ypres (Menin Gate) Memorial 37.

1917 Tuesday 7 August: Private 36417 **Arthur Clive Pepper** aged 19 of 1/4th Battalion the Royal Berkshires died in action in Belgium. Son of Arthur Charles and Mary Ann (Arnold) Pepper of Harpenden, late of Lane's End, Heath and Reach. Ypres (Menin Gate) Memorial 45.

1917 Saturday 11 August: 32269 Private **William James Toms** aged 34 of 2nd Battalion the Bedfords died of wounds in France. Husband of Sarah Jane (Janes, later Cowley) of 88 North Street; son of Henry and Sarah Ann (Sear) Toms of 22 Chapel Path. Étaples Military Cemetery XXV M 13.

1917 Wednesday 15 August: Rifleman 572717 **Harry Stanley Bogg** aged 20 of 5th Battalion the London Regiment was missing, presumed dead, during the Battle of Langemarck. Born in Hampshire, he was living in Luton when he enlisted. Brother of **Gilbert Tom Bogg**; son of Jonathan and Agnes Louisa (Harvey) Bogg of Liscombe. Ypres (Menin Gate) Memorial 52-54.

1917 Thursday 16 August: Rifleman 41765 **James Wesley Foster** aged 19 of 14th (Service) Battalion (Young Citizens) the Royal Irish Rifles, formerly 29503 of 2nd Battalion the Bedfords, was missing, death presumed, during the Battle of Langemarck. He was born in Chalgrave, a ploughboy by 1911. Son of Henry and Elizabeth Sarah (Emerton) Foster of Wingfield, Hockliffe. Tyne Cot Memorial 138-140, 162, 162A-163A.

1917 Thursday 16 August: Corporal/Bombardier 40661 **Sidney Holland** aged 32 of 1st Brigade, the Canadian Field Artillery died in action in France. Born in Totternhoe, he had worked as a coal porter in Leighton before sailing from Liverpool on the White Star Line's *Dominion* for Quebec in July 1910. Letters of administration in lieu of probate were granted to an Edith Taylor, spinster, on whose grave in Leighton-Linslade Cemetery he is commemorated. Of Smith's Falls, Ontario; son of Thomas and Rebecca (Morgan) Holland late of 12 Vandyke Road. Bully-Grenay Communal Cemetery, British Extension IV E 13.

1917 Thursday 16 August: Private 266439 **Arthur James Smith** aged 32 of 1/1st Battalion the O&BLI died in action near St Julien at the Battle of Langemarck (16-18 August). Born in Linslade he moved around with his parents as a child, returning to Linslade to live with his maternal grandmother by 1901, and was a groom when he enlisted. Latterly of Aston Clinton; only brother of **Hortensius Stephen Smith**; husband of Charlotte (Major) of 6 Plantation Road; son of James and Catherine Elizabeth (Thompson), formerly of 37 Old Road, Linslade. Tyne Cot Memorial 96–98.

1917 Thursday 16 August: Pe 203696 **Arthur Woodwards** aged 22 of 1/4th Battalion the O&BLI, formerly 24107 of 3rd Battalion and 20237 of 1/4th Battalion, died when shot by a sniper during the Battle of Langemarck. Born in Wing, he was employed at Bullivant's before he enlisted. Brother of **Ernest Woodwards** and **George Woodwards**; son of Henry and Mary Ann (Taylor) Woodwards of High Street, Wing. Tyne Cot Memorial 96–98.

1917 Thursday 16 August: Private 203691 **William Burrows Woolhead** aged 33 of 1/4th Battalion the O&BLI died in action at the Battle of Langemarck. Born in Wing, he was a bricklayer's labourer before enlisting. Youngest son of Sidney and Ann (Burrows) Woolhead of New Zealand Gardens, Wing. Tyne Cot Memorial 96–98.

1917 Saturday 18 August: Driver T4/035830 **Edward John Smith** aged 24 of 2nd Reserve Park the ASC died of wounds in Belgium. Born in Edlesborough, he was a horse driver at a lime works, probably in Totternhoe. Son of Thomas and Elizabeth (Thorne) Smith of 12 Taskers Row, Edlesborough. Potijze Chateau Lawn Cemetery E 20.

1917 Wednesday 22 August: Private 203174 **Daniel Burrows** aged 37 of 2/4th Battalion the Princess Charlotte of Wales's (Royal Berkshire) Regiment died in action in Belgium. Late of the Star and Garter, High Street South, Dunstable; son of James and Caroline (Peacock) Burrows of 50 Springfield Road, formerly of Lake Street. Tyne Cot Memorial 105–106, 162.

1917 Saturday 22 August: Private 29129 **Alfred Sear** aged 29 or 30 of 4th Battalion the Bedfords died in action near Lens. Born in Heath and Reach, he moved to Dunstable as an engineer's labourer and boarded with a married sister before marrying in 1901. In June 1916 he was drafted to the Western Front and was seriously wounded at the Battle of the Somme. After hospital treatment in England, he returned to France in February 1917. Husband of Mary (Poulton) of 4 Oxford Terrace, Dunstable; son of James and Emma (Giles) Sear late of 5 Mill Road, formerly of Gig Lane, Heath and Reach. Bailleul Road East Cemetery I P 4.

1917 Saturday 22 August: Private 266574 **Ernest Albert Waters** aged 22 of 2/1st Buckinghamshire Battalion the O&BLI, formerly 4144, was reported missing, presumed dead in Belgium. He was a farm worker. Son of Henry and Thirza (Kent) Waters of Station Road, Cheddington. Tyne Cot Memorial 96-98.

1917 Wednesday 22 August: Rifleman B/200882 **William James Windmill** aged 33 of 8th Battalion the Rifle Brigade died in action in Belgium. Born in Billington, he had left the village by 1901 to be a stable boy in Finchley and by 1911 was a domestic gardener boarding in Tottenham. Husband of Amy (Spinks) of North Finchley; son of William James and Ann (Abraham) Windmill of Billington. Tyne Cot Memorial 145-147.

1917 Saturday 25 August: Farrier Sergeant 205073 **Ernest Pollard** aged 23 of 1/1st Royal Bucks Hussars, formerly 755, died of wounds in Egypt. He had enlisted in 1912 and would have been mobilised immediately at the outbreak of war, arriving in Egypt in April 1915. Elder son of Joseph Andrew and Elizabeth (Carter) Pollard of High Street, Wing. Kantara War Memorial Cemetery, B 124.

1917 Tuesday 4 September: Lieutenant Colonel **Arthur Blewitt** aged 56 of the 60th King's Royal Rifle Corps attached to 5th Labour Group died in France of wounds after a bomb explosion. Born in Pinner, he was a career soldier in barracks in York in 1881, captain by 1892 and major by 1902. Twin brother of Annie Blewitt of Heath Manor House. Son of William and Jane (Turner) Blewitt, late of Pinner. Longuenesse (St Omer) Souvenir Cemetery IV D 66.

1917 Monday 17 September: Private 33610 **William Thomas Clare** aged 19 of 8th Battalion the Alexandra, Princess of Wales's Own (Yorkshire) Regiment, formerly 282976 the ASC, died after being wounded at Passchendaele. Born in Eggington, he stayed in the village with his mother and siblings immediately after the death of his father in 1900 but by 1911 was living with his mother and brother in Woburn Road, Hockliffe. Brother of **Joseph Theodore Clare**; son of Albert Theodore and Emma (Clark) Clare of May Cottage, 5 Regent Street. Voormezeele Enclosures No.1 and No. 2 I J 5. (See also Joseph below.)

1917 Thursday 20 September: Private G/21122 **Joseph Theodore Clare** aged 21 of 10th Battalion the West Surreys, formerly 2666 the Royal Fusiliers, died in action at Tower Hamlets Ridge. Born in Eggington, by 1911 he was a farm worker, living with his mother and brother in Woburn Road, Hockliffe. When he enlisted in Luton, he was a smith at an iron works. Brother of **William Thomas Clare**; son of Albert Theodore and Emma (Clark) Clare of May Cottage, 5 Regent Street. Tyne Cot Memorial 14-17, 162-162A. (See also William above.)

1917 Thursday 20 September: Private 3/7430 **Horace Edgar Hubbock**s aged 19 of 2nd Battalion the Bedfords died in action in Belgium. Son of William and Kate Salome (Stevens) Hubbocks of Luton, late of the Stag, Church Street. Tyne Cot Memorial 48-50, 162A.

1917 Thursday 20 September: Private S/21822 **Louis George Janes** aged 20 of 1/4th Battalion the Seaforth Highlanders died in action in Belgium. He had been a poultry boy before leaving for Edinburgh and enlisting. Husband of Theresa Quinn (McEwan) of the North British Station Hotel, Edinburgh; son of James and Caroline (Snoxell) Janes of the Greyhound, Northall. Tyne Cot Memorial Panels 132-135, 162A.

1917 Thursday 20 September: Nurse **Mary Gertrude Tindall** aged 37 of the VAD died at home after surgery following an acute illness. Sister of **Noel Stephen Tindall**; daughter of John and Isabella Mary (Harris) Tindall of Sidmouth, formerly of Beech House, Leighton. Sidmouth Cemetery. (See also Chapter 12.)

1917 Friday 21 September: Private 204357 **Alfred Herbert Adcock** aged 35 of 12th Battalion the East Surreys, formerly 203736 the Bedfords, almost certainly died at the Battle of the Menin Road Ridge. Born in Syston, Leicestershire, he worked for many years in shoe factories until he and his wife moved to Leighton in 1914 where he was a dairyman and licensee of the Royal Oak in Friday Street. He enlisted in Luton on 10 April 1917, although not fit for military service according to his medical record. Husband of Mary Jane (Harris) of 22 North Street; son of Joseph Wallis and Mary (Scarborough) Adcock of Leicester. Tyne Cot Memorial 79-80, 163A.

1917 Friday 21 September: Private 3409 **Sidney Marsh** aged 25 of 3rd Company the Australian Machine Gun Corps died in Belgium. Born in Aldbury, in 1911 he was a tramway conductor in Darlington, living with his mother's brother. Son of Daniel George and Elizabeth Ann (Plumb) Marsh of Stanbridge Crossing, late of Tring Station. Ypres (Menin Gate) Memorial 31.

1917 Saturday 22 September: Gunner 3188894 **George Woodwards** aged 31 of 53rd Battery, Canadian Field Artillery died in France. He was a porter for William Baumbrough, grocer before emigrating to Canada in April 1911, and worked as a timekeeper and clerk in North Bay, Ontario before enlisting in March 1916. Brother of **Ernest Woodwards** and **Arthur Woodwards**; son of Henry and Mary Ann (Taylor) Woodwards of High Street, Wing. Aix-Noulette Communal Cemetery Extension I T 20.

1917 Sunday 23 September: Private (Signaller) 11019 **Percy William Marks** aged 19 of 6th Battalion the Bedfords died the morning after being wounded in the head while making his way to the trenches. A bandsman and songster in the Salvation Army, he was born in Leighton and attended Beaudesert School before becoming apprenticed to carpenter Thomas James Underwood; he enlisted in Luton at the age of 18. Son of Frederick and Ellen Hursley (Lord) Marks of 33a Plantation Road, formerly of 6 Chapel Path. Elzenwalle Brasserie Cemetery II B 5.

1917 Wednesday 26 September: Gnr 147656 **John Gilpin Butcher** aged 35 of 166th Siege Battery the RGA died when a shell burst in the battery. Born in Leighton, he attended Beaudesert School and was apprenticed to a house furnisher in the town, following his trade in Tunbridge Wells by the time he enlisted. Husband of Sarah Annabella (Riddell) of Tunbridge Wells; son of George and Mary Ann Maria 'Polly' (Turney) Butcher of 4 Lake Street. The Huts Cemetery VII C 13.

1917 Wednesday 26 September: Private 30504 **John Chapman** aged 25 of 8th Battalion the King's Own Royal Lancaster Regiment died after being wounded in Belgium. He was a farm labourer before enlisting. Son of Frederick and Ann (Tearle) Chapman of Hockliffe. Tyne Cot Memorial 18-19.

1917 Wednesday 26 September: Private 327298 **William John Clark** aged 20 of 4th Battalion the Suffolk Regiment, formerly G/26153 the London Regiment, was posted as missing, presumed dead, on the first day of the Battle of Polygon Wood. Son of John and Amy Mary (Rowe) Clark of 76 Wing Road. Tyne Cot Memorial 40-41, 162-62A.

1917 Wednesday 26 September: Private G/37164 **Harold Smallbones** aged 29 of 1st Battalion the West Surreys died instantly when a shell exploded where he was sleeping. In 1911 he was living in Northall with his parents, working at Wallace's nurseries until he enlisted with the RFA in Biscot in May

1916. Husband of Lizzie (Lugsden, later Turner) of Luton; son of William and Elizabeth (Janes) Smallbones of Northall. Tyne Cot Memorial 14-17, 162-162A.

1917 Thursday 27 September: Private 235084 **Leonard Oakley** aged 28 of 5th Battalion the O&BLI died while in a Reserve camp between Ypres and Armentières, when a bomb was dropped by an enemy plane. Born in Long Marston, he had lived most of his life in High Street, Wing, and before enlisting was a butcher, probably working for his brother. Youngest child of John and Mary Ann (Luck) Oakley. Westhof Farm Cemetery II E 4.

1917 Wednesday 3 October: Lance Corporal 266113 **William Dickinson** aged 23 of 1/1st Buckinghamshire Battalion the O&BLI died instantly in shellfire while waiting in a trench near St Julien for an attack to start. He was born in Bow, but his mother was from Leighton, so he grew up in Linslade and was a bell ringer at St Barnabas's Church, working at Linslade Nurseries and possibly for the L&NWR until he enlisted at Christmas 1914. Son of Fanny (Lawson) Dickinson and stepson of Thomas Charles Bacchus of 15 Ship Road. His grave was lost during subsequent fighting. Tyne Cot Memorial 96-98.

1917 Thursday 4 October: 29186 Private **Henry Abel** aged 19 of 1/6th Battalion the Royal Warwickshires, formerly 32142 of 3rd Battalion the Northamptonshires, died in action, almost certainly at the Battle of Broodseinde. He was born in Stanbridge, where his father was a butcher. Of 41 Vandyke Road; only child of Arthur and Jane (Olney) Abel of Stanbridge. Tyne Cot Cemetery XIII D 32.

1917 Thursday 4 October: Captain **Alfred Christopher Dancer MC★** aged 24 of 5th Battalion the Dorsetshires died near Poelcapelle. He was born in Heath and Reach where his father was an estate carpenter, and was a pupil both in the village and at Emmanuel School, Wandsworth, where he successfully passed through the Officers' Training Corps. Although offered a commission at the outbreak of war, he chose to enlist with the Surrey Yeomanry as a trooper and saw active service in Gallipoli, gazetted later to the Dorsetshires and taking part in many battles on the Western Front. Husband of Florence Minnie (McKivett) of Wimbledon; son of Thomas and Harriet (Janes) Dancer of Rammamere Farm, Great Brickhill. Tyne Cot Memorial 92. (See also Chapter 17).

1917 Thursday 4 October: Private 325035 **Harry Gardiner** aged 33 of 1/8th Battalion the Royal Warwickshires, formerly 290294 1/4th Battalion the Suffolks, died at the Battle of Broodseinde. Born in Wing, he was a grocery shop manager in Hammersmith when he married in 1909. Husband of Lillian (Gilbert) of Fulham; son of William and Elizabeth (Girling) Gardiner of Handpost, Wing. Tyne Cot Memorial 23-28, 163A.

1917 Friday 5 October: Corporal 36569 **Edward Thomas Sayell** aged 25 of 143rd Company the MGC, formerly 22608 the O&BLI, died after being wounded near St Julien at the Battle of Broodseinde,. He had been wounded at least twice and suffered from shell-shock. Born in Horton, he became a house painter like his father. Husband of Minnie Daisy May (Horne) of 6 Summer Street; son of Walter and Elizabeth Louisa (Jellis) Sayell of 39 Springfield Road. Dozinghem Military Cemetery V H 2.

1917 Saturday 6 October: Corporal 25205 **William Joseph Gadsden** aged 20 or 21 of 6th Battalion the Bedfords died near Passchendaele of wounds received in action there. Born in Peckham, he was working on a farm in Eaton Bray in 1911, his family having recently moved to the village. He enlisted in June 1916 and was drafted to France in the December. Son of William Thomas and Ada (Goss) Gadsden of 3 Chapel Yard, Eaton Bray. Locre Hospice Cemetery III B 24.

1917 Saturday 6 October: Private 41002 **Henry Arthur Hart** aged 34 or 35 of 6th Battalion the Bedfords, formerly 16248 the Royal Fusiliers, then 59625 the Labour Corps, was reported missing following shell fire on support trenches near the Ypres-Menin road during the Battle of Passchendaele, death presumed. Born in Leighton, he was a carter's labourer before enlisting in 1915. Husband of Nellie Augusta (Coles) of 54 Old Road; son of Henry and Elizabeth (Duncombe) Hart of 6 Stanbridge Road. Tyne Cot Memorial 48-50, 162A.

1917 Saturday 6 October: Private PW/5044 **Ernest George Puryer** aged 24 of 2nd Battalion the Duke of Cambridge's Own (Middlesex) Regiment died at No. 53 CCS, Bailleul after an artery in his thigh was ruptured during shelling while awaiting transfer in a school yard. Born in Leighton, he had attended Beaudesert School and was apprenticed to George Faulkner Green, ironmonger, and later employed at Hendon Aircraft Works before enlisting at Mill Hill. He had been 'a devoted temperance worker' and had attended the Hockliffe Street Baptist Chapel. Only child of George William and Elizabeth Ann (Mills) Puryer of 1 South Street. Bailleul Communal Cemetery Extension III E 123.

1917 Sunday 7 October: Lance Corporal 19999 **Frank Heley** aged 19 of 5th Battalion the Dorsetshires died near Poelcapelle. Son of Frederick and Isabella (Lines) Heley of The Court, Slapton (Bedfordshire). Tyne Cot Memorial 92.

1917 Tuesday 9 October: Second Lieutenant **Frederick Thomas Brasington** aged 23 of 9 Squadron the RFC and General List died near Langemarck. Born in Stoke Newington, he was a pupil at the Leighton Gas Works, boarding at 12 Albany Road along with his younger brother. His father had grown up in Wing but had moved to London as a young man. Son of Thomas and Isabella (Gage) Brasington of London. Arras Flying Services Memorial. (See also Chapter 5.)

1917 Tuesday 9 October: Private 3/6996 **George Church** aged 20 of 1st Battalion the Bedfords died in action at the Battle of Poelcapelle, having served on the Western Front for three years. Born in Leighton, he was a sand carter before enlisting and was already a reservist when war broke out. Son of William and Maria (Scott) Church, late of 3 Lammas Walk; half-brother of William Scott of 20 Bedford Street, formerly of 28 Church Street. Tyne Cot Memorial 48-50, 162A.

1917 Tuesday 9 October: Private 7716 **Alfred Coker** aged 35 of 1st Battalion the Bedfords died in action in Belgium. Born in Pitstone, he was a farm labourer when he enlisted in Tring. Husband of Sarah Emily (Burch, later Arnold) of Pitstone; brother of **Samuel George Coker**; son of James Thomas and Sarah (Shillingford) Coker of Town Houses, Pitstone. Hooge Crater Cemetery VIII K 3. (First buried elsewhere.)

1917 Tuesday 9 October: Private 24224 **Charles William Janes** aged 27 of 2nd Battalion the Royal Warwickshires was reported missing, presumed dead, near Poelcapelle. He was born and brought up in Soulbury, where he worked for his father on Rislip Farm. Son of William and Elizabeth (Willmore) Janes, latterly of Bletchley. Tyne Cot Memorial 23-28, 163A.

1917 Tuesday 9 October: Private 32938 **Joseph George Jordan** aged 25 of 16th Battalion the Royal Warwickshires, formerly 29748 of 15th the King's Hussars, was reported missing in action and presumed dead near Poelcapelle. Known as George and born in Wing, he was a stableman in Linslade before enlisting in Aylesbury. Husband of Daisy (Hack) of Ivy Cottage, 89 Vandyke Road; brother of **Lionel Jordan**; son of Henry and Mary (Brown) Jordan of Prospect Place, Wing. Tyne Cot Memorial 23-28, 163A.

1917 Tuesday 9 October: Private 18379 **Frederick James Millins MM★** aged 24 of No 4 Company, 2nd Battalion the Grenadier Guards died in action in Belgium. Born in Cheddington, he was a railway porter in 1911. Youngest son of William Thomas and Dinah (Darvill, later Cooper) Millins of Park Lodge, Mentmore. Tyne Cot Memorial 9. (See also Chapter 17)

1917 Tuesday 9 October: Private 22271 **George Walter Rowe** aged 34 of 1st Battalion the Bedfords, formerly 3rd Battalion, died in action in Belgium. Born in Leighton, he attended Beaudesert School and worked on a farm before moving to Lower Hartshay, Derbyshire to become a miner. Husband of Emily (Linney) of 15 Summer Street; son of George Samuel and Emma (Finch) Rowe of 10 Back Lane. Tyne Cot Memorial 48-50, 162A.

1917 Wednesday 10 October: Gunner 195969 **Ernest William Goodchild** aged 26 of 42nd Battery the RHA and RFA died from wounds at No.1 CCS, having returned to active service after suffering from shell-shock. Born in High Wycombe, he was clerk to a solicitor in Leighton and was well-known locally in connection with Leighton County Court and Linslade Police Court; he was also a popular vocalist. Husband of Alice May (Bailey); son of Thomas Stallwood and Ellen (Martin) Goodchild, all of High Wycombe. Chocques Military Cemetery I M 22.

1917 Thursday 11 October: Private TF/241638 **Ernest Fountain** aged 28 of 4th (Football) Battalion the Duke of Cambridge's Own (Middlesex) Regiment died in shellfire in a front-line trench near Gheluvelt. Born in Eaton Bray, he worked on a farm and as a bricklayer's labourer before enlisting in Bedford in February 1916, having already served in the Bedfordshire Militia. Cousin of **Arthur Janes**; son of Edward and Sarah (Emmerton) Fountain of 6 Bower Lane, Eaton Bray. Tyne Cot Memorial 113-115.

1917 Monday 15 October: Private 28283 **Reginald Francis Miles** aged 24 of 8th Battalion the Somerset Light Infantry, formerly 2566 the Bedfordshire Yeomanry, died in action in Belgium. Of Coronation Cottage, Ashwell Street; son of Richard and Annie (Payne) Miles of 24 Plantation Road, formerly of Wicken. Tyne Cot Memorial 41-42, 163A.

1917 Wednesday 17 October: Private 33051 **Henry Janes** aged 17 or 18 of 8th Battalion the Leicestershires, formerly 3406 of 6th Battalion the Bedfords, died after being wounded in Belgium. Born in Northall, he was a farm labourer in Leighton in 1911. Husband of Ethel Laura (Turney) of 34 Soulbury Road;

son of William and Mary Ann (Wicks) Janes of 46 Bassett Road. Menin Road South Military Cemetery III L 6.

1917 Wednesday 17 October: Private 26961 **Charles Rowland Johnson** aged 32 of 1st Battalion the Bedfords died in a railway accident in France. Born in Hoxton, he moved to Leighton to work as an assistant to his uncle Thomas Henry Munday, a jeweller, and lived with him and two aunts, Sarah (Munday) Vigor and Alexandra Louisa Munday, at 18 Bridge Street. In March 1916 he enlisted in Bedford and was in France by August that year. Husband of Jessie Frances (Furlong) of 14 High Street; brother of **Martin Leslie Johnson**; son of Charles and Annie (Munday) Johnson of Clapton, London. Boulogne Eastern Cemetery VIII I 60.

1917 Friday 19 October: Private 205683 **William Evans** aged 25 of 7th Battalion the Queen's Own (Royal West Kent) Regiment, formerly 3853 the Yeoman Cyclists, died of wounds in Belgium. Born in Leighton, he attended Beaudesert School and worked at a sandpit before enlisting in Luton. Son of Henry and Annie (King) Evans of Luton, formerly of 40 Regent Street. Duhallow ADS (Advanced Dressing Station) Cemetery I E 33.

1917 Friday 19 October: Private 27502 **Frank Page** aged 19 of 5th Battalion the O&BLI died in artillery fire in a front-line trench near the Menin Road, east of Ypres. Born in Wing, he was a member of the Boy Scouts. Youngest child of David and Alice (Burrows) Page of Littleworth. Hooge Crater Cemetery XVII C 7.

1917 Wednesday 24 October: Rifleman A/203426 **Ernest Nicholes** aged 31 of 16th Battalion the King's Royal Rifle Corps, formerly 251155 of 1/16th Battalion the County of London Regiment, died in action in France. Born at the family farm in Ivinghoe, he was apprenticed to an Aylesbury draper in 1901. Son of Charles Henry and Annie Elizabeth (Coltman) Nicholes of Wards Hurst Farm, Ivinghoe. Louverval Military Cemetery B 6.

1917 Friday 26 October: AB Z/1917 **Alfred James Galloway** aged 20 of Anson Battalion the Royal Naval Division was reported missing near Poelcapelle. He was born in Canning Town where his father was working as a carman. Son of William John and Minnie (Dimmock) Galloway of 19 Billington Road. Poelcapelle British Cemetery VII C 8. (See also Chapter 7)

1917 Friday 26 October: Private 44876 **Henry George Hall** aged 33 of 1/5th Battalion the Northumberland Fusiliers, formerly 12127 the Army Catering Corps, was reported missing on 29 October, death in action presumed and officially confirmed in August 1918. Born in Leighton, he had attended Beaudesert School and later worked as a boot salesman in Bedford. Husband of Henrietta Kate (Keech), son of Frederick and Sarah (Hawkins) Hall and stepson of Phoebe (Burrows) Hall, all of Bedford and formerly of 46 Mill Road. Tyne Cot Memorial 19-23, 162.

1917 Sunday 28 October: Private 32050 **Bertie Turney** aged 33 of 6th Battalion the Somerset Light Infantry, formerly 36639 the Devonshires, died at No. 37 CCS, Godewaersvelde, having been gassed and possibly wounded in the front line near Sanctuary Wood on 23 October. An agricultural labourer, he was the organist at Soulbury Methodist Church, his name recorded on the Soulbury First World War Memorial as Herbert. Husband of Annie Elizabeth (Arnold) of Brierley, Soulbury; son of George and Elizabeth (Eggleton) Turney of Soulbury. Godewaersvelde British Cemetery I K 38.

1917 Tuesday 30 October: Private 904468 **William Niven Steadman** aged 27 of 49th Battalion the Canadian Infantry (Alberta Regiment) died in action at Passchendaele. Born in Thornborough, he was educated in Leatherhead and was a farmer when he enlisted with the Canadian Infantry in Edmonton on 6 March 1916. On 9 June 1917 he was in a Canadian General Hospital, having been wounded in his right arm and hand during a raid against enemy lines south of Avion during the 2nd Battle of Arras. Of Battle Bend, Alberta; brother of **John Noel Steadman**; son of the Reverend William and Frances (Niven) Steadman of 53 Dudley Street. Ypres (Menin Gate) Memorial 24, 28, 30.

1917 Tuesday 30 October: Private 331140 **John Waterhouse** aged 25 of 15th Battalion the Sherwood Foresters died in enemy artillery fire in front line trenches near Elverdinghe, 5km north-west of Ypres. He was born near Chapel-en-le-Frith, Derbyshire, and had been a farm labourer before enlisting. Husband of Maud Mary (Spiers) of 38 Springfield Road; son of Joseph and Mary (Brocklehurst) Waterhouse of Derbyshire. Bluet Farm Cemetery II A 44.

1917 Tuesday 30 October: Private 31255 **Frederick John West** aged 33 of 4th Battalion the Bedfords died in action at Passchendaele. Born in Heath and Reach, he enlisted in 1894 and served in South Africa in 1902 before returning to his home village and working for a sand merchant. Husband of

Lily (Pantling) of 16 Union Street; son of John and Maria (Stone) West, late of Heath and Reach. Tyne Cot Memorial 48-50, 162A.

1917 Friday 2 November: Sergeant 10408 **Charles Francis Dudley** aged 28 of D Company, 6th Battalion the Leicestershires, died in action in Belgium. In 1911 he was a farm labourer in his birthplace of Eggington but had moved to Shuttleworth, Leicestershire, before enlisting in August 1914. Son of Alfred and Charlotte (Ludgate) Dudley of Eggington. Tyne Cot Memorial 50, 51.

1917 Friday 2 November: Private 200938 **Edward Holmes MM★** aged 21 of 1/5th Battalion the Bedfords died in action in Palestine during the 3rd Battle of Gaza. Born in Leighton, he attended Beaudesert School and was a member of the Boy Scouts, a labourer when he enlisted at Bedford. Son of Thomas James and Lizzie (Denchfield) Holmes of 58 Hockliffe Street. Gaza War Cemetery XXX B 16. (See also Chapter 17).

1917 Saturday 3 November: Private 200646 **Percival 'Percy' Fiddler** aged 25 of 1/5th Battalion the Bedfords, formerly 4672 the Bedfordshire Territorials, died in action in Palestine. He was born in Chipping Norton and came with his family to Ivinghoe shortly before 1901, moving to Mentmore by 1911 when he was a farm labourer. He had been a member of the Ledburn Sunday School. Son of William and Emma (Hayes) Fiddler of Mentmore. Gaza War Cemetery XXII A 3.

1917 Wednesday 7 November: Private 45599 **John Albert Procter** aged 19 of 3rd Battalion the Suffolks died at 13 Mill Road, having been diagnosed with valvular disease of the heart earlier that year at the Herman de Stern Hospital, Felixstowe. Although John was born in Walworth, his father moved the family back to his own home town of Leighton in 1901-02. He was a steamroller driver before being posted with the 3rd Suffolks on 16 May 1917, although he was in hospital when they boarded. His burial record gives his occupation as tractor driver. Son of John Albert and Elizabeth (Bilton) Procter of 13 Mill Road. Leighton-Linslade Cemetery Grave A 106.

1917 Friday 9 November: Private 47712 **Francis James Ward** aged 40 of 2nd Battalion the Welsh Regiment died in Belgium. Born in Sheep Lane, Heath and Reach, in 1901 he was at Shoebury Barracks, a gunner with the RGA, but was a sandpit labourer in Leighton by 1911. Husband of Susan Louisa (Beaumont) of 28 Union Street; son of Charles and Esther (Windmill) Ward of Stanbridge Road Brickyard. Tyne Cot Memorial 93-94.

1917 Saturday 10 November: Sergeant 43254 **Walter Dennis Toe MM**★ aged 20 of 6th Battalion the Northamptonshires, formerly 3/7407 the Bedfords, died at King's College Hospital, London of gunshot wounds. Born in London he attended Beaudesert School after his father returned with the family to Leighton. Son of Frank Henry and Annie Jane (Goard) Toe of 16 Regent Street. Leighton-Linslade Cemetery Grave CC 101. (See also Chapters 11 and 16)

1917 Thursday 15 November: Captain the Rt Hon **Neil James Archibald Primrose MC**★ aged 34 of 1/1st Battalion the Royal Buckinghamshire Hussars died in action in Palestine. He had been a Privy Councillor, and Member of Parliament for Wisbech Division since 1910. Husband of Lady Victoria Alice Louisa (Stanley, later Bullock) Primrose; son of Archibald Philip, 5th Earl of Rosebery, and Hannah (de Rothschild) Primrose. Ramleh War Cemetery D 49. (See also Chapters 8 and 16)

1917 Sunday 17 November: Major **Evelyn Achille de Rothschild MiD**★ aged 31 of the Royal Buckinghamshire Hussars died in Cairo of wounds. He was brought up at Ascott House, Wing, and after Harrow School and Trinity College, Cambridge, he worked in the family banking house. An all-round sportsman and an excellent equestrian, he rode regularly to hounds, won point-to-point races and bred racehorses. He held a commission in the Hussars before First World War, so was mobilised immediately and reached Egypt in April 1915. Between then and his death he fought in both Egypt and the Dardanelles. Son of Leopold de Rothschild and his wife Marie (Perugia). Buried originally in Cairo Jewish Cemetery. Richon-le-Zion Jewish Cemetery, north-east part. (See also Chapters 8 and 16)

1917 Tuesday 20 November: Private 33801 **William Groom** aged 20 of 8th Battalion the Bedfords died in action, wounded during the British advance at the Battle of Cambrai. He was a Boy Scout, and worked as a wagoner for Jeffrey Sharrett of Yew Tree Farm before the war. Son of Robert and Avis (Fountain) Groom of 16 Bower Lane, Eaton Bray. Ribecourt British Cemetery I B 8.

1917 Tuesday 20 November: Private 330931 **Alfred Wildman** aged 25 of 9th Battalion the Suffolks died in action in France. Born in Eaton Bray, he was still there in 1911, a labourer at a printing works. Son of David and Sarah (Holmes) Wildman of High Street, Eaton Bray. Ribecourt British Cemetery Special Memorial A 9.

1917 Wednesday 21 November: Lance Corporal S/2890 **Frederick John Gurney** aged 32 of 10th Battalion the Rifle Brigade died in action in France. Born in Northall, he lived as a child in Edlesborough and was a butcher's boy in Lidlington by 1901. Ten years later he was married with children and running his own business in East Dulwich. Husband of Katherine Harriet Bemester (Sparrow) of East Dulwich; son of John and Caroline (Goodman) Gurney of Northall, formerly of Leighton Road, Edlesborough. Cambrai Memorial 10, 11.

1917 Wednesday 21 November: Private 205653 **John Roland Sloan Sworder** aged 22 of 101st (Bucks and Berks) Battalion the MGC, formerly 2002 the 1/1st Royal Bucks Hussars, died in action, probably during the Battle of Nebi Samwil. Educated at Beechcroft School, Leighton and Dr Knight's School in Towcester he had spent a year in Vincennes, France before starting work at Maple & Co in Tottenham Court Road, London. A keen sportsman, he enlisted in November 1914 and served in Egypt. Eldest child of John and Mary Jane (Sloan) Sworder of Rothesay, Stoke Road. Jerusalem War Cemetery F 57.

1917 Saturday 24 November: Private G/60145 **Arthur Tucker** aged 24 of 8th Battalion the Royal Fusiliers, formerly 23266 of 7th Battalion the Bedfords, died in action at Cambrai. He was working on a farm when he enlisted in Ampthill. Husband of Sarah Louise (Merridale) of Battlesden Lodge; son of James and Salome (Peacock) Tucker of No. 6 Battlesden. Cambrai Memorial 3, 4.

1917 Sunday 25 November: Private 268759 **Albert Rickett** aged 23 of 12th Battalion the King's (Liverpool) Regiment, formerly 2405 the Bedfordshire Yeomanry died after being wounded at Cambrai. Born in Chalgrave where his father was a shepherd, he remained at New Barn, a farm labourer, until he enlisted. Son of George and Mary (Buckingham) Rickett of New Barn, Chalgrave. Tincourt New British Cemetery II F 13.

1917 Tuesday 27 November: Driver 174345 **John Gates** aged 37 of 131st Field Company the Royal Engineers died from pneumonia at No. 28 General Hospital, Kalamaria. Born in Cheddington, by 1905 he had moved to Lincolnshire and in 1911 was working as a domestic groom at Irnham Hall, with a wife, a son and a mother-in-law to support. Husband of Sarah Jane (Hunt) of Irnham Stables, Grantham; son of Matthew and Mary Ann (Beilby) Gates of Cheddington. Salonika (Lembet Road) Military Cemetery 1293.

1917 Tuesday 27 November: Lance Corporal 11686 **Geoffrey Alfred Sutton** aged 23 of 1st Company, 2nd Battalion the Irish Guards, formerly 1209 of 28th Battalion the London Regiment, was initially reported missing, presumed killed, during the battle of Cambrai but was later discovered to have died of wounds received at Bourlon Wood. Unaccountably after he had received a commission as second lieutenant in 3rd Battalion the Royal Irish Fusiliers, he re-enlisted as a private in the Irish Guards. Born in Eaton Bray, he was educated at home and at Haileybury College. Son of the Reverend Edwin and Annie Hill (Moxhay) Sutton of Grundisburgh, formerly of Eaton Bray. Ontario Cemetery IV A 15.

1917 Thursday 29 November: Private 200832 **Arthur Henry Lancaster** aged 20 of 1/5th Battalion the Bedfords died in action in Palestine. Born in Cheddington, he had lived in Leighton since 1900 and had enlisted there. Son of Harry and Florence Emily (Fountaine) Lancaster of Watford, formerly of 74 Vandyke Road and of Baker Street. Ramleh War Cemetery C 10.

1917 Friday 30 November: Corporal 320774, **Ernest Ambrose Syratt** aged 32 of 2/6th Battalion the London Regiment (City of London Rifles), formerly 2580, died of wounds at No. 62 CCS, Haringhe (Bandaghem). Born in Burcott, he had left home to live with his uncle in Chelsea by the time he was 16 and was a bank clerk before enlisting when war was declared. Husband of Edile Marie (Daeghsel); son of Reuben and Ann (Carter) Syratt of the Six Bells, Burcott. Haringhe (Bandaghem) Military Cemetery I B 16.

1917 Friday 30 November: Private L/14164 **Frederick William Tavener** aged 28 of 8th Battalion the Royal Fusiliers died in shellfire at Cambrai. Born in Ivinghoe Aston, he was a cowman and attended the Wesleyan Methodist Chapel. Son of George and Eliza (Pratt) Tavener of Swan street, Ivinghoe Aston. Cambrai Memorial 3, 4.

1917 Wednesday 5 December: Private 610153 **Harry Janes** aged 37 of 1/19th (County of London) Battalion the London Regiment died in France. He had already been wounded three times and had suffered from shell-shock. In 1911 he was a carman for a removal firm. Brother of **Charles John Janes** and **George Alma Janes**; husband of Elizabeth Caroline (Squirrell) of St Pancras; son of David and Sarah Jane (Emmerson) Janes of Islington, formerly of Bassett Road. Grévillers British Cemetery I C 1.

1917 Sunday 9 December: Private 406061 **Fred Croxford** aged 35 of 1st Battalion the Canadian Infantry (Western Ontario Regiment) died in France. He was born in Heath but was working as a gardener in Handsworth in 1901 and left Liverpool on 4 June 1903 for Quebec aboard the *Ionian* of the Allan Line. Son of William and Phoebe Esther (Gates) Croxford of Norwich, Ontario, formerly of Heath and Reach. Sucrerie Cemetery II C 11.

1917 Monday 17 December: Private 268731 **Thomas Janes Bates** aged 22 of 12th Battalion, the King's (Liverpool) Regiment died of wounds while a prisoner of war at Le Cateau; he had been wounded in the head and captured at the beginning of December during an enemy attack near La Vacquerie, south-west of Cambrai. Before enlisting he had worked with his father, a corn miller and farmer. Brother of **George Bates**; son of George and Mary Ruth (Belgrove) Bates of Grange Mill, Heath & Reach. Le Cateau Military Cemetery V C 2.

1917 Wednesday 26 December: Private/Tpr 205894 **George Elliott** aged 22 of 1/1st Battalion the Royal Buckinghamshire Hussars died at No. 71 General Hospital, Helwan after being wounded. He was born and grew up in Pitstone, where his father was a cattle dealer and butcher. Son of George and Alice (Williams) of Aylesbury, formerly of Pitstone. Cairo War Memorial Cemetery O 84.

1917 Saturday 28 December: Private 20196 **Charles Robinson** aged 24 of 6th Battalion the Royal Munster Fusiliers, formerly 17523 the O&BLI, died in action during the Defence of Jerusalem. Born in Swanbourne, he was a cowman before enlisting, then fought in the Balkans before being transferred when the Fusiliers arrived in Egypt in September 1917. Husband of Mary (Keen) and son of Reuben and Mary Ann (Long, later Pitkin) Robinson, all of Hollingdon. Jerusalem Cemetery X 18.

1918 Saturday 12 January: Private 33874 **John Rayner** aged 28 of 4th Battalion the Bedfords died in action in France. Born in Norfolk, he was a farm labourer and came to Bedfordshire shortly before the outbreak of war. Husband of Florence Kate (Walker, later Eames) of 8 East Street; son of Henry and Eliza (Kirchen) Rayner of Norfolk. Fifteen Ravine British Cemetery IV A 20.

1918 Wednesday 16 January: Lance Corporal G/60052 **William James Roberts** aged 36 of 3/4th Battalion the West Surreys died of wounds in France. Born in Eaton Bray, he grew up there and trained to be a butcher, running his own shop until he enlisted. Husband of Clara (Noah) of High Street, Eaton Bray; son of James and Susannah (Gadsden) Roberts of Great Green Farm, the Rye, Eaton Bray. Tincourt New British Cemetery IV E 35.

1918 Sunday 3 March: Nora Tompkins aged 17 was one of the four women who died at Bute Hospital, Luton from injuries sustained in an explosion at her workplace. She was born in Heath and Reach, shortly after her father's death. Daughter of Frederick and Caroline (Arnold) Tompkins of Lanes End, Heath and Reach. Heath and Reach (St Leonard) churchyard. (See also Chapter 13)

1918 Monday 11 March: Driver 522214 **George Humbles** aged 19 of 483rd (East Anglian) Field Company the RE died in action in France. He was born in Leighton. Brother of **William Humbles**; son of William and Sarah Ann (Sharp) Humbles of 5 Barrow Path. His original grave was destroyed by shellfire. Neuville-Bourjonval British Cemetery Special Memorial 2.

1918 Friday 15 March: Private 26051 **Frederick Adams** aged 53 of the Royal Defence Corps, formerly of the Bedfords, died at home of a malignant stricture of the oesophagus, having been invalided out of the army in 1917. Born in Leighton, by the time he was 11 years old he was a chimney sweep, working for Edward Fensome in Friday Street. He had first enlisted in 1879 and served with the East Surreys in Gibraltar and Egypt, working at the Swan Hotel as an ostler after twelve years with the colours and then enlisting once again in 1915. Father of **Edward George Adams**; husband of Edith (Toms) of 31 Mill Road; son of Sarah Adams. Leighton-Linslade cemetery C 20a.

1918 Thursday 21 March: Private 203211 **Robert Hayes Hankin** aged 20 of 2/5th Battalion the Sherwood Foresters died in France. From the Edmonton Bulletin of 1 March 1930, reporting on the identification after eleven years of his brother Frederick's body: 'Their only other son, Robert, who joined the Bedfordshire Regiment, was reported missing during the great offensive of March 1918.' Born in Islington, he grew up in Heath and Reach along with his older brother Frederick, their three siblings having died as children. He was an under-gardener when he enlisted for the duration of the war in Bedford in June 1916 and had first been sent to France on 26 February 1917. Brother of **Frederick Bernard Hankin**; son of Charles Frederick and Mary Ann Frances (Van Baars) Hankin, of Thomas Street, Heath and Reach, formerly of Islington. Arras Memorial 7.

1918 Thursday 21 March: Private 30612 **Joseph King** aged 27 of 2nd Battalion the Bedfords died without recovering consciousness after being wounded in France. Born in Leighton, he attended Beaudesert School then worked at a sandpit. Brother of **Francis John 'Jack' King**; son of John and Mary (Pratt) King of 24 St Andrew's Street. Pozières Memorial 8, 29.

1918 Thursday 21 March: Private 33078 **Albert Rollings** aged 33 of 8th Battalion the Leicesters, formerly 6402 the Bedfords, died in action on the Somme on the first day of the German Spring Offensive. Born in Eaton Bray, he remained in the village working on farms until he enlisted. Son of Sarah Ann Rollings of Bower Lane, Eaton Bray. Pozières Memorial 29, 30.

1918 Thursday 21 March: Private 28659 **Henry George Stevens** aged 26 of 6th Battalion the Prince Albert's (Somerset) Light Infantry, formerly 35213 the Wiltshires, died in action in France. Born in Leighton, he attended Beaudesert School, later working for a butcher. Son of Arthur John and Elizabeth Ann (Dudley) Stevens of 5 Edward Street. St Souplet British Cemetery I H 35.

1918 Thursday 21 March: Private 32184 **Walter John Wilson** aged 21 of 6th Battalion the Bedfords died in action near Gheluvelt. He was born in Leighton and by 1911 was a farm labourer and the sole financial support of his parents and three siblings, his father having been totally blind for the previous ten years. He enlisted at Luton Corn Exchange early in 1915. Son of William and Sarah (Tearle) Wilson of Church End, Edlesborough, formerly of Summerleys, Eaton Bray. Originally buried in Tower Hamlets Cemetery. Hooge Crater Cemetery XV B 8.

1918 Friday 22 March: Private 293689 **Francis John Quick** aged 20 of 3/10th Battalion the Duke of Cambridge's Own (Middlesex) Regiment attached to 11th Entrenching Battalion, formerly of 1/5th then 2/5th Battalion the Bedfords, died at No. 7 CCS, Tinques, a day after being wounded. Born in Leighton, he had attended Beaudesert School and was a carter at Garside's when he enlisted at Leighton in June 1914. Son of William and Hannah (Pratt) Quick of 92 Bassett Road. Duisans British Cemetery VI E 34.

1918 Saturday 23 March: Private 10141 **Charles Chanin** aged 22 of 16th (the Queen's) Lancers died in action on the Somme with thirty-six others from his regiment. Born in what was to become part of Saskatchewan, Canada, as were some of his siblings, he was an apprentice baker living in Sandy with his parents by 1911. His father had married in 1883 in London but left for Canada alone before 1891, when he was recorded on a census with wife Emma in Assiniboia East. Son of William George and Emma (Hoskins) Chanin of Eaton Bray. Pozières Memorial 5.

1918 Saturday 23 March: Rifleman 374742 **Penrose Frank Coles** aged 19 of 8th (City of London) Battalion (Post Office Rifles) the London Regiment was reported missing, death presumed, during the Battle of St Quentin. Born in Chalgrave, he was appointed assistant postman in Dunstable in 1915. Son of John and Flora Jane Ambridge (Brittain) Coles of Chalgrave. Pozières Memorial 87.

1918 Saturday 23 March: Private 200570 **Herbert Charles Kendall** aged 34 of 7th Battalion the Bedfords, formerly 4400 of 5th Battalion, died in action during the intense fighting around the village of Faillouel, which was encircled by the German Army. He had been seriously wounded in Gallipoli in October 1915 and again in Egypt but, after being shipped home and recovering in England, was transferred into the 7th Battalion in France. Born in Kettering, he was a stonemason before the war and it is his photograph at the top of the home page of www.bedfordregiment.org.uk (2017). Husband of Ellen Elizabeth (Hack) of Heath; son of George Thomas Clarke Kendall and Martha Annie (Roughton) Kendall of the Woolpack, Kettering. Pozières Memorial 28, 29.

1918 Saturday 23 March: Private 267611 **Stanley Miles** aged 21 of 5th Battalion the O&BLI died in action on the Somme. Son of Richard and Mary (Slatter) Miles of Horton, formerly of Main Road, Edlesborough. Pozières Memorial 50, 51.

1918 Sunday 24 March: Private 201515 **Frederick Ruffett** aged 28 of 2nd Battalion the Bedfords died in action at the Somme Crossings. He had fought at the Somme in 1916 and at Arras in 1917. Born in Northall, by 1891 he had moved with his family to Eaton Bray where he worked on a farm. Son of Lewis and Elizabeth (Tompkins) Ruffett of Eaton Bray. Pozières Memorial 28, 29.

1918 Wednesday 27 March: Private 79930 **Albert Samuel** aged 42 of 27th Battalion the Durham Light Infantry, formerly 45298 the King's Own Yorkshire Light Infantry, died in Aylesbury. Born in Leighton, he had moved to Sheffield by 1911, as had his widowed father. Husband of Alice Rose (Ridgway) Samuel of 33 Vandyke Road; son of James and Sarah (Daniels) Samuel late of 3 Edward Street. Leighton-Linslade Cemetery Grave CC 360.

1918 Thursday 28 March: Private 45501 **Walter Garnett** aged 21 of 56th Battalion/Company the Machine Gun Corps (Infantry), formerly G/15871 the Royal West Kent Regiment, died in action near Gavrelle. Born in Leighton, he was a net maker and wire worker there when he enlisted at Bedford. Youngest son of William and Sarah Jane (Hill) Garnett of 27a Plantation Road. Orchard Dump Cemetery IX F 4.

1918 Thursday 28 March: Private 16302 **Albert George Frederick Holyman** aged 35 of 1st Battalion the Hampshires, formerly 9923 the O&BLI, died in action at Haute-Avennes. A grocer's clerk in 1901, by 1911 he had married and was a railway clerk living in Fenny Stratford. Husband of Ada (Vickers) of Willesden, formerly of Fenny Stratford; son of William and Mary Ann (Hedges) Holyman of Edward Street. Arras Memorial 6.

1918 Thursday 28 March: Private G/13302 **William Arthur Smith** aged 30 of 6th Battalion the East Kents (the Buffs) died in action near Mesnil. He was born in Leighton but in 1911 was a straw hat packer living in Luton with his wife and daughter. Husband of Nellie (Clare) of Luton; son of William and Sarah (Roads) Smith, formerly of 47 Vandyke Road. Originally buried elsewhere. Peronne Road Cemetery III H 31.

1918 Monday 1 April: Private 266565 **George Woolhead** aged 21 of 2/1st Bucks Battalion the O&BLI was presumed already to have died near Nesle. Since February 1918 the 2/1st Bucks Battalion had been part of the 25th Entrenching Battalion. He was born in Wing. Son of Thomas and Mary Ann (Bilby) Woolhead of Leighton Road, Wing. Pozières Memorial 50, 51.

1918 Wednesday 3 April: Driver 168889 **William Arthur Dinham** aged 26 of Y.11 Medium Trench Mortar Battery the RFA died in action near Cambrai. Born in Sussex, he had moved to London with his parents shortly afterwards, enlisting in Slough. Husband of Annie (Eames, later Bessant) of 17 Summer Street; son of Charles and Lavinia Finn (Ward) Dinham of Croydon. Philosophe British Cemetery III C 29.

1918 Thursday 4 April: Private 29017 **Ernest Sidney Foster Abery** aged 19 of 4th Battalion the Grenadier Guards died at the Royal Fortress Hospital, Cologne after being taken prisoner. Born in Eastbourne, he moved with his family to Heath and attended Heath National School, then Beaudesert School in Leighton. Son of Ernest and Florence Lizzie (Foster) Abery of Shirley,

Southampton, formerly of Heath and Reach; grandson of Alfred and Louisa (Sanders) Foster of 42 Vandyke Road. Cologne Southern Cemetery VIII C 3.

1918 Friday 5 April: Private 43202 **Harry William Parsons** aged 27 of 6th Battalion the Northamptonshires, formerly 26800 the Bedfords, died in action in France. Born in Drayton Parslow, he lived in Leighton and attended Beaudesert School, and was working as a grocer's assistant when he enlisted. Adopted son of Mary Ann Odell of 14 Chapel Path. Pozières Memorial 54-56.

1918 Monday 8 April: Corporal 12120 **Frederick Charles Higgs** aged 20 or 21 of 6th Battalion the Bedfords died in action in France. He was born in Hockliffe and brought up by his grandparents, working on a farm in the village in 1911. Son of Louisa Higgs of Luton; grandson of Joseph and Sarah (Buckingham) Higgs of Watling Street, Hockliffe. Gommecourt British Cemetery No. 2 IV D 23.

1918 Tuesday 9 April: Private 15510 **George Gaius Horn** aged 21 of 13th Battalion the East Surreys died 'in a battle at Fleurbaix, a bullet killing him as he was serving his Lewis Gun'. Before enlisting he was an errand boy for a brewer. Son of Arthur and Annie (Draper) Horn of Wellcroft, Ivinghoe. Ploegsteert Memorial 6.

1918 Saturday 13 April: Private 35351 **William Smith** aged 19 of 14th Battalion the Royal Warwickshires was reported missing, death presumed during the defence of Nieppe Forest during the Battle of Hazebrouk. Brother of **Peter Smith**; son of Thomas and Mary Ann (Billington) Smith of 52 Old Road. Merville Communal Cemetery Extension III D 13.

1918 Monday 15 April: Private 60351 **Archie Moore** aged 19 of 2nd Battalion the Prince of Wales's Own (West Yorkshire) Regiment died of wounds at a Reserve Field Hospital in France. In June the previous year, during bayonet training at Rugeley Camp, he had fractured his left leg when ordered to jump into a trench on the final assault course. Born in Husbands Bosworth where his father had been a groom at Highfield House, he and his parents moved to Stockgrove some time after he enlisted in December 1916. He was a butcher. Son of James and Catherine (Ward) Moore of Stockgrove. Rosières Communal Cemetery Extension II A 10.

1918 Tuesday 16 April: Private 51656 **Leonard Fensome** aged 20 of 1st Battalion the Lincolnshires, formerly 39431 of 1st and 8th Battalion the

Bedfords, was reported missing, death presumed, at the Bogaert Farm – Stanyzer Cabaret crossroads. Although this was immediately before the Battle of Kemmel, it is considered unofficially to be a part of it. He was born in Dunstable, where his father was a tailor, and lived there at least until 1911, although in 1915 he was fined 5s for obstructing the highway at Chalgrave with a horse and cart. Husband of Clara (Indge) of Chalgrave; son of Samuel and Eliza (Page) Fensome of Dunstable. Tyne Cot Memorial 35-37, 162-162A.

1918 Thursday 18 April: Gunner 65400 **Ernest John Gaskin** aged 27 of X/32nd Divisional Trench Mortar Battery the RFA died 'in the field' after a chlorine gas attack. Born in Leighton, he studied shorthand at evening school before moving to Newington, where he was a grocer's assistant in 1911 before enlisting in Hendon. Son of John Hillier Gaskin and Sarah (Holmes) Gaskin of 16 Vandyke Road. St Sever Cemetery Extension Block F, XI L 4b.

1918 Tuesday 23 April: Private 36540 **William Kenning** aged 21 of 16th Battalion the York and Lancasters, formerly 3205 of 1/5th Battalion the Bedfords, died at the Berks and Bucks Joint Sanatorium, Peppard Common, of dysentery and tuberculosis contracted during his military service. He was a labourer living in High Street, Wing, when mobilised at the outbreak of War; he served in Egypt, was wounded fighting in the Dardanelles in 1915; he was discharged in September 1917 as physically unfit and awarded a Silver War Badge. Husband of Monica Florence (Wosket) of Leamington Spa; son of Thomas and Rose Kenning, late of Bedford. Wing (All Saints) churchyard.

1918 Wednesday 24 April: Corporal 20076 **Charles Smith** aged 22 of D Company, 7th Battalion the Bedfords was reported missing, death presumed, near Cachy during the first tank-to-tank battle at Villers-Bretonneux. Born while his family were living in Paddington, he returned with them to Edlesborough, working for a nurseryman. Son of John and Ann (Cook) Smith of The Green, Edlesborough. Pozières Memorial 28, 29.

1918 Saturday 27 April: Private 40386 **Horace Duncan Flowers** aged 34 of 10th Battalion the South Wales Borderers, formerly 37418 the Bedfords, died in action near Albert. Born in Banbury, he was an accountant's clerk living with his Canadian-born mother and maternal grandmother in Handsworth in 1911 while his father was an unemployed accountant, boarding in Exeter. He lived in King's Heath, Birmingham when he enlisted. Husband of Ethel F. (Kent); son of Horace Edwin and Annie Maria E. (Jones) Flowers of 42b the Crescent, Ashwell Street. Bouzincourt Communal Cemetery Extension II K 13.

1918 Saturday 27 April: Wheeler/Gunner W/5029 **Henry John Hack** aged 25 of 19th Brigade Ammunition Column the RFA died instantly when a shell burst overhead while he was walking with two friends; his companions were unhurt. Born in Leighton, he attended Beaudesert School and had been apprenticed to a tinsmith in 1911 but was later a bricklayer. Son of John and Mary Ann (Dimmock) Hack of Ivy Cottage, 89 Vandyke Road. Outtersteene Communal Cemetery Extension II G 11.

1918 Monday 29 April: Private 42791 **Arthur Charles Brantom** aged 19 of 7th Battalion the Lincolnshires, formerly 157196 of 51st Graduated Battalion the West Surreys, died of wounds in France. Born in Leighton, he was a butcher in 1917 when he enlisted in Luton. Son of Charles and Mary Jane (Elliott) Brantom of Heath Park Cottages, Heath Road. Varennes Military Cemetery I K 26.

1918 Saturday 4 May: Private 291063 **Arthur Thomas Giddings** aged 36 of the Suffolks died at New Military Hospital, Sunderland, from the effects of being gassed. Born in Baldock, he had managed a drapery business in Leighton. His burial record states he was a draper's assistant. Husband of Ada Louise (Newton) of London SE, formerly of 40 Ashwell Street; son of Daniel and Ann (Pateman) Giddings latterly of St Ives, Huntingdonshire. Leighton-Linslade Cemetery CC 8A.

1918 Wednesday 15 May: Driver L/18289 **Arnold Walter Paxton** aged 22 of B Battery, 170th Brigade the Royal Field Artillery died in shellfire near St Amand during a week out of the front line. He was trained for domestic service by a charity in Kensington, the Houseboy Brigade, then enlisted in Liverpool in May 1915 and served in Egypt as well as in France. Son of John and Ellen Elizabeth (Cutler, later Green) Paxton of Wing. St Amand British Cemetery III B 6.

1918 Friday 17 May: Private L/10486 **Benjamin Clarence Strong** aged 22 of 9th Battalion the East Surreys died from 'cardiac weakness' at a German field hospital for prisoners at Flavy-le-Martel. His parents separated by 1899, and he and brother Herbert were boarders together in Rothersfield, Sussex by 1901; in 1911 he was a tailor pupil at the School of Handicrafts at the Chertsey Union workhouse. Aged 15 years and 11 months, he enlisted on 10 July 1912 for twelve years, initially as a stretcher-bearer, and was taught to play the clarinet. Brother of **Francis William Cooper Strong** (**John Stewart**) and **Robert Harold Strong**; son of Robert Bennett and Linda Elizabeth

(Cooper, later Turner) Strong of Hampstead, formerly of Heath and Reach. Annois Communal Cemetery II A 3.

1918 Monday 20 May: Gunner 120791 **Harold Turner** aged 20 of 59th Siege Battery the RGA died in No. 3 CCS, Gézaincourt. He was born in Totternhoe and his family moved around several villages, working on farms. Son of Arthur William and Sarah Ann (Roff) Turner of Pitstone. Bagneux British Cemetery II A 12.

1918 Sunday 26 May: Private 29221 **William John Turney** aged 28 of the RAMC, attached to 2nd Battalion the King's (Liverpool Regiment), died of septicaemia at 143rd Field Ambulance, Salonika. Born in Horton, he worked as a cowman in Slapton before enlisting in Southampton. Son of James and Mary Anne (Brigginshaw) Turney of Church Road, Slapton. Sarigol Military Cemetery C 504.

1918 Monday 27 May: Private 133353 **Sidney Ernest Howe** aged 19 of 50th Battalion the Machine Gun Corps died in action near Craonelle during the German attack on the first day of the 3rd Battle of the Aisne. Called up in June 1917, he had only joined his battalion in France in April 1918. Brother of **Albert Victor Howe**; son of Philip Robert William and Kate (Field) Howe of 24 Waterloo Road, later of 12 Southcourt Avenue. The wooden cross from his grave is mounted on the wall in St Barnabas's Church Linslade. Vendresse British Cemetery I H 13.

1918 Monday 27 May: Second Lieutenant **Lionel Page** aged 24 of 1st Battalion the Worcestershires, formerly 12233 of 6th Battalion the O&BLI, died in action during the 3rd Battle of the Aisne. Brother of **Mark Page** and uncle of **Arthur William Page**; son of George and Rebecca (Woolhead) Page of 52 Springfield Road. Soissons Memorial. (See also Chapter 11)

1918 Tuesday 4 June: Private 33125 **Arthur Thomas Mason** aged 29 of 8th Battalion the Leicestershires, formerly 6299 of 5th Battalion the Bedfords, died while a prisoner of war in Bellicourt. Born in Staffordshire, in 1911 he was living with his parents in Burslem and was working as a canvasser for a baker and confectioner. When he enlisted in Luton in November 1915, he was a grocer's assistant living at 13 Market Square. Son of John and Mary Elizabeth (Goode) Mason of Burslem. Bellicourt British Cemetery II C 5.

1918 Thursday 6 June: Private 23096 **Thomas Henry Teagle** aged 21 of 2nd Battalion the Duke of Edinburgh's (Wiltshire) Regiment died after being wounded. Brother of **Arthur Teagle**; son of Henry and Fanny (Andrews) Teagle of Brook End, Pitstone. Marfaux British Cemetery V H 8.

1918 Monday 17 June: Private 203842 **George Taylor** aged 32 of 2/4th Battalion the O&BLI, formerly 24564 of 5th Battalion, died near Nesle, between Amiens and Saint Quentin. Originally buried in Nesle German Cemetery, he may have been captured during the Third Battle of the Aisne. He was born in Wing and before enlisting was a bricklayer's labourer. Husband of Lily (Rolls, later Guess) of Littleworth; son of Sarah Taylor. Roye New British Cemetery IV D 13.

1918 Tuesday 18 June: Lance Corporal 30447 **George Bates** aged 25 of 1/1st Bedfordshire Yeomanry, 1st Division Cavalry of the Line, died of wounds received in action in France. Born in Heath and Reach, he was working in the family corn-milling business when he enlisted in Bedford. Brother of **Thomas Janes Bates**; son of George and Mary Ruth (Belgrove) Bates of Grange Mill, Heath and Reach. Abbeville Communal Cemetery Extension IV B 16.

1918 Thursday 20 June: Captain **William Reginald Guy Pearson MiD★** aged 21 of the RAF, formerly of 17th Battalion the Royal Fusiliers and the ASC, died as the result of a collision at 1,000ft while practising aerial combat in Avro 504J B8604 at No. 4 Training Depot Station, Hooton. He had been credited with at least seven 'kills' before becoming an instructor, and was regarded as a very safe and skilful pilot. Educated at Berkhamsted School, he enlisted aged 18 and was commissioned immediately as temporary second lieutenant in the ASC. He transferred to the RFC in France, and served as an observer before training as a pilot. He was born in Lancashire, after which the family moved to Islington where his sister Kathleen Mary was born. In about 1905 they moved to the Manor House, 14 Lake Street and then to the Cedars, in Church Square. His sister was the children's author, Mary Norton. Son of Dr Reginald Spencer and Minnie Savile (Hughes) Pearson of Stockwell, formerly of the Cedars. Eastham (St Mary) Churchyard E 4.

1918 Thursday 28 June: Private 802279 **Wilfred Turney** aged 33 of 18th Battalion the Canadian Infantry (Western Ontario Regiment) died of wounds in France. In 1901 he was a stationary engine stoker living with his family in Ivinghoe but had emigrated to Canada before 1911. Son of Ambrose and Emily

Ann (Deeley) Turney of Vicarage Lane, Ivinghoe. Gézaincourt Communal Cemetery Extension I N 2.

1918 Thursday 4 July: Private 2865 **Albert Brand** aged 29 of 59th Battalion Australian Infantry, AIF, died in action at the Battle of Hamel. Born in Wing, he emigrated to Australia in January 1911 and was a fireman in New South Wales before enlisting in September 1916. Brother of **Joseph Brand**; son of Joseph and Sarah Ann (Rogers) Brand of High Street, Wing. Méricourt-L'Abbé Communal Cemetery Extension III E 9.

1918 Saturday 6 July: Pioneer 365900 **William Benjamin Reeve** aged 18 of Tyne Electrical Engineers, the RE, died at the Alexandra Hospital, Cosham. Born in Leighton, he had attended Beaudesert School and was a hydraulic pump driver when he enlisted in May 1917. Son of William Benjamin and Harriett (Sapwell) Reeve of 8 Plantation Road. Leighton-Linslade Cemetery K 159. (See also Chapter 11.)

1918 Monday 8 July: Private 122654 **Albert Doggett** aged 27 of 50th Battalion the MGC died of wounds while a prisoner of war, captured on 9 April 1918 at the Battle of Estaires, during the Battle of the Lys. Born in Wing, he was a railway guard, and lived in Hackney with his wife and children until he joined the army in August 1917. Husband of Florence (Neaves); son of William and Emma (Dunham) Doggett of Stewkley Road, Wing. Cologne Southern Cemetery VIII A 24.

1918 Monday 8 July: Driver T4/263014 **William Humbles** aged 24 of 580th Company the ASC died at Frensham Hill Military Hospital. Born in Leighton, he worked as a farm labourer before enlisting in Luton. Brother of **George Humbles**; son of William and Sarah Ann (Sharp) Humbles of 5 Barrow Path. Leighton-Linslade Cemetery CC 275.

1918 Wednesday 17 July: Rifleman A/205169 **Joseph Stone** aged 19 of 16th Battalion the King's Royal Rifle Corps died from meningitis at Avesnes War Hospital. He had worked for the L&NWR. Son of Joseph and Annie (Pratt) Stone of the Maltings, Heath and Reach. Avesnes-Sur-Helpe Communal Cemetery B 91.

1918 Friday 20 July: Private 17048 **Amos Lugsden** aged 21 of 2nd Battalion the Duke of Wellington's (West Riding) Regiment died in action in France. He worked for grocer Ernest Howlett in Luton in 1911 and later for a chemist.

After enlisting he was a driver with the ASC but was posted to the Duke of Wellington's. Brother of **Albert Lugsden**, **Arthur Joseph Lugsden** and **Fred Lugsden**; son of David and Sarah Ann (Rollings) Lugsden of High Street, Eaton Bray. Marfaux British Cemetery VII A 7.

1918 Sunday 21 July: Private TR/10/43048 **Joseph George Newbury** aged 34 of 51st Battalion the Royal Sussex Regiment, formerly 14983 the East Lancashires, died from pneumonia at Thetford Military Hospital. He had been invalided back to England in 1917 because of ill-health. Born in Heath and Reach, he attended Beaudesert School and was apprenticed to a blacksmith before working in Luton for the GNR as a stable man and railway porter. Husband of Alice Elizabeth (Lawson, later Heeley) of Rugby, formerly of Luton; son of Joseph and Emily (Cherry) Newbury of 41 Church Street. Leighton-Linslade Cemetery CC 277.

1918 Saturday 27 July: Private 29168 **Ernest Taylor** aged 30 of 1/6th Battalion the Duke of Wellington's (West Riding) Regiment died in No. 3 Australian CCS, Brandhoek, of gunshot wounds to his back, forehead and neck. Born in Cheddington, he worked on a farm before moving to Yorkshire where he was a goods porter before enlisting in Huddersfield. Husband of Elizabeth (Firth, formerly Kelly) of Huddersfield; son of William and Mary (Baker) Taylor of Mentmore. Esquelbecq Military Cemetery III D 14.

1918 Sunday 4 August: Private 40651 **Leonard Moore** aged 23 of 2nd Battalion the Royal Dublin Fusiliers, formerly 2687 the Suffolk Yeomanry, died of cardiac paralysis and diphtheria at Tincourt Hospital having been taken prisoner on 23 March. Son of Alfred and Louisa (Lawson) Moore of 40 Regent Street, formerly of Heath and Reach. Tincourt New British Cemetery IX E 15.

1918 Monday 5 August: (Private 31534) **John William Henry Bock** aged 31 formerly of the RAMC, died of tuberculosis aggravated by his army service. He worked as a gardener before volunteering on 3 September 1914 and served in Malta before being discharged as physically unfit in February 1917 and awarded a Silver War Badge. He was born in Linslade but his mother died when he was a toddler and he was brought up by uncles in Wing. Husband of Mary Jane (Hedges) of Wingrave; son of John Louis and Elizabeth (Mead) Bock. Wingrave (St Peter & St Paul) churchyard.

1918 Tuesday 6 August: Private 78826 **Richard Edward Botterill** aged 18 of 11th Battalion the Royal Fusiliers (City of London Regiment), formerly

37026 of 4th Battalion the East Surreys, died in action during the defence of Amiens. Born in Duston, he moved to Leighton after 1911. Husband of Winifred Emily (Horn) of 22 Mill Road; son of Richard and Elizabeth Kate (Poole) Botterill of Duston. Franvillers Communal Cemetery Extension II B 10.

1918 Tuesday 6 August: Private 17280 **Albert Room** aged 32 of 2nd Battalion the Bedfords died of wounds in France. He was born in Edlesborough and worked on farms both there and in Eaton Bray. Son of Charles and Elizabeth (Hazzard) Room of Moor End, Eaton Bray. Dive Copse British Cemetery III K 25.

1918 Wednesday 7 August: Lance Corporal 30598 **Edward Cyril Sinfield** aged 28 of 2nd Battalion the Bedfords died near Corbie-sur-Somme. Married by 1911, he was a straw-plait dyer. Inside All Saints Church, Tilsworth is an oak hymn number board with a small brass plate bearing his name. In 1920, his widow and daughter emigrated to Australia. Husband of Daisy Laura (Willison) and son of Samuel and Ellen (Crawley) Sinfield, all of Tilsworth. Pozières Memorial 28, 29.

1918 Thursday 8 August: Private 61026 **John William Auger** aged 35 of 9th Battalion the Royal Fusiliers (City of London Regiment), formerly 14697 of 8th Battalion the West Surreys, died in action in France, his body being found between the lines by a burial party. He had been wounded in March 1917. Born in Walworth, he and his brother were basket makers boarding with the Bierton family at 33 Lake Street in 1911. Husband of Maud Louisa (Bierton) of Ivy Cottage, Regent Street; son of John and Emily (Flower) Auger of Camberwell. Vis-En-Artois Memorial 3.

1918 Thursday 8 August: Private G/95560 **Arthur Charles Halsey** aged 18 of the Royal Fusiliers posted to 2/4th Battalion the London Regiment (Royal Fusiliers) died in action in France. He had tried to enlist when under-age in 1915 but his father had intervened; as the lad was so keen, it was suggested that he remain in the service until eligible for draft. Son of Alfred and Caroline (Richardson) Halsey of Ladysmith Lane, Ivinghoe. Vis-en-Artois Memorial 3.

1918 Friday 9 August: Private 202505 **Sidney Dyer** aged 29 of 2/4th Battalion the Princess Charlotte of Wales's (Royal Berkshire) Regiment died a prisoner of war. At the age of 2, he was with his mother and two siblings in Leighton Buzzard Workhouse; ten years later he and a younger brother were boarded-out children living at Lawford's Farm, Heath Road. His mother was no longer able to look after her children or had died before 1911, when he was a farm worker living with his grandmother and an uncle in Edlesborough. Brother of **Lewis Dyer**; son of Sarah Dyer, late of Eaton Bray. Berlin South-Western Cemetery VI C 8.

1918 between Thursday 15 August and **15 November**: Private 12144 **Henry Shackleton** aged 18 of 6th Battalion the South Wales Borderers was presumed to have died in Germany, possibly after being taken prisoner, while working on roads and barbed wire defences near Kemmel south-west of Ypres. He was born in Fenny Stratford, but brought up in Leighton Buzzard. Brother of **Joseph Benjamin Shackleton/Wise**; son of John William and Sophia (King) Shackleton of Friday Street. Tyne Cot Memorial.

1918 Wednesday 21 August: Private 42036 **Walter George Aris** of 2nd Battalion the Suffolks, formerly TR/9/9723 Training Reserve, died from wounds on the way to a base hospital in France. Born in Tingewick, he was still there with his family in 1911 and was a Salvation Army helper, working at a Co-operative Society when he enlisted in Bedford. Son of George and Clara Eleanor (Blackwell) of 77 South Street, formerly of Tingewick. Bac-du-Sud British Cemetery III A 11.

1918 Thursday 22 August: Private 41972 **Frank Brantom** aged 18 of 7th Battalion the Norfolks, formerly the East Surreys then the Hertfordshire Yeomanry, died, wounded in action, near Cambrai. Born in Linslade, he moved away with his parents but returned to work as a coach builder at Morgan's before being conscripted. Only surviving child of William Joseph and Mary Ann (Stevens) Brantom of Newport Pagnell, formerly of 4 Springfield Road. Beacon Cemetery, Sailly-Laurette VI E 5.

1918 Thursday 22 August: Sergeant 10296 **John Pugh** aged 35 or 36 of 12th Battalion the MGC, formerly 14686 the O&BLI, died during the advance in Flanders, south-west of Armentières. He was born in Ledsham, Cheshire and had been butler to Sir Dyce Duckworth before enlisting. Husband of Emily (Tearle) of Wing; son of John and Elizabeth (Wilcoxon) of Willaston. Norfolk Cemetery, Becordel-Becourt I D 31.

1918 Thursday 22 August: Private G/63810 **Peter Smith** aged 18 of the Middlesex Regiment (attached to 1/19th Battalion the London Regiment) died during an attack on enemy lines during the Battle of Albert. He was an engine cleaner on the L&NWR before being called up following his 18th birthday. Brother of **William Smith**; son of Thomas and Mary Ann (Billington) Smith of 52 Old Road. Bray Vale British Cemetery I C 4.

1918 Friday 23 August: Private 33066 **Ralph Neale** aged 28 of 1/1st Battalion the Hertfordshires, formerly 6th Battalion the Bedfords, died near Achiet-le-Grand. Born in Heath and Reach, he was a farm labourer before enlisting in Leighton. Son of George and Emily (Tame) Neale of Reach Green, Heath and Reach. Originally buried in Bucquoy Community Cemetery. Serre Road Cemetery No. 2 X G 17.

1918 Friday 23 August: Private 20014 **William Alec Stevens** aged 22 of 1st Battalion the Bedfords died in action in France. He was born in Heath and Reach and in 1911 was a telegram boy living at the sub-post office in Simpson; he later enlisted in Ampthill. Of 72 St Andrew's Street; son of Sarah Ann Stevens and grandson of George and Elizabeth Stevens, all formerly of Birds Hill, Heath and Reach. Achiet-le-Grand Communal Cemetery Extension IV P 11.

1918 Sunday 25 August: Second Lieutenant **John Alfred Lee** aged 18 of No. 55 Squadron the RAF died when flying over enemy lines. Born in Sussex, he was living in Totternhoe by 1901 with his parents. After his family moved to Leighton, he attended Beaudesert School. Son of John and Letitia Laura (Correll) Lee of Kempston, formerly of Grove Road. Charmes Military Cemetery I A 18. (See also Chapter 5.)

1918 Sunday 25 August: Able Seaman R/564 **George Albert Matthews** aged 22 of Machine Gun Battalion the RN Division was shot in the head when sheltering in a shell hole during the 2nd Battle of Bapaume. He was born in Bletchley where his father was an L&NWR porter, but lived in Linslade from the age of 6 and was a munitions worker before joining the RNVR on 22 December 1916. Son of William and Frances (Grimble) Matthews of 15 Stoke Road. Vis-En-Artois Memorial 1, 2.

1918 Tuesday 27 August: Private 32139 **Herbert Kent MM★** aged 20 of 4th Battalion the Bedfords died of wounds in France. Son of Ernest Edward and Emily Annie (Rowe) Kent of Ledburn. Vis-En-Artois Memorial 4, 5. (See also Chapter 17.)

1918 Thursday 29 August: Gunner 147379 **Henry Edward Griffith** aged 39 of 116th Siege Battery the RGA died at the German Military Hospital in

Dercy-Mortiers. Born in Epsom, where his father was a stud groom, he moved to Crafton, Wing when his father's work took him to the breeding stud there. He enlisted in Paris. Son of Joseph and Mary (Griffith) Griffith of Grove Place. Originally buried in Crécy-sur-Serre German Cemetery. Chauny Communal Cemetery British Extension 5 B 2.

1918 Sunday 1 September: Private G/63272 **Frederick Groves** aged 34 of 19th London Regiment attached to the Duke of Cambridge's Own (Middlesex) Regiment, formerly 21665 the Suffolks, died in action during the 2nd Battle of Bapaume. Born in Leighton, he was a horseman at a hotel, enlisting in Bedford. Son of Thomas and Emily (Parker) Groves of 6 Ashwell Street. Vis-En-Artois Memorial 8-9.

1918 Sunday 1 September: Sergeant G/2186 **Augustus Housden Roser DCM★** aged 29 of 8th Battalion the East Surreys died in action near Sailly-Saillise. Born in Wimbledon, he attended school and was later a grocer's assistant before enlisting there. Some time after 1911 his parents came to Leighton where they remained for several years. Son of John Thomas and Agnes Elizabeth (Housden) Roser of 55 North Street. Combles Communal Cemetery Extension II D 31. (See also Chapter 17)

1918 Thursday 5 September: Private 42235 **Cyril George Day** aged 19 of 7th Battalion the Norfolks died after being wounded near Mametz during the 2nd Battle of the Somme. Born in Leighton, he had attended Beaudesert School and then worked as a dental mechanic. He enlisted as a trooper with the Hertfordshire Yeomanry in Luton and promoted to lance corporal, was later transferred to the Stafford Yeomanry and then joined the Norfolks. Only child of George and Emilie Louisa (Foster) Day of 27 Hockliffe Road. Vis-En-Artois Memorial 4.

1918 Wednesday 11 September: Private 16681 **John Thomas Osborne** aged 28 of 8th Battalion the Bedfords died near his home, having been discharged on 25 August 1916 as unfit for service; whilst in a trench with a machine gun in Ypres on 3 January 1916 he was blown up by a mine and both legs were broken causing permanent damage. He was a farm labourer aged 25 years 11 months, living at Reach Green, Heath and Reach, when he enlisted on 9 September 1914. His burial record names him, correctly, as John Thomas Gibson, labourer. Of 38 Baker Street; son of Henry Thomas Osborne and Mary Gibson; stepson of Martha (Baxter) Osborne, late of Shenley Church End. Leighton-Linslade Cemetery H 42.

1918 Tuesday 17 September: Corporal 56249 **Stephen Rose** aged 27 of 12/13th Battalion the Northumberland Fusiliers, formerly R/4/0 66258 of the ASC, died in Rouen after being wounded. He was a groom in Chippenham in 1911 and his future wife, born in Eaton Bray, was in service a few miles away in Seend. Husband of Agnes Elizabeth (Tompkins) of Moor End Lane, Eaton Bray; son of James and Emma Emily (Smith) Rose of Chippenham. St Sever Cemetery Extension III L 22.

1918 Wednesday 18 September: Private 41148 **Arthur Joseph Lugsden** aged 19 of 9th Battalion the Norfolks died after being wounded at Holnon Wood. Brother of **Albert Lugsden**, **Amos Lugsden** and **Frederick Lugsden**; son of David and Sarah Ann (Rollings) Lugsden of High Street, Eaton Bray. Trefcon British Cemetery B 41.

1918 Friday 20 September: Private 50983 **Herbert Going** aged 19 of 6th Battalion the Northamptonshires died after being wounded, almost certainly at the Battle of Épehy. Born in Stony Stratford, he enlisted in Bedford. Brother of **Leopold Francis Harold Going** and **William John Going**; son of Frederick and Harriet Salt (Perry) Going of 29 Mill Road. Doingt Communal Cemetery Extension I B 6.

1918 Friday 20 September: Private G/89270 **Arthur Teagle** aged 20 of 1st Battalion the Duke of Cambridge's Own (Middlesex) Regiment died in action in France. Brother of **Thomas Henry Teagle**; son of Henry and Fanny (Andrews) Teagle of Brook End, Pitstone. Villers Hill British Cemetery II C 23.

1918 Saturday 21 September: Private 25623 **Ralph Adkins** aged 29 of 9th Battalion the Duke of Wellington's (West Riding) Regiment, formerly 25204 the Somerset Light Infantry and previously 5674 the West Surreys, died in action in France. Born in Leighton, he attended Beaudesert School and was a grocer's assistant. He had moved to Aldershot and married, before enlisting in Winchester on 5 December 1915. Husband of Margaret (O'Connell) of Aldershot; son of George and Eliza (Roe) Adkins of 11 Hartwell Grove. Vis-En-Artois Memorial 6.

1918 Saturday 21 September: Private 29676 **William Henry Tew (Two)** aged 19 of 1st Battalion the West Surreys died in action near Manancourt. Born in Billington, he attended school in Aspley Guise while living with his paternal grandparents in Wavendon, later moving to Billington to live with an uncle and aunt. Brother of **Edward John Tew (Two)**; son of Joseph Paul and Mary Ann

(Pratt) Tew late of Heath and Reach; grandson of Henry and Emma (Pilgrim) Two of Billington Crossing. Villers Hill British Cemetery VI D 18.

1918 Sunday 22 September: Sergeant 260003 **Edward James Harris** aged 35 of D Company, 10th Battalion the Sherwood Foresters, formerly 200012 the Bedfords, died in action at Gauche Wood. Born in Linslade, he was a house painter when he enlisted in Leighton. Husband of Catherine (Gatwood) of 40 Stanbridge Road; son of James West and Sarah Jane 'Jenny' (Kightley) Harris of 17 Wing Road. Arras Memorial Bay 7; his body was later recovered and buried at Gauche Wood Cemetery Grave 5.

1918 Wednesday 25 September: Tpr L/11282 **Henry Bertram Turney** aged 27 of 1/1st Battalion Queen Mary's Regiment (the Surrey Yeomanry) died during an advance on horseback from Salonika. Born in Leighton, he worked in the family business (his father was a general hawker) before marrying. Husband of Helen (Dimmock) of the Ram, 8 St Andrew's Street; son of Thomas and Elizabeth Louisa (Heley) Turney of North Street. Doiran Memorial.

1918 Monday 30 September: Private 65482 **Ernest John Goodman** aged 28 of 26th Battalion the Royal Fusiliers, formerly 32990 the East Surreys, died of wounds in Belgium. Born in Stanbridgeford, he was in Leighton by 1911, when his father was a verger at All Saints church; by then Ernest was a grocer's assistant, boarding in Bedford. Son of William and Caroline (Cooper) Goodman of 3 Hockliffe Road. Vlamertinghe New Military Cemetery XIV F 2.

1918 Tuesday 1 October: Private G/25462 **Horace Charles Andrews** aged 19 of 11th Battalion the West Surreys, formerly 3092 of 3rd Battalion the O&BLI, died in action near the Wervicq to Menin railway line. Born in Leighton he attended Beaudesert School and was apprenticed to gas fitter William Jellis when he enlisted in Luton in May 1917. Son of Simeon and Phoebe (Buckingham) Andrews of 63 Hockliffe Road, late of 40 Regent Street. Tyne Cot Memorial 14-17, 162-162A.

1918 Tuesday 1 October: Private 30341 **Percy Bunker** aged 32 of King's Company, 1st Battalion the Grenadier Guards died at No. 34 CCS, Grevillers after being wounded, probably during the Battle of the Canal du Nord (27 September – 1 October). Born in Olney, he was brought up in Linslade and was apprenticed at 13 as a clerk for the L&NWR. He maintained his connection with St Barnabas's Church after he moved away, and worked in the Euston coaching superintendent's office where he remained from 1906 until he was conscripted in August 1917. Husband of Margaret Emily (Stevens) of Leighton; son of Benjamin and Anne (Gibbs) Bunker of Buckingham. Grévillers British Cemetery XIV B 6.

1918 Tuesday 1 October: Private 98225 **Alfred Joseph Dudley** aged 27 of 2/2nd (North Midland) Field Ambulance the RAMC died of dysentery at No. 39 Stationary Hospital, Fort Gassin. Named as Albert Joseph on the CWGC website, his birth was registered as Alfred Joseph in Leighton in 1892; he still lived in the town when he enlisted in Luton in November 1915, working in his father's cabinet-making, furniture sales and undertaker business in North Street. Husband of Alice Mary (Groom) of 60 Springfield Road; the only surviving child of Joseph Jabez and Frances Elizabeth (Adams) Dudley of 60 and 62 North Street. Aire Communal Cemetery IV E 10.

1918 Wednesday 2 October: CSM 8030 **Ernest Rufus Matthews MM★** aged 28 of 2nd Battalion the Suffolks died after being wounded in the hip during the attack on Rumilly-en-Cambrensis. Born in Stanbridge, he had attended Beaudesert School and was a printer in 1910 when he enlisted in Bedford; by 1911 he was with the regiment in Aldershot. Husband of Ethel Margaret (Crowe), latterly of Wandsworth; son of James Jabez and Mary Ann (Boskett) Matthews of Chapel Path, formerly of 5 Edward Street. Grévillers British Cemetery XV E 11. (See also Chapter 17)

1918 Friday 4 October: Private 18314 **Arthur Charles Pilgrim MM★** aged 30 of 14th Battalion the Royal Warwickshires, formerly 22952 of the Somerset Light Infantry, died at Le Tréport Military Hospital after being wounded, probably in the 2nd Battle of Bapaume, during the 2nd Battle of the Somme. He had been a labourer for a sand merchant, then a railway porter and had worked at the Hunt Hotel stables before enlisting, serving in Italy and France. He had married on 5 July 1917 and his wife and father visited him before he died. Husband of Lizzie (Jakeman); son of Arthur and Ellen Pilgrim of 5 Stoke Road. Mont Huon Military Cemetery VIII H 2B. (See also Chapter 17.)

1918 Saturday 5 October: Lieutenant **John 'Jack' Auguste Pouchot DCM★** aged 20 of 56 Squadron the RAF, formerly 2159 Rifleman of 16th Battalion the London Regiment Queens Westminster Rifles, died near Le Cateau. Born in London, he moved to Leighton in 1904 when his parents bought the tenancy of the Bell, Market Square; a few years later his parents separated. After his mother's tragic death from burns after a fire at the hotel in 1911, he returned to London and lived with foster parents. Only child of Auguste François Pouchot of Pimlico and of Emily Marian (Holdom) Pouchot late of the Bell, Market Square. Marcoing British Cemetery I C 20. (See also Chapters 5 and 16)

1918 Monday 7 October: Private M2/074637 **Arthur George Bullen** aged 27 of 37th Division Mechanical Transport (MT) Company the ASC died in action near the Hindenburg Line. His parents lived in New Road in 1891 and, although born in Rickmansworth in 1892, he was with them in Ivinghoe by 1901. Ten years later he was a footman to Lady Penrhyn at Ham Court, Upton-upon-Severn. Husband of Susan Hannah (Gobey) Bullen of Croydon; son of Richard Henry and Amy Annie (Selvey) Bullen of 1 Church Road, Ivinghoe. HAC (Honourable Artillery Company) Cemetery VIII C 24.

1918 Monday 7 October: Private 14006 **Ralph Kenneth Foxon** aged 22 of 7th Battalion the Duke of Edinburgh's (Wiltshire) Regiment, formerly 14565 the O&BLI, died in action during the breaching of the Hindenburg Line near the village of Beaurevoir. The sixth son to be drafted, he enlisted in Oxford in 1915. Son of George Thomas and Mary (Chandler) Foxon of 35 Beaudesert. Guizancourt Farm Cemetery Row D Grave 29.

1918 Monday 7 October: Private 66471 **William Richard Watson** aged 23 of 99th Field Ambulance the RAMC died at No. 46 CCS, Delsaux Farm of wounds probably sustained at Bailleul. Born in Watford he grew up in Linslade, where he was a bell ringer at St Barnabas Church. Before enlisting on 11 September 1915 he had been a clerk on the L&NWR for six years, starting as an apprentice before his 14th birthday, and had attended Leighton Buzzard Evening School from 1909 to 1912. Son of William Richard and Sarah Elizabeth (Ford) Watson of Sunny Bank, Rosebery Avenue. Delsaux Farm Cemetery I B 1.

1918 Tuesday 8 October: Acting Lance Corporal 22937 **Frederick Joseph Rolls** aged 22 of 1st Battalion the Hertfordshires died in action in France. Born in Potsgrove, he worked in domestic service as a house boy before enlisting in Ampthill. Son of Thomas and Sarah Jane (Snoxell) Rolls of Sandhouse, Heath and Reach. Naves Communal Cemetery Extension III C 6.

1918 Saturday 12 October: Corporal 165692 **Frederick William Joynson** aged 25 or 26 of 101st Battalion the Machine Gun Corps (Infantry), formerly 1151 the Royal Buckinghamshire Hussars, died after being wounded in France/

Belgium. Of Bridge Street; son of Alfred William and Ellen Emily (Harding) Joynson of Hughenden. Lijssenthoek Military Cemetery XXX B 18.

1918 Tuesday 15 October: Private 505198 **George Reginald Farr Cropley** aged 23 of 1/13th (County of London) Battalion (Kensington), formerly 3817 of 5th Battalion the London Regiment, died of wounds in Belgium. In 1911 he was a GPO messenger boy in Catford. Son of Samuel Farr and Jane Elizabeth (Keech) Cropley of 124 Wing Road, formerly of Catford; grandson of George and Hannah (Horne) Keech late of 41 Mill Road. Lijssenthoek Military Cemetery XXX D 6.

1918 Thursday 17 October: Private 29472 **James Monk** aged 24 of 2nd Garrison Battalion the O&BLI died at his home. He was a cowman on a local farm in 1911. Son of William and Elizabeth Ann (Gadsden) Monk of the Lock House near the Brownlow, Ivinghoe. Ivinghoe (St Mary), south of church.

1918 Saturday 19 October: Private 83889 **Sidney Baines** aged 31 of 18th Squadron the MGC (Cavalry), formerly 8785 of 5th Battalion the Bedfords, died of malaria in Alexandria. Born in Heath and Reach, he was a sand pit labourer, moving to Luton where he enlisted in December 1915. Husband of Nellie Elizabeth Holding of Luton; son of William Finch and Annie Jane (Heley) Baines of Heath and Reach. Damascus Commonwealth War Cemetery Grave B 111.

1918 Saturday 19 October: Gnr 157838 **Ralph William Creamer** aged 23 of 19th Brigade Ammunition Column the Royal Field Artillery died of malaria in Syria having been sent with the Mediterranean Expeditionary Force to Salonika in 1917. From there he went to Egypt and fought in Gaza. He was a farm worker in 1911 but a carman when he enlisted in Luton shortly before his 21st birthday. Son of Frederick Samuel and Kate (Culverhouse) Creamer of Chalgrave. Originally buried in the Damascus Protestant Cemetery. Damascus Military Cemetery A 56.

1918 Wednesday 23 October: Private G/82005 **Joseph Wright Biggs** aged 19 of C Company, 26th Battalion the Royal Fusiliers died in Belgium. Born in Holloway, he had moved to Heath and Reach with his family by 1905. Son of Joseph and Kate Elizabeth (Wright) Biggs of Thomas Street, Heath and Reach. Harlebeke New British Cemetery VI D 11.

1918 Wednesday 23 October: Private 200487 **Frederick George Jakeman** aged 20 of 2nd Battalion the Bedfords died in action in France. Born in Leighton, he had attended Beaudesert School but was unemployed in 1911. Son of Daniel and Sarah Jane (Squires) Jakeman of 66 North Place, Plantation Road. Highland Cemetery II B 7.

1918 Wednesday 23 October: Private 50030 **Frank Alexander Randolph Richardson** aged 19 of 2nd Battalion the Northamptonshires died near Bayreuth, a POW since being captured on 27 May 1918 at the beginning of the Battle of the Aisne. Son of Amos Harry and Mary Elizabeth (Meades) Richardson of Aylesbury Road, Wing. Niederzwehren Cemetery, Kassel IV K 1

1918 Thursday 24 October: Private 203768 **Alfred Charles Lake** aged 38 or 39 of 2/6th Battalion the Royal Warwickshires died in action liberating the village of Vendegies-sur-Écaillon during the Battle of the Selle. He was born in Stewkley, moving to High Street, Wing when he was a boy, where he was a labourer before enlisting. Son of Thomas and Ann (Illing) Lake, late of High Street, Wing. Canonne Farm British Cemetery A 4.

1918 Monday 28 October: Sapper WR/270169 **Albert George Robinson MSM★** aged 33 of 18th Light Railway Company the RE died at No. 41 CCS, Le Cateau, of injuries from an accident. He lived in Linslade and worked at Bletchley as a railway goods guard before enlisting. Born in Soulbury, Husband of Ada Mary (Randall), latterly of Burcott Hall Farm, Wing; son of Arthur George and Emma (Cox) Robinson of Brook Cottages, Soulbury. Roisel Communal Cemetery Extension I E 19. (See also Chapter 17)

1918 Monday 28 October: Corporal 5172 **Grenville Lawrence Towers** aged 31 of 2/5th Battalion the Bedfords died at his home, the Swan Hotel, his heart weakened by several bouts of rheumatic fever. Born in Leighton, he had enlisted but his health was such that he was almost immediately discharged as medically unfit. In 1914 was driving a motor-tram in Luton. His burial record has his occupation as munitions worker. Son of William Green and Catherine 'Kitty' (Collins) Towers of the Swan Hotel, 52 High Street. Leighton-Linslade Cemetery D18.

1918 Wednesday 30 October: Second Lieutenant **John Carter** aged 26 of 10th Kite Balloon Section the RAF, formerly Lance Corporal 54258 of 22nd Brigade the RFA, died when a stray shell hit his billet as he slept. Husband of Dorothy Blanche (Young) of Hampshire; son of Humphrey and Emma (Ginger) Carter of Ivinghoe. St Souplet British Cemetery II A 13.

1918 Wednesday 30 October: Private 68867 **Ernest Woodwards** aged 34 of 105th Company the Labour Corps, formerly 36634 of the West Surreys, died of wounds at 72nd Field Ambulance, near St Aubert. He was a milkman in Willesden before enlisting. Brother of **Arthur Woodwards** and **George Woodwards**; husband of Rose Hannah Gertrude (Wilhelm) later of Finchley; eldest son of Henry and Mary Ann (Taylor) Woodwards of High Street, Wing. St Aubert British Cemetery V A 17.

1918 Friday 1 November: Sergeant Mechanic 207333 **Arthur Albert Tompkins** aged 33 of the RAF, formerly F7333 of the RNAS, died at 2nd Scottish General Hospital, Edinburgh of a perforated duodenal ulcer and peritonitis. Born in Cheddington he was a carpenter by 1901, like his father, and was living in Kensington. He had been attached to HMS *Hyacinth*, serving on the Cape and East Africa station, but at the time of of his death was stationed at RAF Turnhouse. Husband of Emma Mary (Edwards) Tompkins of Harlesden; son of Arthur Jethro and Ann Sophia (Clark) Tompkins of Aylesbury, formerly of Cheddington. Cheddington (St Giles), left of main path.

1918 Saturday 2 November: Sergeant 16999 **Arthur William Foster MM★** aged 21 of 2nd Battalion the Machine Gun Corps died at No. 6 General Hospital, Rouen. Born in Stewkley, he moved with his family to Ivinghoe and then to Billington where he worked on a farm. Son of Alfred and Harriet Annie (Jones) Foster of Billington. St Sever Cemetery Extension S III L 6. (See also Chapter 17)

1918 Sunday 3 November: Private GS/239103 **Ezra Samuel Francis Emerson** aged 24 of 43rd Garrison Battalion the Royal Fusiliers, formerly 2927 the Huntingdon Cyclists Battalion, attached to the Royal West Kent Regiment, died at No. 30 General Hospital, Calais. He had been transferred to 43rd Garrison Battalion, considered unfit for front-line duty. In 1911 he was a baker's labourer. Son of John and Ann (Peppiatt) Emmerson of Dunstable, formerly of Regent Street, Summerleys, Eaton Bray. Les Baraques Military Cemetery, Sangatte VI C 6A.

1918 Monday 4 November: Shoeing Smith 54648 **Charles Richard Allder** aged 38 of 3rd (Lahore) Division Ammunition Column the Royal Horse and Royal Field Artillery died of malaria after being wounded in Egypt. Born in Stewkley, he married in Kentish Town in 1906 while working as a platelayer;

after his son was born in Hampstead, he brought the family home to Stewkley and by 1911 was working there as a horsekeeper on a farm, moving to Heath and Reach before the birth of a daughter in 1912. Husband of Hilda Pearcey (Owers) of Heath and Reach; son of Frederick Williamson and Sarah Ann (Tofield) Allder of North End, Stewkley. Ramleh War Cemetery EE 5.

1918 Monday 4 November: Private 43949 **Martin Leslie Johnson** aged 19 of 10th Battalion the Essex Regiment, formerly 50188 the Bedfords, died in action in France. Born in Hoxton, he was living in Leighton when he enlisted in Luton. Brother of **Charles Rowland Johnson**; son of Charles and Annie (Munday) Johnson, of Clapton, London; nephew of Thomas Henry Munday of 18 Bridge Street. Preux-Au-Bois Communal Cemetery Grave A 29.

1918 Tuesday 5 November: Private G/17193 **Arthur Baker** of 2nd Battalion the Royal Sussex Regiment died after being wounded during the attack on the Sambre-Oise Canal. Born in Eaton Bray, he was with his parents in Chapel Yard in 1901 but his mother died and his father remarried, moving to Dunstable, and he lived with his maternal grandfather in High Street in the village. Son of Joseph George and Mary Ann (Goodman) Baker of Dunstable, formerly of Eaton Bray. Premont British Cemetery 11 A 21.

1918 Tuesday 5 November: Rifleman R/26323 **Archibald James Tilbrook** aged 32 of 4th Battalion the King's Royal Rifle Corps died a day after being wounded during the 2nd Battle of the Sambre. Born in Maidstone, he worked at the Faith Press in Wing Road and was an active member of St Barnabas's Church. Husband of Lilian Norah (Holmes) of 25 Dudley Street; one of two sons of James and Dora Louisa (Brown) Tilbrook of Maidstone to die on active service. Fontaine-Au-Bois Communal Cemetery D 16.

1918 Thursday 7 November: Private 51337 **Charles Mason** aged 22 of 1st Battalion the Somerset Light Infantry died of wounds in France. He was born in Marsworth and in 1901 he and his family were at Cook's Wharf, Pitstone (technically Marsworth), having moved to Cheddington by 1911 where he worked on a farm. Husband of Margery (Mason) late of Tollesbury; son of William and Mary Ann (Wesley) Mason of Seabrook, Cheddington. Queant Road Cemetery I B 2.

1918 Friday 8 November: Private PW/6452 **Thomas Hyde** aged 27 of 1/8th Battalion the Duke of Cambridge's Own (Middlesex) Regiment died when hit by a shell. He had been wounded in the knee in August 1917 and admitted to a stationary hospital in Rouen. The joint stiffened and he was sent to Ireland on garrison duty but during the last German 'push' he was again drafted to France. Born in Leighton, he attended Beaudesert School and was a bricklayer's labourer before enlisting in his home town. Husband of Margaret Lucy (Rogers) and son of William Thomas and Mary Jane (Rowe) Hyde, all of 28 East Street. Blaugies Communal Cemetery, near the north-west corner.

1918 Sunday 10 November: Gunner 168715 **Daniel Randall** aged 23 of D Battery, 160th (Wearside) Brigade RFA died in action. He was a shepherd in his birthplace, Wing, before enlisting in Watford. Husband of Ethel (Lambourne) of 22 Union Street; son of Joseph and Martha (Bull) Randall of Church Street, Wing. Terlincthun British Cemetery VII D 40.

1918 Tuesday 12 November: Private 18933 **Arthur Harold Kemsley** aged 30 of 6th Battalion the Queen's Own (Royal West Kent) Regiment died of Spanish influenza while a prisoner of war in Altdamm (now in Poland), having been captured on 30 November 1917 at the Battle of Lateau Wood. In 1911 he was a printer in his birthplace of Sittingbourne; he later married in Aylesbury and moved to Northampton, then to Linslade. He enlisted in November 1915, serving from May 1916. Husband of Elsie (Tompkins) of 39 New Road; one of three sons of George and Agnes Eliza (Milgate) Kemsley of Sittingbourne to die on active service. Berlin South-Western Cemetery XIX A 11.

1918 Wednesday 13 November: Spr 522217 **Samuel Walter Stevens** aged 28 of 157th Field Company the RE died at No. 15 CCS, Don of pneumonia following influenza. He was a bricklayer, like his father. Husband of Elizabeth Ellen (Mead) of 12 Plantation Road; son of William and Catherine (Scrivener) Stevens of 50 Plantation Road. Don Communal Cemetery I B 35.

1918 Wednesday 13 November: Private 241391 **Edward Stone** aged 24 of 425th Agricultural Company the Labour Corps 'succumbed at 15.20h' to pneumonia at the Military Hospital, Hounslow. In 1911 he was a sandpit labourer. Husband of Louisa (Birch, later Smith) of Uxbridge; son of Frederick and Annie (Tompkins) Stone of Reach Green, Heath and Reach. Cowley (Middx) (St Laurence) churchyard.

1918 Thursday 14 November: Air Mechanic 1st Class 246611 **Percy William Avery** aged 27 of the RAF died from pneumonia at Chichester Military Hospital. He was born in Aston Clinton but his family were in Leighton by 1901; he attended Beaudesert School and was first a confectioner's assistant, becoming a baker by the time he enlisted in the RNAS on 16 January 1918, being transferred to the RAF at its inception later that year. Son of William Joseph and Alice May (Ridgway) Avery of Ashwell Street. Leighton-Linslade Cemetery B 382a. (See also Chapter 5)

1918 Sunday 17 November: Private 43798 **Leslie Payne** aged 20 of the Samoan Relief Force died from a fever aboard SS *Talune*, returning from Samoa to New Zealand, and was buried at sea. Born in Leighton, he appears to have left for New Zealand before 1911. He was a drover living in Matai Street, Inglewood when his name appeared on the 1916-17 New Zealand Army Reserve Rolls for 1st Division Taranaki (North Island) and on 4 May 1918 he enlisted in the New Zealand Defence Force, his occupation being station hand. Brother of **Archibald James Payne**; son of George and Mary Ann (Turney) Payne of Harley House, 54 North Street. Wellington Provincial Memorial.

1918 Sunday 17 November: Corporal 15719 **Robert Sproat** aged 25 of 8th Battalion the Somerset Light Infantry died after being discharged, no longer physically fit for war service, on 26 June 1917. Born in Northumberland, he had been a miner before enlisting 14370 the Northumberland Fusiliers in Cramlington. Shortly after leaving the army, he married in Heath and Reach. Husband of Lilian May (Whiting, later Dickens) of Heath and Reach; son of Matthew and Emily (Docherty) Sproat of Cramlington, Northumberland. Heath and Reach Cemetery B 142.

1918 Tuesday 19 November: Corporal 42703 **Arthur Kempster** aged 25 of 3rd Brigade the Canadian Field Artillery died from influenza and the effects of mustard gas. Born in Crafton, he and his younger brother were assistant butchers in 1911, living in Wealdstone. Son of George and Sarah (Jakeman) Kempster of Crafton. Wingrave Congregational Chapel Yard.

1918 Thursday 21 November: Private 143266 **Herbert Randall** aged 28 of 432nd Agricultural Company, Labour Corps died of pneumonia, probably in Wing. Born in Burcott, he was a labourer when he enlisted in the O&BLI. Son of George and Emma (Smith) Randall of Northampton, formerly of Wing. Wing (All Saints) churchyard.

1918 Friday 22 November: Lance Corporal 16828 **Philip Varney** aged 29 of 7th Battalion the O&BLI, transferred 121277 to 203rd Area Employment Company the Labour Corps, died at No. 27 CCS, Kavalla in Salonika. Born in Mentmore, he had attended Sunday school in Ledburn and in 1911 was a farm labourer there. Son of Henry and Maria (Green) Varney of Ledburn. Dedeagatch British Cemetery 77.

1918 Sunday 24 November: Pioneer 341418 **Ernest Frank Odell** aged 20 of Bedfordshire A Signal Depot the RE, formerly Trooper 245749 of 9th Yeomanry Cyclists Corps (2/1st Battalion the West Kent Yeomanry), died at No. 2 General Hospital, Le Havre from influenza and broncho-pneumonia. Born in Leighton, he attended the Baptist chapel. Son of Charles and Annie Matilda (Mercy) Odell of 47 Dudley Street, formerly of 32 Lake Street. Ste Marie Cemetery Division 62, IV D 8.

1918 Friday 29 November: Private 37214 **George Griffin** aged 41 of A Company 1/5th Battalion the Bedfords died at one of the general hospitals in Alexandria of pneumonia contracted after he had been wounded. Born in Leighton where his father was a coal dealer and carter, he was a carman's labourer when he enlisted. Husband of Phillis (Lathwell) of 27 North Street; son of George and Elizabeth (Rackham) Griffin of 95 North Street. Alexandria (Hadra) War Memorial Cemetery C 280.

1918 Saturday 30 November: Sergeant 12161 **Frank Ernest Stone** aged 30 of No. 3 (Western) Aircraft Repair Depot the RAF died of influenza and broncho-pneumonia at Beaufort War Hospital, Bristol. Born in Linslade, he moved as a young man to Gravesend where he was a solicitor's clerk before becoming a clerk in the RFC in October 1915, reaching the rank of sergeant in October 1917, before being transferred to the RAF at its formation. Son of William and Emily Ann (Boddington) Stone late of Linslade. Bristol (Arnos Vale) Cemetery, Screen Wall 4 723.

1918 Tuesday 3 December: Private 61638 **Robert Smith** aged 25 of 103rd Company the Labour Corps, formerly 39039 of 35th Labour Battalion the Royal Fusiliers, died at Aylesbury Military Hospital. Born in Kilburn while his father was briefly a railway platelayer there, he attended Beaudesert School and in 1911 was a house painter, working for a builder. His burial record has his date of death as 4 November, his occupation as painter. Brother of **James Smith**; son of William and Agnes (Ellaway) Smith of 70 St Andrew's Street. Leighton-Linslade Cemetery E 7.

1918 Tuesday 10 December: Private G/15833 **Robert Macdonald** aged 44 of 5th Battalion the Royal Fusiliers died after falling from a night train at Chelmscote, between Linslade and Stoke Hammond while he was travelling to his home in Innellan, Argyll; he awoke disorientated and opened the carriage door. Born in Blantyre, Lanarkshire and previously employed as a mercantile clerk, he enlisted in 1916 under the Derby Scheme and was gassed in March 1918, from which he was recovering. Son of the Reverend Robert and Catherine (Cameron) Macdonald, late of Blantyre. Old Linslade (St Mary's) churchyard.

1918 Wednesday 11 December: Private D/14850 **Harold Hill** aged 30 of the Duke of Lancaster's Own Yeomanry, formerly 1872 the Hertfordshire Yeomanry and D/14850 the Corps of Dragoons, died of pneumonia at Alexandria Hospital. In September 1914 he enlisted in Hertford and served in Egypt from July 1915. He is named in army records as Harry Hills. Only son of George and Lucy (Monk) Hill of 4 Dudley Street. Alexandria (Hadria) War Memorial Cemetery Plot H Grave 31.

1918 Friday 27 December: Private 313015 **Ernest Woodcraft** aged 22 of 1/7th Battalion the Royal Highland Regiment, formerly 6360 the Gloucestershire Regiment and WR/273147 the Royal Engineers, died at No. 22 CCS, Cambrai of influenza. He was born in Eaton Bray but had left home by 1911 to work as a mill hand for printers in Hemel Hempstead. Brother of **Harry Woodcraft**; son of John and Elizabeth (Fountain) Woodcraft of Bower Lane, Eaton Bray. Cambrai East Military Cemetery IV A 4.

1918 Saturday 28 December: Private 38386 **William Thomas Halsey** aged 18 of 52nd Graduated Battalion the Devonshires died at Aylesbury Military Hospital while home on leave; a signal maroon, found by his 10-year-old brother Arthur, exploded after being ignited, death according to the Register of Soldiers' Effects being from 'accidental wounds from a bomb on furlough'. Son of William and Susan Charlotte (Inns) Halsey of Church Road, Ivinghoe. Ivinghoe (St Mary) churchyard 455.

1918 Monday 30 December: Gunner 227555 **Henry James 'Harry' Beilby** aged 21 of the RGA died of encephalitis at the Connaught Hospital, Aldershot. By 1901 his mother was dead and the two boys went with their father to live with his sister. Son of Arthur and Ellen Maria (Sayell) Beilby of Blenheim Cottages, Cheddington. Cheddington (St Giles), north-west of church.

1918 Tuesday 31 December: Sapper 288438 **Richard Percy Butcher** aged 33 of Imperial Signal Company the RE died in German East Africa after an illness. Born in Leighton, he was a post office clerk before enlisting and a freemason. Husband of Elizabeth (Osmond) of 41 Billington Road; son of George and Mary Ann Maria 'Polly' (Turney) Butcher of 4 Lake Street. Dar Es Salaam (Upanga Road) Cemetery VII A 3.

1919 Monday 20 January: Sergeant **Eric Ashley Broad** aged 39 of the Australian Army Service Corps died at the Public Hospital in Perth, having being demobilised three months earlier with valvular disease of the heart, broncho-pneumonia and influenza. In April 1898 he had sailed on the P&O mail boat *Britannia* for Australia where he ran a poultry farm near Perth for some years, but despite his hard work, lack of experience and capital led to bankruptcy in 1910 and he was a motor mechanic and driver when he enlisted in April 1915. Probate was granted three times (in 1920, 1929 and 1930) to his unmarried sister Charlotte Hilda; in 1927 five shillings and a penny lay in his State Savings account, still unclaimed. Son of the Reverend John Ashley and Catherine (Tiplady) Broad of Cheddington Rectory. Perth (Karrakatta) General Cemetery Anglican HA 474.

1919 Thursday 23 January: Corporal M2/134079 **Harold Percy Timms** aged 32 of Mechanised Transport the ASC, attached F Anti-Aircraft Battery the RFA, died of pneumonia at his wife's family home, Ley Farm, Eaton Bray. Born in Aspley Guise he and his family moved several times before settling in Dunstable; he somehow managed to meet and marry a girl from Eaton Bray, although she lived with relatives in Chiswick in 1901. He was a carpenter before enlisting. Brother-in-law of **John Theodore Pratt**; husband of Elsie Gadsden (Pratt, later Pryer) and son of Joseph Harper and Sarah (Gadsden) Timms, all of Eaton Bray. Dunstable Cemetery B 58.

1919 Friday 7 February: Private/Lance Corporal 13585 **William Samuel Whybrow** aged 24 of C Company, 1st Battalion the Bedfords died of pneumonia at Mapperley Hall Red Cross Hospital, Nottingham, where he was convalescing from wounds received in action. Born in Leighton, he had attended Beaudesert School and was a house boy in 1911, living with his parents. His burial record incorrectly names him as James instead of Samuel. Son of Joseph and Millicent Jane (Coleman) Whybrow of 36 East Street. Leighton-Linslade Cemetery E 8.

1919 Sunday 16 February: Corporal SE/13778 **Percy Harold Dimmock** aged 24 of 14th Veterinary Hospital the AVC died of pneumonia at No. 1 South African General Hospital, Abbeville. Born in Leighton, he attended Beaudesert

School and before enlisting had worked as a grocer's assistant. Only brother of **Frank Dimmock**; son of Reuben and Alice (Haynes) Dimmock of 46 Mill Road. Abbeville Communal Cemetery Extension V F 4.

1919 Wednesday 19 February: Private R4/144337 **William John Blew** aged 24 of the Remount Depot the ASC, died from influenza at Royal Victoria Hospital Netley, Hampshire. A groom before enlisting in October 1915, he was at the Swaythling Remount Depot throughout the First World War. Son of Henry and Mary Ann (Dunn) Blew of School Lane, Wing. Netley Military Cemetery Plot C E 2004.

1919 Monday 24 February: Private 721304 **William George Bates** aged 31 of 2/24th Battalion the London Regiment died of pneumonia in Lambeth. His parents, both born in the Tring area, had moved their family to Lambeth in 1911 where they all worked in the boot trade, but had returned by 1919. Son of Alfred Foster and Mary Ann (Saunders) Bates of North East Cottage, Ivinghoe. Ivinghoe (St Mary), east of church.

1919 Monday 10 March: Sapper 563264 **Ralph Sanford** aged 29 of BB Cable Section the RE, formerly 2500 the Middlesex Regiment, died at the Royal Free Hospital, Grays Inn Road from illness contracted in France. He was born and grew up in Leighton, attending Beaudesert School and working as an ironmonger's assistant until he joined the RE (Electrical Division, Searchlight Section) in 1914. His burial record states he was an ironmonger. Son of Robert and Matilda (Brandon) Sanford of 19 Dudley Street. Leighton-Linslade Cemetery CC 96.

1919 Wednesday 12 March: Private M2/178158 **William John Randall MM★** aged 26 of 13th Siege Battery, Ammunition Column the ASC died at No. 41 Stationary Hospital, Poulainville. Born in Burcott, in 1911 he was a groom living in Ledburn in the same household as his future wife, and later became chauffeur to Lord Rosebery's estate manager Charles Claude Edmunds. Husband of Ellen Elizabeth (Sayell, later Fountain) of Ledburn; son of George and Emma (Smith) Randall of Wing. St Pierre Cemetery XIV E 1.

1919 Thursday 23 March: Private 201296 **Archibald Thomas Kember** aged 26 of 4th Battalion the Royal Sussex Regiment, transferred 361818 to 800th Area Employment Company the Labour Corps, died from heart failure while on the staff at a prisoner of war camp at Sidi Bishir, Alexandria, Egypt. He had previously been severely wounded during his three years in action on the Eastern Front. Born in Leighton, he was living in Heath Street, Hampstead and working as a draper's assistant in 1911. Son of William Walter and Sarah Ann (Rogers) Kember of The Croft, Stanbridge Road, late of 4 High Street. Alexandria (Hadra) War Memorial Cemetery Grave C 211.

1919 Sunday 20 April: George Newman, formerly AB R/3191 Nelson Battalion the RNVR died in the Western Hospital, Fulham. Drafted into the RNVR in June 1917 he served as an infantryman in France until invalided out in February 1919 suffering from tuberculosis, attributable to war service. He was a farm horseman before enlisting. Son of Henry and Sarah (Strange) Newman of Slapton. Slapton (Holy Cross) churchyard.

1919 Wednesday 7 May: Private 266170, formerly 3343, **Arthur Edwin Cutler** aged 22 of 2/1st Buckinghamshire Battalion the O&BLI died of tuberculosis contracted during his military service. Born in Wing, he was a farm labourer before enlisting soon after his 18th birthday in January 1915. He served on the Western Front for over a year before being transferred to the Territorial Force Depot and was invalided out of the army as physically unfit in January 1918. Son of John and Lucy (Smallbones) Cutler of Aylesbury Road, Wing. Wing (All Saints) churchyard.

1919 Thursday 15 May: Commander **Noel Stephen Tindall** aged 38 of base ship HMS *Egmont* died at Bighi Naval Hospital, Malta, of broncho-pneumonia. He was born in Leighton where his father was a partner in Bassett, Son and Harris Bank until its amalgamation with Barclays in the 1890s. Brother of **Mary Gertrude Tindall**; husband of Elizabeth Rose (Horne) of Bay View, Bantry, County Cork; son of John and Isabella Mary (Harris) Tindall of Sidmouth, formerly of Beech House, Leighton. Malta (Capuccini) Naval Cemetery Protestant Grave 69.

1919 Monday 2 June: Corporal 28435 **Thomas Cyril James Lambert Stevens** aged 31 of the Royal Gloucestershire Hussars, formerly of 20th Hussars, died of malaria in Leighton at his parents' home, the Unicorn, Lake Street. He enlisted on 5 November 1914 and served in France, where he was wounded, and then in Egypt where he contracted malaria. He was born in Linslade but spent much of his childhood at the Unicorn, where his parents were licensees, before boarding at a school in Towcester. In 1902 he had left England for the USA for the first time and was a prosperous rancher and married by the time he enlisted. Son of James and Kate (Lambert) Stevens of the Unicorn Hotel, 10 Lake Street. Leighton-Linslade Cemetery B 571A.

1919 Tuesday 8 July: Private 35648 **David Lansbury** aged 21 of 1st Battalion the Essex Regiment died of pulmonary tuberculosis, contracted while on active service. He was a farm labourer when he enlisted on 2 March 1916 but was discharged on 31 May 1918, no longer physically fit for war service. He left Étaples for England on the HMHS *Newhaven* and received the Silver War Badge along with a pension. Son of John and Mary Ann (Capp) Lansbury of 6 Sheep Lane, Potsgrove. Potsgrove (St Mary) churchyard.

1919 Saturday 19 July: Private 41318 **Frank Dimmock** aged 20 of 3rd Battalion the Prince of Wales's (North Staffordshire) Regiment, formerly of 52nd (Graduated) Battalion the Bedfords, died of tuberculous peritonitis at the Military Hospital, Curragh. Born in Leighton, he had attended Beaudesert School and worked as a grocer's errand boy on leaving school but a wire worker when he enlisted in September 1916. He was transferred after being posted to France but in March 1918 was invalided to England from No. 14 General Hospital, Wimereux with trench foot. Only brother of **Percy Harold Dimmock**; son of Reuben and Alice (Haynes) Dimmock of 46 Mill Road. Leighton-Linslade Cemetery K 277.

1919 Sunday 3 August: George Cosby aged 22, formerly Private 22590 the Bedfords, died at Corbetts Hill Farm. He enlisted in September 1915 but was discharged with a Silver War Badge two years later, suffering from Addison's Disease since being gassed while on active service. He worked for a grocer before enlisting and his burial record states he was a grocer's assistant. Of 53 Plantation Road; son of Frederick and Emily (Reeve, later Underwood) Cosby of 6 Friday Street. Leighton-Linslade Cemetery K 237.

1919 Friday 12 September: Private 18942 **Wilfred Charles Horley** aged 22 of 4th Battalion the Bedfords died at the Princess Alice Home, Upton Towers, Slough. On several occasions he survived being buried by shells but lost the use of his limbs after being shot through the spine in March 1918. Son of Frederick and Emma (Seabrook) Horley of Church End, Hockliffe. Hockliffe (St Nicholas), near north-west corner.

1919 Friday 17 October: Lieutenant **Alfred Stone** aged 25 of 3rd Battalion the Suffolks died in France. In 1911 he was a baker's assistant. Son of George and Sarah Ann (Newbury) Stone of 1 Woburn Road, Heath and Reach. Étaples Military Cemetery XLV D1.

1919 Thursday 23 October: Private 25672 **Herbert William Bray** aged 32 of 11th Battalion the Royal Berkshires died from the effects of a gas attack near Cambrai in 1918. Invalided home to recover, he was transferred to 95472 the Labour Corps. He was born and lived in Wing, a house boy in 1901 and a gardener in 1911. Husband of Laura Ellen (Foulkes) of Wing; son of Frank and Emma (Brooker) Bray of Frogmore Cottages, Wing. Wing (All Saints) churchyard.

1920 Saturday 13 March: Private G/73105 **Arthur Thomas Lathwell** aged 27 of 13th Battalion the Middlesex Regiment, formerly 7432 of 1/6th Battalion the Essex Regiment, died at the Royal Bucks Hospital, Aylesbury from the effects of a fever contracted in the East. He enlisted in 1915 and in August 1916 served with the Essex Regiment in Egypt, thence to Gaza; he also saw service during the Vadar Offensive of September 1918. He was a drover before enlistment and his burial record has labourer. Of 7 East Street, where he lived with an uncle and aunt, George and Catherine Favell, after the death of his mother. Son of Ephraim and Sarah Ann (Samuel) Lathwell of 9 East Street. Leighton-Linslade Cemetery K 165.

1920 Sunday 11 April: Alec Janes aged 24, formerly Lance Corporal 252 of the East Kents (the Buffs) and Private 401102 the Labour Corps, died in the Throat Hospital, Golden Square, London as a result of his war service. He was born in Leighton Buzzard and attended Beaudesert School and, although in poor health, he enlisted soon after war was declared. Husband of Grace (Fuggle) and son of John and Elizabeth Ann (Hartley) Janes, all of 80 Church Street. Leighton-Linslade Cemetery GG 2A.

1920 Saturday 12 June: Private 26020 **Arthur Cook** aged 44 of 2nd Battalion the O&BLI, formerly 2467 of 3rd Battalion and of the Royal Berkshires, died in Buckinghamshire. He had served in the Boer War and had been awarded two clasps to his medal but was discharged on 7 February 1919, having contracted typhoid in November 1918. Born in Ivinghoe, he was a council road worker, living with his wife and her mother 'near the railway bridge' in 1911. Husband of Louisa (Wesley) of Pitstone; son of George and Fanny (Evans) Cook, late of 2 Ship End, Pitstone. Pitstone (St Mary).

1920 Thursday 15 July: Private 18736 **William Frederick Taylor** aged 45 of 4th Battalion the Bedfords, transferred to 518902 the Labour Corps, died in Hertfordshire. In 1891 he was apprenticed to his father, a jeweller, at 49 High Street and by 1911 was married with nine children and running his own business at 61 High Street, Stony Stratford. Husband of Edith Anne (Stanbridge) of Stony Stratford; son of Thomas Frederick and Elizabeth (Stears) Taylor of 36 Plantation Road. St Albans (Hatfield Road) Cemetery Mil. E 6.

1923 Tuesday 12 June: Henry Richard Stone aged 30, formerly of the O&BLI, died of tuberculosis contracted during his war service. He was born in Soulbury, but had been a footman in London before enlisting. Son of John and Ellen Jane (Woolhead) Stone of Brook Cottages, Soulbury. Soulbury (All Saints) churchyard.

1925 shortly before **17 August: Horace William Pratt** aged 29 of 1st Battalion the Norfolks died in Heath and Reach from the effects of his war service. Son of Horace and Annie (Neal) Pratt of Fox Corner, Heath and Reach. Heath and Reach (St Leonard).

1927 Thursday 21 July: Rifleman G/21379 **Percy Francis Hedges** aged 30 of 1st Battalion the West Surreys, formerly 1st and 6th Battalions, died at his home in Cheddington of pulmonary phthisis. He was born and raised in Cheddington and was a newspaper boy in 1911. He enlisted on 11 December 1915, served for almost four years before being discharged on 18 July 1919, unfit for active service, and was awarded the Silver War Badge the following August. Son of Arthur and Ruth (Coker) Hedges of the Old Inn, Cheddington. Cheddington (St Giles) churchyard.

1933 Monday 1 May: Cyril James Turner aged 39, formerly Corporal 22430 of 6th Battalion the O&BLI, died in a convalescent home in Reading. Born in Cheddington, he was a gardener in the village in 1911 but was a railwayman there after his discharge from the army in 1919 as permanently unfit since being wounded, for which he received the Silver War Badge. Husband of Marjory Frances Beatrice (Tompkins) of Mentmore Road, Cheddington; son of Frederick and Sarah Jane (Sayell) Turner of Station Road, Cheddington. Cheddington (St Giles) churchyard.

1934 Thursday 31 May: Arthur Thomas Seabrook aged 35, formerly Private 40830 of 7th Battalion the Duke of Cornwall's Light Infantry died in the Buckinghamshire Lunatic Asylum, Stone. He enlisted one month after his 18th birthday and was discharged two years later with a Silver War Badge, unfit due to sickness. The inscription on his headstone reads: 'A victim of the Great War'. Son of William and Jane Elizabeth (Church) Seabrook of 33 New Road. Old Linslade (St Mary's) churchyard.

APPENDIX A

TIMELINE 1914–1918

1914

JUNE
Archduke Franz Ferdinand of Austria is assassinated by a Bosnian Serb nationalist.

JULY
Austria–Hungary declares war on Serbia. Russia defends Serbia.

AUGUST
Germany declares war on Russia, then on France (Russia's ally) and invades Belgium. Belgium appeals to Britain and Britain declares war on Germany. Events escalate and Europe is divided into the Central Powers (Germany, Austria-Hungary and later Turkey and their allies) and the Triple Entente (Britain and the British Empire, France, Russia and their allies). Albania, Belgium, the Netherlands, Norway, Spain and Sweden remain neutral. General French's 'contemptible little army', all professional volunteer soldiers, begin to embark for France and engage with more than twice as many German troops at the Battle of Mons. There are thousands of casualties; both sides use quick-firing artillery and machine guns to devastating effect. Private Ernest Samuel Richard Mead from Leighton of the 19th Royal Hussars is there, armed with his sword. 'I shall never forget when the first shot was fired.' The BEF retreats and for the first time Britain finds it necessary to begin recruiting a large army, known as Lord Kitchener's Army. LB Reservists are called up immediately. The 1914 Defence of the Realm Act is given royal assent to control communications, the nation's ports and subject civilians to the rule of military courts. The 7th Battalion the Royal Warwickshires pass through Leighton, staying only a few days. An appeal is made for the services of ladies willing to assist in running a Red Cross hospital in Leighton Buzzard, should it be found necessary to fit one up. Alice (Bromhead) Bassett is President of the Leighton Buzzard Division of the Soldiers' and Sailors' Families Association, 'to whom enquiries may be addressed.'

SEPTEMBER

The German advance towards Paris draws French and British soldiers to counter-attack in the Battle of the Marne. The two sides try to outflank each other to the north and to the Belgian coast; the 'Race to the Sea' begins. The Germans are pushed back to the River Aisne where they hold their line. Both sides dig in, defensive lines are drawn across north-east France; a war of attrition begins, and four years of trench warfare on the Western Front. Miller William Simmons offers a bonus of £3 to anyone with a month's residence in the two towns who is accepted for Lord Kitchener's Army before 12 September and forty-eight people receive this. The amount of work in hand at Morgan's has not altered since war was declared.

OCTOBER

The 1st Battle of Ypres begins. The town is strategically located along the roads leading to the Channel ports in Belgian Flanders. but the British fail to break through German lines. Troops from the British Empire and from the French colonies in Africa join the Allies. Germany fires shells containing tear-gas. The first detachment of 3,000 or 4,000 troops, expected for some days, arrives in the towns by train. A harmonium and a clock at a Leighton school are damaged by troops. The All Saints church organist and director of the LB Operatic Society, Ralph Richardson-Jones, joins the Yeomanry.

NOVEMBER

Turkey declares war on Russia, Britain, France and Serbia. David Lloyd George, in his War Budget, announces that income tax will double in 1915 to pay for the conflict and duty on beer and tea will be raised. Almost 4,000 troops are billeted in the towns 'and will probably stay a month' – this will drag on until April. A special constables' guard is in place at the Sand House Pumping Station in Heath. Eight Belgian refugees who have been enjoying the hospitality of private families move into the second house in Heath Road to be furnished by the Wesleyan Committee.

DECEMBER

Haig commands the newly-formed First Army. The Second Army is formed at the same time. This is the year of the Christmas Day truce, which Linslade man Reginald Alfred Cornish of the Queen's Westminster Rifles witnesses. More troops arrive in the towns. New blue uniforms are issued and rumour has it that all the men will soon receive khaki uniforms. Company Sergeant Major George Hutchinson has been joined by his wife Elizabeth and their children who are billeted in 31A Plantation Road; his 12-year-old daughter Margaret dies on 18 December and is buried in Vandyke Road (Leighton-Linslade) Cemetery, her headstone paid for by her father's comrades of 12th Battalion the West Yorkshire Regiment.

1915

JANUARY

Germany uses chemical gas on the Eastern Front. Along with the list of men who have enlisted, published weekly in the *LBO*, there is this message: 'Men who have not responded to the requirements of their country are urged to answer the appeal.' Brown's advertise for iron moulders and improvers at their Victoria Ironworks.

FEBRUARY

Germany announces that it will sink ships carrying supplies to or from Britain. The billeted soldiers play inter-regimental football at the Stoke Road ground; the match raises £3 0s 6d for the Linslade Invalid Kitchen Fund.

MARCH

The Mediterranean Expeditionary Force is formed. Indicator nets aid in the destruction of German submarine *U8* off Folkestone. The RFC carries out aerial photography in preparation for the Battle of Neuve Chapelle, despite bad weather, and for the first time an attack front is mapped to a depth of 1,450yd (1,400m). Corporal H. Guess is with the Bedfords, and is one of only four of the fourteen in his trench to survive. Leighton and Linslade have each 'contributed to the Colours' 5 per cent of their combined population of 9,046.

APRIL

The Allies attack the Ottoman forces, but their attempted amphibious landing to take the peninsula of Gallipoli fails; the Allies are unable to break out of their beachheads. By the end of the campaign in January 1916, the number of New Zealand and Australian casualties exceeds 11,000. There is stalemate on Western Front. Germany uses chlorine gas against the French at Ypres. This is the first large-scale use of gas and its effects are devastating. The Somersets and the West Yorks leave the towns for Halton but not before a marching regimental band has startled a horse pulling a sand-cart and Hubert Michael Hyde, aged 5, has been run over and dies of his injuries.

MAY

A coalition government is formed. U-Boats patrol Atlantic and Mediterranean trade routes and Germany issues warnings before a torpedo sinks a civilian passenger liner, RMS *Lusitania*, off the coast of Ireland. Among the dead are 128 Americans. There are Zeppelin air raids on London. More hospitals are opened in large private and public buildings. Women take on men's work and the Board of Agriculture forms the Women's Land Army. The last troops, the 10th York & Lancasters, leave Linslade for Halton Camp. Band of Hope workers are said to have been amongst 'the most regular promoters of temperance canteens and innocent recreations for the men.'

JUNE

German airship LZ-37 is destroyed near Ghent by Lieutenant Reginald 'Rex' Warneford of the RNAS, the first to be successfully attacked from the air. Joseph Elliott, aged 74, of Grove Road tries to enlist but is not accepted. Margaret Gotzheim of the Crown, regarded as an alien enemy, is fined £20 for travelling more than 5 miles from her home without a permit; she was recognised by the Luton police. Bricklayer's labourers erecting the new factory for government work in Union Street (Bullivant's) down tools and demand higher wages of Willis, the contractor. They leave the premises and are immediately replaced.

JULY

The 1915 Munitions of War Act becomes law, giving the Ministry of Munitions the power to declare factories controlled establishments, and through a system of certificates and of tribunals, restrict the freedom of workers to leave, also regulating the wages, hours and conditions of munitions workers. The 1915 National Registration Act is passed, requiring all men and women between the ages of 15 and 65 to register their address. In the poorer neighbourhoods of Leighton and Linslade, the enumerators have to fill in many of the registration forms themselves, as the people are unable to write. Leighton Buzzard Wool Sale attracts only a small attendance; the highest price is 49s 7d per tod (28lbs). The town is expecting from 1,500 to 1,800 men of the Royal Field Artillery; the police provide billets in Lake Street and Grove Road for the advance party of 100 men. Page's Park having been chosen for the horse lines, a good deal of training is also to be carried out there.

AUGUST

The landing at Suvla (Dardanelles) begins with 5th Battalion the Bedfords among the troops, and two cavalrymen from the Leighton area die in the Battle of Scimitar Hill. A fire at the Swan Hotel stables is caused by a soldier throwing down a match after lighting his cycle lamp. A further detachment of men arrive to join the artillery training camp in Page's Park. In the evening the men are making good use of the Wesleyan classroom for reading and writing.

SEPTEMBER

The British first release asphyxiating gas on a large scale at the Battle of Loos, causing casualties among their own men. A flag day in aid of the RSPCA fund for sick and wounded horses raises £41 17s 5d from Leighton and Heath.

OCTOBER

Lord Derby's Group Scheme is launched to increase voluntary enlisting, classifying men by marital status and age. Military service tribunals are introduced and the *LBO* gives detailed reports weekly. Many letters arrive from those recently billeted in the towns, some cheerful, some harrowing. A new lighting order is enforced by Leighton Police: all external lights must be extinguished except for railway or munition works, which must be kept low or shaded. Linslade, being in a different county, continues to light up.

NOVEMBER

The Cabinet War Committee has its first meeting and the Port and Transit Executive Committee is formed. Canvassing under Lord Derby's Scheme is being actively conducted in the towns by a representative committee. All Saints holds afternoon services without sermons, for the benefit of those unwilling to leave home after dark now that there is no street lighting.

DECEMBER

The Group Scheme ends. The 20th Annual Christmas Fat Stock Sale of oxen, cows, sheep and pigs takes place in Church Square with 'well up to the average established in recent years.' At a sale in Leighton Buzzard £700 is raised by the Bedfordshire Branch of the British Farmers' Red Cross Fund. Private Andrew Kirk of the Royal Warwickshires, formerly billeted in Leighton, writes from a hospital in England. He is one of a party of returned prisoners of war from Germany. At a meeting of the LBUDC, the first matter to give rise to contention is the positioning of a boundary wall at Bullivant's new wire works.

1916

JANUARY

On 27 January the 1916 Military Service Act introduces compulsory conscription into the Reserve of all single men aged 18 to 41. Some conscientious objectors are sent to work settlements. Britain introduces the Summer Time Act from 21 May to 1 October. There is a great decrease in tramps at Leighton Workhouse, many having given up the road and joined the services. The *LBO* stops running its weekly roll of honour.

FEBRUARY

Germany plans an offensive on a series of forts around the town of Verdun, to lure the French Army into defending it and to be destroyed. This strategy fails but with a horrendous casualty toll. Miss B of Dudley Street seeks work: 'Advertiser, keen on Milk or Bread Round, during the duration of the war; early riser; punctual; can drive; used to all weather.'

MARCH
The 1916 Military Service Act comes into force, imposing the conscription of all single men aged 18 to 41. The first public meeting of the local military service tribunal is held. Among the formal exemptions for a shoeing smith, a horse slaughterer and men on munition work, there is an application on behalf of the council surveyor, and two months' postponement is agreed.

APRIL
British and Indian forces in Mesopotamia (Iraq) are crushed by the Turks at Kut. Martial law is proclaimed in Dublin. Miss Kate Blewitt of Heath Manor House is Registrar of District VIII (Leighton Buzzard) Women's County War Agricultural Committee.

MAY
The German fleet attempts to shell the English coast and attack part of the British fleet but meets the full force of the British Navy off the coast of Denmark, at Jutland. Britain loses more ships than Germany, failing to destroy the German High Seas Fleet but causing it to retreat and remain confined in its North Sea and Baltic ports for the rest of the war. Germany then relies on U-boats to attack British supply lines. These create havoc. The Irish Rebellion collapses. Daylight Saving is introduced in Britain and a second Military Service Act extends compulsory conscription to married men aged 18 to 41. A tender of £5 is accepted for sheep grazing in the recreation ground by Bryan Welch of Stafford House, a shire horse breeder. An All Saints Vestry meeting reports that £19 has been spent on aircraft insurance.

JUNE
Heavy fighting around Ypres continues; Germany temporarily seizes Hill 62 from Canadian troops.

JULY
The Battle of the Somme begins, part of a joint offensive by the Allies on their fronts in France, Italy and Russia. Haig hopes to end the deadlock with an artillery bombardment to silence the German guns and allow his infantry to break through. This fails because the Germans dig in and aim their machine guns at the charging Allied soldiers. Nearly 20,000 British soldiers die on the first day. Although news of their deaths does not arrive immediately, there are at least eleven local casualties during the first week. Money is raised for the Comforts Fund for Leighton soldiers

on active service at a whist drive and dance at the Corn Exchange, organised by the Women's Unionist and Tariff Reform Association. James Robinson, proprietor of the basket works, dies.

AUGUST

The propaganda film *The Battle of the Somme* premières in London, giving audiences their first realistic impression of a battlefield on the Western Front. Approximately 20 million Britons see the film during the first six weeks of its release. A baker advertises: 'Wanted, a man thoroughly good at Bread and Smalls (ineligible for service). Help given. Permanency. Box No. 25, *Reporter* Office, Market Square.'

SEPTEMBER

Tanks are introduced on the Somme battlefield by the British, but there are so few that they have little impact. Cities and towns in several counties are attacked simultaneously by twelve German naval Zeppelins. An illustration of the military version of the Tielocken Burberry topcoat, 'no buttons to fasten or lose', accompanies an advertisement naming their Leighton agent, Henry Stanley Willard of 35 High Street.

OCTOBER

The Board of Agriculture appoints a Royal Commission on Wheat Supplies. The price of a loaf of bread rises to 10d, its highest ever. Bakers are accused of increasing their prices before the government can introduce legislation to control prices.

NOVEMBER

The first German daylight aeroplane raid on London takes place by a lone aeroplane. The Battle of the Somme ends with the Allies having advanced just 5 miles. There are over half a million casualties on each side. Local newspapers appeal for biographical details of local officers and men who fall in the service of the country. A Russian Flag Day held in Leighton raises £59 6s 3d.

DECEMBER

Lloyd George replaces Asquith as Prime Minister and Lord Derby is appointed Secretary of State for War. The restriction of Christmas leave means that of the 1,000 local men in the army, few are spending the holiday with their relatives. With very little in the way of munitions work to make up for the earnings of the men now in the army, Leighton is feeling the influence of the war more than most towns.

1917

JANUARY

People who go out at night in charge of perambulators are advised that these come under the term 'vehicles', and close attention should be paid to the new Lighting Order; they must display two lighted lamps, a white one showing to the front and a red one to the rear.

FEBRUARY

Germany retreats to a carefully prepared line of defences – the Hindenburg Line – and resumes its U-boat campaign against commercial ships headed from America to Britain; there are many American civilian casualties. Prisoners of war in Britain work on the land. John Richard Hunt of the Bell Hotel, Leighton, pleads not guilty to failing to close his licensed premises as respects members of HM Forces.

MARCH

British forces push the Turks back in Palestine and capture Baghdad. Under a misapprehension, the Leighton Tribunal had been dealing with Group Scheme volunteers.

APRIL

The USA declares war on Germany. The Battles of Arras continue at Vimy Ridge and the Scarpe simultaneously. A Leighton man is there with the Canadian Infantry. Henry James Fish, keeper of the Ewe and Lamb, is fined £1 on each of two offences against the Aliens' Restriction Order in respect of a Russian visitor to his house.

MAY

After huge losses in April, the Atlantic Trade Convoy Committee is appointed to protect merchant shipping. The first National Kitchen is opened by Queen Mary in Westminster Bridge Road, London, providing cheap meals for those affected by food shortages. A royal proclamation encourages a voluntary reduction in bread consumption. The Linslade War Savings Committee organises a food economy and war savings exhibition with lectures at the Forster Institute.

JUNE

The Battle of Messines Ridge begins with the British Army exploding nineteen mines in the early hours of 7 June. The first American troops arrive in Britain. Receipts for the Red Cross Society on Buckinghamshire Day from the Linslade, Wing Grove and Edlesborough district total £311.

JULY

The action at Ypres begins on 31 July, centred upon the village of Passchendaele. The Women's Army Auxiliary Corps is formed and the British royal family changes its surname from Saxe-Coburg to Windsor. Brantom's seedsmen advertise Karswood Spice which will double egg output, and by so doing, automatically defeat the German submarine campaign.

AUGUST

The 2nd Battle of Ypres continues with the Battles of Langemarck and Hill 70 at Lens. Two battalions of the O&BLI are among the troops. The Ministry of Reconstruction is formed, responsible for administrative reform, the role of women in society, employment, industrial relations and housing.

SEPTEMBER

Germany uses artillery shells containing mustard gas against the Russians at Riga. The first group of repatriated British prisoners of war reaches England from Switzerland. Two hundred thousand women are now estimated to be working on the land. Brown's demonstrate their 'Overtime' tractors, useful during the current serious shortage of labour and the demands on the agricultural industry to increase the food supply. The military appeals against a three-month exemption for Ernest Lee, house furnisher and undertaker; he will not be called until 15 October.

OCTOBER

Canadian troops capture the village of Passchendaele; there are 250,000 casualties. British troops attack the Yser Canal, in Boesinghe. On the first day of the Battle of Broodseinde, the attack by the Australian and New Zealand Army Corps reaches the high ground just below the summit of the Broodseinde Ridge. Four local men die during this battle. Zeppelin L53 drops bombs on Heath and Reach. Leighton's Urban District Council resolves that the only street lighting should be at the Roebuck corner of Hockliffe Street by an oil lamp, to be extinguished at 10.30p.m.

NOVEMBER

The Bolsheviks, led by Lenin, seize power and Russia begins to leave the war, signing an armistice in December. In the peace treaty Germany gains large swathes of eastern Europe. The Battle of Cambrai begins and the first major tank attack takes place with 324 British tanks. Among those fighting are 8th Battalion the Bedfords. The Ministry of National Service is formed, and the Air Force (Constitution) Act, 1917 passed. A substantial country house, Bossington, in 5 acres with carriage drive and lime avenue, is offered 'For Sale At War Price'.

DECEMBER

The United States declares war on Austro-Hungary. All hostilities on the Eastern Front are suspended. The British capture Jerusalem and General Edmund Allenby, Commander-in-Chief of the Egyptian Expeditionary Force, dismounts and enters the city on foot in respect for the Holy City, posting guards to protect all sites held sacred by the Christian, Muslim and Jewish religions. Nationwide sugar rationing is introduced. Arthur Roberts of the Rye, Eaton Bray pays 5s 6d costs for failing to post up a list of persons, over 16 years of age, employed by him.

1918

JANUARY

The Air Ministry is formed. Food rationing extends to tea, butter and margarine. Thomas Handy Bishop, harness-maker, dies aged 78. The directors of Morgan's present a set of instruments to the works band which has recently been formed. Bedfordshire War Agricultural Committee announces that a camp is being arranged in Leighton, where German prisoners will be placed who are skilled agriculturists. They will be available to farmers within a radius of 5 miles of the town.

FEBRUARY

Dover is shelled by a U-boat. The Ministry of Information is created, and women aged over 30 win the right to vote. Meat and fat rationing begins in London and the Home Counties. After seven weeks the milk vendors' strike in Leighton is over. The Linslade Food Control Committee provides 4oz of butter for every inhabitant of the combined Wing and Eaton Bray Rural Districts. Leighton Buzzard people, who did not participate in the scheme, regard this as only another reason to regret the refusal of the Leighton Committee to join the combined district.

MARCH

Russia withdraws from the war and Germany moves troops from the Eastern to the Western Front. The Allied Blockade Committee is formed to regulate trade more effectively.

APRIL

The Military Service (No. 2) Act raises the age limit to 51.

MAY

Germany's spring offensive in France brings it a huge breakthrough on a 50-mile front south of Arras; it pushes the Allies back 40 miles, but the overstretched German Army is unable to sustain its attack. American troops begin to arrive in great numbers. The 1916 Summer Time Act receives royal assent. A photographer, Percy John Baker, is fined £1 for using motor spirit illegally.

JUNE

The Representation of the People Act 1918 is passed in the House of Commons, giving the vote to all men over the age of 21 and to women over the age of 30. Some 'jolly girls' from the training centre at Leighton for the Women's Land Army attend a recruiting rally in Tring. The local Post of the Comrades of the Great War is strong enough to be formed into a branch.

JULY

French forces launch a surprise attack, the beginning of the Hundred Days Offensive, and Germany retreats across the River Marne. The government protests against the Sand and Gravel Agreement of May 1918, regarding the export of sand and gravel from the Netherlands for German use. In War Savings Week, Linslade is endeavouring to raise £5,000, a sum equal to £1 10s per head of population, for national purposes.

AUGUST

Reinforced by American troops, the Allies carry out a series of sustained attacks and begin with the Battle of Amiens. In a series of battles the German Army is pushed further east and the German commanders privately concede that the war is lost. A gas explosion wrecks the meter house and board room of the Leighton Buzzard Gas Co. at night, causing people to think that there is a Zeppelin raid. A total of £2,000 is raised by the Linslade War Savings Committee during an aeroplane week.

SEPTEMBER

The Allied forces retake Passchendaele. Influenza, pneumonia and malaria cause many deaths.

OCTOBER

The Allies have by now taken control of almost all of German-occupied France and part of Belgium; Germany asks for an armistice. This is the month of the highest mortality from the Spanish 'flu pandemic in Britain.

NOVEMBER

Before the Allied armies can invade Germany, an armistice is signed, bringing the war on the Western Front to an end. In a train carriage at Compiègne in northern France, the Germans surrender and agree to withdraw their forces from France and Belgium and the fighting ceases at 11.00 a.m. on 11 November 1918. Prisoners of war and serving soldiers begin to return. Leighton Buzzard is in the throes of the influenza epidemic with a good proportion of the population affected. The day and evening schools have had to be closed. As far as is known, only one death has occurred. Jack Rowe, a Leighton munition worker, pleads guilty to leaving a train in motion, protesting against the overcrowding of munition trains on the Dunstable line, and is let off with a caution. Three performances of the pantomime *Aladdin* raise a substantial sum for the local Red Cross fund.

APPENDIX B

The key to local memorials on which casualties named in Chapter 18 are commemorated.

Leighton Buzzard and Linslade

Leighton Buzzard	War Memorial 1914–18 and 1939–45	Church Square	*1*
Leighton Buzzard	Baptist Church brass plaque 1914–18 and 1939–45	Hockliffe Street	*2*
Leighton Buzzard	Beaudesert School 1914–18	Royal British Legion, West Street	*3*
Leighton Buzzard	Buzzard Scout Troop	Buzzard Scout Hut, Grovebury Road	*4*
Leighton Buzzard	London County and Westminster Bank 1914–18	Natwest Bank, 27 High Street	*5*
Leighton Buzzard	Post Office 1914–18 and 1939–45	Church Square	*6*
Leighton Buzzard	Salvation Army 1914–18 and 1939–45	Lammas Walk	*7*
Linslade	War Memorial 1914–18 and 1939–45	Mentmore Road	*8*
Linslade	War Memorial 1914–18 and 1939–45	St Barnabas	*9*
Linslade	War Memorial 1914–18	St Barnabas bell ringing chamber	*10*
Linslade	Missing – for transcription see Imperial War Museum website	Faith Press	*11*

Elsewhere in Bedfordshire and Buckinghamshire

Battlesden	brass plaque inside church	St Peter and All Saints	12
Billington	Roll of Honour 1914 – 1918 and plaque	St Michael and All Angels	13
Chalgrave		Tebworth Memorial Hall	14
Cheddington	War Memorial	St Giles	15
Eaton Bray	War Memorial 1914-18 and 1939-45	St Mary the Virgin	16
Eaton Bray	War Memorial 1914-18 and 1939-45	Wesleyan Chapel	17
Edlesborough	War Memorial	St Mary the Virgin	18
Eggington	War Memorial 1914-18 and 1939-45	St Michael	19
Heath and Reach	War Memorials 1914-18 and 1939-45 obelisk and inside church	St Leonard	20
Hockliffe	Memorial inside church 1914-1919	St Nicholas	21
Ivinghoe	War Memorial	St Mary the Virgin	22
Ledburn	-	(see Mentmore)	-
Luton	George Kent Ltd Roll of Honour	Luton Museum and Art Gallery, Wardown Park	23
Mentmore	War Memorial	St Mary the Virgin	24
Northall	-	(see Edlesborough)	
Pitstone		Memorial Hall	25
Potsgrove	Brass plaque inside church	St Mary the Virgin	26
Slapton	Memorial inside church 1914-1919	Holy Cross	27
Soulbury	War Memorial 1914-18 and 1939-45	All Saints	28
Tilsworth	Roll of Honour	All Saints	29
Wing	War Memorial 1914-18 and 1939-45	All Saints	30

APPENDIX C

The first surname and forename or initials given are as transcribed from the first memorial, variants follow. To identify the memorials, please refer to the key in Appendix B

surname	forename(s)	memorial code	page(s)
Abel	H. (Henry)	1	286
Abery	Sidney (Ernest Sidney Foster)	3	300
Adams	E.G. (Edward George)	1, 3	241
Adams	F. (Frederick)	1	297
Adams	J. (James)	1, 3	242
Adcock	A.H. (Alfred Herbert)	1	284
Allder	Charles R. (Charles Richard)	20	318
Alldritt	Lionel (Thomas Frederick Lionel)	3	261
Andrews	H.C. (Horace Charles/Charles)	1, 2, 3	313
Archer	P. C. (Percy Charles)	15	261
Aris	W.G. (Walter George)	1, 7	309
Ashby	John	12, 26	231
Atkins (Adkins)	R. (Ralph)	1	312
Auger	J.W. (John William)	1	308
Avery	P.W. (Percy William)	1, 3	320
Baines	Sidney	20	316
Baker	Arthur	16, 17	319
Baker	James	3, 20	277
Baker	S.W. (Stanley Wallace)	1, 3	246
Banwell	William	20	272
Bates	George	20	305
Bates	Thomas J. (Thomas Janes)	20	296
Bates	W.G. (William George)	22	325

Beaumont	R.J. (Robert James)	1, 3	277
Beckett	Arthur John	Abinger Common	242
Beilby	H. (Harry/Henry James)	15	323
Bierton	J. (Joseph)	1	263
Biggs	Joseph W. (Joseph Wright)	20	316
Birch	Albert Edward	21	265
Bird	Albert	14	237
Blew	William (William John)	30	325
Blewitt	Arthur	20	283
Bock	John (John William Henry)	30	307
Bodsworth	P.T. (Percy Thomas)	8, 9	243
Bogg	Gilbert (Gilbert Tom)	28	257
Bogg	Harry (Harry Stanley)	28	281
Bolton	A. (Albert)	1, 30	227
Bond	William (William Ernest)	24	276
Bonham	A. (Alfred)	22	260
Boon	C. (John Charles)	1	260
Botterill	Edward (Richard Edward)	20	307
Boyce	F. (Frederick)	1	253
Brand	Albert (Alfred)	30	306
Brand	Joseph	30	269
Brandom	W. (William John)	1, 3	238
Bransom	H. (Henry)	1, 3	275
Brantom	Arthur (Arthur Charles)	3, 20	303
Brantom	Frank	4	309
Brantom	W.H. (William Harper)	3, 8, 9	248
Brasington	F.T. (Frederick Thomas)	1	288
Bray	Herbert (Herbert William)	30	328
Brazier	E. (Ernest)	8, 9	244
Briggs	H.S. (Herbert Stanley)	2, 8, 9	276
Broad	E.A. (Eric Ashley)	15	324
Brown	B.F. (Bertie Frank)	1, 3	255
Brown	J. (James Frederick)	1	276
Bryant	Frank (Francis William)	30	264
Bull	James	24, 30	239

Bullen	Arthur George	London (Virtual)	315
Bunker	Henry Charles Elliott	29	249
Bunker	Percy	Buckingham	313
Burrows	Daniel	none found	228
Burrows	Leopold Charles	Stockwell	282
Butcher	J.G. (John Gilpin)	1	285
Butcher	R.P. (Richard Percy)	1, 6	323
Carey	John Herbert	none found	269
Carter	J. (John)	22	317
Chandler	J. (Joseph)	15	265
Chanin	Charles	16	298
Chapman	John	21	285
Chase	Frederick	21	249
Chaundy	John Henry	Gloucester	248
Cheshire	Claude	4	277
Chevens	John	20	247
Church	G. (George)	1	288
Clare	J.T. (Joseph Theodore)	1	283
Clare	W.T. (William Thomas)	1	283
Claridge	Lawrence Braham	Whitgift School	244
Clark	W.J. (William John)	8, 9	285
Clarke	John William	12, 26	259
Clarke	Joseph	12, 26	269
Cleaver	F.W. (Frederick William)	1	275
Coker	Alfred	25	288
Coker	Samuel (Samuel George)	25	232
Coles	Penrose Frank	14	299
Collins	James Henry	Potters Bar	269
Cook	A.J. (Albert John)	1, 3	249
Cook	Arthur	25	328
Cook	Charles	21	272
Cooper	A. (Alfred)	15	245
Cooper	William John	none found in UK	264
Cornish	E. (Ernest Edward)	1, 3	266
Cornish	R.A. (Reginald Alfred)	3, 8, 9	246

Cornwell	John 'Jack' Travers	Bishopsgate, Hornchurch	245
Cosby	G. (George)	1	327
Costin	Fred	16	271
Crabb	John William	burial only found	230
Crabtree	William	none found	232
Creamer	Joseph (Joseph Henry)	21	278
Creamer	Ralph William	21	316
Crook	Mervyn Cecil	none found	266
Cropley	George Reginald Farr	London (Virtual)	316
Croxford	Frederick (Fred)	20	296
Cutler	Arthur (Arthur Edwin)	30	326
Dancer	Alfred Christopher	20	286
Dawson	A.J. (Alfred John)	1, 3, 4, 11	272
Dawson	W. (William James)	1, 3	230
Day	C.G. (Cyril George)	1, 3	311
de Rothschild	Evelyn (Evelyn Achille)	30	293
Dean	W.E. (William Edward)	1, 2	264
Deeley	John	16, 17	249
Dickenson (Dickinson)	W. (William)	8, 9, 10	286
Dickins (Dickens)	Henry (Harry)	28	231
Dimmock	F. (Frank)	1, 3	327
Dimmock	P.H. (Percy Harold)	1, 3	324
Dinham	W.A. (William Arthur)	1	300
Doggett	Albert	30	306
Dudley	A.J. (Alfred/Albert Joseph)	1, 2, 3	314
Dudley	F.C. (Charles Francis)	19	292
Dunford	E.T. (Ernest Thubron)	8, 9	270
Dunham	Stanley Harold	Watford	260
Dyer	Lewis	none found	228
Dyer	Sidney	none found	308
Eggleton	W. (William Thomas)	1, 3	251
Elliott	George	25	296

Elmer	Thomas	Swanbourne	275
Emerton	Albert Oliver	14	270
Emmerson (Emerson)	Ezra Samuel Francis	16	318
Evans	W. (William)	1, 3	290
Fallick	Robert Henry	Aldingbourne	279
Farnham	George (George Robert)	16, 17	236
Faulkner	A.J. (Alec Joseph)	1, 3	238
Fensome	Leonard	14	301
Fiddler	Percy (Percival)	24	292
Flowers	Horace Duncan	none found	302
Foster	Arthur William	none found	318
Foster	James Wesley	14	281
Fountain	Ernest	16, 17	289
Fountaine	Sidney (Sidney James)	30	250
Foxon	R.K. (Ralph Kenneth)	1, 3	315
Freeman	John	12, 20, 26	232
Freeman	William	20	249
Fripp	J.D. (John Trude)	1	241
Gadsden	William Joseph	16	287
Gale	B.P. (Baron Percy)	15	239
Galloway	A.J. (Alfred James)	1	290
Gardiner (Gardener)	Harry	30	286
Garforth	William (William Godfrey Willoughby)	30	235
Garnett	G. (George)	1	267
Garnett	W. (Walter)	1	300
Gaskin	E.J. (Ernest John)	1, 3	302
Gates	J. (John)	15	294
Gibbs	C.F. (Cyril Frederick)	1, 3	257
Giddings	A.T. (Arthur Thomas)	1	303
Ginger	J. (Joseph)	1	247
Girling	L. (George Leonard)	1	269
Going	F.H. (Leopold Francis Harold)	1	251

Going	H. (Herbert)	1, 3	312
Going	W.J. (William John)	1	252
Goodchild	Ernest (Ernest William)	none found	289
Goodman	E.J. (Ernest John)	1	313
Gordon	Henry William	none found	262
Green	C.H. (Cecil Henry)	1	258
Griffin	G. (George)	1	322
Griffiths	H. E. (Henry Edward)	1	310
Groom	Edward	16, 17	266
Groom	F. C. (Frederick Charles)	1, 7	278
Groom	William	16	293
Groves	F. (Frederick)	1	311
Guess	Sidney	30	243
Gurney	Frederick John	London (Virtual)	294
Gutteridge	Harry Dennis	Luton	262
Hack	W.J. (Henry John)	1, 3	303
Haggerwood (Wood)	Henry (Henry Hagger)	20	233
Hall	C. (Charles)	1, 3	243
Hall	H.G. (Henry George)	1, 3	291
Hall	William (William George)	3	254
Halsey	C. (Arthur Charles)	22	308
Halsey	G. (George Charles)	1	248
Halsey	W. (William Thomas)	22	323
Hammerton	John (John Thomas)	30	258
Hankin	Frederick B. (Frederick Bernard)	3, 20	252
Hankin	Robert H. (Robert Hayes)	20	297
Hardy	Frederick James	16	256
Harris	C. (Charles)	1	273
Harris	E.J. (Edward James)	1	313
Hart	A.H. (Henry Arthur)	8, 9	287
Hart	W. (William)	1, 3	260
Healing	Kenneth	5	271
Hedges	P. (Percy Francis)	15	329

Heley	Frank	27	288
Heley	J. (Thomas John)	1, 3	257
Higgs	Frederick (Frederick Charles)	21	301
Hill	C. (Charles)	8, 9	250
Hill (Hills)	H. (Harold/Harry)	8, 9	323
Hodge	Herbert	none found	237
Holland	G.L. (George Lewis)	8, 9	234
Holland	J.H. (James Henry)	8	239
Holland	S. (Sidney)	1	281
Holmes	E. (Edward T.)	1, 3, 4	292
Holmes	George (George Walter)	20	230
Holmes	W.R. (William George)	1, 3	235
Holyman	Albert George Frederick	none found	300
Horley	Albert	20	260
Horley	Wilfred C. (Wilfred Charles)	21	327
Horn	A. (Alfred)	1	270
Horn	G. (George Gaius)	22	301
Horn (Horne)	J. (John)	1, 3	256
Horne	Dennis (Dennis Arthur)	30	237
Howe	A.V. (Albert Victor)	8, 9	273
Howe	C.A. (Charles Arthur)	8, 9, 10	235
Howe	S.E. (Sidney Ernest)	8, 9	304
Hubbocks	Horace Edgar	none found	284
Humbles	G. (George)	1, 3	297
Humbles	W. (William)	1	306
Humphrey	Reginald George	Brentford	252
Hurkett	Albert William	London (Virtual)	229
Hyde	R.J. (Richard James)	1, 3	231
Hyde	T. (Thomas)	1, 3	319
Jackson	Arthur	16, 17	270
Jakeman	F.G. (Frederick George)	1, 3	317
Janes	Alec	burial only found	328
Janes	Arthur	16, 17	255
Janes	C. (Claud/Claude)	1, 3, 8, 9	273
Janes	Charles (Charles William)	28	288
Janes	Charles John	London (Virtual)	273

Janes	G.A. (George Alma)	1	258
Janes	H. (Harry)	1, 7	295
Janes	Henry	28	289
Janes	Louis G. (Louis George)	18	284
Janes	Thomas William	3, 23	264
Jeffery	Reuben	24	273
Jenkins	George	21	240
Johnson	C.R. (Charles Rowland)	1, 2	290
Johnson	M.L. (Martin Leslie)	1	319
Jordan	J.G. (Joseph George)	1, 30	288
Jordan	Lionel	30	236
Joynson	Frederick William	none found	315
Keen	G. (George)	1, 2, 3	244
Kember	A. (Archibald Thomas)	1	325
Kempster	Arthur	24, 30	321
Kempster	T.G. (Thomas George)	1, 4	252
Kemsley	A.H. (Arthur Harold)	8, 9	320
Kendall	Herbert Charles	Kettering	299
Kennett	Albert Edward	Australian (Virtual)	261
Kenning	William	30	302
Kent	Herbert	24	310
Kimble	Levi (Levi John)	28	228
King	Archie William	29	238
King	F.J. (Francis John (Jack))	1	251
King	G.A. (George Arthur)	1, 4	245
King	Harry John (Henry John)	29	234
King	J. (Joseph)	1	298
Kingham	Arthur John	14	257
Kiteley	T.W. (Thomas William)	1, 3	278
Knight	Albert	18	277
Knightley	Percy Edward	Bethnal Green	263
Lake	Charles (Alfred Charles)	30	317
Lancaster	A.H. (Arthur Henry)	1, 3	295
Lansbury	David	12, 26	327
Lathwell	Arthur Thomas	burial only found	328

Lawrence	R. (Richmond)	8, 9	275
Lawson	J. (John/Jack)	1, 3	233
Leach	F.C. (Frederick Charles)	19	259
Lee	J.A. (John Alfred)	1, 3	310
Lovell	Sidney (Sidney Frederick)	30	271
Luck	E.L. (Edward Lewis)	1	256
Luck	H.J. (Hayward James)	1	255
Luck	S. J. (Sidney James)	1	267
Lugsden	Albert (Albert Frederick)	16, 17	247
Lugsden	Amos	16, 17	306
Lugsden	Arthur J. (Arthur Joseph)	16, 17	312
Lugsden	Frederick (Fred)	16, 17	266
Macdonald	Robert	burial only found	322
Major	J. (John)	1	239
Marks	P.W. (Percy William)	1, 3, 7	285
Marsh	Sidney	Aldbury	284
Martin	H.E. (Horace Edmund)	8, 9	246
Mason	A.T. (Arthur Thomas)	1	304
Mason	C. (Charles)	15	319
Matthews	E.R. (Ernest Rufus)	1, 3	314
Matthews	G.A. (George Albert)	8, 9	310
McCubbin	A. (Alec/Alexander)	1, 3	234
Mead	F. (Frank)	1	271
Mead	F.C. (Frederick Charles)	1, 3	274
Mead	J.J. (James Joseph)	1, 3	280
Mead	William	27	267
Meager	W.C. (William Charles)	8, 9	243
Meakins	Cyril (Cyril Samuel)	16	232
Meggison	Joseph	none found	268
Miles	P. (Percy Thomas)	22	268
Miles	R. (Reginald Francis)	1	289
Miles	Stanley	none found	399
Millins	F.J. (Frederick James)	15, 24	289
Missenden	R.W. (Reginald William)	8, 9	247
Money	Harry	20	245

Monk	J. (James)	22	316
Moore	Archie	Husbands Bosworth	301
Moore	L. (Leonard)	1	307
Nash	W. (William)	1	253
Neale	Ralph	20	310
Newbury	J.G. (Joseph George)	1, 3	307
Newman	George	27	326
Nicholes	E. (Ernest)	22	290
Nicker	G.F. (George Frederick)	8	227
Norman	James	Sandy	262
North	Herbert (Herbert Henry)	21	280
Oakley	Leonard	30	286
Odell	E.F. (Ernest Frank)	1,3	322
Orchard	Jack (John)	28	235
Osborne (Gibson)	John Thomas	burial only found	311
Ostler	Walter Hollingsworth	Dunstable	262
Paddock	Frank (William Francis)	16	268
Page	A.W. (Arthur William)	8, 9	248
Page	Frank	30	290
Page	L. (Lionel)	8, 9	304
Page	M. (Mark)	4, 8, 9	234
Page	W. (William Albert Charles)	1, 3	275
Pantling	H.J. (Horace James)	1, 3, 7	271
Pantling	L. (Leonard)	1, 3	249
Pantling	S.J. (Sydney John)	1, 3	246
Paragreen	Frederick (Frederick Arthur)	20	230
Parker	J.H. (James Henry)	1	262
Parsons	W. (Harry William)	1, 2, 3	301
Paxton	Arnold (Arnold Walter)	30	303
Paxton	James (Jim)	30	227
Payne	A.J. (Archibald James)	1	263
Payne	L. (Leslie)	1	321
Pearson	A.A. (Arthur Albert)	1	236

Pearson	Arthur J. (Arthur John)	20	264
Pease	W.G. (William James)	1, 30	253
Pepper	Arthur Clive	Harpenden	281
Peppiatt	William	18	249
Perry	F.E. (Frederick Ernest)	1	236
Phillips	R.E. (Richard Edward/Thomas)	1	255
Phillips (Philips)	F. (Frank Charles)	1, 3	229
Pickering	Frank	30	250
Piggott	John	29	272
Pilgrim	A.C. (Arthur Charles)	8, 9	314
Plummer	A.G. (Alfred George)	1	276
Plummer	Edward Joseph (Ted)	London (Virtual)	243
Pollard	Ernest	30	283
Pope	William James	none found	265
Potts	George	24	234
Pouchot	A.J. (John/Jack Auguste)	1, 3	314
Pratt	Cuthbert	13	274
Pratt	G. (George)	1, 3	230
Pratt	Harry (Henry George)	30	274
Pratt	Horace (Horace William)	20	329
Pratt	John T. (Theodore John)	16, 17	253
Primrose	Neil (Neil James Archibald)	24	293
Procter	J.A. (John Albert)	1	292
Pugh	John	30	309
Puryer	E.G. (Ernest George)	1, 2, 3	287
Quick	F.J. (Francis John)	1, 3	298
Quick	H.A. (Harold Arthur)	1, 7	238
Randall	Daniel	30	320
Randall	Edward (Edward John)	30	240
Randall	Harold (Harold Victor)	30	279
Randall	Herbert	30	321
Randall	William (William John)	24	325
Rayner	J. (John)	1	296
Redding	T.E. (Thomas Edmund)	1, 3	270
Reeve	W. (William Benjamin)	1, 3	306

Richards	E. (Ernest Edward)	15	258
Richardson	Frank (Frank Alexander Randolph)	30	317
Richmond	F.R. (Frederick Robert)	1	265
Richmond	H.S. (Harold Stedman)	1	254
Rickard	Joseph	25	241
Rickett	Albert	14	294
Rimington	Oscar	30	259
Roberts	S. (Sidney)	1	270
Roberts	William J. (William James)	16, 17	296
Robinson	Albert G. (Albert George)	28	317
Robinson	Charles	28	296
Robinson	Frank Charles	none found	257
Robinson	W. (William)	8, 9	229
Rodgers	Harold	Kilnhurst	230
Roff	Ernest	27	272
Rogers	Albert	18	254
Rogers	E.T. (Thomas)	Chicheley	240
Rogers	Joseph	30	259
Rollings	Albert	16, 17	298
Rollings	Mark	16, 17	276
Rolls	Frederick John (Frederick Joseph)	12, 20, 26	315
Room	Albert	18	308
Rose	G.T. (George Thomas)	1, 7	237
Rose	Percival	20	242
Rose	Stephen	16	312
Roser	Augustus Housden	London (Virtual)	311
Rowe	Ernest John	Canadian (Virtual)	233
Rowe	G.W. (George Walter)	1, 3	289
Rowland	William (William John)	25	280
Ruffett	Frederick	16, 17	299
Ruffett	J. (William John)	22	259
Ruffhead	F.C. (Frederick Charles)	1, 3	247
Russell	George Arthur	none found	277

Samuel	A. (Albert)	1	299
Samuel	Noel Stephen	none found	257
Sanford	R. (Ralph)	1, 3	325
Saunders	Albert Edward	London (Virtual)	244
Sayell	E.T. (Edward Thomas)	8, 9	287
Sayell	G. (George)	15	274
Sayell	Samuel	24	278
Seabrook	Arthur Thomas	burial only found	329
Seabrook (Smith)	A.J. (Arthur John)	15	260
Sear	Alfred	Dunstable	282
Seddon	R.J. (Robert Joseph)	8, 9, 10	260
Shackleton	H. (Henry)	1	309
Shackleton (Wise)	J.B. (Joseph Benjamin)	1	255
Shepherd	S. (Sidney Charles)	1, 3	251
Sinfield	Edward Cyril	29	308
Smallbones	Harold (Harold J)	16, 17	285
Smith	A.J. (Arthur James)	1	281
Smith	Charles	18	302
Smith	Edward J (Edward John)	18	282
Smith	H. (Harry)	1, 3, 4, 11	267
Smith	Hortensius Stephen	none found	266
Smith	J. (James)	1, 3	238
Smith	J. (Joseph)	1, 2, 3	235
Smith	James	13	261
Smith	P. (Peter)	8, 9	309
Smith	R. (Robert)	1, 3	322
Smith	Samuel	30	247
Smith	W. (William)	8, 9	301
Smith	W.A. (William Arthur)	1, 3	300
Sproat	Robert	20	321
Staines	Henry (Henry John)	30	250
Steadman	J. N. (John Noel)	1	268
Steadman	W.N. (William Niven)	1	291

Stevens	H.G. (Henry George)	1, 3	298
Stevens	T.J. (Thomas Cyril James Lambert)	1	326
Stevens	W. (William Alec)	1	310
Stevens	W. (William)	1, 3	280
Stevens	W.S. (Samuel Walter)	1, 3	320
Stibbon	Thomas	none found	279
Stone	Alfred	20	327
Stone	Edward	20	320
Stone	Frank Ernest	burial only found	322
Stone	Henry R. (Henry Richard)	28	329
Stone	Joseph	20	306
Strong	Benjamin C. (Benjamin Clarence)	20	303
Strong	Robert H. (Robert Harold)	20	232
Strong (Stewart)	Francis W. (John/Francis William Cooper)	20	279
Sturman	Arthur	19	254
Summers	Cyril Henry Gerald	Padbury	245
Sunderland	A.J.E. (Alfred Joseph Elton)	19	279
Sutton	Geoffrey A. (Geoffrey Alfred)	16	295
Sworder	J.R.S. (John Roland Sloan)	8, 9	294
Syratt	Ernest (Ernest Ambrose)	30	295
Tavener	F. (Frederick William)	22	295
Taylor	E. (Ernest)	15, 24	307
Taylor	George	30	305
Taylor	William (William Frederick)	St Albans	328
Teagle	Arthur	London (Virtual)	312
Teagle	Thomas Henry	none found	305
Tew (Two)	E.J. (Edward John)	1	229
Tew (Two)	William (William Henry)	20	312
Thompson	A. (Amos)	1, 20	244
Thorpe	Harry (Harry Archibald)	none found	237
Tilbrook	A.J. (Archibald James)	1, 4, 9, 11	319
Timms	Harold P. (Harold Percy)	16, 17	324

Tindall	Mary Gertrude	Sidmouth	284
Tindall	Noel Stephen	Sidmouth	326
Toe	W.D. (Walter Dennis)	1, 3	293
Tofield	Frederick J. (Frederick Joseph)	28	241
Tompkins	A.A. (Arthur Albert)	15	318
Tompkins	E.O. (Ernest/Edward Oliver)	8, 9	278
Tompkins	H.S. (Horace Sidney)	15	239
Tompkins	Nora (Norah)	20, 23	297
Toms	W. (William James)	1, 3	281
Tooley	H.A.R. (Harold Augustus Rupert)	1	231
Towers	G.L. (Grenville Lawrence)	1	317
Tucker	Arthur	12, 26	294
Tucker	Edward	21	262
Turner	C.J. (Cyril James)	15	329
Turner	Harold	25	304
Turney	Alfred (Alfred Henry)	28	256
Turney	Bert	28	228
Turney	H.B. (Henry Bertram)	1, 3	313
Turney	Herbert (Bertie)	28	291
Turney	Robt J. (Robert James/Joseph)	3, 27	240
Turney	W. (Wilfred)	22	305
Turney	William J. (William John)	27	304
Underwood	T. (Thomas)	1, 3	233
Varney	Philip	24	321
Varney	Reginald Thomas	Newport Pagnell	245
Vasey	Francis John	Australian (Virtual)	251
Wadelin	Arthur	28	243
Walker	J. (Jack)	8, 9	231
Ward	F. (Francis James)	1	292
Waring	Fred (Frederick)	25	268
Warr	Benjamin William Green	Fenny Stratford	250
Waterhouse	John	none found	291
Waters	E.A. (Ernest Albert)	15	283
Watson	W.R. (William Richard)	8, 9, 10	315

Weaver	Frank Thomas	none found	280
Webb	George (Frederick George)	20	256
Weedon	Ernest	16, 17	258
Weedon	Frederick (Frederick William)	16, 17	269
Wells	G. (George)	22	228
Wernham	J. (James)	1, 2, 3	256
West	F.J. (Frederick John)	1	291
Whitaker	Frank	Cublington	274
Whitbread	A.E. (Albert Edward)	8, 9	253
Whitbread	L.G. (Leonard George)	1, 3	242
White	E. (Edwin)	8, 9	239
White	S. (Samuel)	8, 9	234
Whiting	Edwin Joseph	St Albans Abbey	241
Whitman	B.F. (Bernard Frank)	1	274
Whybrow	W.S. (William Samuel/Samuel William)	1, 3	324
Wildman	Alfred	16	293
Willis	G.E. (George Edgar)	8, 9	252
Wilson	Walter J. (Walter John)	18	298
Windmill	William James	none found	283
Woodall	Harold	March	249
Woodcraft	Ernest	16, 17	323
Woodcraft	Harry	16, 17	263
Woodwards	Arthur	30	282
Woodwards	Ernest	30	318
Woodwards	George	30	285
Woolhead	George	30	300
Woolhead	George	12, 26	267
Woolhead	Thomas	20	276
Woolhead	William (William Burrows)	30	282

BIBLIOGRAPHY

In order to piece together the events described in this book researchers consulted many sources. Among the most important were the local newspapers, principally the *Leighton Buzzard Observer,* but also the *Bedfordshire Advertiser, Luton Times and Advertiser, North Bucks Times, Bucks Herald and Northampton Mercury.*

Much information was gleaned from original documents held by the Bedfordshire Record Office, the Public Record Office at Kew, the Imperial War Museum, Doncaster Record Office, the RAF Air Historical Branch, the Western Front Association and the London & North Western Railway Society.

Many websites and genealogical records were consulted and crosschecked to produce the most comprehensive list of all the casualties from the area, including all those on local war memorials and some who are not. These sources are too many to list.

Among the other publications consulted were:
Brown, Maureen, *Linslade's Role in the First World War, Transactions*
Darby, Hanna, *Leighton Buzzard's Monolith*
Dingwall, R.P., *Narrow Gauge Tracks in the Sand*
Dunn, Captain J.C., *The War the Infantry Knew, 1914-18*
Haythornthwaite, Philip J., *The World War One Source Book*
Heritage, T.R., *The Light Track from Arras*
Holt, Toni and Valmai, *Battlefields of the First World War*
Howard E.D. (editor), *Modern Foundry Practice*
Jane's Encyclopaedia of Aviation
Leleux, Sydney, *Leighton Buzzard Light Railway*
Liddell Hart, B.H., *History of the First World War*
Robertson, Bruce, *British Military Aircraft Serials, 1912–1966*
Sharp, Dan, *Duelling Above the Trenches – Sopwith Aircraft of the Great War*
Storey, Neil R., *Animals in the First World War*
Western Front Association Journal, *Stand To!* September 2015

INDEX